lonely planet

D0834621

Discover
Italy

Contents

Throughout this book, we use these icons to highlight special recommendations:

 The Best…
Lists for everything from bars to wildlife – to make sure you don't miss out

Don't Miss
A must-see – don't go home until you've been there

 Local Knowledge Local experts reveal their top picks and secret highlights

 Detour
Special places a little off the beaten track

If you like…
Lesser-known alternatives to world-famous attractions

These icons help you quickly identify reviews in the text and on the map:

 **Sights**

Eating

Drinking

 Sleeping

Information

This edition written and researched by

Alison Bing

Abigail Blasi, Cristian Bonetto, Gregor Clark, Joe Fullman, Duncan Garwood, Paula Hardy, Robert Landon, Virginia Maxwell, Olivia Pozzan, Brendan Sainsbury, Donna Wheeler, Nicola Williams

Milan,
the Lakes &
Piedmont

p109

Venice,
Veneto &
Bologna

p157

Florence,
Tuscany &
Umbria

p213

Rome &
the Vatican

p51

Naples,
Pompeii &
the Amalfi Coast

p273

p311

Sicily &
Southern Italy

● Venice, Veneto & Bologna

- Legendary Venice
- Culinary Bologna & Veneto
- Glimpse Heaven Inside St Mark's Basilica
- Admire Propaganda at the Ducal Palace
- Meet the Venetian Masters
- Clamour for More at Verona's Roman Arena
- Bologna's Quadrilatero

● Florence, Tuscany & Umbria

- Duomo, Florence
- Sacred Assisi
- Develop a Celebrity Crush at the Accademia
- Actually Enjoy Politics at Palazzo Pubblico
- Chianti Landscape
- Feel Small in San Gimignano
- Orvieto's Cathedral

● Rome & the Vatican

- Museo e Galleria Borghese
- Colosseum
- Vatican Museums
- St Peter's Basilica
- Roman Forum
- Roman Catacombs
- Trastevere

● Milan, the Lakes & Piedmont

- Milan Fashion & Design
- Lake Como
- Da Vinci's Last Supper
- Get Wowed atop Milan's Duomo
- Live Bellagio's *Dolce Vita*
- Window-shop Milan's Quadrilatero d'Oro
- Turin's Eataly

● Naples, Pompeii & the Amalfi Coast

- Ruins of Pompeii
- Sing in the Blue Grotto
- Get a Positive Outlook in Positano
- Become Speechless in Ravello
- Turn Back Time at Museo Archaeologico Nazionale
- Make a Meal of the Centro Storico

Contents

Plan Your Trip   On the Road

Contents

On the Road

In Focus

Survival Guide

This Is Italy

Packing your bags for every possible Italian adventure is a challenge – yet Italy makes it look easy, with 47 Unesco World Heritage sites, 20 champion soccer teams, 40 European Union–acclaimed cheeses and (get this) one million vineyards, all crammed into a country the size of a Prada clutch.

Just come as you are, and let Italy show you how it's done. In a couple of days you'll have a new wardrobe; in a week you'll be on a Vespa, making gestures that could get you arrested elsewhere. You've got places to go: an Amalfi Coast beach, maybe an opera in a Roman amphitheatre, or your pick of Italy's year-round festivals. You don't have to wait for Venice Carnevale or yet another World Cup victory to party in the streets – any old saint's day or country *sagra* (harvest fair) will do.

Hungry? Ah, that's Italy's favourite word. Thanks to ancient volcanoes and an unusually sunny disposition, there's always some local, seasonal speciality bursting with flavour, and it will be delivered to you atop the best pasta or risotto you will have in this lifetime. City-state turf battles long fought by armies are now waged by *pizzaioli* (pizza-makers) over the correct thickness of a crust – best not to get the Neapolitans and Romans started. Just eat and smile, which should be easy.

Maybe it's the Mediterranean diet, but Italy wears its millennia of turbulent history extraordinarily well. Roman towns like Pompeii, Herculaneum and Ostia Antica were so well preserved by their masks of mud or volcanic ash, you'll swear they're not a day over 1950 years old. But Italy also offers glimpses into the future, with cutting-edge design showcases during Milan's Salone Internazionale del Mobile and a recent boom in contemporary art museums in Venice, Turin, Naples and Rome. For big ideas, major meals and outsized personalities, Italy has your dream vacation in the bag.

> 66
> Italy wears its millennia of turbulent history extra-ordinarily well.
> 99

Gondola ride (p171), Venice
JEAN-PIERRE LESCOURRET/LONELY PLANET IMAGES ©

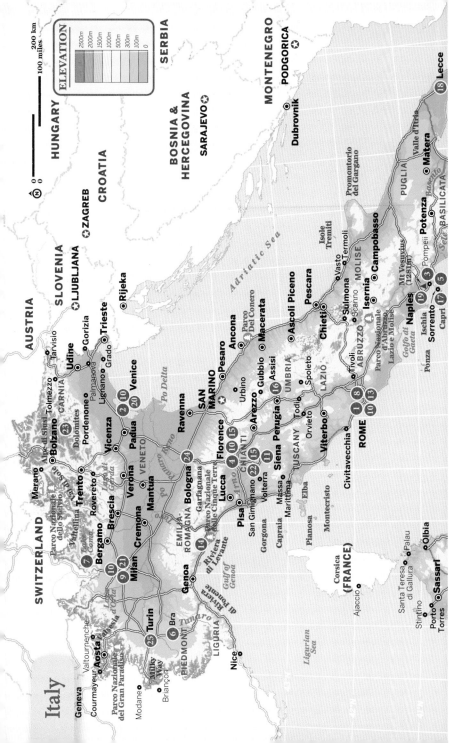

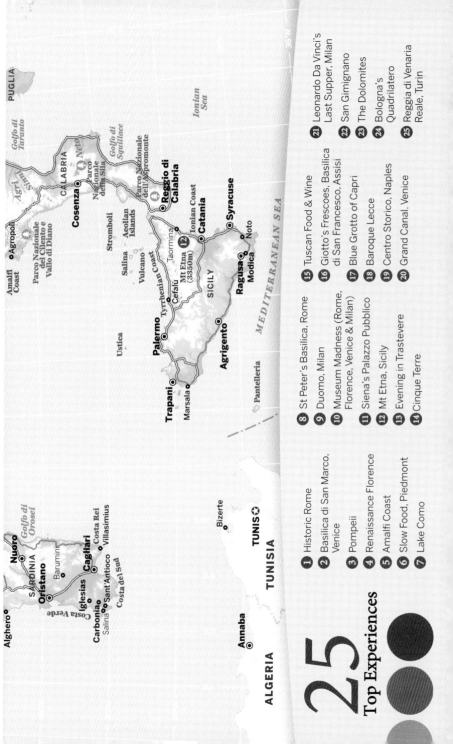

25 Top Experiences

1. Historic Rome
2. Basilica di San Marco, Venice
3. Pompeii
4. Renaissance Florence
5. Amalfi Coast
6. Slow Food, Piedmont
7. Lake Como
8. St Peter's Basilica, Rome
9. Duomo, Milan
10. Museum Madness (Rome, Florence, Venice & Milan)
11. Siena's Palazzo Pubblico
12. Mt Etna, Sicily
13. Evening in Trastevere
14. Cinque Terre
15. Tuscan Food & Wine
16. Giotto's Frescoes, Basilica di San Francesco, Assisi
17. Blue Grotto of Capri
18. Baroque Lecce
19. Centro Storico, Naples
20. Grand Canal, Venice
21. Leonardo Da Vinci's Last Supper, Milan
22. San Gimignano
23. The Dolomites
24. Bologna's Quadrilatero
25. Reggia di Venaria Reale, Turin

25 Italy's Top Experiences

Historic Rome

Once *caput mundi* (capital of the world), Rome was spawned by a wolf-suckled wild boy (according to legend), grew to be Western Europe's first superpower, became the spiritual centrepiece of the Christian world, and is now the repository of over 2500 years worth of European art and architecture. From the Pantheon (p73) and the Colosseum (p72) to Michelangelo's Sistine Chapel (p89) and controversial Caravaggios (p77), there's simply too much to see in one visit. So do as countless others have done before you, toss your coin into the Trevi Fountain (p80) and promise to return. Colosseum

Venice's Basilica di San Marco

Stepping through the portals of San Marco (p185), try to imagine what it might have been like for an illiterate, burlap-clad medieval peasant glimpsing those shimmering gold mosaic domes for the first time. It's not such a stretch – once you see those millions of tiny gilt tesserae cohere into a singular heavenly vision, every leap of human imagination since the 12th century seems comparatively minor.

Pompeii

Nothing piques human curiosity quite like a mass catastrophe and few can beat the ruins of Pompeii (p298), a once thriving Roman town frozen for all time in its 2000-year-old death throes. Wander Roman streets, the grassy, column-lined forum, the city brothel, the 5000-seat theatre and the frescoed Villa dei Misteri, and ponder Pliny the Younger's terrifying account of the tragedy: 'Darkness came on again, again ashes, thick and heavy. We got up repeatedly to shake these off; otherwise we would have been buried and crushed by the weight'.

The Best...
Underground Sights

ROMAN CATACOMBS
Rome's subterranean city of the dead, from popes to paupers. (p95)

MATERA
A town of cave-dwellings carved out along a ravine, complete with cave hotels and churches. (p346)

CATACOMBE DI SAN GENNARO
Two stories of grand, frescoed graves in caves. (p290)

ST PETER'S BASILICA
Book ahead to enter a tunnel to the tomb of St Peter under the Basilica. (p90)

Renaissance Florence

From Brunelleschi's red-tiled dazzler, the Duomo (p226), to Michelangelo's greatest hits, *David* (p231) and *The Birth of Venus* (p227), Florence contains 'the greatest concentration of universally renowned works of art in the world' according to Unesco. Whereas Rome and Milan have been torn down and rebuilt many times, central Florence looks much as it did in 1550, with stone towers and cypress-lined gardens. The effect is rather like a Renaissance painting, which of course makes perfect sense when you think about it. Duomo

The Best...
Shopping Destinations

MILAN
Street fashion competes with Fashion Week runways to define Italian style. (p135)

FLORENCE
Exquisite stationery, butter-soft leather goods, rare wines and heavenly scented candles. (p241)

VENICE
Modern artisan-made statement pieces, from marble-paper cocktail rings to Murano glass chandeliers. (p200)

SICILY
Sunny ceramics, vintage marionettes, marzipan treats and sweet Marsala wine. (p329)

Amalfi Coast

With its scented lemon groves, flower-strewn cliff sides, tumbling sherbet-hued towns and bobbing fishing boats, the Amalfi Coast still claims the crown as the prettiest coast on the peninsula. Cinque Terre may argue, but Hollywood divas and starry-eyed day-trippers insist that the stretch from Sorrento (p299) to Positano (p305) is the least developed and most beautiful. Positano

Piedmont's Slow Food Zone

Piedmont (p147) offers a staggering menu. Compare the size of the human stomach to the scale of Eataly, the Turin factory converted into a showcase for Slow Food specialities (p152), and you might despair of ever making it through the gauntlet of tasting counters. For a mellower gastronomic experience, day-trip to the small Piedmont town of Bra, where Slow Food was founded.

Lovely Lake Como

Formed at the end of the last Ice Age, dazzling Lake Como, nestled in the shadow of the Rhaetian Alps, is the most spectacular of the Lombard lakes, its grand Liberty-style villas home to movie moguls and Arab sheikhs. Surrounded on all sides by luxuriant greenery, among the lake's siren calls are the landscaped gardens of Villa Serbelloni (p146), Villa Carlotta (p145) and Villa Balbianello (p145), which blush pink with camellias, azaleas and rhododendrons in April and May.

St Peter's Basilica

Many a Renaissance genius was defeated by the same puzzle: how do you build a suitable shrine for apostle and church founder, St Peter, while making room for all humanity within its portals? Michelangelo topped everyone with a novel solution: cutting corners. Instead of resting St Peter's dome squarely on angular supports, Michelangelo lifted it high above a rippling colonnade that allows light to flood the vast basilica interiors. The basilica (p90) remains squarely grounded over St Peter's tomb, but Michelangelo's dome adds boundless glory.

The Best...
Unbelievable Architecture

ALBEROBELLO
Stone cottages that look like cupcakes with white icing. (p345)

VENICE BIENNALE
In even-numbered years, Venice's ancient Arsenale shipyards become a launching platform for avant-garde architecture. (p191)

FIERA MILANO
Massimiliano Fuksas upstages Italy's biggest design fair with pavilions that resemble billowing glass sails. (p132)

LEANING TOWER
Tilted climbs are even giddier on moonlit summer nights. (p244)

Milan's Duomo

Six centuries in the making, Milan's Duomo (p143) is the grand finale of International Gothic and a monument to Milanese determination. Candoglia marble had to be hauled from suburban docks via a canal system, aided by Leonardo Da Vinci–designed hydraulic locks. By the time the cathedral took shape, Renaissance replaced Gothic as a favoured global style. But Milan continued its singular monument, and an enthusiastic Napoleon offered to finance its completion. Since Napoleon never did pay up, Milanese claim full credit for this wonder.

The Best...
Modern Art Museums

MAXXI
Conceptual architect Zaha Hadid's splashy new contemporary art-star showcase. (p91)

PUNTA DELLA DOGANA
Provocative art fills ancient warehouses revamped by architect Tadao Ando. (p184)

MUSEO D'ARTE CONTEMPORANEA
Art innovations, from Arte Povera found-material sculpture to site-specific video art. (p147)

MADRE
From Jeff Koons' uberkitsch *Wild Boy and Puppy* to Rebecca Horn's Neapolitan-esque *Spirits*. (p285)

10 Museum Madness

A browse through your art history textbook will highlight the names of seminal movements such as classical, Renaissance, mannerist, baroque, futurist and metaphysical – all of which were forged in Italy by a pantheon of artists including Giotto, Da Vinci, Michelangelo, Botticelli, Bernini, Caravaggio, Carracci, Boccioni, Balla and de Chirico. Find the best of them in Rome's Galleria Borghese (p92) and new MAXXI gallery (p91), Florence's Uffizi (p227), Venice's Galleria dell'Accademia (p181), and Milan's Museo del Novecento (p122). *Doni Tondo*, Michelangelo, Galleria degli Uffizi (p227 and p232), Florence

Siena's Palazzo Pubblico

A medieval monument like no other, Siena's Town Hall (Palazzo Pubblico; p252) is missing a lot of the usual grim Gothic decor. There are no sinister gargoyles peering from the eaves, or fire-and-brimstone *Last Judgments* predicting dire consequences for sinners. Instead, Siena's soaring, striking brick town hall is focused on the here and now, with Ambrogio Lorenzetti's *Allegory of Good and Bad Government* frescoes supplying Siena's town council with a medieval-cartoon mission statement: collect taxes, end corruption, avoid war, and don't forget to party.

Mt Etna

Known to the Greeks as the 'column that holds up the sky', Mt Etna (p334) is Europe's largest volcano and one of the world's most active. The ancients believed the giant Tifone (Typhoon) lived in its crater and lit up the sky with regular, spectacular pyrotechnics. At 3323m, it towers above Sicily's Ionian Coast, and since 1987 its slopes have been part of the Parco Naturale dell'Etna, an area that encompasses both alpine forests and the forbiddingly black summit.

Evening in Trastevere

Millennia ago, the sound of a stampede might've signalled a surprise attack on this Roman legionnaires' quarter. Now it's the noise of platform pumps clomping *sampietrini* (cobblestones) toward Piazza Santa Maria in Trastevere (p85) on the nightly *passeggiata* (stroll), off to conquer happy-hour buffets, or to claim a corner of the fountain for a gossip session. The crowd is international, but the fashion, flirtation and street theatre is quintessentially Roman.

Cinque Terre

For the sinful inhabitants of the Cinque Terre's (p154) five villages – Monterosso al Mare, Vernazza, Corniglia, Manarola and Riomaggiore – penance involved a lengthy and arduous hike up the vertiginous cliff side to the local village sanctuary there to appeal for forgiveness. Scale the same sanctuary trails today through terraced vineyards and *macchia*-covered hillsides, and it's hard to think of a more benign punishment as the heavenly views unfurl.

Riomaggiore (p155)

The Best...
Natural Wonders

MT ETNA
Scale the slopes of Europe's most vocal volcano. (p334)

CINQUE TERRE
Secluded coves perfect for pirates, with rocky bluffs, turquoise waters, tiered vineyards and terraced lemon groves that could cure entire cities of scurvy. (p154)

VILLA CARLOTTA
Orange-blossom bowers and camellias perfume leisurely spring strolls in a Prussian princess' garden along Lake Como. (p145)

VULCANO
Black-sand beaches, thermal mud baths and bubbling hot springs beneath an island volcano. (p330)

The Best...
Street Markets

MERCATO DI BALLARÒ
A Sicilian market with the flavours and colourful characters of a Middle Eastern souk. (p322)

RIALTO MARKETS
The market that launched Venice's trading empire still sells produce and lagoon seafood – juicy gossip gratis. (p161)

PORTA PORTESE
Rome's flea market stretches for blocks: sunglasses, comics and even kitchen sinks. (p104)

MERCATO DI PORTA NOLANA
Vendors peddle pastries and buffalo-milk mozzarella with a chorus of sing-song chants. (p291)

OLIVIER CIRENDINI / LONELY PLANET IMAGES ©

RICHARD I'ANSON / LONELY PLANET IMAGES ©

Tuscan Food & Wine Hotspots

Break bread with celebrity restaurateur Fabbio Picchi at members' club Teatro del Sale (p239) and sample simple, heart-warming, belly-filling Tuscan cooking. The secret ingredient of Tuscan food is, well, the ingredients. In a land of legendary flavours, from San Miniato truffles to wild-boar sausages and hunks of bluish *bistecca alla fiorentina,* Tuscan farmers still tend to their pigs and cows, olives and grapes, with the pride of artisans. Sample the very best at Il Santo Bevitore (p239) and La Bottega (p255). Central Market (p234), Florence

Giotto's Frescoes, Basilica di San Francesco, Assisi

During the grim days of the Black Death, Giotto di Bondone brought living colour to his daring naturalistic frescoes for the Basilica di San Francesco in Assisi (p263). He revealed a human side to spiritual figures that sparked a renaissance. Such is the continued devotion these frescoes inspire that after being shattered by a 1997 earthquake, they were painstakingly reconstructed from thousands of fragments.

Blue Grotto of Capri

Some Italian place names embellish the facts (Amalfi's Emerald Grotto is more of a mossy green) but the water in this sea-cave on the isle of Capri really does glow an ethereal blue. Squeeze through the mouth of the cave in a rowboat and experience an optical effect no amusement park ride with artificial lighting can capture (sorry, Disney). No wonder Romans built a shrine to appease the local water sprite: this grotto (p301) casts a spell on all who enter.

Baroque Lecce

The extravagant architectural character of many Puglian towns is due to the local style of *Barocco Leccese*. Local craftsmen vied for ever greater heights of creativity, carving sandstone facades with swirling vines, gargoyles and strange zoomorphic figures. Lecce's Basilica di Santa Croce (p344) is the high point of a style that was so outrageously busy, the Marchese Grimaldi said it made him think a lunatic was having a nightmare. Basilica di Santa Croce (p344), Lecce

The Best...
Food & Wine Regions

EMILIA-ROMAGNA
Italy's gastronomic Holy Grail, home to *prosciutto di Parma, parmigiano reggiano* (Parmesan) and balsamic vinegar. (p209)

PIEDMONT
Truffles, gorgonzola, chocolate and Barolo beckon in the home of the Slow Food Movement. (p147)

NAPLES & SURROUNDS
Real-deal pizza and *mozzarella di bufala* (buffalo mozzarella) meet crispy *sfogliatelle* (ricotta-filled pastries). (p291)

SICILY
Cuisine with a kick and Arabic undertones, from wild-caught tuna and *arancini Siciliani* (risotto balls) to handcrafted marzipan and ricotta-stuffed *cannoli*. (p322)

Street Life in Naples' Centro Storico

19

There's nothing like waking up to the sound of the Porta Nolana market (p291). What a feast for the senses! It's as similar to a North African bazaar as to a European market: fruit vendors raucously hawking their wares in Neapolitan dialect, swordfish heads casting sidelong glances at you across heaps of silvery sardines on ice, the irresistible perfume of lemons and oranges, and the warm, just-baked aroma of *sfogliatella* pastries.

The Best...
Hill Towns

RAVELLO
Artists' retreats are interrupted by romantic seacliff sunsets. (p306)

ORVIETO
Truffles, ceramics, white wines and apocalyptic omens inside a pretty pink cathedral. (p267)

MONTALCINO
Medieval town perched atop vineyards, with Brunello wine tastings in the town castle's cellar. (p254)

URBINO
The ideal Renaissance city on a hill, from gracious palaces to glorious frescoes. (p263)

GETTY CITY COMMISSION /LONELY PLANET IMAGES ©

Grand Canal

20

Other capitals can keep their grand boulevards: Venice's Grand Canal (p176) makes all other byways seem downright pedestrian. Drifting is the only way to cover this shimmering stretch of the imagination, from the controversial modern fish-tail Calatrava Bridge to the lacy pink Gothic Ducal Palace. Grand buildings lining the waterway span centuries and architectural styles, from medieval Moorish Gothic to 21st-century postmodern baroque. Gondolas tied to striped mooring poles bob in Grand Canal waves, as though bowing at passing dignitaries in their sleek teak taxi-boats. Traffic never looked this good.

RICHARD I'ANSON / LONELY PLANET IMAGES ©

Leonardo Da Vinci's Last Supper

In Da Vinci's *Last Supper* (p127), apostles leap out of their chairs in shock as Jesus calmly reports that one of them will betray him. For his dynamic mural, Da Vinci used a trick street artists now take for granted: applying wet paint onto a dry wall, instead of the medieval wet-on-wet fresco technique. The experimental mix proved unstable, but even badly faded, this Renaissance breakthrough shows indelible genius.

San Gimignano

Medieval hill towns dot the Tuscan hillside, but this one's more of an exclamation mark. Eleven medieval skyscrapers loom over tiny San Gimignano (p256), where neighbourly competition for status fuelled a 14th-century tower-building boom – until the plague rendered such artificial distinctions irrelevant. Centuries later, the town's towering ambitions have paid off: one of Tuscany's premier attractions, San Gimignano is now a Unesco World Heritage site.

The Dolomites

Scour the globe and you'll find plenty of taller, bigger, more geologically volatile mountains, but few can match the romance of the pink-hued, granite Dolomites (p192). Maybe it's their jagged summits dressed in vibrant spring skirts of wildflowers or the skiers that zigzag their valleys in winter, but this tiny pocket of northern Italy has produced some of the most daring mountaineers on the planet.

23

The Best...
Peak Performances

LA SCALA
Verdi premieres set standards for opera's toughest crowds – they've made grown tenors cry, but the intermission commentary is priceless. (p135)

ROMAN ARENA, VERONA
Roman games seem tame compared to epic productions in this open-air Roman amphitheatre. (p206)

LA FENICE
From Rossini to Stravinsky, this gilded jewel-box theatre has lured the world's best. (p199)

TEATRO SAN CARLO
Freshly restored, Italy's largest opera house is set to steal La Scala divas' thunder. (p292)

Bologna's Quadrilatero

Roman traders once hawked their wares in this ancient market district, and surprisingly little has changed in the Quadrilatero (p209). Via Pescherie Vecchie (Old Fishmongers' Street) still sells its namesake product, and you can hear knives being sharpened on whetstones along Via Caprarie (Butchers' Street). Best of all are the delicatessens, with backlit *prosciutto di parma* (cured Parma hams) hanging in shop windows like Tiffany jewels. Pack a picnic to enjoy under Bologna's porticos, and taste why the Quadrilatero has been foodie central for millennia.

The Best...
Beaches

VIESTE
Sandy beaches with shimmering blue waters, backed by striking white bluffs. (p341)

BAGNI REGINA GIOVANNA
Snorkle through the ruins of an ancient Roman villa. (p299)

ISCHIA
Island spa retreat, with natural hot springs on private beaches. (p304)

LIDO DEL FARO
Luxe beach getaway on the isle of Capri, with a private beach, swimming pool and onsite seafood restaurant. (p302)

TAORMINA
Take the cable car from the cliff-side beach to coves bobbing with fishing rowboats. (p333)

(25)

Turin's Reggia di Venaria Reale

Equivalent to the Medicis in Florence and the Borgheses in Rome, Turin's Savoy princes had a penchant for extravagant royal palaces – but they clearly outdid themselves in Italy's mini-Versailles, the Reggia di Venaria Reale (p149). This non-too-modest hunting lodge of Duke Carlo Emanuele II is one of the largest royal residences in Europe, and the mammoth €200 million restoration of this Unesco-certified building involved the preservation of 1.5 million sq ft of stucco and plasterwork and 11,000 sq ft of frescoes.

Italy's
Top Itineraries

Florence to Rome World Heritage Wonders

5 DAYS

Italy is home to an enviable 47 Unesco World Heritage Sites, with 38 more on the short list for confirmation. Cover some of Italy's most celebrated sites on this brief trip – and see how many make your own list of all-time favourite destinations.

Adriatic Sea

FLORENCE ①

SAN MARINO

② SAN GIMIGNANO

③ SIENA

④ ASSISI

Tyrrhenian Sea

⑤ ROME

① Florence (p226)

Florence's historic centre is a Unesco World Heritage Site. Here you don't have to hunt for treasures: the **Duomo** and its **Battistero**, the **Basilica di Santa Maria Novella** and the **Palazzo Vecchio** make Renaissance razzle-dazzle hard to miss. Circle the monuments, then devote an afternoon to the **Uffizi** and the next morning to the **Galleria dell'Accademia**.

FLORENCE ➲ SAN GIMIGNANO
🚌 **1¼ hours** 14 buses daily. 🚗 **One hour** SP1 to Poggibonsi, then SR2 to RA3.

② San Gimignano (p256)

On day three, head to skyscraping San Gimignano, famous for its mini-Manhattan of medieval towers. Step into the town's **basilica** for 14th-century frescoes, including di Bartolo's hungry devil, and sleep in a medieval townhouse at **Hotel L'Antico Pozzo**.

SAN GIMIGNANO ➲ SIENA
🚌 **One to 1½ hours** 10 buses Monday to Saturday. 🚗 **One to 1½ hours** Take RA3 (Siena–Florence superstrada).

③ Siena (p250)

Cappuccino kick-starts day four in **Il Campo**. Admire the **Palazzo Pubblico**, see the stunning inlaid marble floors of the **Duomo**, then view its exterior from your room at **Campo Regio Relais**.

SIENA ➲ ASSISI
🚌 **2½ to three hours** Daily bus to Perugia, then hourly Perugia–Assisi train. 🚗 **One to 1½ hours** SS326 to Perugia, then SS75 (Ospedalicchio exit).

④ Assisi (p263)

Pause for reflection on day five in the Unesco–heralded home of St Francis. His life unfolds in glowing colour in Giotto's **Basilica di San Francesco** frescoes.

ASSISI ➲ ROME
🚌 **Two to 2½ hours** Hourly trains leave for Rome via Foligno. 🚗 **2½ to three hours** Take SS75 to Perugia, then A1 to Rome.

⑤ Rome (p64)

For Romans, the classic **Centro Storico** stroll involves gossip under the **Pantheon**'s stone portico, espresso at **Tazza d'Oro** and pizza at **Pizzeria da Baffetto**.

Spanish steps and Chiesa della Trinità dei Monti (p79)

RICHARD I'ANSON/LONELY PLANET IMAGES ©

33

5 DAYS

Rome to Pompeii
Ancient Rome's Greatest Hits

Ancient Rome didn't just fall – it was smothered in volcanic ash, buried in mudslides, and stomped underfoot. But in Italy, millennia-old Roman artefacts have been found remarkably intact, from temple altars to brothel menus. See the relics of Italy's late, great civilisation.

ROME ①
② OSTIA ANTICA
Golfo di Gaeta
NAPLES ③
⑤
HERCULANEUM ④
POMPEII
Adriatic Sea
Tyrrhenian Sea

1 Rome (p64)

Experience the city as ancient Romans did. Swing by the **Roman Forum** to hear news, and pray to the gods for peace, marriage and success in politics. Stop by the **Mercati di Traiano**, the three-storey market where silks and spices from every corner of the empire were sold. Don't miss the **Colosseum**, or the obligatory photo with a gladiator – tipping is customary, flirting optional.

ROME ◐ OSTIA ANTICA
🚌 **45 minutes** From Stazione Porta San Polo, catch Ostia–Lido train. 🚗 **30 minutes** Take A12 toward Fiumicino; take the Scavi exit.

2 Ostia Antica (p84)

On day two, follow ancient Romans fed up with chariot traffic, and take a day trip down to Ostia Antica. Traces of this 2300-year-old resort town were buried during medieval floods, but archaeologists have recently uncovered spa complexes with wrestling rings, restaurants with frescoed menus and even ancient door-less latrines.

ROME ◐ NAPLES
🚌 **1¼ to 1¾ hours** 42 Rome–Naples trains daily, including Frecciarossa (High Velocity). 🚗 **Two to three hours** Take A1 south.

3 Naples (p284)

In Naples, ancient Rome lurks around every corner. Roman bakeries and laundries hide under church floors at **Chiesa e Scavi di San Lorenzo Maggiore**; a city of the dead can be found in **catacombs** under Naples' vibrant streets; and palatial **Museo Archaeologico Nazionale** is littered with looted antiquities, from Pompeii mosaics to vividly illustrated menus for Roman brothels. On day four, explore Roman secret passages by candlelight with

Napoli Sotterranea, emerging for dinner at legendary **Pizzeria Gino Sorbillo**.

NAPLES ◐ POMPEII
🚌 **35 minutes** Frequent, fast service. 🚌 **30 minutes** Every half hour. 🚗 **45 minutes** Take A3 south.

4 Pompeii (p298)

Talk about unlucky: Pompeii was recovering from an AD 63 earthquake when Mt Vesuvius erupted, burying the town. Today, the remarkable preservation allows visitors to see how citizens died – plaster casts of adult victims trying to shelter children are especially poignant – but also how ancient Romans lived, between wars and disasters.

POMPEII ◐ HERCULANEUM
🚌 **25 minutes** Frequent service from Pompeii to Ercolano-Scavi station and Naples. 🚗 **30 minutes** Take A3 north.

5 Herculaneum (p299)

The eruption that buried Pompeii caused mudslides in Herculaneum, and this Roman city is arguably even better preserved. Looters were lax here, leaving fossilised home decor, gorgeous mosaics and a statue of Hercules urinating.

Pompeii (p298)
GREG ELMS/LONELY PLANET IMAGES ©

10 DAYS

Rome to Barolo
Gourmet Grand Tour

Earn the ultimate gourmet bragging rights on an Italian adventure that leads you by the tastebuds from cappuccino in Rome to decadent deli in Bologna, red wine in Verona, chocolate in Turin, Slow Food feasts in Bra, truffles in Alba, ending with a world-class nightcap in Barolo..

❶ Rome (p64)

After experiencing Michelangelo's **Sistine Chapel**, summit the dome of **St Peter's**, then hit **Hostaria Dino e Tony** for *pasta all'amatriciana*. Sightseeing in **Centro Storico** is a fine excuse for gelato at **Gelateria Giolitti** and drinks in **Campo de' Fiori**.

ROME ➲ BOLOGNA
🚊 2¼ to four hours 42 Rome–Naples trains daily, including Frecciarossa (High Velocity).
🚗 3¾ hours Take A1 north.

❷ Bologna (p207)

Explore cutting-edge art at **MAMbo**, then browse the **Quadrilatero**, where medieval porticos shelter mouth-watering deli displays. The next day, whip up a feast with a **La Vecchia Scuola Bolognese** cooking course or leave it to the professionals at **Drogheria della Rosa**.

BOLOGNA ➲ VERONA
🚊 1½ hours Hourly departures.
🚗 1½ hours Take A22 north.

❸ Verona (p204)

Fair Verona is where Shakespeare set his scene, and romance is aided by Veneto's famed wines at **Piazza delle Erbe** and the annual **VinItaly**. Catch a summer outdoor opera at the ancient **Roman Arena**.

VERONA ➲ TURIN
🚊 Three to four hours Several trains daily; change in Milan. 🚗 Three to 3½ hours Take the A21 via Piacenza to avoid Milan traffic.

Bologna (p207)
© DAVID NOTON PHOTOGRAPHY / ALAMY

❹ Turin (p147)

Devote a day to Turin's excellent **museums**, with frequent fuel stops at **historic cafes**. Stay the night in converted-car-factory **Le Meridien Art + Tech**, before diving into **Eataly**, where tastings and culinary workshops double as meals.

TURIN ➲ BRA
🚊 One hour Frequent commuter trains.
🚗 One hour Take A6 south to Marene; exit to SS231 east to Bra.

❺ Bra (p152)

The home of Slow Food is the little town of Bra, where artisans make chocolates, cheeses and cured meats from historic recipes. Dine upstairs from Slow Food HQ at **Osteria del Boccondivino,** and sleep in a winery at **Albergo Cantine Ascheri**.

BRA ➲ ALBA
🚊 15 to 30 minutes Frequent commuter trains.
🚗 30 minutes Take E74 east.

❻ Alba (p152)

Head straight to the source of Italy's white truffles and celebrated red wine. Get an edible education with **cooking classes, winery tours** and **truffle-foraging** excursions, and stay at comfortable **Hotel San Lorenz**.

ALBA ➲ BAROLO
🚊 20 minutes Trains every hour.
🚗 20 minutes Take SP3 south.

❼ Barolo (p152)

This tiny village makes Italy's most prized food-friendly wines, offering bargain **Enoteca Regionale** tastings in a castle dungeon. The town's namesake red is stunning with truffle-laced meals at **Hotel Barolo**.

10 DAYS

Naples to Palermo
Seaside Splendours

Vertiginous cliffs, pastel-hued fishing villages, sun-drenched Mediterranean flavours: this trip takes in seriously stunning coasts. Peak beach season is late summer, so book July-August accommodation well ahead.

① NAPLES
CAPRI ② ③ POSITANO
Golfo di Salerno
Golfo di Taranto
Tyrrhenian Sea
⑤ AEOLIAN ISLANDS
Ionian Sea
④ TAORMINA

❶ Naples (p284)

Begin your seaside getaway in hyperactive Naples, its **centro storico** home to Graeco-Roman ruins, baroque churches and the ultra-hip **MADRE** museum of contemporary art. Sample Neapolitan pizza and produce at the **Mercato di Porta Nolana**, and enjoy baroque masterpieces and splendid vistas at the **Certosa di San Martino**.

NAPLES ➔ CAPRI
🚢 **40 to 50 minutes** Ferries leave from Molo Beverello; some hydrofoils depart Mergellina.

❷ Capri (p300)

On day four, catch a ferry from Naples to dazzling Capri. Take a boat trip into the incandescent **Blue Grotto** and indulge in *la dolce vita* on **Piazza Umberto I**. Day five options include taking a **diving course**, riding the **seggiovia** for panoramas, or exploring imperial ruins at **Villa Jovis**.

CAPRI ➔ POSITANO
🚢 **30 to 40 minutes** Direct hydrofoil service in summer; via Sorrento autumn to spring.

❸ Positano (p305)

The Amalfi Coast's most photogenic town is short on sights but big on charm – a fine excuse to explore boutique-lined streets or soak up the sun on **Spiaggia Grande**.

POSITANO ➔ TAORMINA
🚢 **10½ hours** Overnight ferry from Naples
✈ **One hour** Fly from Naples to Messina or Catania, connected to Taormina by train.
🚆 **6½ hours** Train from Naples to Taormina, with ferry between Villa San Giovanni and Messina.

❹ Taormina (p333)

Unwind in jet-set-favourite Taormina, with its rowboats to **Isola Bella** for lazy beachside lounging and its medieval streets selling local ceramics. In summer, don't miss concerts in Taormina's iconic amphitheatre, **Teatro Greco**.

TAORMINA ➔ AEOLIAN ISLANDS
🚢 **Three hours** Take the train to Milazzo, where frequent summer ferries depart for the Aeolian Islands.

❺ Aeolian Islands (p330)

Spend a couple of days on the stunning Aeolian Islands, surrounded by crystal-clear waters. **Lipari** has an impressive citadel museum; **Vulcano** offers therapeutic hot springs and black-sand beaches; and verdant, flower-strewn **Salina** sprinkles pasta with island-grown capers.

Vulcano (p330), Aeolian Islands
HOLGER LEUE/LONELY PLANET IMAGES ©

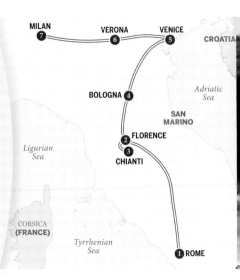

2 WEEKS

Rome to Milan Classic Cities

While Italy's riches could easily take a lifetime to explore, two weeks will allow you a respectable taste of its astounding architectural, artistic, culinary and geographic diversity. The focus here is on the big-hitters, with a speedy side trip thrown in.

❶ Rome (p64)

Spend your first day exploring ancient must-see sights such as the **Imperial Forum** and the **Capitoline Museum**, before aperitivo hour at **Salotto 42**. The following day, take in the cultural riches of the **Vatican** before a rustic Roman feast in **Trastevere**. On day three, meet masterpieces at **Museo e Galleria Borghese** and flip a coin into the **Trevi Fountain** to ensure a return visit.

ROME ➡ FLORENCE
🚃 1½ to four hours Two to three trains per hour.
🚗 Three hours Take A1 north.

❷ Florence (p226)

Head to the Renaissance jewel of Florence and take in the whole of the city from the top of the **Duomo** before spending the afternoon at the **Uffizi**. Save the next morning to say 'ciao' to *David* at the **Galleria dell'Accademia**, before checking out the **Central Market** and watching the sun sink behind **Ponte Vecchio**.

FLORENCE ➡ CHIANTI
🚌 One hour Buses depart hourly for Greve in Chianti. 🚗 40 minutes to one hour Take SR222 south.

❸ Chianti (p255)

Take a break from Italy's urban intensity with a bike tour to the vine-draped hills of Chianti. Indulge in a little wine tasting, soak up the sun-blessed Tuscan countryside and pedal back to Florence in time for a dinner at **L'Osteria di Giovanni**.

FLORENCE ➡ BOLOGNA
🚃 35 minutes to 1½ hours Two to three trains hourly. 🚗 1½ hours Take A1 north.

❹ Bologna (p207)

The following morning it's time to travel north to food-obsessed **Bologna**. Take in art and medieval architecture on **Piazza Maggiore** before diving into the delis of the **Quadrilatero**. Finally, whet your appetite for dinner by climbing **Torre degli Asinelli**.

Chianti (p255), Tuscany
GLENN VAN DER KNIJFF/LONELY PLANET IMAGES ©

VENICE ⟳ VERONA

🚊 1¼ to 2¼ hours At least three trains hourly.
🚌 1¾ hours Take A4 west.

6 Verona (p204)

On day 12, travel west to the setting of Romeo and Juliet – **Verona**. Fall head-over-heels for the city's beautiful churches and *palazzi*, including Romanesque **Basilica di San Zeno Maggiore** and Renaissance **Loggia del Consiglio**. If you're visiting between July and September, don't miss opera at the **Roman Arena**.

VERONA ⟳ MILAN

🚊 1¼ to two hours Trains every half-hour.
🚌 1¾ to two hours Take A4 west.

7 Milan (p122)

Complete your adventure in high-octane Milan, home of the outlandishly Gothic **Duomo**, high-fashion **Galleria Vittorio Emanuele II** and legendary opera house **La Scala**. Make sure you're booked to see Leonardo Da Vinci's **The Last Supper**. If you miss out, get your cultural fix at the **Pinacoteca di Brera** before a wardrobe overhaul in the fashionista heartland **Quadrilatero d'Oro**.

BOLOGNA ⟳ VENICE

🚊 1¼ to 2¼ hours Frequent trains, some via Mestre. 🚌 20 minutes Take A13 north; park at Tronchetto, Venice's parking garage.

5 Venice (p170)

Arriving in Venice on day eight, allow the wonder to sink in. Bask in the architectural glories of **Piazza San Marco**, stroll winding streets to the **Rialto Bridge**, and sample rare Veneto vintages at **I Rusteghi**. Discover modern art at **Peggy Guggenheim Collection** and **Punta Della Dogana**, and follow fraternal-twin masterpieces at **I Frari** and **Scuola Grande di San Rocco** with cocktails in **Campo Santa Margherita**. Explore the outer lagoon islands to find glass on Murano, colour-blocked houses on Burano, and perhaps overnight in Ernest Hemingway's writer's retreat on Torcello.

Italy Month by Month

Top Events

- ⊛ **Settimana Santa,** March to April
- ⊛ **Festa di San Gennaro,** May, September & December
- ⊛ **La Biennale di Venezia,** June to October
- ⊛ **Estate Romana,** June to September
- ✖ **Festival delle Sagre,** September
- ✖ **Fiera del Tartufo,** November

January

Following hot on the heels of New Year is Epiphany. In the Alps and Dolomites, it's ski season, while in the Mediterranean south winters are mild and crowd-free, although many resort towns are firmly shut.

⊛ Regata della Befana

Witches in Venice don't ride brooms: they row boats. Venice celebrates Epiphany with a fleet of brawny men dressed up as witches (*befane*).

✪ Ski Italia

Italy's top ski resorts are in the northern Alps and the Dolomites, but you'll also find resorts in the Apennines, Le Marche and even Sicily. The best months of the season are January and February.

February

Short and accursed, is how Italian's describe February. In the mountains the ski season hits its peak in line with school holidays. Further south its chilly but almond trees start to blossom and carnival season warms things up.

⊛ Carnevale

In the period leading up to Ash Wednesday, many Italian towns stage pre-Lenten carnivals. Venice's Carnevale (www.carnevale.venezia.it) is the most famous.

✖ Mostra Mercato del Tartufo Nero

An early spring taste of truffles from the gastronomic Umbrian town of Norcia. Thousands of visitors sift through booths tasting all things truffle, and other speciality produce (www.neronorcia.it).

(left) Carnevale, Venice
RUTH EASTHAM & MAX PAOLI/LONELY PLANET IMAGES ©

March

The weather in March is capricious: sunny, rainy and windy all at once. March 21st is the official start of Spring, but things only really start to open up for the main season during Easter week.

🎋 Settimana Santa

On Good Friday, the pope leads a candlelit procession to the Colosseum, and on Easter Sunday, he gives his blessing. In Florence, a cartful of fireworks explodes in Piazza del Duomo.

April

Spring has sprung and April sees the Italian peninsula bloom. The mountains of Sicily and Calabria are carpeted with wildflowers, while the gardens of the Italian north show off their tulips and early magnolias.

🎯 Settimana del Tulipano

Tulips erupt in bloom in the grounds of Villa Taranto on Lake Maggiore. The dahlia path and dogwood are also in bloom in what is considered one of Europe's finest botanical gardens.

🎋 Vinitaly

Sandwiched between the Valpolicella and Soave wine regions, Verona hosts the world's largest wine fair, VinItaly (www.vinitaly.com). Over five days, 4,000 international exhibitors offer liquid education with wine tastings, lectures and seminars.

May

The month of roses and early summer produce makes May a perfect time to travel, especially for walkers. The weather is warm but not too hot and prices throughout Italy are good value. It's also patron saint season.

🎋 Processione dei Serpari

The strangest patron saint day is held in Cocullo, Abruzzo. A statue of St Dominic is draped with live snakes and carried in the Snake-Charmers' Procession.

🎋 Festa di San Gennaro

As patron saint days go, Naples' Festa di San Gennaro has a lot riding on it – namely securing the city from volcanic disaster. The faithful gather in the cathedral to see San Gennaro's blood liquefy. If it does, the city is safe. Repeat performances take place on 19 September and 16 December.

June

The summer season kicks off in June. The temperature cranks up quickly, beach *lidi* (resorts) start to open and some of the big summer festivals commence. June 2 is the Anniversary of the Republic, a national holiday.

🎋 La Biennale di Venezia

Held June-October in odd-numbered years, the Venice Art Biennale (p191) is one of the art world's most prestigious events. Architecture events are held September-November of even-numbered years, and performing art events are held annually spring-summer.

🎋 Festival dei Due Mondi

Held in the Umbrian hill town of Spoleto from late June to mid-July, the Spoleto Festival (www.spoletofestival.it) is an international arts event, featuring music, theatre, dance and art.

July

School is out and Italians everywhere are heading out of cities and to the mountains or beaches for their summer holidays. Prices and temperatures rise. Many cities host summer art festivals.

🌠 Ferragosto

One of Italy's biggest holidays. It marks the Feast of the Assumption, but even before Christianity, the Romans honoured their gods on Feriae Augusti. Naples celebrates with particular fervour.

🌠 Venice International Film Festival

The Mostra del Cinema di Venezia (p191) is held at the Lido and attracts the international film glitterati with its red-carpet premieres and glamour.

September

This is a glorious month to travel in Italy. Summer waxes into autumn and the start of the harvest season sees lots of local *sagre* (food festivals) spring up.

❌ Festival delle Sagre

On the second Sunday of September over 40 communes in the Piedmont province of Asti put their wines and local gastronomic products on display (www.festivaldellesagre.it).

🌠 Regata Storica

On the first Sunday in September, a floating parade of boaters in period dress are followed by gondola and other boat races along the Grand Canal in Venice.

October

October is a fabulous time to visit the south, when the days still radiate with late summer warmth and the *lidi* are emptying out. Further north the temperature starts to drop and summer festivals come to an end.

🌠 Il Palio

Daredevils in tights thrill the crowds with this chaotic bareback horse race around the piazza in Siena. Preceding the race is a parade in medieval costume.

🌠 Estate Romana

Between the end of June and September, Rome puts on a summer calendar of events that turn the city into an outdoor stage. The programme encompasses music, dance, literature and film, and events are staged in some of Rome's most attractive venues.

August

August in Italy is hot, expensive and crowded. Everyone is on holiday and while it may no longer be true that everything is shut, many businesses and restaurants do close for part of the month.

Salone Internazionale del Gusto

Hosted by the Piedmont-based Slow Food Movement, this biennial food Expo is held in Turin in even-numbered years.

November

Winter creeps down the peninsula in November, but there's plenty going on. This is truffle season, and also time for the chestnut harvest and mushroom picking.

Ognissanti

Celebrated all over Italy as a national holiday, All Saints Day on the 1st November commemorates the Saint Martyrs, while the 2nd November, All Souls Day, is set aside to honour the deceased.

Fiera del Tartufo

From Alba (www.fieradeltartufo.org) and Asti in the north to Tuscany's San Miniato (www.san-miniato.com), November is prime truffle-time.

Opera Season

Italy is home to four of the world's great opera houses: La Scala in Milan, La Fenice in Venice, Teatro San Carlo in Naples and Teatro Massimo in Palermo. The season traditionally runs from mid-October to March, although La Scala opens later on St Ambrose Day, the 7th of December.

December

The days of alfresco living are firmly at an end. December is cold and Alpine resorts start to open for the early ski season. Looming Christmas festivities warm things up though.

Natale

The weeks preceding Christmas are studded with religious events. Many churches set up nativity scenes known as *presepi* – Naples is especially famous for these. On Christmas, the Pope gives Midnight mass in St Peter's Square.

Far left: Il Palio, Siena
Left: Regata Storica, Venice

What's New

For this new edition of Discover Italy, our authors have hunted down the fresh, the transformed, the hot and the happening. These are some of our favourites. For up-to-the-minute recommendations, see lonelyplanet.com/italy.

1 MAXXI, ROME
Winner of the 2010 Stirling Prize for architecture, Rome's new MAXXI gallery, designed by Zaha Hadid, curves and coils like Kubrick's Space Odyssey interiors (p91).

2 CINQUE TERRE TRAILS
New National Park bike trails (complete with bike rental) have opened along the Cinque Terre (p154).

3 SICILIAN FLIGHTS
Sicily's Trapani airport is busy expanding. Ryanair have added 13 new routes, including flights from Scandinavia and Eastern Europe (p330).

4 MUSEO DEL VINO, BAROLO
Barolo's new interactive wine museum was designed by François Confino (behind Turin's fab film museum). There's a different wine tasting every day (p152).

5 VENISSA, MAZZORBO
Dine on rising-star Paola Budel's inspired lagoon cuisine at Venissa. If you're lucky you may get to sample the estate's new vintage of the heritage island-grown Dorona grape (p190).

6 NEW VIEWS AT ARA PACIS, ROME
Richard Meier's minimalist museum housing Augustus' Arch of Peace incited architectural turf warfare between modernists and traditionalists by blocking views of a baroque church. Peace is at hand: a Meier-approved plan to dismantle the offending wall is in the works (p81).

7 GRAND HOTEL PIAZZA BORSA, PALERMO
Wake up feeling like a million bucks after a sound night's sleep in the Sicilian Stock Exchange, re-opened in 2010 as a luxe hotel with Jacuzzi suites (p327).

8 ALESSI FLAGSHIP, MILAN
Whimsical home decor has a new home in Milan's swanky Quadrilatero d'Oro, where purple spotlighting illuminates Martí Guixé's displays that look like minimalist sacrificial altars (p135).

9 METRO TO EATALY, TURIN
New metro service now provides easy access to Turin's major suburban attraction: a Fiat factory transformed by Renzo Piano into an industrial-chic complex of art, hotels, and Eataly (p150).

10 FAMILY APARTMENTS, TUSCANY
Available on a nightly basis, Kristin and Kaare's family-friendly apartments in Lucca fill a big gap in Tuscany's accommodation market. They also organise tours and cooking courses (p247).

11 PALAZZO GRIMANI, VENICE
Venice's Palazzo Grimani is open to the public after nearly 30 years of restoration. It houses Doge Grimani's Graeco-Roman antiquities and high-calibre temporary exhibitions (p188).

Get Inspired

📖 Books

○ **Christ Stopped at Eboli** (1947) Carlo Levi's bitter-sweet tale of an exiled dissident doctor.

○ **History** (1974) War, sexual violence and a mother's struggles define Elsa Morante's controversial novel.

○ **The Baron in the Trees** (1957) Italo Calvino's tragicomic fable is a metaphor for Italy's postwar reinvention.

○ **The Name of the Rose** (1980) A medieval murder mystery from literary heavyweight Umberto Eco.

○ **The Snack Thief** (2000) A maverick cop on his toes in Andrea Camilleri's whodunit.

🎬 Films

○ **Il Postino** (1994) Massimo Troisi plays Italy's most adorable postman.

○ **La Dolce Vita** (1960) Federico Fellini's tale of hedonism, celebrity and suicide in 1950s Rome.

○ **Pane e Tulipani** (2000) A housewife runs away to Venice, pursued by an amateur detective.

○ **Caro Diario** (1994) Director/actor Nanni Moretti looks for the meaning of life in Rome on a Vespa.

○ **Gomorra** (2008) In-your-face mafia exposé based on Roberto Saviano's best seller.

🎵 Music

○ **Mina** (Mina) Best-selling album from Italy's foremost female rocker.

○ **Crêuza de mä** (Fabrizio de André) Bob Dylan–esque poetry in Genovese dialect.

○ **Stato di Necessità** (Carmen Consoli) Guitar riffs and soulful lyrics from Sicily's favourite singer/songwriter.

○ **Suburb** ('A67) Neapolitan rock-crossover group 'A67 collaborate with anti-mafia activists.

🖱 Websites

○ **Delicious Italy** (www.deliciousitaly.com) Find a cooking course; research Italian food and wine.

○ **Ente Nazionale Italiano per il Turismo** (www.enit.it) The Italian national tourist board's website.

○ **Life in Italy** (www.lifeinitaly.com) Italian news in English, everything from current affairs to fashion.

○ **Lonely Planet** (lonely planet.com) Country-specific information, forums and articles.

⏱ Short on time?

This list will give you instant insight into the country.

Read *The Leopard* (1958) Giuseppe di Lampedusa's epic tale of Sicily's Independence upheavals is Italy's all-time best seller.

Watch *Bicycle Thieves* (1958) Vittorio di Sica's poignant tale of an honest man trying to provide for his son in postwar Rome.

Listen *La Traviata* (1955) Diva Maria Callas embodies Verdi's fallen woman in La Scala's production by film-maker Luchino Visconti.

Log on www.tweetaly.com offers Italian updates on the arts, festivals, recipes and more.

Barolo wine
ALAN BENSON/LONELY PLANET IMAGES ©

●●● Need to Know

Currency
Euro (€)

Language
Italian

ATMs
Readily available in cities and towns.

Credit Cards
Visa and MasterCard widely accepted.

Visas
Generally not required for stays under 90 days (or for most EU nationals; exceptions include the UK and Ireland).

Mobile Phones
European and Australian phones work; other phones should be set to roaming. Use a local SIM card for cheaper local calls.

Wi-Fi
Irregular wi-fi hotspots often require payment.

Internet Access
Bring ID for internet cafes.

Driving
Drive on the right; steering wheel is on the left side of the car. By law, turn on headlights on all motorways.

Tipping
Optional 10% for good service.

When to Go

Dry climate
Warm to hot summer, mild winter
Warm to hot summer, cold winter
Mild summer, cold winter
Cold climate

Milan
GO Dec–Mar (skiing) & Sep

Venice
GO Feb–Mar & Sep–Nov

Rome
GO Apr–May, Jul & Nov–Dec

Naples
GO May–Jun & Sep

Palermo
GO Sep–Oct

High Season
(Jul–Aug)
○ Queues at big sights and on the road, especially August

○ Prices skyrocket for Christmas, New Year and Easter

○ Late December to March high season in the Alps and Dolomites

Shoulder
(Apr–Jun & Sep–Oct)
○ Good deals on accommodation, especially in the south

○ Spring is best for festivals, flowers and local produce

○ Autumn is best for warm weather and the grape harvest

Low Season
(Nov–Mar)
○ Prices at their lowest – up to 30% lower than in high season

○ Many sights and hotels closed in coastal and mountainous areas

○ A good period for cultural events in large cities

Advance Planning

○ **Three months before** Shop for flight deals, book accommodation if travelling during peak times and research classes.

○ **One month before** Scan local websites for special events or festivals on during your stay, and book tickets where possible.

○ **One week before** If taking prescription medications, ask your physician for a signed and dated letter describing your condition and medication. Scan or photocopy all important documents (passport, driving licence), reconfirm accommodation bookings and make key restaurant reservations.

Your Daily Budget

Budget up to €100

- Dorm beds €15-25
- Double room in a budget hotel €50-100
- Pizza and pasta €8-12
- Excellent markets and delis for self-catering

Midrange €100-200

- Double room in a hotel €80-180
- Lunch and dinner in local restaurants €25-45

Top end over €200

- Double room in four- or five-star hotel €200-450
- Top restaurant dinner €50-150

Exchange Rates

Australia	A$1	€0.73
Canada	C$1	€0.72
Japan	¥100	€0.96
New Zealand	NZ$1	€0.56
UK	UK£1	€1.16
US	US$1	€0.74

For current exchange rates see www.xe.com

What to Bring

- **Clothing** Smart casual clothes – T-shirts, shorts and dusty sandals don't cut it in bars and restaurants in fashion-conscious Italy.
- **ID** Passport or Italian ID card obligatory for hotel check-in and internet cafes. Valid licence and car documents required if driving.
- **Insurance** Ensure comprehensive coverage for theft, cancellations and medical expenses, and car insurance if driving.

Arriving in Italy

Aeroporto Leonardo Da Vinci-Fiumicino

Trains and buses To Rome centre every 30 minutes from 6am to 11pm

Night bus Hourly from 12.30am to 5am

Taxis €40 set fare; 45 minutes

Aeroporto Milano Malpensa

Malpensa Express and Shuttle To Milan centre every 30 minutes from 5am to 10.30pm

Night bus Limited services between 11pm and 5am

Taxis €79 set fare; 50 minutes

Aeroporto Capodichino

Airport shuttle To Naples centre every 20 minutes from 6.30am to 11.40pm

Taxis €19 set fare; 30 minutes

Getting Around

- **Air** Best for travellers on tight schedules.
- **Boat** Frequent ferries and hydrofoils connect Italy's islands to mainland ports.
- **Bus** Handy for smaller towns, Italy's extensive bus network spans local to intercity routes.
- **Car** Rental is limited to persons aged 25 years or over.
- **Train** Italy's extensive and affordable train network spans high-speed intercity to slower regional services.

Accommodation

- **Agriturismi** Farmstays range from few-frills rustic to pool-side chic.
- **B&Bs** Affordable and popular, from a room in a family home to self-contained studio apartments.
- **Convents and monasteries** Tranquillity and an early curfew define Italy's more spiritually inclined slumbering options.
- **Hotels** An extensive range of options spanning cheap-and-nasty dosshouses near stations to uberluxe retreats.
- **Pensioni** Modest, smaller-scale hotels, usually family-run.
- **Villa rentals** Self-contained accommodation in picturesque rural dwellings.

Be Forewarned

- **Appropriate attire** Cover torsos, shoulders and upper legs when visiting religious sites.
- **Petty theft** Be mindful of personal possessions, especially in crowded public areas.
- **Public holidays** Many restaurants and shops close for at least part of August.

Rome & the Vatican

When high culture meets street culture, it's pure Roman romance. Rome has impressive credentials: it ran an empire for a millennium, starred in dozens of classic films, created more than enough artistic masterpieces to fill its many palaces and maintains a close (if complicated) relationship with the Pope.

But when you see this city in action, it's the beginning of an epic crush. Priests in designer shades march through the Vatican chatting on mobile phones; politicians toss silk ties over their shoulders to gorge on gelato on baroque piazzas; safety-helmeted fashionistas throw farewell kisses as they roar down ancient cobblestone lanes on their scooters. You'll have to excuse the rushed goodbyes – with a packed calendar of arts festivals, alternative underground events, and reservations at legendary trattorias, Romans are usually running late for some fabulous date. Join them, and discover for yourself why all roads lead to Rome.

Trevi Fountain (p80)

St Peter's Basilica (p90)

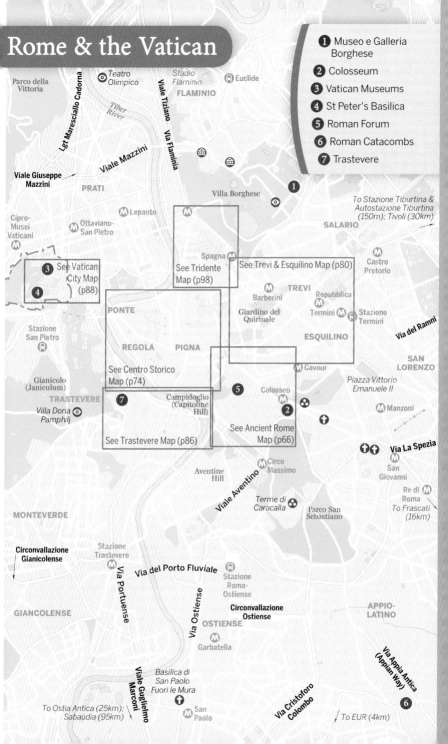

Rome & the Vatican Highlights

① Museo e Galleria Borghese

What makes the Museo e Galleria Borghese so special is there are so many important artworks in a relatively compact space. The result is less museum fatigue and a journey that takes you from the Roman period to golden-age masters like Caravaggio, Bernini, Borromini, Titian and Canova...just to name a few!

Need to Know

ONLY TWO HOURS? On the ground floor, see the gladiatorial mosaics. Upstairs, see Canova's Venere Vincitrice, the Caravaggios and Raphael's paintings **See our author's review, p93.**

Don't Miss List

BY ALESSIO ZITO, TOUR GUIDE

1 VENERE VINCITRICE

Antonio Canova's depiction of Napoleon's sister, Paolina Borghese, as *Venere Vincitrice* (Venus Victorious) is sublime. You could spend hours marvelling at how Canova managed to make the figure 'sink' into the cushions. The way the drapery flows so effortlessly over her body is equally impressive.

2 RATTO DI PROSERPINA

Gian Lorenzo Bernini's sculpture *The Rape of Proserpina* (1621-2) is incredible in that its twisting composition allows the simultaneous depiction of Pluto's abduction of Proserpina, their arrival in the underworld and her praying for release. To experience the narrative, start from the left, move to the front, and then view it from the right.

3 RITRATTO DI GIOVANE DONNA CON UNICORNO

Raphael's portrait *The Young Woman with a Unicorn* (c 1506) was inspired by da Vinci's *The Lady with an Ermine* (1490). The painting originally depicted a woman holding a dog, a symbol of fidelity. But when the marriage did not take place, scholars believe, Raphael replaced the dog with a unicorn, a symbol of chastity or virginity.

4 SATIRE SU DELFINO

In Sala VII, the 'Egyptian Room', you'll find the *Satyr on a Dolphin,* dating from the 2nd century and probably intended for a fountain. The piece is believed to have inspired Raphael's design for the figure of Jonah and the Whale in the Chigi Chapel inside the Chiesa di Santa Maria del Popolo (p77).

5 BACCHINO MALATO

Of the many Caravaggio paintings, *Sick Bacchus* (1592-5) is particularly intriguing for its portrayal of the god of heady pleasures as a pale, tired-looking youth. Scholars believe the self-portrait was executed when Caravaggio was suffering from malaria. Cardinal Scipione Borghese, who formed the Borghese art collection, was a strong believer in the young artist's talent, buying pictures rejected by those who had commissioned them.

Colosseum

Even before stepping foot into the ancient stadium, most visitors are gob-smacked to step out of the metro station to find the Colosseum looming before them. Not only is this Roman arena impressive for its size and endurance, but its well-preserved condition makes for an evocative insight into ancient life.

Need to Know

BEST ROUTE Go to the 2nd floor for exhibitions and the views, then head down to the arena **TICKETS** Buy online (www.pierreci.it) to avoid queuing **See our author's review on p72.**

Don't Miss List

BY VINCENZO MACCARRONE,
COLOSSEUM STAFF MEMBER

1 ARENA
The arena had a wooden floor covered in sand to prevent combatants from slipping, and to soak up blood. Gladiators arrived directly from their training ground via underground passageways, and were hoisted onto the arena by a complicated system of pulleys.

2 CAVEA AND THE PODIUM
The cavea, for spectator seating, was divided into three tiers: knights in the lowest, wealthy citizens in the middle and plebs at the top. The podium – close to the action but protected by nets made of hemp – was reserved for emperors, senators and VIPs.

3 FACADE
The exterior mimics the Teatro di Marcello (p65); the walls were once clad in travertine, with statues in the niches on the 2nd and 3rd storeys. On the top level are holes which held wooden masts supporting the Velarium (a canvas awning over the arena).

4 TEMPORARY EXHIBITIONS
The 2nd floor hosts some fantastic exhibitions, either about the Colosseum or on the wider history of Rome. Walk past the bookshop to the end of the corridor and look towards the eastern side of the Roman Forum (p68) – there's a wonderful view of the Tempio di Venere e Roma (Temple of Venus and Rome), hard to see from the ground.

5 PERFECT PHOTO
Towards closing time, the Colosseum is bathed in a beautiful light. For great views of the building, head up Colle Oppio (Oppio Hill) right above the Colosseo metro station, or up Colle Celio (Celio Hill) opposite the Palatino and Colosseum exit.

Vatican Museums

Modesty may be a cardinal virtue, but it doesn't apply to the Pope's palace, which is also home to the glorious Vatican Museums (p89). The highlight of these miles of museum is the Sistine Chapel, with Michelangelo's iconic ceiling of God bringing Adam to life with a touch. Don't miss the Raphael rooms and priceless Renaissance paintings – and if you're with kids, say hello to the resident mummies. Ceiling, Sistine Chapel (p89)

St Peter's Basilica

The Vatican City may be the world's smallest independent state, but it has a landmark befitting one of the grandest. St Peter's (p90) was built by a brain trust of Renaissance architects and capped by Michelangelo's dome, which offers views over Bernini's colonnade-framed piazza. Inside you'll find Michelangelo's moving Pietá, priceless papal jewels, Bernini's gilded altar, and serene light streaming in from every angle.

Roman Forum

With a little imagination and a handy illustration of the Roman Forum (p68), you can picture this archaeological site as it was thousands of years ago: an urban hub where business was conducted, gossip exchanged, gods worshipped, politics debated and flirting attempted (not necessarily in that order). Though Rome has since taken on a different form, its essential functions still mimic its ancient Forum.

Roman Catacombs

Underneath Rome there's another Rome, with more than half a million people – only none of them are alive. Along the Appia Antica are miles of tunnels and over 30 catacombs (p95) with Roman graves, including early Popes and Christian martyrs. Some tombs are frescoed, others graffitied by medieval pilgrims who venerated them, but the most fascinating are simple graves from millennia ago marked with touching remembrances from family members.

Trastevere

The *trasteverini* (neighbourhood natives) consider themselves the true descendants of ancient Rome, and they've got the attitude and some of the city's oldest churches to back them up. Trastevere (p85) is a visual charmer, with ivy-tickled facades along old lanes – but it's the remaining *trasteverini* that give ancient Trastevere its modern edge, with fearless scooter moves and a serving of street sass during the nightly *passegiata* (stroll).

Rome & the Vatican's Best...

Freebies

○ Walking into a rain shower inside the **Pantheon** (p73)

○ Watching Rome's street fashionistas parade past the **Spanish Steps** (p79)

○ Viewing priceless treasures for free on the last Sunday at the **Vatican Museums** (p89)

○ Joining Sunday morning guided walking tours of the **Appia Antica** (p91)

○ Receiving Papal blessings on Sundays at noon in **St Peter's Square** (p90)

Sweeping Views

○ **Dome of St Peter's Basilica** (p90) Thank Michelangelo for dizzying views over Rome and the Pope's backyard

○ **Caffè Capitolino** (p101) Watch flocks of starlings form storm clouds over Rome's domes

○ **Gianicolo** (p103) See church spires catch Rome's golden late-afternoon light

○ **Palatine** (p65) Scan the Roman Forum from the city's ancient Beverly Hills

○ **Il Vittoriano** (p73) Take the elevator for Roman panoramas

Local Drink Orders

○ The ultimate summer pick-me-up: *granita di caffè* (shaved-ice coffee) at **CaffèTazza d'Oro** (p102)

○ Your choice of 1200 wines, including sentimental local favourite white Est! Est!! Est!!! at **Cavour 313** (p101)

○ Frothy, sweet *gran caffe* espresso at **Caffè Sant'Eustachio** (p101)

○ *Grattachecca al limone* (lemon ice, vodka optional) along the Tevere during **Estate Romana** (p103)

○ *Cioccolato caldo con panna* (cocoa with whipped cream) at **Bar San Calisto** (p103)

Modern Classics

⊙ An ancient army barracks reinvented by architect Zaha Hadid into a contemporary art showcase, **Maxxi** (p91)

⊙ New interpretations of classical symphonies in the Renzo Piano–designed **Auditorium Parco della Musica** (p104)

⊙ Fedoras rocked by Humphrey Bogart and Al Capone at **Borsalino** (p104)

⊙ Organic cosmetics made by monks at **Ai Monasteri** (p104)

⊙ Emperor Augustus' monument to peace inside Richard Meier's controversial **Museo dell'Ara Pacis** (p81)

Left: Spanish Steps and Chiesa della Trinità dei Monti (p79) ; **Above:** St Peter's Square (p88)

Need to Know

ADVANCE PLANNING

⊙ **One month before** Book a tour of the Tomb of St Peter (p90). Scan the Auditorium Parco della Musica (p104) website (www.auditorium. com) for upcoming events

⊙ **Two weeks before** Book dinner at Agata e Romeo (p99) and visits to view Palazzo Farnese frescoes (p78)

⊙ **One week before** Purchase tickets online to the Vatican Museums (p89) and Museo e Galleria Borghese (p92), and reserve guided tours of the Colosseum (p92)

⊙ **Two days before** Reserve tables at Beer & Fud (p100) or Ditirambo (p97)

RESOURCES

⊙ **Roma Turismo** (www. roma turismo.it) Official Rome Tourist Board site; also has an airport office near arrivals

⊙ **Enjoy Rome** (www. enjoyrome.com) Private tourist office that runs tours and publishes the free, useful *Enjoy Rome* city guide

⊙ **Pierreci** (www.pierreci. it) Cultural event calendar and online tickets for major sights and exhibitions

⊙ **In Rome Now** (www. inromenow.com) Handy entertainment listings, though advertising-heavy

GETTING AROUND

⊙ **Air** Major airlines fly to/ from Leonardo da Vinci (Fiumicino). Low-cost carriers use Ciampino

⊙ **Bus** Handy connections between Roma Termini station and Centro Storico

⊙ **Metro** Useful for Ancient Rome and Vatican City

⊙ **Train** To/from Fiumicino airport and Ostia Antica

⊙ **Tram** Handy for Auditorium Parco della Musica and Trastevere

⊙ **Walk** Perfect to explore Rome's distinct neighbourhoods

BE FOREWARNED

⊙ **Museums** Most close on Monday

⊙ **Restaurants** Many close in August for the summer break, and stay open late in summer

⊙ **Pickpockets** Operate on transport and at tourist sites

Rome Walking Tour

Cover two thousand years of history and a dozen priceless masterpieces with a stroll around Rome's historical centre – perfect for a lazy morning, or to fill the pausa (downtime) between lunch and when shops re-open in the afternoon.

WALK FACTS

- **Start** Largo di Torre Argentina
- **Finish** Palazzo Farnese
- **Distance** 2km
- **Duration** Two hours

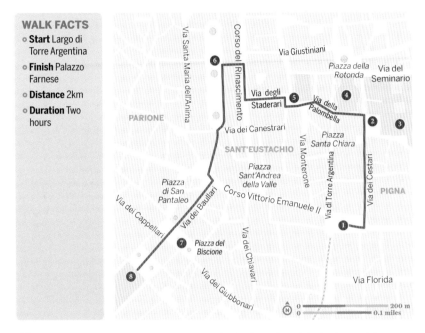

❶ Largo di Torre Argentina

At the centre of Rome's transit hub is a fenced-off archaeological site, where stray cats stalk the ruins of four Republic-era temples and nap peacefully on the site of Julius Caesar's assassination in 44 BC. From here, walk a couple blocks up Via dei Cestari.

❷ Elefantino

If getting your luggage home seems like a tricky prospect after shopping in Rome, consider Bernini's hapless elephant, who's stuck carrying a 6th century BC Egyptian obelisk while balancing on a pedestal. Elefantino's long trunk is reaching toward his back, as though trying to scratch an itch under the obelisk – like most Romans, Bernini finds poignant humour in absurd situations.

❸ Chiesa di Santa Maria Sopra Minerva

Behind the sympathetic Elefantino is another beloved local landmark: Rome's only Gothic church, built atop a Roman temple to the goddess Minerva. Inside, soaring, vaulted ceilings are frescoed with starry skies, and Filippino Lippi captures sunshine in his luminous 1488-92 Carafa Chapel frescoes.

④ Pantheon

Around the corner awaits an ancient Roman marvel. Built in 27 BC, the dome of the Pantheon remains the largest unreinforced concrete dome ever built. For the full effect, stand in the centre of the floor, and look up at the open skylight in the centre of the dome. The coffered poured-concrete sides seem to swirl as they soar upwards in a dizzying, uplifting optical effect. Consecrated as a Christian church in 608, the Pantheon houses the tombs of Raphael and Victor Emmanuel II.

⑤ Caffè Sant'Eustachio

From the Pantheon, follow signs towards Piazza Navona, stopping off for the signature foamy, sweet *gran caffe* espresso at the cafe many Romans claim is the city's best.

⑥ Piazza Navona

Welcome to Rome's showplace, where street artists, touts and pigeons compete for attention with Bernini, creator of the Fontana dei Quattro Fiumi, and Borromini, responsible for the Chiesa di Sant'Agnese in Agone. From the 17th to 19th century, the square was flooded on weekends so that mock naval battles and other entertainment could be staged here.

⑦ Campo de' Fiori

Across Corso Vittorio Emanuele II, the Campo de' Fiori is a colourful Roman street market by day and a foreign-student party scene by night, with non-stop international flirting.

⑧ Palazzo Farnese

Beyond the campo is this stately Renaissance *palazzo* (palace). Romans still bemoan that this Michelangelo-refurbished palace was rented to the French Embassy, limiting access to superb frescoes by Annibale Carracci (book visits in advance) – but according to 17th century records, Palazzo Farnese's worst tenant was scandalous Queen Christina of Sweden, whose staff burned painted doors for kindling.

Rome In...

TWO DAYS

On day one, follow the walking tour, opposite. Afterwards, ditch your guidebook and wander the boutique-lined streets around Piazza Navona and the Pantheon until lunchtime. Fuel up with espresso at Tazza d'Oro before taking on ancient Rome: the Colosseum, the Roman Forum and Palatino (Palatine Hill). Explore the Capitoline museums, and take a late-afternoon breather at Caffè Capitalino overlooking Rome before your evening in Trastevere. On day two, hit the Vatican, marvelling at St Peter's Basilica and the Sistine Chapel in the Vatican Museums.

FOUR DAYS

On day three, check out the Trevi Fountain, the Spanish Steps and the Museo e Galleria Borghese. At night, head to Campo de' Fiori for a drink, and find some thin-crust Roman pizza. Next day, visit the Museo Nazionale Romano: Palazzo Massimo alle Terme before exploring the Jewish Ghetto and backstreets such as Via del Governo Vecchio. Round off your visit with drinks and dining in San Lorenzo.

Foot from statue of Emperor Constantine, Capitoline Museum (p69)
JEAN-PIERRE LESCOURRET/LONELY PLANET IMAGES ©

Discover Rome & the Vatican

ROME

Pulsating, seductive and utterly disarming, the Italian capital is an epic, monumental metropolis that will steal your heart. There are just too many reasons to fall in love: artistic masterpieces, operatic piazzas, romantic corners and cobbled lanes. Rome also boasts a busy cultural calendar with arts festivals and an alternative underground scene.

History

According to myth, Rome was founded on the Palatino (Palatine Hill) by Romulus and Remus, the twin sons of vestal virgin Rhea Silva and the God of War, Mars. Following the fall of Tarquin the Proud, the last of Rome's seven Etruscan kings, the Roman Republic was founded in 509 BC. Julius Caesar, the last of the Republic's consuls, was assassinated in 44 BC, leaving Mark Antony and Octavian to fight for the top job. Octavian prevailed and, with the blessing of the Senate, became Augustus, the first Roman emperor.

Augustus ruled well, and the city enjoyed a period of political stability and unparalleled artistic achievement – a golden age which the Romans yearned for again as they endured the depravities of Augustus' successors Tiberius, Caligula and Nero. But the city bounced back and by AD 100 it had a population of 1.5 million and was the undisputed *Caput Mundi* (capital of the world). It couldn't last, though, and when Constantine moved his power base to Byzantium in 330, Rome's glory days were numbered. In 455 it was routed by

Basilica di San Giovanni in Laterano (p83)

the Vandals and in 476 the last emperor of the Western Roman Empire, Romulus Augustulus, was deposed.

Christianity had been spreading since the 1st century AD thanks to the underground efforts of apostles Peter and Paul, and under Constantine it received official recognition. In the late 6th century Pope Gregory I did much to strengthen the Church's grip over the city, laying the foundations for its later role as capital of the Catholic world. At the behest of the city's great papal dynasties – the Barberini, Farnese and Pamphilj, among others – the leading artists of the 15th and 16th centuries were summoned to work on projects such as the Sistine Chapel and St Peter's Basilica. But the enemy was never far away, and in 1527 the Spanish forces of Holy Roman Emperor Charles V ransacked Rome.

Another rebuild was in order, and it was to the 17th-century baroque masters Bernini and Borromini that Rome's patrons turned. Exuberant churches, fountains and *palazzi* sprouted all over the city, as these two bitter rivals competed to produce ever-more virtuosic masterpieces.

The next makeover followed the unification of Italy and the declaration of Rome as its capital. Post-Fascism, the 1950s and '60s saw the glittering era of *la dolce vita* and hasty urban expansion, resulting in Rome's sometimes wretched suburbs. A clean-up in 2000 had the city in its best shape for decades, and in recent years some dramatic modernist building projects have given the Eternal City some edge, such as Richard Meier's Museo dell'Ara Pacis and Massimiliano Fuksas' ongoing Centro Congressi in EUR.

◎ Sights

Ancient Rome

PALATINE HILL   Archaeological Site
(Palatino; Map p66; ☏ 06 3996 7700; www.pierreci.it; Via di San Gregorio 30; adult/reduced incl Colosseum & Roman Forum €12/7.50, audioguides €5; ☼ 8.30am-1hr before sunset)
According to legend, this is where Romulus killed his twin and founded Rome in 753 BC. The emperor Augustus lived here all his life and successive emperors built increasingly opulent palaces.

Most of the Palatino as it appears today is covered by the ruins of Emperor Domitian's vast complex, which served as the main imperial palace for 300 years. On entering the complex from Via di San Gregorio, head uphill until you come to the first recognisable construction, the **stadio**, probably used by the emperors for private games and events.

On the other side of the *stadio* are the ruins of the huge **Domus Augustana**,

Trevi Fountain (p80)
WILL SALTER/LONELY PLANET IMAGES ©

Ancient Rome

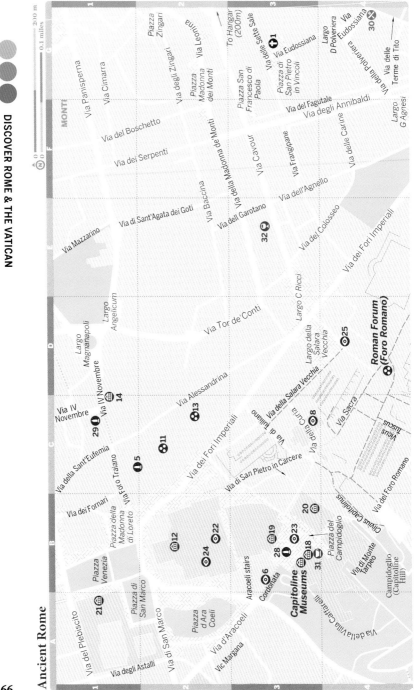

200 m
0.1 miles

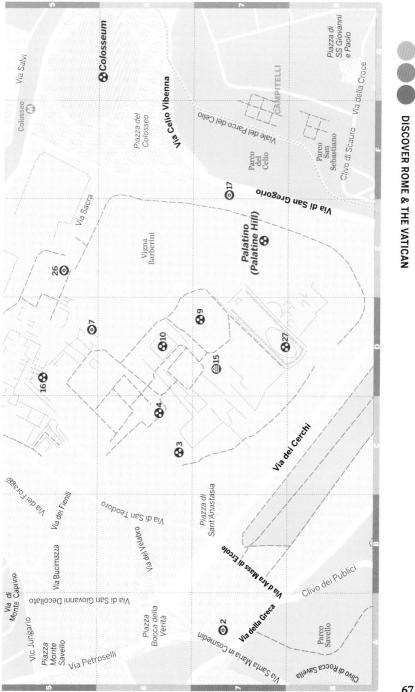

DISCOVER ROME & THE VATICAN

Colosseum

Via Salvi

Colosseo Ⓜ

Piazza del Colosseo

Via Celio Vibenna

Via Sacra

Viale del Parco del Celio

CAMPITELLI

Parco del Celio

Parco San Sebastiano

Clivo di Scauro

Piazza di SS Giovanni e Paolo

Via della Croce

Vigna Barberini

Ⓣ 17

Via di San Gregorio

Ⓣ 26

Ⓣ 7

Palatino (Palatine Hill)

Ⓣ 16

Ⓣ 10

Ⓣ 9

Ⓣ 15

Ⓣ 27

Ⓣ 4

Ⓣ 3

Via dei Foraggi

Via dei Fienili

Via Bucimazza

Via di Monte Caprino

Vic Jungario

Piazza Monte Savello

Via di San Giovanni Decollato

Via del Velabro

Via di San Teodoro

Via dei Cerchi

Piazza di Sant'Anastasia

Piazza Bocca della Verità

Via Petroselli

Via Santa Maria in Cosmedin

Ⓣ 2

Via d a Mass di Ercole

Via della Greca

Clivo dei Publici

Parco Savello

Clivo di Rocca Savella

67

Ancient Rome

the emperor's private residence. In 2007 a mosaic-covered vaulted cavern was discovered more than 15m beneath the Domus. Some believe this to be the *Lupercale*, a cave believed by ancient Romans to be where Romulus and Remus were suckled by a wolf. The grey building near the Domus Augustana houses the **Museo Palatino** and its collection of archaeological artefacts. North of the museum is the **Domus Flavia**, the public part of the palace complex.

Among the best-preserved buildings on the Palatino is the **Casa di Livia**, northwest of the Domus Flavia. Home to Augustus' wife Livia, it was built around an atrium leading onto what were once reception rooms, decorated with frescoes of mythological scenes, landscapes, fruits and flowers. In front is the **Casa di Augusto** (entry in groups of 5; ⊙11am-4.30pm Mon, Wed, Sat & Sun), Augustus' separate residence, which contains superb frescoes in vivid reds, yellows and blues.

Northeast of the Casa di Livia lies the **criptoportico**, a 128m tunnel where Caligula was perhaps murdered, and which Nero used to connect his Domus Aurea with the Palatino. Nowadays it's used to stage temporary exhibitions.

The area west of this was once Tiberius' palace, the Domus Tiberiana, but now the site of the 16th-century **Orti Farnesiani**, one of Europe's earliest botanical gardens.

ROMAN FORUM   Archaeological Site
(Foro Romano; Map p66; ☑06 3996 7700; www.pierreci.it; Largo della Salara Vecchia; adult/reduced incl Colosseum & Palatino €12/7.50, audioguides €5; ⊙8.30am-1hr before sunset) Today an impressive, if rather confusing, sprawl of ruins, the Roman Forum was once a gleaming complex of marble-clad temples, proud basilicas and vibrant public spaces: the gleaming heart of an ancient city. For highlights, see p70.

IMPERIAL FORUMS   Archaeological Site
(Map p66) The ruins over the road from the Roman Forum are known collectively as the Imperial Forums (Fori Imperiali).

Constructed between 42 BC and AD 112 by successive emperors, they were largely buried in 1933 when Mussolini built Via dei Fori Imperiali. Excavations have since unearthed much of them, but work continues and visits are limited to the Mercati di Traiano (Trajan's Markets), accessible through the **Museo dei Fori Imperiali** (Map p66; 06 06 08; www.mercatiditraiano.it; Via IV Novembre 94; adult/reduced €11/9; 9am-7pm Tue-Sun, last entry 6pm). From the main hallway, a lift whisks you up to the **Torre delle Milizie** (Militia Tower), a 13th-century red-brick tower, and the upper levels of the **Mercati di Traiano**. These markets, housed in a three-storey semicircular construction, hosted hundreds of traders selling everything from oil and vegetables to flowers, silks and spices.

Little that's recognisable remains of the **Foro di Traiano** (Trajan's Forum), except for some pillars from the **Basilica Ulpia** and the **Colonna di Traiano** (Trajan's Column), whose minutely detailed reliefs celebrate Trajan's military victories over the Dacians (from modern-day Romania).

PIAZZA DEL CAMPIDOGLIO
Piazza

(Map p66) This elegant piazza, designed by Michelangelo in 1538, is the centrepiece of the Campidoglio (Capitoline Hill), one of the seven hills on which Rome was founded. You can reach the piazza from the Roman Forum, but the most dramatic approach is via the **Cordonata**, the graceful staircase that leads up from Piazza d'Ara Coeli. At the top, the piazza is bordered by three *palazzi*: Palazzo Nuovo to the left, **Palazzo Senatorio** straight ahead, and Palazzo dei Conservatori on the right. Together, Palazzo Nuovo and Palazzo dei Conservatori house the **Capitoline Museums**, while Palazzo Senatorio is home to Rome's city council.

In the centre, the bronze equestrian **statue of Marcus Aurelius** is a copy. The original, which dates from the 2nd century AD, is in the Capitoline Museums.

If You Like…
Ancient Rome

If glimpses of the Colosseum, Roman Forum and Roman Catacombs sparked your interest in ancient history, find out how Romans once lived in these splendid ruins:

1 AREA ARCHEOLOGICA DEL TEATRO DI MARCELLO E DEL PORTICO D'OTTAVIA
(Map p74; Via del Teatro di Marcello; 9am-7pm summer, 9am-6pm winter) Portico d'Ottavia is Rome's oldest *quadriporto* (four-sided porch), originally constructed in 146 BC and home of the city's fish market until the 19th century. Beyond the portico is Teatro di Marcello, a 20,000-seat theatre planned by Julius Caesar and finished around 13 BC.

2 TERME DI CARACALLA
(06 399 67 700; Viale delle Terme di Caracalla 52; adult/reduced incl Mausoleo di Cecilia Metella & Villa dei Quintili €6/3, audioguide €5; 9am-1hr before sunset Tue-Sun, 9am-2pm Mon year-round) Starting in AD 217, the Caracalla baths cleaned 1600 of Rome's unwashed masses at a time – while slaves sweated in 9.5km of underground tunnels to keep the plumbing and heating running. Opera is performed amid the ruins each summer.

3 MUSEO NAZIONALE ROMANO: PALAZZO MASSIMO ALLE TERME
(Map p80; 06 399 67 700; www.pierreci.it; Largo di Villa Peretti 1; adult/reduced €7/3.50, audioguide €4; 9am-7.45pm Tue-Sun) The mesmerising 1st century 'Boxer' is a highlight of the classical sculpture collection downstairs, but upstairs is an indoor garden paradise of 30BC to 20 BC frescoes, preserved from the villa retreat of emperor Augustus' wife Livia Drusilla.

CAPITOLINE MUSEUMS   Art Galleries
(Musei Capitolini; Map p66; 06 06 08; www.museicapitolini.org; Piazza del Campidoglio 1; adult/reduced €12/10, audioguide €5; 9am-8pm Tue-Sun, last admission 7pm) The world's oldest national museums were founded in 1471 when Pope Sixtus IV donated a few bronze sculptures to the city, forming the nucleus of what is now one of Italy's finest collections of classical art.

Roman Forum

In ancient times, a forum was a market place, civic centre and religious complex all rolled into one, and the greatest of all was the Roman Forum (Foro Romano). Situated between the Palatino (Palatine Hill), ancient Rome's most exclusive neighbourhood, and the Campidoglio (Capitoline Hill), it was the city's busy, bustling centre. On any given day it teemed with activity. Senators debated affairs of state in the **Curia ❶**, shoppers thronged the squares and traffic-free streets, crowds gathered under the **Colonna di Foca ❷** to listen to politicians holding forth from the **Rostrum ❷**. Elsewhere, lawyers worked the courts in basilicas including the **Basilica di Massenzio ❸**, while the Vestal Virgins quietly went about their business in the **Casa delle Vestali ❹**.

Special occasions were also celebrated in the Forum: religious holidays were marked with ceremonies at temples such as the **Tempio di Saturno ❺** and the **Tempio di Castore e Polluce ❻**, and military victories were honoured with dramatic processions up Via Sacra and the building of monumental arches like the **Arco di Settimio Severo ❼** and the **Arco di Tito ❽**.

The ruins you see today are impressive but they can be confusing without a clear picture of what the Forum once looked like. This spread shows the Forum in its heyday, complete with temples, civic buildings and towering monuments to heroes of the Roman Empire.

TOP TIPS

Get grandstand views of the Forum from the Palatino and Campidoglio.

Visit first thing in the morning or late afternoon; crowds are worst between 11am and 2pm.

In summer it gets hot in the Forum and there's little shade, so take a hat and plenty of water.

Colonna di Foca & Rostrum

The free-standing, 13.5m-high Column of Phocus is the Forum's youngest monument, dating to AD 608. Behind it, the Rostrum provided a suitably grandiose platform for pontificating public speakers.

Campidoglio (Capitoline Hill)

Admission

Although valid for two days, admission tickets only allow for one entry into the Forum, Colosseum and Palatino.

Tempio di Saturno

Ancient Rome's Fort Knox, the Temple of Saturn was the city treasury. In Caesar's day it housed 13 tonnes of gold, 114 tonnes of silver and 30 million *sestertii* worth of silver coins.

JONATHAN SMITH / LONELY PLANET IMAGES ©

GEOFF STRINGER / LONELY PLANET IMAGES ©

Tempio di Castore e Polluce

Only three columns of the Temple of Castor and Pollux remain. The temple was dedicated to the Heavenly Twins after they supposedly led the Romans to victory over the Etruscans.

Arco di Settimio Severo

One of the Forum's signature monuments, this imposing triumphal arch commemorates the military victories of Septimius Severus. Relief panels depict his campaigns against the Parthians.

Curia

This big barnlike building was the official seat of the Roman Senate. Most of what you see is a reconstruction, but the interior marble floor dates to the 3rd-century reign of Diocletian.

Basilica di Massenzio

Marvel at the scale of this vast 4th-century basilica. In its original form the central hall was divided into enormous naves; now only part of the northern nave survives.

Julius Caesar RIP

Julius Caesar was cremated on the site where the Tempio di Giulio Cesare now stands.

Via Sacra

Tempio di Giulio Cesare

Casa delle Vestali

White statues line the grassy atrium of what was once the luxurious 50-room home of the Vestal Virgins. The virgins played an important role in Roman religion, serving the goddess Vesta.

Arco di Tito

Said to be the inspiration for the Arc de Triomphe in Paris, the well-preserved Arch of Titus was built by the emperor Domitian to honour his elder brother Titus.

GLENN BEANLAND/LONELY PLANET IMAGES ©

Don't Miss **The Colosseum**

A monument to merciless power, the Colosseum (Colosseo) remains the most thrilling sight in Rome, even as a ruin. Built by the emperor Vespasian (r AD 69–79), the Colosseum was inaugurated in AD 80. To mark the occasion, Vespasian's son and successor Titus (r 79–81) held 100 days and nights of games, during which 5000 animals were slaughtered. Trajan (r 98–117) topped Titus' blood-sport record, holding a 117-day marathon killing spree involving 9000 gladiators and 10,000 animals.

The **arena** had a wooden floor covered in sand to soak up the blood and prevent the combatants from slipping on their own blood, sweat and tears. Trap doors led to underground chambers and passageways beneath the arena floor, an area known as the **hypogeum**. The **cavea** (spectator seating area) was divided into three tiers: knights sat in the lowest tier, wealthy citizens in the middle and lowly plebs in the cheap seats up top. The broad terrace in front of the tiers of seats is the **podium**, once reserved for emperors, senators and VIPs.

The top tier and hypogeum have recently been opened to the public for visits. Visits to these areas are possible on guided tours, which must be booked in advance and cost €8 on top of the normal Colosseum ticket price. For first-hand insights on the Colosseum, see p57.

THINGS YOU NEED TO KNOW

Map p66; ✏ 06 399 67 700; Piazza del Colosseo; adult/reduced incl Roman Forum & Palatino €12/7.50, audioguides €5.50; ☺ 8.30am-1hr before sunset

The entrance is in **Palazzo dei Conservatori**, where you'll find the original core of the sculptural collection on the 1st floor. Before you head upstairs, take a moment to admire a mammoth head, hand and foot from a 12m-high statue of Constantine that originally stood in the Roman Forum.

Making The Most Of Your Euro

You can buy the following discount cards at any of the monuments or museums listed (or online at www.pierreci.it).

○ **Appia Antica Card** (adult/reduced €7.50/4.50, valid seven days) For the Terme di Caracalla, Mausoleo di Cecilia Metella and Villa Quintili.

○ **Archaeologia Card** (adult/reduced €23/13, valid seven days) For entrance to the Colosseum, Palatino, Roman Forum, Terme di Caracalla, Palazzo Altemps, Palazzo Massimo alle Terme, Terme di Diocleziano, Crypta Balbi, Mausoleo di Cecilia Metella and Villa Quintili.

○ **Roma Pass** (www.romapass.it, €25, valid three days) Includes free admission to two museums or sites (choose from a list of 38) as well as reduced entry to extra sites, unlimited public transport within Rome, and reduced entry to other exhibitions and events. The Roma Pass is also available at Comune di Roma tourist information points.

Upstairs, the Pinacoteca contains paintings by Titian, Tintoretto, Reni, Van Dyck, Rubens and Caravaggio.

Palazzo Nuovo contains some real show-stoppers. Chief among them is the *Galata Morente* (Dying Gaul), a Roman copy of a 3rd-century BC Greek original that movingly depicts the anguish of a dying Frenchman.

IL VITTORIANO Monument
(Map p66; Piazza Venezia; admission free; ⊙9.30am-5.30pm summer, 9.30am-4.30pm winter) For Rome's best 360-degree views, take the **Roma dal Cielo** (adult/reduced €7/3.50; ⊙9.30am-6.30pm Mon-Thu, to 7.30pm Fri-Sun) lift from the side of the building up to the very top of this monument, begun in 1885 to commemorate Italian unification and honour Victor Emmanuel II.

PALAZZO VENEZIA Palazzo
(Map p66; Piazza Venezia) The first of Rome's great Renaissance palaces. For centuries it served as the embassy of the Venetian Republic, although its best known resident was Mussolini, who famously made speeches from the balcony overlooking the square.

To see inside, visit the sprawling, undervisited **Museo Nazionale del Palazzo Venezia** (☏06 678 01 31; Via del Plebiscito 118; adult/reduced €4/2; ⊙8.30am-7.30pm Tue-Sun) with its superb Byzantine and early Renaissance paintings and an eclectic collection of jewellery, tapestries, ceramics, bronze figurines, arms and armour.

BOCCA DELLA VERITÀ Monument
(Map p66; Piazza della Bocca della Verità 18; donation €0.50; ⊙9.30am-4.50pm) A round piece of marble once used as an ancient manhole cover, the *Bocca della Verità* (Mouth of Truth) is one of Rome's great curiosities. Legend holds that if you put your hand in the carved mouth and tell a lie, it will bite your hand off.

The mouth lives in the portico of the beautiful, medieval **Chiesa di Santa Maria in Cosmedin**. Originally built in the 8th century, the church was given a major revamp in the 12th century, when the seven-storey bell tower and portico were added and the floor was decorated with Cosmati inlaid marble.

Centro Storico

FREE **PANTHEON** Church
(Map p74; Piazza della Rotonda; admission free, audioguide €5; ⊙8.30am-7.30pm Mon-Sat, 9am-6pm Sun) The city's best preserved ancient monument dates from around

73

Centro Storico

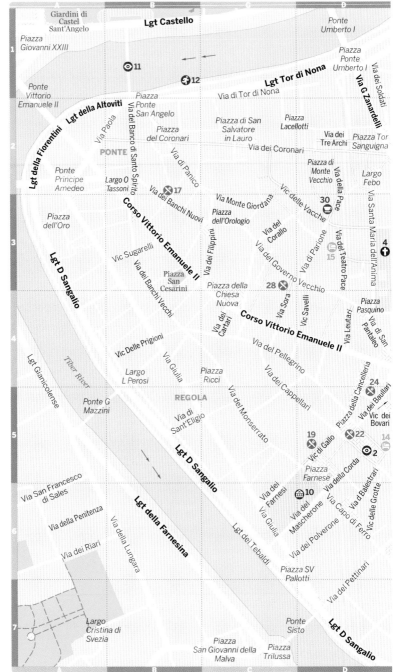

DISCOVER ROME & THE VATICAN

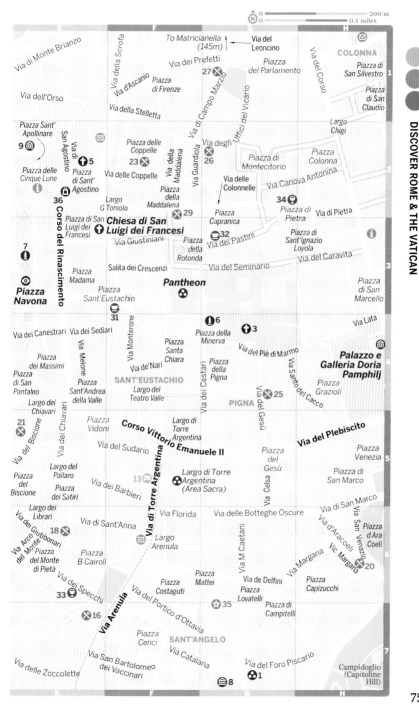

To Matricianella
(145m)

Via del
Leoncino

Via di Monte Brianzo

Via della Scrofa

Via dei Prefetti

COLONNA

Piazza di
San Silvestro

Via d'Ascanio

Piazza
di Firenze

27

Via di Campo Marzio

Piazza
del Parlamento

Via del Corso

Piazza
di San
Claudio

Via dell'Orso

Via della Stelletta

Uffici del Vicario

Largo
Chigi

Piazza Sant'
Apollinare

9

Via di Sant'Agostino

Piazza delle
Coppelle

Via della Maddalena

Via degli Uffici del Vicario

Piazza di
Montecitorio

Piazza
Colonna

5

23

26

Piazza delle
Cinque Lune

Piazza
di Sant'
Agostino

Via delle Coppelle

Via Guardiola

Via delle
Colonnelle

Via Canova Antonina

36

Largo
G Toniolo

Piazza
della
Maddalena

34

Corso del Rinascimento

Piazza di San
Luigi dei
Francesi

**Chiesa di San
Luigi dei Francesi**

29

Piazza
Capranica

Piazza di
Pietra

Via di Pietra

7

Via Giustiniani

Piazza
della
Rotonda

32

Via dei Pastini

Piazza di
Sant'Ignazio
Loyola

Via del Caravita

Piazza
Madama

Salita dei Crescenzi

Via del Seminario

Piazza
di San
Marcello

**Piazza
Navona**

Piazza
Sant'Eustachio

Pantheon

31

Via dei Canestrari

Via dei Sediari

Via Monterone

6

3

Via Lata

Piazza della
Minerva

Via del Piè di Marmo

Piazza
dei Massimi

Via Melone

Piazza
Santa
Chiara

Via de'Nari

Piazza
di San
Pantaleo

Piazza
Sant'Andrea
della Valle

SANT'EUSTACHIO

Largo del
Teatro Valle

Via dei Cestari

Piazza
della
Pigna

Via Santo del Cacco

**Palazzo e
Galleria Doria
Pamphilj**

Piazza
Grazioli

Largo dei
Chiavari

21

Via del Biscione

Via dei Chiavari

Piazza
Vidoni

Corso Vittorio Emanuele II

Largo di
Torre
Argentina

PIGNA

Via del Gesù

25

Via del Plebiscito

Via del Sudario

Via di Torre Argentina

Piazza
del
Gesù

Piazza
Venezia

Largo del
Pallaro

Piazza
del
Biscione

Piazza
dei Satiri

Via dei Barbieri

Largo di Torre
Argentina
(Area Sacra)

13

Via Celsa

Piazza di
San Marco

Largo dei
Librari

Via di Sant'Anna

Via Florida

Via delle Botteghe Oscure

Via di San Marco

18

Via Arco del Monte

Via dei Giubbonari

Largo
Arenula

Via San Venanzio

Piazza
d Ara
Coeli

Piazza
del Monte
di Pietà

Piazza
B Cairoli

Via M Caetani

Via d'Aracoeli

Via Margana

Vic Margana

20

33

Via dei Specchi

Via Arenula

Piazza
Costaguti

Piazza
Mattei

Via de Delfini

Piazza
Lovatelli

Piazza
Capizucchi

35

16

Via del Portico d'Ottavia

Piazza di
Campitelli

Piazza
Cenci

SANT'ANGELO

Via Catalana

Via delle Zoccolette

Via San Bartolomeo
dei Vaccinari

Via del Foro Piscario

Campidoglio
(Capitoline
Hill)

8

1

0   200 m
0   0.1 miles

Centro Storico

AD 120, when Emperor Hadrian built over Marcus Agrippa's original temple (27 BC) – you can still see Agrippa's name inscribed on the pediment. Considered the Romans' most important architectural achievement, it was the largest dome in the world until the 15th century and is still the largest unreinforced concrete dome ever built. Its harmonious appearance is due to a precisely calibrated symmetry – its diameter is exactly equal to the Pantheon's interior height of 43.3m.

PALAZZO E GALLERIA DORIA PAMPHILJ   Museum
(Map p74; ☏ 06 679 73 23; www.dopart.it; Via del Corso 305; adult/reduced €10.50/7.50; ⏱10am-5pm, last admission 4.15pm) You wouldn't know it from the grimy exterior, but this 15th century palace houses an extraordinary collection of works by Raphael, Tintoretto, Brueghel, Titian, Caravaggio, Bernini and Velázquez. Masterpieces abound but look out for Titian's powerful *Salomè con la testa del Battista* (Salome with the Head of John the Baptist) and two early works by Caravaggio: *Riposso durante la fuga in Egitto* (Rest During the Flight into Egypt) and *Maddalene Penitente* (Penitent Magdalen). The collection's undisputed star is the Velázquez portrait of Pope Innocent X, who grumbled that the depiction was 'too real'.

CHIESA DI SANTA MARIA SOPRA MINERVA   Church
(Map p74; Piazza della Minerva; ⏱8am-7pm Mon-Fri, 8am-1pm & 3.30-7pm Sat & Sun) Bernini's much-loved **Elefantino** sculpture trumpets the presence of Rome's only Gothic church, built on the site of an ancient temple to Minerva. Inside, you'll find two superb 15th-century frescoes by

Filippino Lippi and one of Michelangelo's lesser-known sculptures, *Cristo Risorto* (Christ Bearing the Cross; 1520). An altarpiece of the Madonna and Child in the second chapel in the northern transept is attributed to Dominican friar and painter Fra Angelico, who is also buried in the church.

MUSEO NAZIONALE ROMANO: PALAZZO ALTEMPS   Museum

(Map p74; 📞 06 683 35 66; www.pierreci.it; Piazza Sant'Apollinare 44; adult/reduced €7/3.50; ⏰9am-7.45pm Tue-Sun, last admission 7pm) Prize exhibits include the 5th-century *Trono Ludovisi* (Ludovisi Throne), a carved marble throne depicting Aphrodite being plucked from the sea as a newborn babe. The wall frieze (about half of which remains) depicts the 10 plagues of Egypt and the Exodus, while the walls of the Sala delle Prospettive Dipinte are decorated with landscapes and hunting scenes seen through trompe l'œil windows.

PIAZZA NAVONA   Piazza

(Map p74) Laid out on the ruins of an arena built by Domitian in AD 86, Piazza Navona was paved over in the 15th century and for almost 300 years hosted the city's main market.

Of the piazza's three fountains, Bernini's high-camp **Fontana dei Quattro Fiumi** (Fountain of the Four Rivers) dominates. Depicting personifications of the Nile, Ganges, Danube and Plate rivers, it's festooned with a palm tree, lion and horse and topped by an obelisk. Legend has it that the figure of the Nile is shielding his eyes from the **Chiesa di Sant'Agnese in Agone** (www.santagneseinagone.org; ⏰9.30am-12.30pm & 3.30-7pm Tue-Sat, 9am-1pm & 4-8pm Sun), designed by Bernini's bitter rival, Borromini. The truth, more boringly, is the gesture indicates that the source of the Nile was unknown at the time.

CAMPO DE' FIORI   Piazza

(Map p74) Noisy, colourful 'Il Campo' is a major focus of Roman life: by day it hosts a

---

♥ **If You Like…**
Controversial Caravaggios

As you'll notice in Palazzo e Galleria Doria Pamphilj (p76) and Capitoline Museums (p69), Caravaggio painted religious figures as down-to-earth Romans you might see on local street-corners – perhaps because he used prostitutes as models. Never shy of scandal, Caravaggio dispenses with haloes and uses dramatic *chiaroscuro* (light and dark) shading to highlight saints at their most vulnerable moments in these churches:

1 **CHIESA DI SAN LUIGI DEI FRANCESI**
(Map p74; Piazza di San Luigi dei Francesi; ⏰10am-12.30pm & 4-7pm, closed Thu afternoon) This 1589 baroque French church showcases Caravaggio's shocking realism in *The Calling of Saint Matthew*, *Saint Matthew and the Angel* and *The Martyrdom of Saint Matthew* (notice Caravaggio's self-portrait behind the assassin).

2 **CHIESA DI SANT'AGOSTINO**
(Map p74; Piazza di Sant'Agostino; ⏰7.45am-noon & 4-7.30pm) This early Renaissance church contains Raphael's 1512 Isaiah fresco and Caravaggio's *Madonna dei Pellegrini* (Madonna of the Pilgrims), which caused an uproar when it was unveiled in 1604 for showing Mary barefoot and her two devoted pilgrims as filthy beggars.

3 **CHIESA DI SANTA MARIA DEL POPOLO**
(Map p98; 📞06 361 08 36; Piazza del Popolo; ⏰7am-noon & 4-7pm Mon-Sat, 8am-1.30pm & 4.30-7.30pm Sun) Built in 1099 to exorcise the ghost of Nero, who was buried here – hence the creepy kneeling skeleton mosaic in Raphael's Chigi Chapel (completed by Bernini). Left of the altar are two Caravaggio masterpieces: the 1600-01 *Conversion of St Paul* and *Crucifixion of St Peter* – both initially rejected by church leaders.

---

much-loved market, while at night it morphs into a raucous open-air pub. Towering over the square is the Obi-Wan-like form of Giordano Bruno, a monk who was burned at the stake for heresy in 1600.

Top 5 Film Locations

○ **Trevi Fountain** (p80) Scene of Anita Ekberg's sensual dip in *La Dolce Vita*.

○ **Bocca della Verità** (p73) Gregory Peck goofs around with Audrey Hepburn in *Roman Holiday*.

○ **Piazza Navona** (p77) In *Eat Pray Love* Julia Roberts finds ice-cream solace in front of the Chiesa di Sant'Agnese in Agone.

○ **Piazza di Spagna** (p79) Drama over drinks at the foot of the Spanish Steps in *The Talented Mr Ripley*.

○ **Pantheon** (p73) Tom Hanks checks out Raphael's tomb in *Angels and Demons*.

PALAZZO FARNESE Palazzo

(Map p74; www.ambafrance-it.org, in Italian & French; Piazza Farnese; admission free, under 15yr not admitted; ☾tours 3pm, 4pm & 5pm Mon & Thu, by appointment only) One of Rome's greatest Renaissance *palazzi,* Palazzo Farnese was started in 1514 by Antonio da Sangallo the Younger, continued by Michelangelo and finished by Giacomo della Porta. Nowadays, it's the French Embassy and open only to visitors who've booked a guided tour – get a booking from the website. Visits (in Italian or French) take in the Galleria dei Carracci, home to a series of frescoes by Annibale Carracci, said by some to rival those of the Sistine Chapel.

MUSEO EBRAICO
DI ROMA Synagogue, Museum

(Jewish Museum of Rome; Map p74; ☎06 6840 0661; www.museoebraico.roma.it; Via Catalana; adult/reduced €10/4; ☾10am-6.15pm Sun-Thu, 10am-3.15pm Fri summer, 10am-4.15pm Sun-Thu, 9am-1.15pm Fri winter) Rome's Jewish com-

Left: Spanish Steps and Chiesa della Trinità dei Monti;
Below: Trevi Fountain (p80)

(LEFT) RICHARD I'ANSON/LONELY PLANET IMAGES ©; (BELOW) JON DAVISON/LONELY PLANET IMAGES ©

munity is one of Europe's oldest, dating from the 2nd century BC. Between 1555 and the late 19th century, and then again during WWII, Rome's Jews were confined to the area known as the Jewish Ghetto, now a lively and atmospheric neighbourhood. The museum, housed in Europe's second-largest synagogue, chronicles the engrossing historical, cultural and artistic heritage of the city's Jewry. You can also book one-hour guided walking tours of the Ghetto (adult/reduced €8/5) at the museum.

Tridente & Trevi
PIAZZA DI SPAGNA & THE SPANISH STEPS   Piazza, Museum
(Map p98) The **Piazza di Spagna** was named after the Spanish Embassy to the Holy See, and so were the Spanish Steps, although they were designed by the Italian Francesco de Sanctis in 1725 and lead to the **Chiesa della Trinità dei Monti**. Overlooking the steps, the **Keats-**

Shelley Memorial House (Map p98; ☏06 678 42 35; www.keats-shelley-house. org; Piazza di Spagna 26; adult/reduced €4.50/3.50; ☏10am-1pm & 2-6pm Mon-Fri, 11am-2pm & 3-6pm Sat) is where the 25-year-old Keats died of tuberculosis in 1821 after an obviously unsuccessful trip to Rome to improve his health, and is now an evocative museum housing poems, letters and memorabilia of Keats, Shelley, Byron and their friends.

PIAZZA DEL POPOLO & AROUND   Piazza, Churches, Museum
(Map p98) For centuries the site of public executions, this elegant ellipse was laid out in 1538 to provide a suitably grandiose entrance to what was then the main northern gateway into the city. Guarding its southern end are Carlo Rainaldi's twin 17th-century baroque churches, **Chiesa di Santa Maria dei Miracoli** and **Chiesa**

Trevi & Esquilino

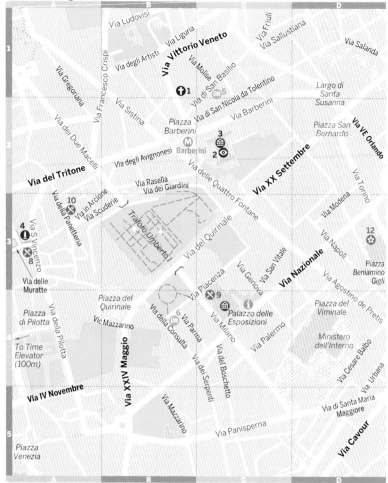

di Santa Maria in Montesanto, while over on the northern flank is the **Porta del Popolo**, created by Bernini in 1655 to celebrate Queen Christina of Sweden's defection to Catholicism. In the centre, the 36m-high **obelisk** was brought by Augustus from Heliopolis, in ancient Egypt, and moved here from the Circo Massimo in the mid-16th century. To the east are the **Pincio Hill Gardens**.

TREVI FOUNTAIN Fountain
(Fontana di Trevi; Map p80) This fountain almost fills an entire piazza, and is Rome's most famous fountain, its iconic status sealed when Anita Ekberg splashed here in *La Dolce Vita*. The flamboyant baroque ensemble was designed by Nicola Salvi in 1732 and depicts Neptune's chariot being led by Tritons with sea horses – one wild, one docile – representing the moods of the sea.

TIME ELEVATOR Cinema
(off Map p80; ☏ 06 6992 1823; www.time
elevator.it; Via dei Santissimi Apostoli 20; adult/
reduced €12/9; ☉ 10.30am-7.30pm; 🚻) There
are three programs, but the one to see is
Time Elevator Rome, a 45-minute virtual
journey through 3000 years of Roman
history. Shows kick off half-past every
hour, and children and adults alike love
the panoramic screens, flight-simulator
technology and surround-sound system.
Note that children under five aren't ad-

mitted and anyone who suffers motion
sickness should probably give it a miss.

MUSEO DELL'ARA PACIS Museum
(Altar of Peace; Map p98; ☏ 06 820 59 127;
www.arapacis.it; Lungotevere in Augusta; adult/
reduced €9/7, audioguide €3.50; ☉ 9am-7pm
Tue-Sun) Richard Meier's minimalist
glass-and-marble pavilion echoes the
surrounding Fascist architecture, and
many Romans detest this first modern
construction in Rome's historic centre
since WWII. The wall dividing the busy
Lungotevere in Augusta from Piazza
Augusto Imperatore has been criticised
for obscuring the baroque façade of the
church of San Rocco all'Augusteo, but it
will soon be dismantled, according to new
plans approved by the architect.

The Mysterious Case of the Trevi Coins

Legend has it that throwing a coin in the Trevi Fountain ensures you'll return to Rome, and visitors hedging their bets throw about €3000 into the Trevi per day. This money is meant to be collected daily and donated to the Catholic charity Caritas – but in 2002, police discovered that an unemployed 50-year-old man who goes by the name D'Artagnan (real name: Roberto Cercelletta) had been raiding the fountain for change for 34 years.

D'Artagnan was banned from the fountain, and new security measures were put in place – but he returned to the fountain a few days later, and publicly slashed his belly in protest. The ban lasted a year, until a court ruled that since the money was discarded, it could not technically be considered stolen.

Eight years later, another scandal erupted when a TV company secretly filmed the fountain and discovered that D'Artagnan and some helpers were still collecting Trevi coins with the apparent complicity of the police. In the following days, D'Artagnan staged another belly-slashing protest, clambering onto the rocks surrounding the fountain to display his wounds. Rome's mayor, Gianni Alemanno, now plans to pass legislation to make removal of coins from the Trevi Fountain a criminal offence.

Inside is the less-controversial **Ara Pacis Augustae** (Altar of Peace), Augustus' great monument to peace. One of the most important works of ancient Roman sculpture, the vast marble altar (it measures 11.6m by 10.6m by 3.6m) was completed in 13 BC. Of the reliefs, the most important depicts Augustus at the head of a procession, followed by priests, the general Marcus Agrippa and the entire imperial family.

CHIESA DI SANTA MARIA DELLA CONCEZIONE   Church

(Map p80; ☑ 06 487 11 85; Via Vittorio Veneto 27; admission by donation; ☺9am-noon & 3-6pm Fri-Wed) Descend into the Capuchin cemetery below and you'll be gobsmacked. Between 1528 and 1870, the Capuchin monks used the bones of 4000 of their departed brothers in a most macabre take on interior decoration with vertebrae used as fleurs-de-lis and femur light fixtures.

GALLERIA NAZIONALE D'ARTE ANTICA: PALAZZO BARBERINI   Art Gallery

(Map p80; ☑ 06 2258 2493; www.galleria borghese.it; Via delle Quattro Fontane 13; adult/reduced €5/2.50; ☺9am-7.30pm Tue-Sun, ticket office closes 7pm) Many high-profile baroque architects worked on 17th-century **Palazzo Barberini**, including rivals Bernini and Borromini. Today the palace houses works by Raphael, Caravaggio, Guido Reni, Bernini, Filippo Lippi, Holbein, Titian and Tintoretto – not to mention the mesmerising ceiling of the main salon, the *Triumph of Divine Providence* (1632–39) by Pietro da Cortona.

Esquilino, Monti & San Lorenzo

BASILICA DI SANTA MARIA MAGGIORE   Church

(Map p80; ☑ 06 6988 6800; Piazza Santa Maria Maggiore; audioguide €5; ☺7am-7pm) One of Rome's four patriarchal basilicas (the others being St Peter's, San Giovanni in Laterano and San Paolo Fuori-le-Mura), this church is decorated by glimmering 13th-century mosaics. The great interior retains its original 5th-century structure, with a fine example of 12th-century Cosmati paving and 5th-century mosaics in the triumphal arch and nave, depicting Old Testament scenes. Binoculars will come in handy. In the upper **loggia** (☎ 06 6988 6802; admission €5; ⊗ 2-5pm), you'll find iridescent 13th-century mosaics.

BASILICA DI SAN PIETRO IN VINCOLI   Church
(Map p66; ☎ 06 488 28 65; Piazza di San Pietro in Vincoli 4a; ⊗ 8am-12.30pm & 3.30-7pm Apr-Sep, 8am-12.30pm & 3-6pm Oct-Mar) Pilgrims and art-lovers flock to this basilica for two reasons: to see St Peter's chains and to see Michelangelo's tomb of Pope Julius II. The church was built in the 5th century to house the chains that bound St Peter when he was imprisoned in the Carcere Mamertino. To the right of the altar is Julius' monumental tomb. At its centre is Michelangelo's buff *Moses*, with two small horns sticking out of his head. Subject of much curiosity, the horns were inspired by a mistranslation of a biblical passage: where the original said that

rays of light issued from Moses' face, the translator wrote 'horns'. Michelangelo was aware of the mistake, but gave Moses horns anyway.

San Giovanni to Testaccio
BASILICA DI SAN GIOVANNI IN LATERANO   Cathedral
(Piazza di San Giovanni in Laterano 4; audioguides €5; ⊗ 7am-6.30pm) Founded by Constantine in AD 324, this was the first Christian basilica built in the city and is still Rome's official cathedral and the pope's seat as the bishop of Rome. The central bronze doors were moved here from the **Curia** in the Roman Forum, while to their right is the Holy Door, which is only opened in jubilee years.

On the first pilaster in the right-hand nave is an original, if incomplete, fresco by Giotto. While admiring it, cock your ear towards the next pilaster, where a monument to Pope Sylvester II (r 999–1003) is said to sweat and creak when the death of a pope is imminent. To the left of the altar, the beautiful **cloister** (admission €2; ⊗ 9am-6pm) was built by the Vassalletto family in the 13th century. The

Pantheon (p73)

GLENN BEANLAND/LONELY PLANET IMAGES ©

Detour:
Ostia Antica

Look out, Pompeii: excavations are uncovering ancient Roman restaurants, menus, even toilets at **Ostia Antica** (✒06 563 52 830; www.ostiantica.info, in Italian; Viale dei Romagnoli 717; adult/child €6.5/free, parking €2.50, site map €2; ☺8.30am-7pm Tue-Sun Apr-Oct, to 6pm Mar, to 5pm Nov-Feb). An outbreak of malaria forced citizens to flee in the 5th century AD, and river silt preserved artefacts dating from 300BC to 300AD, including:

Squeaky-clean Ostia Antica's 20 bath complexes included block-long **Terme di Nettuno**, where mosaics show Neptune driving his chariot past sea monsters, mermaids and mermen. Athletes used to train here in the **Palaestra**, where mosaics show boxers and wrestlers in action.

Next to the baths, Agrippa's **theatre** held audiences of up to 3000. In the entryway, you can still see original stucco decoration.

After pleasure came business: behind the amphitheatre is **Piazzale delle Corporazioni**, merchant headquarters, with mosaics representing Ostia's varied business interests.

The **Thermopolium** restaurant has a fresco over the bar advertising the menu, an excavated kitchen, and a fountain courtyard where Romans once gossiped over happy hours.

Across from the Thermopolium are a sociable crescent of **toilets**, so bathroom-goers could continue conversations face-to-face.

Statues and sarcophagi are located in the **museum**, along with mercifully modern toilets, a cafeteria/bar and a gift shop.

To get there, by car, take Via del Mare or the A12 toward Fiumicino, and follow the signs for the Scavi (Ruins). By train, take metro line B to Piramide, exit to Stazione Porta San Paolo, and catch the Ostia Lido train to Ostia Antica.

twisted columns were once completely covered with inlaid marble mosaics, remnants of which can still be seen.

SCALA SANTA & SANCTA SANCTORUM   Church
(Piazza di San Giovanni in Laterano 14; Scala/Sancta free/€3.50; ☺Scala 6.15am-noon & 3.30-6.45pm summer, 6.15am-noon & 3-6.15pm winter, Sancta 10.30-11.30am & 3-4pm, closed Wed am & Sun year-round) The **Scala Santa** is said to be the staircase that Jesus walked up in Pontius Pilate's palace in Jerusalem. Consequently you can only climb it on your knees. At the top of the stairs, the **Sancta Sanctorum** (Holy of Holies) was the popes' private chapel and contains spectacular 13th-century frescoes.

BASILICA DI SAN CLEMENTE   Church
(www.basilicasanclemente.com; Via di San Giovanni in Laterano; admission church/excavations free/€5; ☺9am-12.30pm & 3-6pm Mon-Sat, noon-6pm Sun) The medieval church features a marvellous 12th-century apse mosaic depicting the Trionfo della Croce (Triumph of the Cross) and some wonderful Renaissance frescoes in the Chapel of St Catherine, to the left of the entrance. Steps lead down to the 4th-century basilica inferiore, mostly destroyed by Norman invaders in 1084, but with some faded 11th-century frescoes illustrating the life of San Clement. Follow the steps down another level and you'll come to a 1st-century Roman house and a dark, 2nd-century temple to Mithras, with an altar showing the god slaying a bull. Be-

neath it all, you can hear the eerie sound of a subterranean river, running through a Roman Republic-era drain.

Trastevere & Gianicolo

PIAZZA SANTA MARIA IN TRASTEVERE
Piazza

(Map p86) With its network of cobbled lanes, flapping washing hung between 17th-century ivy-draped facades, and crumbling ochre buildings, Trastevere is bewitchingly pretty, and gets packed on summer evenings. It's glittering heart is this piazza with its central fountain, a 17th-century restoration of the Roman orginal.

BASILICA DI SANTA MARIA IN TRASTEVERE
Church

(Map p86; ✆ 06 581 48 02; Piazza Santa Maria in Trastevere; ✆7.30am-9pm) Begun in AD 337, a major overhaul in 1138 saw the addition of the Romanesque bell tower and glittering facade. Inside, the 12th-century mosaics are the stars. Beneath this, six mosaics by Pietro Cavallini illustrate the life of the Virgin (c 1291).

VILLA FARNESINA
Historical Building

(off Map p86; ✆06 6802 7268; Via della Lungara 230; adult/reduced €5/4; ✆9am-1pm Mon-Sat) A gorgeous 16th-century villa that features some awe-inspiring frescoes by Sebastiano del Piombo, Raphael and the villa's original architect, Baldassare Peruzzi. The most famous frescoes are in the Loggia of Cupid and Psyche on the ground floor, which are attributed to Raphael, who also painted the Trionfo di Galatea (Triumph of Galatea) in the room of the same name.

BASILICA DI SANTA CECILIA IN TRASTEVERE
Church

(Map p86; ✆ 06 589 92 89; Piazza di Santa Cecilia 22; basilica free, Cavallini fresco & crypt each €2.50; ✆basilica & crypt 9.30am-12.30pm & 4-6.30pm, Cavallini fresco 10am-12.30pm Mon-Sat) Dedicated to the patron saint of music, this ancient church features a stunning 13th-century fresco by Pietro Cavallini in the nuns' choir. Beneath the church you can visit the excavations of a maze of Roman houses, one of which is thought to have been that of the young Cecilia.

Foccacia pizzas, Rome

ALAN BENSON/LONELY PLANET IMAGES ©

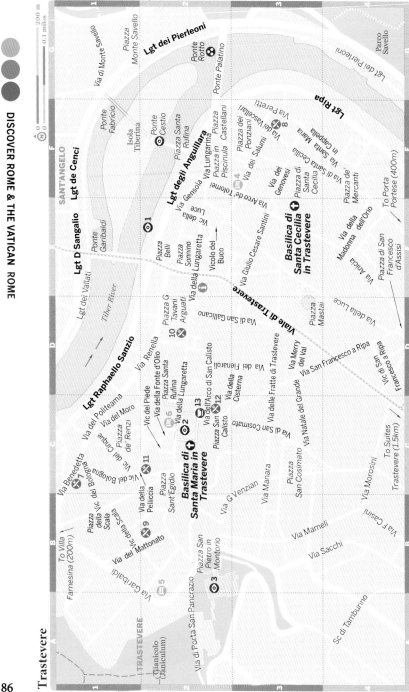

Trastevere

200 m
0.1 miles

SANT'ANGELO

TRASTEVERE

Gianicolo
(Janiculum)

To Villa
Farnesina (200m)

Lgt Raphaello Sanzio

Tiber River

Lgt dei Vallati

Lgt D Sangalio

Lgt de Cenci

Lgt dei Pierleoni

Piazza
Monte Savello

Via di Monte Savello

Ponte
Rotto

Parco
Savello

Lgt dei Pierleoni

Ponte Palatino

Lgt di Ripa

Ponte
Fabricio

Isola
Tiberina

Ponte
Cestio

Piazza Santa
Rufina

Lgt degli Anguillara

Ponte
Garibaldi

Via Peretti

Via dei Vascellari

Piazza in
Piscinula

Piazza
Castellani

Piazza dei
Ponziani

Via Santa Maria
in Cappella

Via Gensola

Via Lungarina

Vic. Arco de' Tolomei

Via della
Luce

Via dei Genovesi

Via dei Salumi

Piazza di
Santa
Cecilia

Piazza dei
Mercanti

Basilica di
Santa Cecilia
in Trastevere

To Porta
Portese (400m)

Via di Santa Cecilia

Piazza
Belli

Piazza
Sonnino

Via della Lungaretta

Vicolo del
Buco

Via Giulio Cesare Santini

Via della
Madonna dell'Orio

Piazza di San
Francesco d'Assisi

Via Anica

Piazza
Tavani
Arguati

Viale di Trastevere

Via di San Gallicano

Piazza
Mastai

Via della Luce

Via del Politeama

Via del Moro

Via Benedetta

Via della
Fonte d'Olio

Via Renella

Vic. del Piede

Piazza Santa
Rufina

Via della Lungaretta

Piazza G

Via del
Fienaroli

Via delle Fratte di Trastevere

Via Merry
del Val

Via San Francesco a Ripa

Vic. di San
Francesco a Ripa

Piazza de
Renzi

Via del Cinque

Piazza
di Bologna

Vic. del Bologna

Via della
Scala

Via della
Pelliccia

Piazza
Sant'Egidio

Basilica di
Santa Maria in
Trastevere

Via dell'Arco di San Calisto

Piazza San
Calisto

Via della
Cisterna

Via di San Cosimato

Via Natale del Grande

To Suites
Trastevere (1.5km)

Via Morosini

Via di Porta San Pancrazio

Via del Mattonato

Piazza San
Pietro in
Montorio

Via G Venzian

Piazza
San Cosimato

Via Manara

Via Mameli

Via Sacchi

Via F Casini

Sc. di Tamburino

Via Garibaldi

Don't Miss **Vatican Museums**

The Vatican Museums deliver 7km of sublime thrills. Don't miss these highlights:

Pinacoteca The papal picture gallery is packed with masterpieces, including Raphael's last work, *Transfiguration* (1517-20), and Leonardo da Vinci's unfinished *St Jerome* (c1480).

Museo Gregoriano Egizio (Egyptian Museum) Treasures taken from Egypt in Roman times range from ancient mummies to astonishingly lifelike Fayum death-mask portraits c 250AD.

Museo Pio-Clementino *Apollo Belvedere* and 1st-century *Laocoön* grace the **Cortile Ottagono** (Octagonal Courtyard), while sea monsters and centaurs gallop underfoot in the **Sala Rotonda** (Round Room) floor mosaic.

Museo Gregoriano Etrusco The upper level of Belvedere Palace houses mysterious talismans from Etruscan tombs, storytelling Greek vases and Roman treasures.

Stanze di Raffaello (Raphael Rooms) To decorate the private apartments of Pope Julius II, Raphael and his assistants filled these rooms with frescoes and Raphael's *School of Athens*, featuring great thinkers gathered around Plato and Aristotle – and himself, naturally (Raphael is second from the right).

Sistine Chapel (Capella Sistina) The Vatican's masterpiece is the ceiling of this 15th-century chapel, where papal conclaves elect the pope. Michelangelo's 800-sq-metre ceiling fresco illustrates Genesis, including *Creation of Adam,* which shows God bringing Adam to life. Michelangelo covered the chapel's 200-sq-metre west wall with souls facing the wrath of God. After his *Last Judgment* was unveiled in 1541, Pope Pius IV had one of Michelangelo's students cover some of Michelangelo's naked bodies with fig leaves.

THINGS YOU NEED TO KNOW

Map p88; 📞 06 698 84 676; www.vatican.va, tickets & tours http://biglietteriamusei.vatican.va/musei/tickets; Viale Vaticano; adult/reduced €14/8, last Sun of month free, guided tours adult/reduced €31/24; 🕙9am-6pm Mon-Sat, last admission 4pm, 9am-2pm last Sun of month, last admission 12.30pm; present email booking confirmation and passport for entry

JEAN-PIERRE LESCOURRET/LONELY PLANET IMAGES ©

Don't Miss St Peter's Basilica

Rome's most spectacular church is also a monument to artistic genius. The original basilica built by Constantine in the 4th century had fallen into disrepair until Bramante began a radical re-design in 1506. But St Peter's owes most to Michelangelo, who took over the project in 1547 and designed the dome.

The cavernous 187m-long **interior** is dotted with spectacular works of art, including Michelangelo's hauntingly beautiful **Pietá** on the right as you enter. Supported by four spiral columns and made with bronze taken from the Pantheon, Bernini's 29m-high **baldachin** rises over the high altar, above St Peter's grave.

To climb the **dome**, look for the entry to the right of the basilica. An elevator takes you halfway up and, from there, it's a 320-step climb to reach the top. The panoramic views are worth it, but the steep, narrow staircase is not recommended for anyone with claustrophobia or vertigo.

Through a door on your left, the **Museo Storico Artistico** sparkles with priceless artefacts, including a communion-wafer box by Donatello and the 6th-century Crux Vaticana, a cross studded with jewels.

Excavations have uncovered what archaeologists believe is the **Tomb of St Peter**, which can only be visited on a 90-minute guided tour booked by emailing the **Ufficio Scavi**.

THINGS YOU NEED TO KNOW

Map p88; www.vatican.va; Piazza San Pietro; audioguides €5; ⊙7am-7pm summer, 7am-6pm winter; appropriate attire required (no shorts, miniskirts or bare shoulders); **dome** (with/without elevator €7/5; ⊙8am-5.45pm summer, 8am-4.45pm winter); **Museo Storico Artistico** (Treasury; adult/reduced €6/4; ⊙9am-6.15pm summer, 9am-5.15pm winter); **Tomb of St Peter** (admission €10, age 15yrs & up); **Ufficio Scavi** (Excavations Office; Map p88; ☎06 698 85 318; scavi@fsp.va)

PONTE SANT'ANGELO   Bridge

(Map p74) In the 17th century, Bernini and his pupils sculpted the figures of angels that line this pedestrian walkway, orginally built by Hadrien in AD 134.

Villa Borghese & Around

MUSEO NAZIONALE DELLE ARTI DEL XXI SECOLO (MAXXI)   Art Gallery

(📞06 321 01 81; www.fondazionemaxxi.it; Via Guido Reni 2f; adult/reduced €11/7; ⏱11am-7pm Tue, Wed, Fri & Sun, 11am-10pm Thu & Sat) More than the exhibitions of contemporary art and architecture, the real attraction here is the building itself. Anglo-Iraqi architect Zaha Hadid has remodelled a former barracks into a light-filled showroom of snaking white walkways, staircases, and acres of glass, cement and steel.

GALLERIA NAZIONALE D'ARTE MODERNA E CONTEMPORANEA   Art Gallery

(📞06 3229 8221; www.gnam.beniculturali.it; Viale delle Belle Arti 131; adult/reduced €8/4; ⏱8.30am-7.30pm, last admission 6.45pm Tue-Sun) Set in a vast belle époque palace are works by some of the most important exponents of modern Italian art. There are canvases by the *macchiaioli* (the Italian Impressionists) and futurists Boccioni and Balla, as well as several impressive sculptures by Canova and major works by Modigliani and De Chirico. International artists are also represented, with works by Degas, Cezanne, Kandinsky, Klimt, Mondrian, Pollock and Moore.

MUSEO NAZIONALE ETRUSCO DI VILLA GIULIA   Museum

(📞06 322 65 71; www.ticketeria.it; Piazzale di Villa Giulia 9; adult/reduced €4/2; ⏱8.30am-7.30pm, last admission 6.30pm Tue-Sun) Italy's finest collection of pre-Roman Etruscan treasures is in Villa Giulia, Pope Julius III's 16th-century pleasure palace, including the Euphronios Krater, a celebrated Greek vase that was returned to Italy in 2008 after a 30-year tug of war between the Italian government and New York's Metropolitan Museum of Art.

Southern Rome

BASILICA DI SAN PAOLO FUORI LE MURA   Church

(📞06 6988 0800; Via Ostiense 190; ⏱6.45am-6.30pm) The biggest church in Rome after St Peter's (and the world's third-largest) stands on the site where St Paul was buried after being decapitated in AD 67. Built by Constantine in the 4th century, it was largely destroyed by fire in 1823 and much of what you see today is a 19th-century reconstruction. However, many treasures survived the fire, including the 5th-century triumphal arch, with its heavily restored mosaics, and the gothic marble tabernacle over the high altar.

Doom-mongers should check out the papal portraits beneath the nave windows. Every pope since St Peter is represented and legend has it that when there is no room for the next portrait, the world will fall. There are eight places left.

The stunning 13th-century Cosmati mosaic work in the **cloisters** (admission free; ⏱9am-1pm & 3-6pm) of the adjacent Benedictine abbey also survived the 1823 fire.

VIA APPIA ANTICA   Historical Site

(Appian Way; 🚍) Heading southeast from Porta San Sebastiano, the Via Appia (Appian Way) was known to the Romans as the *regina viarum* (queen of roads). Named after Appius Claudius Caecus, who laid the first 90km section in 312 BC, it was extended in 190 BC to reach Brindisi, some 540km away on the southern Adriatic coast. Flanked by some of the city's most exclusive private villas, as well as Roman tombs, the long cobbled road is a great place for a walk or cycle. The road is best known for its catacombs – around 300km of underground tunnels were used as burial chambers by the early Christians (see the boxed text, p95).

If you're planning on really seeing the sights, think about buying the Appia Antica Card (see boxed text, p73). The **Appia Antica Regional Park Information Point**(📞06 513 53 16; www.parcoappiaantica.org; Via Appia Antica 58-60; ⏱9.30am-1.30pm & 2-5.30pm Mon-Sat, 9.30am-5.30pm Sun, to 4.30pm daily winter) is very informative.

You can buy a map of the park here and hire **bikes** (per hour/day €3/10). The park authorities organise a series of free guided tours, on foot and by bike, on Sunday mornings.

 Tours

BATTELLI DI ROMA
Boat
(Map p74; ☎ 06 9774 5498; www.battellidiroma. it; adult/reduced €16/12) Runs hour-long hop-on hop-off cruises along the Tiber between Ponte Sant'Angelo and Ponte Nenni. Trips depart at 10am from Ponte Sant'Angelo, 10.10pm from Isola Tiberina, and then hourly until 6.30pm.

TRAMBUS 110OPEN
Bus
(☎ 800 281281; www.trambusopen.com; family/ adult/reduced €50/20/18; ⏱every 15min 8.30am-8.30pm) This open-top, double-decker bus departs from Piazza dei Cinquecento in front of Termini station, and stops at the Colosseum, Bocca della Verità, Piazza Venezia, St Peter's, Ara Pacis and Trevi Fountain. The entire tour lasts two hours but the tickets are valid for 48 hours and allow you to hop on and off as you please. Get tickets online, on board, from the info boxes on Piazza dei Cinquecento or the Colosseum, or from authorised Trambus Open dealers.

TRAMBUS ARCHEOBUS
Bus
(☎ 800 281281; www.trambusopen.com; family/ adult €40/12; ⏱half-hourly 9am-4.30pm) This is a stop-and-go bus that takes sightseers down Via Appia Antica, stopping at points of archaeological interest; for ticket points, see p92.

BICI & BACI
Bike, Scooter
(☎ 06 482 84 43; www.bicibaci.com; Via del Viminale 5; €35; ⏱10am, 3pm & 7pm Mar-Oct, by request Nov-Feb) Bici & Baci runs daily bike tours of central Rome, taking in the historical centre, Campidoglio and the Colosseum, as well as tours on vintage Vespas and in classic Fiat 500 cars.

 Sleeping

Although Rome doesn't have a low season as such, the majority of hotels offer discounts from November to March (excluding the Christmas and New Year

---

Rome for Kids

A three-day, child-friendly itinerary is available at http://piccolituristi. turismoroma.it, or you can design your own around these kid-friendly top spots:

○ **Colosseum** (p72) Pose with gladiators and tour underground prisons.

○ **Villa Borghese** (p92) In Villa Borghese, **Casina di Raffaello** (☎ 06 428 88 888; www.casinadiraffaello.it; Viale della Casina di Raffaello) is a well-equipped daycare centre with a nice little playground, a small library and a soft play area. Accessing the facilities costs €5 per child.

○ **Explora** (☎ 06 361 37 76; www.mdbr.it; Via Flaminia 82; adult/child over 3yrs/child 1-3yrs/child under 1yr €7/7/3/free; ⏱9.30am-7.30pm Tue-Sun Sep-Jul, 11.30am-7pm Tue-Sun Aug) Museum dedicated to kids under 12. Visits by guided tour only; bookings advised, essential at weekends. Outside there's a free playground open to all.

○ **Time Elevator** (p80) A giddy ride through Roman history; not for the under 5s.

○ **Via Appia Antica and the Catacombs** (p95) Bike ancient roads and explore Rome's spooky underground city of the dead (best for age 12 and up).

EPI/ IMAGEBROKER ©

Don't Miss **Villa Borghese**

This Roman villa has it all: a splendid ground-floor sculpture gallery with intricate Roman floor mosaics and over-the-top frescoes; an upstairs picture gallery packed with masterpieces; and a picnic-perfect park.

A tour of the sculpture highlights kicks off in Sala I with Antonio Canova's daring depiction of Napoleon's sister, Paolina Bonaparte Borghese, reclining topless as *Victorious Venus* (1805–08). But Gianlorenzo Bernini's spectacular sculptures steal the show – Daphne's hands seem to morph into leaves before your eyes in the swirling *Apollo and Daphne* (1622–25) in Sala III, and Persephone seems to be turning into untouchable stone as Pluto's hand presses into her thigh in Sala IV's *Rape of Persephone* (1621–22).

Painting highlights include: Caravaggio getting the party started in Sala VIII with his dissipated-looking *Bacchus* (1592–95), followed by his creepy but gorgeous *Madonna with Serpent* (1605–06); *St John the Baptist* (1609–10), probably Caravaggio's last work; and his *David with the Head of Goliath* (1609–10) – Goliath's severed head is said to be a self-portrait.

Upstairs, Raphael shows his emotional range, from the pathos of his *Deposition* (1507) to his fanciful *Lady with a Unicorn* (1506). Romance is a recurring theme, from Correggio's erotic *Danae* (1530–31) in Sala X to Titian's early masterpiece, *Amor Sacro e Amor Profano* (Sacred and Profane Love; 1514) in Sala XX.

Cardinal Scipione Borghese created the gardens as a getaway for his powerful family in the 17th century, and they're still perfect for carefree picnics and family fun. Bike hire is available at Via delle Belle Arti for about €5/15 per hour/day.

THINGS YOU NEED TO KNOW

📞 06 3 28 10; www.galleriaborghese.it; Piazzale del Museo Borghese 5; adult/reduced €8.50/5.25, audioguides €5; ⏱ 9am-7pm Tue-Sun, prebooking necessary

period), and some also offer discounts in August. In Rome, a room occupancy tax is added to the regular accommodation bill of €2 per person per night for a maximum of 10 days in *agriturismi,* B&Bs, guesthouses, and one-, two- and three-star hotels, or €3 per person per night for a maximum of 10 days in four- and five-star hotels. Prices quoted in this chapter do not include the tax.

Accommodation Options

You'll find a full list of accommodation options (with prices) at www.060608.it. If you arrive without a reservation, there's a **hotel reservation service** (☎06 699 10 00; booking fee €3; ☉7am-10pm) next to the tourist office at Stazione Termini.

The following agencies all offer online booking services.

Bed & Breakfast Association of Rome (www.b-b.rm.it) Lists B&Bs and short-term apartment rentals.

Bed & Breakfast Italia (www.bbitalia.com) Rome's longest-established B&B network.

Cross Pollinate (www.cross-pollinate.com) Has B&Bs, private apartments and guesthouses.

Sleeping Rome (www.sleepingrome.com) Offers B&B and has good short-term apartment rentals.

Centro Storico

HOTEL CAMPO
DE' FIORI   Boutique Hotel   €€€
(Map p74; ☎06 687 48 86; www.hotelcampo defiori.com; Via del Biscione 6; s €170-220, d €200-270, 2-person apt €130-150, 4-person apt €180; ❄ @ ⊛ ⚑) This rakish four-star has the lot – sexy decor, an enviable location just off Campo de' Fiori, attentive staff and a panoramic roof terrace. The hotel also offers 11 apartments in the vicinity, ideal for families.

TEATROPACE 33   Hotel   €€
(Map p74; ☎06 687 90 75; www.hotelteatropace. com; Via del Teatro Pace 33; s €69-150, d €110-240; ❄) In a former cardinal's residence, this friendly three-star has 23 beautifully appointed rooms decorated with parquet

flooring, damask curtains and exposed wood beams.

ARGENTINA
RESIDENZA   Boutique Hotel   €€
(Map p74; ☎06 6819 3267; www.argentina residenza.com; Via di Torre Argentina 47; r €120-200; ❄ ⊛) This quiet boutique hotel is hidden on the 3rd floor of a building on Largo di Torre Argentina. All the bustle of the piazza will seem a very long way away as you slip into your jacuzzi and relax in your tastefully modern wood-beamed room.

Tridente & Trevi

VILLA SPALLETTI TRIVELLI   Hotel   €€€
(Map p80; ☎06 4890 7934; www.villaspalletti.it; Via Piacenza 4; r €330-345; ℗ ❄ @ ⊛) With 12 elegant rooms in a glorious mansion in central Rome, you can overlook the gardens of the Quirinale or the estate's own Italian garden.

HOTEL PANDA   Hotel   €
(Map p98; ☎06 678 01 79; www.hotelpanda. it; Via della Croce 35; s with/without bathroom €80/68, d with/without bathroom €108/78; ⊛) Only 50m from the Spanish Steps, the Panda's clean rooms are smallish but nicely furnished, and there are several triples with a bed on a cosy mezzanine.

BABUINO 181   Boutique Hotel   €€€
(Map p98; ☎06 3229 5295; www.romeluxury suites.com/babuino; Via del Babuino 181; r €180-250; ❄ ⊛) A beautifully renovated old palazzo in the heart of the shopping district, Babuino offers discreet luxury, with gorgeous rooms with touches such as a Nespresso machine and fluffy bath robes.

DAPHNE B&B   B&B   €€
(Map p80; ☎06 8745 0086; www.daphne-rome. com; Via di San Basilio 55; d with bathroom €140-235, without bathroom €100-150; ❄ @ ⊛) Boutique B&B Daphne is a gem. Run by an American-Italian couple, it has chic, sleek, comfortable rooms, helpful English-speaking staff, top-notch breakfasts and the loan of a mobile phone for your stay.

RAI/IMAGEBROKER ©

Don't Miss **Roman Catacombs**

Rome's persecuted Christian community built a network of subterranean burial grounds outside the city walls in the first centuries AD, as laws dictated. Corpses in sheets were placed in niches in soft stone walls, which were sealed with marble or terracotta. In about 800AD, after frequent invasions, the bodies of popes and Christian martyrs were moved to basilicas inside the city walls. The catacombs were abandoned and many were forgotten.

Since the mid-19th century, more than 30 catacombs in the Rome area have been excavated by archaeologists. All the following catacombs can be visited through guided tours in English, Italian, French, German and Spanish.

Catacombs of San Callisto Founded at the end of the 2nd century and named after Pope Calixtus I, this became the official cemetery of the newly established Roman Church. In tunnels stretching over 20km, archaeologists have found the tombs of half a million people, including seven popes martyred in the 3rd century.

Catacombs of San Sebastiano Housing frescoes, stucco, epigraphs and three perfectly intact mausoleums on the second level, as well as fascinating graffiti left by visiting pilgrims sometime after 258 AD, when early saints were entombed here.

Catacombs of San Domitilla Stretching underground across 17km, they are illuminated with early Christian wall paintings, and dotted with graves marked with such touching dedications, such as the one by Aurelius Ampliatus to his wife Aurelia: 'An incomparable spouse, a truly chaste woman who lived 25 years, two months, three days and six hours'.

THINGS YOU NEED TO KNOW

Catacombs of San Callisto (🕿 06 513 01 580; Via Appia Antica 110 & 126; www.catacombe.roma.it; adult/reduced €8/4; ⊙ 8.30am-noon & 2.30-5pm Thu-Tue, closed Feb, to 5.30pm Apr-Sept); **Catacombs of San Sebastiano** (🕿 06 785 03 50; www.catacombe.org; Via Appia Antica 136; catacombs adult/reduced €8/4; ⊙ 8.30am-noon & 2-5pm Mon-Sat, closed Nov, to 5.30pm Apr-Sept); **Catacombs of San Domitilla** (🕿 06 511 03 42; Via delle Sette Chiese 283; adult/reduced €8/4; ⊙ 9am-noon & 2-5pm Wed-Mon, closed Jan)

CROSSING CONDOTTI   Guesthouse   €€€

(Map p98; ☎06 6992 0633; www.crossing condotti.com; Via Mario de' Fiori; r €180-300; ❄🤝) A five-room place, this is one of Rome's new breed of upmarket guest-houses, where all the fittings, linen and comforts are top-notch, and the pretty (though not large) rooms have lots of character and antique furnishings.

Trastevere & Giancolo

DONNA CAMILLA SAVELLI   Hotel   €€€

(Map p86; ☎06 58 88 61; www.hotelsavelli. com; Via Garibaldi 27; r €230-450; P ❄ @ 🤝) A converted convent that was originally designed by great baroque architect Bor-romini with 78 beautifully updated rooms, some overlooking the lovely cloister garden or with views of Rome.

ARCO DEL LAURO   B&B   €€

(Map p86; ☎9am-2pm 06 9784 0350, 346 2443212; Via Arco de' Tolomei, 27; s €75-125, d €95-145; ❄🤝) With only six rooms, this fab B&B in an ancient *palazzo* is a find. Beds are comfortable, showers are pow-erful and the owners are eager to please.

VILLA DELLA FONTE   B&B   €€

(Map p86; ☎06 580 37 97; www.villafonte.com; Via della Fonte dell'Olio 8; s €110-145, d €135-170; ❄🤝) A 17th-century building in a street off Piazza Santa Maria in Trastevere with only five rooms, all of which are simply decorated but have pretty outlooks, good bathrooms and comfortable beds covered with lovely linen.

Vatican City & Around

HOTEL BRAMANTE   Hotel   €€

(Map p88; ☎06 6880 6426; www.hotelbramante. com; Vicolo delle Palline 24-25; s €100-160, d €150-220; ❄🤝) Housed in the 16th-century building that was home to architect Domenico Fontana before Pope Sixtus V banished him from Rome, Hotel Bramante's 16 rooms are full of antiques and rustic elegance.

 Eating

Ancient Rome

HOSTARIA DA NERONE   Trattoria   €€

(Map p66; ☎06 481 79 52; Via delle Terme di Tito; meals €35; ☺Mon-Sat) This old-school,

Outdoor dining, Centro Storico, Rome

WILL SALTER/LONELY PLANET IMAGES ©

family-run trattoria is not the place for a romantic dinner or a special-occasion splurge, but if you're after a filling meal after exploring the Colosseum, it does the job. Tourists tuck into classic Roman pasta and salads on the few outside tables, while in the yellowing, woody interior, visiting businessmen cut deals over *saltimbocca* and tiramisu.

Centro Storico

CASA COPPELLE Modern Italian €€
(Map p74; ☑06 6889 1707; www.casacoppelle. it; Piazza delle Coppelle 49; meals €35) Brick walls, books, flowers and subdued lighting set the romantic scene for simple yet delicious food.

PIZZERIA DA BAFFETTO Pizzeria €
(Map p74; ☑06 686 16 17; Via del Governo Vecchio 114; pizzas €6-9; ☺6.30pm-1am) Meals are raucous, chaotic and fast, but the thin-crust pizzas are spot on and the vibe is fun. There's also a **Baffetto 2** (Map p74; Piazza del Teatro di Pompeo 18; ☺6.30pm-12.30am Mon-Fri, 12.30-3.30pm & 6.30pm-12.30am Sat & Sun) near Campo de' Fiori.

DITIRAMBO Modern Italian €€
(Map p74; ☑06 687 16 26; www.ristorante ditirambo.it; Piazza della Cancelleria 72; meals €35; ☺closed Mon lunch) This hugely popular new-wave trattoria offers a laid-back, unpretentious atmosphere and innovative, organic cooking. Book ahead.

ANTICO FORNO ROSCIOLI Bakery €
(Map p74; Via dei Chiavari 34; pizza slice from €2; ☺7.30am-8pm Mon-Fri, to 2.30pm Sat) Join the lunchtime crowds for a slice of pizza (the *pizza bianca* is legendary) or a freshly baked pastry. There's also a counter serving a selection of hot pasta dishes and vegetables.

AR GALLETTO Traditional Italian €€
(Map p74; ☑06 686 17 14; www.ristorantear gallettoroma.com; Piazza Farnese 102; meals €35-40; ☺Mon-Sat) Good, honest Roman food, a warm local atmosphere and dazzlingly set exterior tables. Roast chicken is the house speciality (*galletto* means little rooster).

GINO Trattoria €€
(Map p74; ☑06 687 34 34; Vicolo Rosini 4; meals €30; ☺Mon-Sat) Hidden away down a narrow lane close to parliament, Gino's is perennially packed with gossiping politicians. Join the right honourables for well-executed staples such as *rigotoni alla gricia (*pasta with cured pig's cheek) and meatballs, served under hanging garlic bulbs and gaudily painted vines. No credit cards.

ENOTECA CORSI Osteria €
(Map p74; ☑06 679 08 21; Via del Gesù 88; meals €25; ☺lunch Mon-Sat) The look is rustic and the atmosphere one of cheery organised chaos. On offer are homey dishes prepared using good, fresh ingredients, and the menu follows the culinary calendar (so if it's *gnocchi,* it's a Thursday).

ALFREDO E ADA Traditional Italian €
(Map p74; ☑06 687 88 42; Via dei Banchi Nuovo 14; meals €20; ☺Mon-Fri) For a taste of a authentic Roman cooking, head to this tiny brick-arched and wood-panelled place. It's distinctly no-frills – the wine list consists of two choices, red or white – but the food is filling, warming and just like *nonna* would have cooked it.

Tridente & Trevi

🖋PALATIUM Enoteca €€
(Map p98; ☑06 6920 2132; Via Frattina 94; meals €40; ☺11am-11pm Mon-Sat, closed Aug) Conceived as a showcase of Lazio's bounty, this sleek *enoteca* close to the Spanish Steps serves excellent local specialities, such as *porchetta* (pork roasted with herbs), artisan cheese and delicious salami, as well as an impressive array of Lazio wines (try lesser-known drops such as Aleatico). *Aperitivo* is a good bet, too.

OPEN COLONNA Restaurant €€€
(Map p80; ☑06 4782 2641; Via Milano 9a; meals €20-80; ☺noon-midnight Tue-Sat & Sun lunch) Spectacularly set at the back of Palazzo delle Esposizioni, superchef Antonello Colonna's superb, chic restaurant is tucked away on a mezzanine floor under an extraordinary glass roof. There's a more basic but still delectable fixed

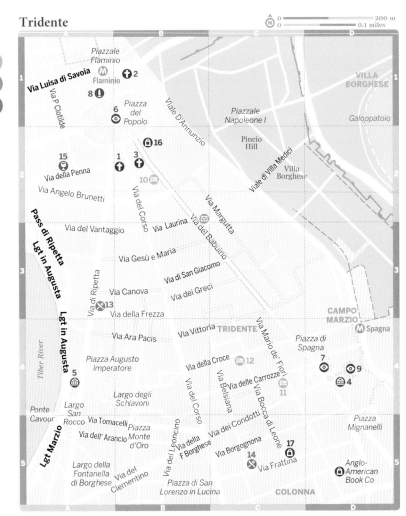

two-course lunch or buffet for €15, and Saturday and Sunday brunch at €28.

LA BUCA DI RIPETTA Restaurant **€€€**
(Map p98; ☎ 06 321 93 91; Via di Ripetta 36; meals €50; ☺daily) Try the *zuppa rustica con crostini di pane aromatizzati* (country-style soup with rosemary-scented bread) or the *matolino di latte al forno alle erbe con patate* (baked suckling pork with potatoes) and you'll be fuelled for either more sightseeing or a serious snooze.

ANTICO FORNO Sandwich Shop **€**
(Map p80; ☎ 06 679 28 66; Via delle Muratte 8; ☺7am-9pm) Near the Trevi Fountain, Antico Forno is one of Rome's oldest bakery shops, and its well-stocked deli counter has a grand array of freshly baked *panini*, focaccia and pizza.

Esquilino, Monti & San Lorenzo

L'ASINO D'ORO Modern Italian **€€**
(☎ 06 4891 3832; Via del Boschetto 73; meals €40) Unfussy yet innovative, with dishes

Tridente

such as slow-roasted rabbit in a rich berry sauce and desserts that linger in the memory. For such excellent food, this intimate, informal yet classy place is one of Rome's best deals, especially for the set lunch.

AGATA E ROMEO Modern Italian €€€
(Map p80; ☏06 446 61 15; Via Carlo Alberto 45; meals €120; ⌚Mon-Fri) Chef Agata Parisella designs and cooks menus, offering creative uses of Roman traditions, while husband Romeo curates the wine cellar and daughter Maria Antonietta chooses the cheeses. Bookings essential.

FORMULA 1 Pizzeria €
(☏06 445 38 66; Via degli Equi 13; pizzas from €6; ⌚6.30pm-1.30am Mon-Sat) At this basic, historic San Lorenzo pizzeria, waiters zoom around under whirring fans delivering tomato-loaded bruschetta, fried zucchini flowers, *supplì al telefono* and bubbling thin-crust pizza.

TRIMANI WINE BAR Enoteca €€
(Map p80; ☏06 446 96 30; Via Cernaia 37b; meals €40; ⌚Mon-Sat, closed 2 weeks Aug) This is a top-of-the-range wine bar, with a delectable range of dishes – from oysters to lentil soup to salami and cheeses served with mustard and jam – plus a choice of over 4500 international wines.

DA FELICE Traditional Italian €€
(☏06 574 68 00; Via Mastro Giorgio 29; meals €40; ⌚Mon-Sat) Highlights include glorious *tonnarelli cacio e pepe* (square-shaped pasta with pecorino Romano cheese and black pepper) and wonderful roast lamb.

San Giovanni to Testaccio

TRATTORIA DA BUCATINO Trattoria €€
(☏06 574 68 86; Via Luca della Robbia 84; meals €30; ⌚Tue-Sun) Ask for a table upstairs (with wood panels, Chianti bottles and a mounted boar's head) and dig into huge portions of Roman soul food. The *bucatini all'amatriciana* is a must.

VOLPETTI PIÙ Traditional Italian €
(Via Volta 8; meals under €15; ⌚10.30am-3.30pm & 5.30-9.30pm Mon-Sat) One of the few places in town where you can sit down and eat well for less than €15, Volpetti Più is a sumptuous *tavola calda*, offering an opulent choice of pizza, pasta, soup, meat, vegetables and fried nibbles.

Trastevere & Giancolo

GLASS HOSTERIA Creative Italian €€€
(Map p86; ☏06 5833 5903; Vic del Cinque 58; meals €70; ⌚dinner Tue-Sun) Trastevere's foremost foodie address, the Glass Hosteria is a breath of fresh air in the neighbourhood, a modernist-styled, sophisticated setting with cooking to match.

PARIS Traditional Italian €€
(Map p86; ☏06 581 53 78; Piazza San Calisto 7a; meals €45; ⌚Tue-Sat, lunch Sun, closed 3 weeks Aug) An old-school Roman restaurant set in a 17th-century building, Paris is the best place outside the Ghetto to sample

Top 5 for Gelato

○ **San Crispino** (☎06 679 39 24) Via della Panetteria (Map p80; Via della Panetteria 42; ⊗noon-12.30am Mon, Wed, Thu & Sun, noon-1.30am Fri & Sat); Piazza della Maddalena (Map p74; Piazza della Maddalena 3; ⊗noon-12.30am Mon, Wed, Thu & Sun, noon-1.30am Fri & Sat) The delicate, strictly natural and seasonal flavours are served only in tubs (cones would detract from the taste).

○ **Alberto Pica** (Map p74; ☎06 686 84 05; Via della Seggiola 12; ⊗8.30am-2am Mon-Sat year-round, 4pm-2am Sun, closed 2 weeks Aug) In summer, it offers flavours such as *fragolini de bosco* (wild strawberry) and *petali di rosa* (rose petal), but flavours feature seasonal specialities throughout the year.

○ **Fior di Luna** (Map p86; ☎06 6456 1314; Via della Lungaretta 96; ⊗noon-1am) A small artisanal ice creamery in Trastevere, it only uses fresh, seasonal ingredients, and is the ideal place to stop when you're wandering around Rome's prettiest district after dinner.

○ **Gelateria Giolitti** (Map p74; ☎06 699 12 43; Via degli Uffici del Vicario 40; ⊗7am-2am) Gregory Peck and Audrey Hepburn swung by this historic gelateria in *Roman Holiday* and it used to deliver marron glacé to Pope John Paul II.

○ **Ara Coeli** (Map p74; ☎06 679 50 85; Piazza d'Aracoeli 9; ⊗11am-11pm) Close to the base of the Campidoglio, Ara Coeli is handily located and offers more than 40 flavours of excellent organic ice cream, semicold varieties, Sicilian granita and yoghurt.

Roman-Jewish cuisine, such as delicate *fritto misto con baccalà* (deep-fried vegetables with salt cod) and *carciofi alla giudia* (Jewish-style artichokes).

DA LUCIA Trattoria **€€**
(Map p86; ☎06 580 36 01; Vicolo del Mattonato 2; meals €30; ⊗Tue-Sun) On a cobbled back-street that is classic Trastevere, Da Lucia serves up a cavalcade of Roman speciali-ties including *trippa all romana* (tripe with tomato sauce) and *pollo con peperoni* (chicken with peppers), as well as bounti-ful antipasti and possibly Rome's best tiramisu. Cash only.

DA ENZO Trattoria **€€**
(Map p86; ☎06 581 83 55; Via dei Vascellari 29; meals €25; ⊗Mon-Sat) This snug dining room with rough yellow walls and lots of character serves up great, seasonally based Roman meals, such as spaghetti with clams and mussels or grilled lamb cutlets.

BEER & FUD Pizza **€**
(Map p86; ☎06 589 40 16; Via Benedetta 23; meals €25; ⊗6.30pm-1am Tue-Sun, closed Aug) This buzzing, vaulted pizzeria wins plau-dits for its small menu of organic pizzas, *crostini* and delicious fried things (potato, pumpkin etc) and has a microbrewery on site. Save room for dessert. Book ahead.

Vatican City & Around

MONDO ARANCINA Sicilian **€**
(Via Marcantonio Colonna 38; arancine from €2) All sunny yellow ceramics, cheerful crowds and tantalising deep-fried snacks, including the classic fist-sized *arancine*, fried rice balls stuffed with *ragù* and peas.

ANGELI A BORGO Traditional Italian **€€**
(Map p88; ☎06 686 96 74; www.angeliaborgo. com; Borgo Angelico 28; pizzas from €5.50, meals €25-30) Just a few blocks back from St Peter's, this laid-back restaurant pizzeria with a high brick ceiling, yellow walls and an ample menu offers wood-fired pizzas

and focaccia, abundant pasta and exceptional tiramisu.

HOSTARIA DINO E TONY Trattoria €€
(off Map p88; ☎06 3973 3284; Via Leone IV; meals €30-35; ⏰Mon-Sat) Kick off with the monumental antipasto, a minor meal in its own right, before plunging into its signature dish, *rigatoni all' amatriciana*. No credit cards.

CACIO E PEPE Trattoria €
(☎06 321 72 68; Via Avezzana 11; meals €25; ⏰closed Sat dinner & Sun) Romans flock here in droves for *cacio e pepe* – fresh *bucatini* slicked with buttery cheese and pepper – followed by *pollo alla cacciatora* (hunter's chicken).

 **Drinking**

Ancient Rome
CAFFÈ CAPITOLINO Cafe
(Map p66; Capitoline Museums, Piazzale Caffarelli 4; ⏰Tue-Sun) Hidden behind the Capitoline Museums, this stylish rooftop cafe commands memorable views. You don't need a ticket to drink here – it's accessible via an entrance that is located behind Palazzo dei Conservatori.

CAVOUR 313 Wine Bar
(Map p66; ☎06 678 54 96; www.cavour313.it; Via Cavour 313; dishes €7-14; ⏰10am-3.30pm & 7pm-midnight, closed Aug) Situated close to the Colosseum and the Forum, wood-panelled, intimate wine bar Cavour 313 offers sensational wine (over 1200 labels to choose from), cold cuts, cheeses and daily specials.

Centro Storico
CAFFÈ SANT'EUSTACHIO Cafe
(Map p74; Piazza Sant'Eustachio 82; ⏰8.30-1am Sun-Thu, to 1.30am Fri, to 2am Sat) The famous *gran caffè* is created by beating the first drops of espresso and several teaspoons of sugar into a frothy paste, then adding the rest of the coffee on top. Specify if you want it *amaro* (bitter) or *poco zucchero* (with a little sugar).

OPEN BALADIN Bar
(Map p74; www.openbaladin.com; Via degli Specchi 6; ⏰12.30pm-2am) A designer beer bar near Campo de' Fiori, Open Baladin has more than 40 brews on tap and up to a

Caffè Sant'Eustachio

100 bottled beers, mainly produced by Italian artisanal breweries.

SALOTTO 42   Bar

(Map p74; www.salotto42.it; Piazza di Pietra 42; ⊙10am-2am Tue-Sat, to midnight Sun & Mon) A hip, glamorous lounge bar, complete with vintage armchairs, sleek sofas and a collection of two-tonne design books. Run by an Italian-Swedish couple, it has an excellent *aperitivo* spread and serves a Sunday brunch (€15).

CAFFÈ TAZZA D'ORO   Cafe

(Map p74; Via degli Orfani 84; ⊙Mon-Sat) One of the city's best cafes offers a range of delicious coffee concoctions, such as *granita di caffè*, a crushed-ice coffee with a big dollop of cream, and *parfait di caffè*, a €3 coffee mousse.

BAR DELLA PACE   Cafe

(Map p74; Via della Pace 5; ⊙9am-3am Tue-Sun, 4pm-3am Mon) Inside it's gilded baroque and mismatched wooden tables; outside locals and tourists strike poses over their Campari against a backdrop of ivy.

Tridente & Trevi

SALOTTO   Bar

(Map p98; Via della Penna 22; ⊙noon-3am) As part of the art deco Hotel Locarno, this bar has a lovely Agatha Christie-era feel, and a greenery-shaded outdoor terrace in summer. Cocktails cost €16.

Esquilino, Monti & San Lorenzo

SOLEA CLUB   Bar

(☎328 9252925; Via dei Latini 51; ⊙9pm-2am) With lots of vintage sofas, chairs, and cushions on the floor, this baroque bar has San Lorenzo hipsters lounging all over the floor, drinking the so-mean-they-snarl mojitos. Fun.

San Giovanni to Testaccio

IL PENTAGRAPPOLO   Wine Bar

(Via Celimontana 21b; ⊙noon-3pm & 6pm-1am Tue-Sun) A few blocks from the Colosseum, these attractive star-vaulted rooms offer 250 labels to choose from and about 15 wines by the glass. There's live jazz or soul on Thursday, Friday and Saturdays nights and a daily *aperitivo* (6pm to 8.30pm).

Trastevere & Gianicolo

BAR SAN CALISTO Bar
(Map p86; ☎ 06 589 56 78; Piazza San Calisto 3-5; ⏲ 6-2am Mon-Sat) Those in the know head to the down-at-heel 'Sanca' for its basic, stuck-in-time atmosphere and cheap prices (a beer costs €1.50). It's famous for its chocolate – drunk hot with cream in winter, eaten as ice cream in summer.

Vatican City & Around

PASSAGUAI Wine Bar
(Map p88; www.passaguai.it; Via Leto 1; ⏲ 10am-2am Mon-Sat; 🛜) A cavelike basement wine bar, Passaguai has a few outdoor tables and feels pleasingly off the beaten track. There's a good wine list and range of artisanal beers, and the food – such as cheeses and cold cuts – is tasty, too. Free wi-fi.

 **Entertainment**

For events, check out the following:

Romac'è (www.romace.it, in Italian; €1) Rome's most comprehensive listings guide comes complete with a small English-language section; it's published every Wednesday.

Trova Roma, Comes as a free insert with *La Repubblica* every Thursday.

Wanted in Rome (www.wantedinrome. com; €1) An English-language magazine that contains listings of festivals, exhibitions, dance shows, classical music events, operas and cinema releases. It's published every second Wednesday.

Estate Romana (www.estateromana.comune. roma.it) From mid-June to mid-September, most of the city's clubs and music joints close but this festival brings outdoor concerts, open-air cinema and temporary markets to Rome summer nights.

Music

AUDITORIUM PARCO
DELLA MUSICA Cultural Centre
(☎06 8024 1281; www.auditorium.com; Viale
Pietro de Coubertin 30) Designed by Renzo
Piano, the Auditorium Parco della Musica
is home to Rome's top orchestra – the
world-class Orchestra dell' Accademia
Nazionale di Santa Cecilia (www.santa
cecilia.it).

Opera

TEATRO DELL'OPERA DI ROMA Opera
(Map p80; ☎06 4807 8400; www.operaroma.it;
Piazza Beniamino Gigli; ☾box office 9am-5pm
Mon-Sat, 9am-1.30pm Sun) This theatre has
an impressive history: it premiered Puc-
cini's *Tosca,* and Maria Callas sang here.
Rome's indoor opera season runs from
December to June, then moves outside in
summer, to the spectacular setting of the
Terme di Caracalla.

Clubbing

RIALTOSANTAMBROGIO
Cultural Centre
(Map p74; ☎06 68133 640; www.rialto.roma.it;
Via di San'Ambrogio 4) Located in the Ghetto,
this ancient building centred around a
courtyard holds central Rome's best
clubbing nights, exhibitions and art-house
cinema.

CONTE STACCIO Nightclub
(www.myspace.com\contestaccio; Via di Monte
Testaccio 65b; ☾8pm-5am) With an under-the-
stars terrace and an arched interior, Conte
Staccio is one of the most popular venues
on the Testaccio clubbing strip, serving
up a regular menu of DJs and live-music
performances.

ALEXANDERPLATZ Live Music
(☎06 3974 2171; www.alexanderplatz.it; Via
Ostia 9; ☾7am-2pm Sep-Jun) The top jazz
joint in Rome attracts top international
performers and a passionate, knowledge-
able crowd. The performances start at
around 10pm.

 **Shopping**

BORSALINO Accessories
(Map p98; ☎06 3265 0838; Piazza del Popolo 20;
☾10am-7.30pm Mon-Sat, 10.30am-7.30pm Sun)
Borsalino is *the* Italian hatmaker, favoured
by 1920s criminal Al Capone, Japanese
Emperor Hirohito and Humphrey Bogart.
Think fedoras, pork-pie styles, felt cloches
and woven straw caps.

FAUSTO SANTINI Shoes
(Map p98; ☎06 678 41 14; Via Frattina 120;
☾11am-7.30pm Mon, 10am-7.30pm Tue-Sat,
11am-2pm & 3-7pm Sun) Style mavens adore
Roman designer Fausto Santini for his
simple, architectural shoe designs. Colours are beautiful and the quality impeccable. For bargains, check out the outlet
shop, **Giacomo Santini** (Map p80; Via Cavour
106), where stock from previous seasons
is discounted up to half-price.

AI MONASTERI Cosmetics
(Map p74; www.monasteri.it; Corso del Rinascimento 72) This apothecary-like shop stocks
all-natural cosmetics, sweets, honeys,
jams and wines, all made by monks. Stock
up on sage toothpaste, rose shampoo,
cherry brandy and a mysterious-sounding
elixir of love.

PORTA PORTESE FLEA MARKET Market
(Piazza Porta Portese) With thousands of
stalls selling everything from rare books
and spare bike parts to Peruvian shawls
and MP3 players, it's crazily busy and a
lot of fun.

Information

Medical Services
Rather than go to a *pronto soccorso* (Accident and
Emergency) department, you can try calling the
Policlinico Umberto I (☎06 49971, first aid 06
49979501; Viale del Policlinico 155) , located near
Stazione Termini.
You can also call a private doctor to come
to your hotel or apartment. Try Roma Medica
(☎338 622 4832; 24 hr).

Tourist Information

Enjoy Rome (Map p80; ☎06 445 18 43; www.
enjoyrome.com; Via Marghera 8a; ⏰9am-5.30pm
Mon-Fri, 8.30am-2pm Sat) An excellent private
tourist office that runs tours and publishes the
free and useful *Enjoy Rome* city guide.

Rome Tourist Board (APT; ☎06 06 08; www.
romaturismo.it; ⏰9am-6pm) Has an office at
Fiumicino airport in Terminal B, International
Arrivals.

Comune di Roma (City Council; ☎06 06 08;
www.060608.it; ⏰9am-9pm) Tourism
information points across Rome and a
multilingual information line provide information
on culture, shows, hotels and transport; you
can also book theatre, concert, exhibition and
museum tickets. The Comune also publishes the
monthly 'What's On' pamphlet *L'Evento,* as well
as *Un Ospite a Roma* (A Guest in Rome; www.
unospitearoma.it, www.aguestinrome.com).

❶ Getting There & Away

Air

Rome's main international airport, **Leonardo da
Vinci** (FCO; ☎06 6 59 51; www.adr.it), better
known as Fiumicino, is on the coast 30km west
of the city. The much smaller **Ciampino Airport**
(CIA; ☎06 6 59 51; www.adr.it), 15km
southeast of the city centre, is the hub
for low-cost carriers such as **Ryanair**
(www.ryanair.com) and **easyJet**
(www.easyjet.com).

Car & Motorcycle

Car-hire is available at both
airports and Stazione
Termini from the following:

Avis (☎06 481 43 73;
www.avisautonoleggio.it)

Europcar (☎06 488 28
54; www.europcar.com)

Hertz (☎06 474 03 89;
www.hertz.com)

Maggiore National
(☎06 488 00 49;
www.maggiore.com)

Basilica di Santa Maria Maggiore (p82)
WILL SALTER/LONELY PLANET IMAGES ©

Train

Almost all trains arrive at and depart from
Stazione Termini (Map p80), Rome's principal
station. Train information is available from the
train information office (⏰6am-midnight) next
to platform 1, online at www.ferroviedellostato.it,
or (if you speak Italian) by calling ☎89 20 21.

❶ Getting Around

To/From the Airport

From Fiumicino airport, the following transport is
available:

Leonardo Express train (adult/child €14/free)
Journey time is 30 minutes between Fiumicino
and Termini; departures every 30 minutes.

FR1 train (one way €8) Connects the airport
to Trastevere, Ostiense and Tiburtina stations
every 15 minutes (hourly on Sunday and public
holidays).

SIT bus (☎06 591 68 26; www.sitbusshuttle.
it; one way €8) Regular departures from Via
Marsala outside Stazione Termini to/from
Fiumicino. Journey time is one hour.

Airport Shuttle (06 420 13 469; www. airportshuttle.it) Transfers to/from your hotel for €25 for one person, then €6 for each additional passenger.

Taxi The set fare to/from the city centre is €40, which is valid for up to four passengers with luggage. Note that taxis registered in Fiumicino charge a set fare of €60, so make sure you catch a Comune di Roma taxi.

From Ciampino airport, the following transport is available:

Terravision bus (www.terravision.eu; one way/ return €4/8) Twice hourly departures to/from Via Marsala outside Stazione Termini. Journey time is 40 minutes.

SIT bus (www.sitbusshuttle.com; one way/return €6/8) Leaves regularly from Via Marsala outside Stazione Termini; journey time is 45 minutes.

Airport Shuttle (06 420 13 469; www. airportshuttle.it) Transfers to/from your hotel for €25 for one person, then €5 for each additional passenger.

Taxi The set rate to/from the airport is €30.

Car & Motorcycle

ACCESS & PARKING Most of the historical centre is closed to normal traffic from 6.30am to 6pm Monday to Friday, from 2pm to 6pm Saturday, and from 11pm to 3am Friday to Sunday. Restrictions also apply in Trastevere (6.30am-10am Mon-Sat, 11pm-3am Fri-Sun), San Lorenzo (9pm-3am Fri-Sun), Monti (11pm-3am Fri-Sun) and Testaccio (11pm-3am Fri-Sun). If you're staying in this zone, contact your hotel, which will fax the authorities with your number plate, thus saving you a fine. There's a comprehensive list of carparks on www.060608.it – click on the transport tab and car parks.

Public Transport

TICKETS Rome's public transport system includes buses, trams, metro and a suburban train network. Children under 10 travel free. Buy tickets at *tabacchi*, newsstands and from vending machines at main bus stops and metro stations. They must be purchased before you start your journey and validated in the yellow machines on buses, at the entrance gates to the metro or at train stations.

Single (BIT; €1) Valid for 75 minutes on buses or trams, or for one metro ride.

Daily (BIG; €4) Unlimited travel until midnight of the day of purchase.

Three-day (BTI; €11) Unlimited travel for three days.

Weekly (CIS; €16) Unlimited travel for seven days.

Villa d'Este (p107), Tivoli

Detour:
Tivoli: Villa Adriana & Villa D'Este

Rome's glitterati have escaped the heat of summers and scandals in Tivoli for millennia – and now you can join them at two Unesco World Heritage royal retreats: Villa Adriana and Villa d'Este. Emperor Hadrian's sprawling, 2nd-century AD Villa Adriana, 5km outside Tivoli, is more like a town than a villa, while 16th-century Villa d'Este is a High Renaissance pleasure palace. You can visit both in a day, if you start early.

An intrepid traveller and architect, Hadrian personally designed much of **Villa Adriana** (☎06 399 67 900; adult/reduced €8/4, parking €2; ⏰9am-7pm, last admission 5.30pm), with inspiration from buildings he'd seen around the world. Enjoy an imperial stroll under the portico-shaded **pecile** (Athenian-style building), along a canal representing the Nile, and through the underground gallery at Hadrian's private retreat, the **Teatro Marittimo**, built on a manmade island. Pack a picnic to feast in the gardens.

When Cardinal Ippolito d'Este redecorated the place in 1551, this former Benedictine convent became sumptuous **Villa d'Este** (☎199 766 166, 0445 230310; www.villadestetivoli.info; Piazza Trento; adult/reduced €8/4; ⏰8.30am-1hr before sunset Tue-Sun). Mannerist frescoes cover villa walls indoors, and the romantic gardens are dotted with stone gargoyles and 100 fantastical fountains that are wonders of Renaissance engineering – Gianlorenzo Bernini designed one with an organ inside that still plays, using water pressure. Picnics aren't allowed; try the stylish on-site cafe or nearby **Trattoria del Falcone** (☎0774 312358; Via del Trevio 34; meals €30; ⏰Wed-Mon), a stone-walled bistro serving classic pasta dishes since 1918.

Tivoli is located about 30km east of Rome via the A24, and is accessible by Cotral bus from outside the Ponte Mammolo station on metro line B (€1.60, every 15 minutes, 50 minutes). Information is available from the **tourist information point** (☎07 743 13 536; ⏰9am-5.30pm) on Piazza Garibaldi, where the bus arrives.

PASSES The Roma Pass comes with a three-day travel pass valid within the city boundaries. The Vatican and Rome card (1/2/3 days €19/21/25) provides unlimited travel on all public transport within the city and on the Open buses operated by Roma Christiana (p92).

BUSES Buses and trams are run by ATAC (☎06 57 003; www.atac.roma.it). The main bus station (Map p80; Piazza dei Cinquecento) is in front of Stazione Termini, where there's an information booth (⏰7.30am-8pm). Buses generally run from about 5.30am until midnight, with limited services throughout the night.

METRO Rome has two metro lines, A (orange) and B (blue), which cross at Termini, the only point at which you can change from one line to the other.

Taxi

Official licensed taxis are white with the symbol of Rome on the doors. In town (within the ring road), flag fall is €2.80 between 7am and 10pm on weekdays, rising to €4 on Sundays and holidays, and €5.80 between 10pm and 7am. Then it's €0.92 per km. Note that when you call for a cab, the meter is switched on immediately and you pay for the cost of the journey from wherever the driver receives the call.

You can book a taxi by phoning the Comune di Roma's automated taxi line (☎060609) or calling a taxi company direct.

La Capitale (☎06 49 94)

Pronto Taxi (☎06 66 45)

Radio Taxi (☎06 35 70)

Milan, the Lakes & Piedmont

Never mind its age, northwest Italy thoroughly enjoys modern living. Sure, the region is known for gilded Bellagio villas, palatial museums, and the ultimate faded glory: Leonardo Da Vinci's *Last Supper*. But far from being overshadowed by this rich heritage, northwest Italy puts it to work with fashion photo shoots, avant-garde art collections and digital-image technology. With its obsessive attention to well-designed detail, Milan carries off work and play with equal flair: watch and learn how to eat (happy hour buffets), where to relax (the Lakes) and when to work that runway (Fashion Week or Saturdays at the club).

Grand Napoleonic boulevards criss-cross its centre, but Turin is defined by its industrial-chic, arty edge. Turin's picturesque Piedmont and Cinque Terre hinterlands are also absurdly delicious. Here in the home of Slow Food, entire Piedmontese towns seem topped with gooey fontina cheese, lavished with white truffles, and awash in Barolo.

Duomo (p123), Milan
DAN HERRICK/LONELY PLANET IMAGES ©

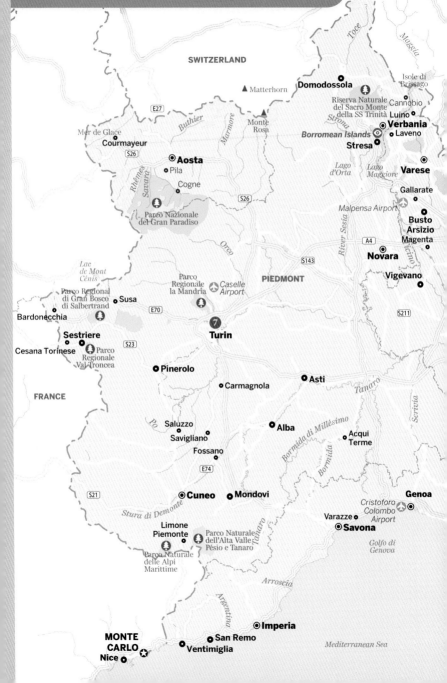

Milan, the Lakes & Piedmont

SWITZERLAND

▲ Matterhorn

Domodossola

Isole di Brissago

Riserva Naturale del Sacro Monte della SS Trinità

Cannobio

Luino

Monte Rosa

Borromean Islands

Verbania

Laveno

Stresa

Mer de Glace

Buthier

Marmore

Courmayeur

Aosta

Pila

Lago d'Orta

Lago Maggiore

Varese

Cogne

Gallarate

Rhêmes Savara

Malpensa Airport

Busto Arsizio

Parco Nazionale del Gran Paradiso

Orco

Magenta

River Sesta

Ticino

Novara

Vigevano

Lac de Mont Cénis

Parco Regionale la Mandria

Caselle Airport

PIEDMONT

Parco Regionale di Gran Bosco di Salbertrand

Susa

Bardonecchia

Sestriere

Turin

Cesana Torinese

Parco Regionale Val Troncea

Pinerolo

FRANCE

Carmagnola

Asti

Tanaro

Scrivia

Saluzzo

Po

Savigliano

Alba

Bormida di Millèsimo

Acqui Terme

Fossano

Bormida

Cuneo

Mondovi

Genoa

Cristoforo Colombo Airport

Varazze

Stura di Demonte

Savona

Limone Piemonte

Parco Naturale dell'Alta Valle Pésio e Tanaro

Tanaro

Golfo di Genova

Parco Naturale delle Alpi Marittime

Arroscia

Argentina

MONTE CARLO

Imperia

San Remo

Mediterranean Sea

Nice

Ventimiglia

0 — 50 km
0 — 25 miles

Parco Nazionale dello Stelvio
S38
S38
A2
A13
Chiavenna
3
Lago di Mezzola
Lago di Como
S38
Sondrio
Adda
Parco dell'Adamello
Sarca
E45
Lugano
Lenno
Varenna
Bellagio
Parco Regionale degli Orobie Valtellinesi
Serio
Laglio
Triangolo Lariano
Enna
Cernobbio
Lecco
Parco Regionale Bergamasche
San Pellegrino Terme
Como
Lago di Annone
Adda
Brembo
Oglio
Lago d'Iseo
Mella
Lago d'Idro
Parco Regionale dell'Alto Garda Bresciano
Monte Baldo
Saronno
Bergamo
Dalmine
Cherio
Cesano Maderno
Monza
Oglio
Treviglio
Parco Regional del Serio
Brescia
Orio al Serio
Lago di Garda
Milan
SS11
A4
Desenzano del Garda
Colombare
Verona
Crema
Serio
LOMBARDY
SS9
Lodi
Chiese
River Mincio
Pavia
Parco Adda Sud
Cremona
Mantua
Lago Superiore
Po
A21
Trebbia
A22
Secchia
Parma
Reggio Emilia
Panaro
LIGURIA
A15
Camogli
Rapallo
A12
Portofino
Vara
Parco Nazionale delle Cinque Terre
Vernazza
La Spezia
Corniglia
Sarzana
Riomaggiore
Lerici
Porto Venere

1 Milan Fashion & Design
2 Lake Como
3 Da Vinci's *Last Supper*, Milan
4 Duomo, Milan
5 Bellagio
6 Quadrilatero d'Oro, Milan
7 Eataly, Turin

Milan, the Lakes & Piedmont Highlights

① Milan Fashion & Design

Milan is defined not by its landmark buildings, but by what Milanese put inside them – especially all those living-room corners and bedroom closets. Milan's showcases for fashion and home decor designers draw international crowds; this city will find any excuse to dress up and redecorate. Above: Living cocktail bar (p134); Top Right: Triennale Design Museum (p132); Bottom Right: Milan Men's Fashion Week

Need to Know

NIGHTLIFE LISTINGS
Milano2night (http://milano
.tonight.eu) **MOST FASHION-
ABLE NON-FASHION
EVENT** Milano Film Festival
(www.milanofilmfestival.it)
See p132.

Milan Don't Miss List

BY CLAUDIO BONOLDI, FASHION & DESIGN PHOTOGAPHER

1 SALONE DEL MOBILE

April's Salone del Mobile (international furniture fair; p132) is the busiest time to visit Milan, but it's also the best. You don't actually need to see the fair – just go see the glass FieraMilano (p132) building from outside, then head into **Fiera Fuoresalone** (http://fuorisalone.it), the international selection of works by emerging designers held in a satellite pavilion.

2 FASHION WEEK

Unless you're in the business, skip the runway shows and go to fashion events instead. Hotel roofs, old factories, and other places normally closed to the public host parties, and after the relief of getting through runway presentations, the mood is upbeat.

3 TRIENNALE DESIGN MUSEUM

Milan's design museum (p132) showcases classic design objects that put Milan and Italy on the map – Memphis Group teapots, Gio Ponti chairs – as well as experimental approaches. Some shows are inspiring, some are frustrating, but it's always interesting to notice your reaction to design.

4 HAPPY HOUR

The most fashionable scene in Milan is also the cheapest. From 6pm to 8:30pm, you can get access to an entire buffet for the price of a drink. Around Arco della Pace are a dozen classic happy hour places, including Living (p134) – very stylish, sometimes snobbish. For cocktails with friendly people in a trendy location, try **Bar Rita** (02 837 2865; Via Angelo Fumagalli 1; noon-midnight) in Navigli.

5 STREET FASHION PHOTO-OPS

Corso Garibaldi is where you'll find people dressed to be admired – but for street fashion that's a little freaky, don't miss the scene weekdays at Corso di Porta Ticinese. For fashion photo shoots, Cimitero Monumentale (Milan's cemetery) makes an evocative setting with weathered statuary. But for inspiration, the Duomo (p143) is obligatory.

113

Lake Como

Lake Como (Lago di Como) is the most spectacular of Italy's northern lakes. The surrounding mountains plunge straight into the water, which is edged with lots of small, characterful villages where you can always find a little peace and quiet. Below: Villa Balbianello (p145), Lenno; Top Right: Fried fish, Como (p142); Bottom Right: Gardens at Villa Carlotta (p145), Tremezzo

Need to Know

WINTER Most hotels close, but small, family-run hotels are still good bets for a relaxing stay **TRANSIT** Trains connect Como and Milan; buses run from Como to Bellagio **See p146.**

2

Lake Como Don't Miss List

BY RITA ANNUNZIATA,
LAKE COMO NATIVE & TOUR GUIDE

1 WALKING TRAILS & TOURS

Walking tours of the mountains surrounding the towns of Bellagio (p146), Lenno (p144), and Tremezzo (p145) offer an insight into the lake's lesser-known villages and landscapes. The 6km walk from Bellano to Varenna along the ancient Viandante trail is particularly beautiful. On the western shore, head to the Chiesa di San Martino, 400m above tiny Cadenabbia, for spectacular views. You'll find information on walking trails and tours at the local tourist offices.

2 ROMANTIC GARDENS

Quite simply, Lake Como's gardens are marvellous. To catch the spring blooming of azaleas, rhododendrons and camellias, visit before 10 May. Among the most beautiful gardens are those of Villas Serbelloni (p146), Balbianello (p145) and Carlotta (p145). In summer, enchanting classical concerts are held in some of the gardens, mostly at Villa Carlotta. For schedules, check the villas' websites or those of the local tourist offices.

3 GASTRONOMIC ENCOUNTERS

You'll find lots of wonderfully atmospheric restaurants and trattorias around the lake, such as Albergo Silvio's (p146) lofty restaurant. Or book a table at **Locanda dell'Isola Comacina** (☎ 0344 55083; www.comacina. it; return shuttle boat from Sala Comacina €6), on the lake's only island. Expect lots of fresh vegetables, local trout and fabulous fried chicken. Owner Benvenuto will tell you about the island's long and complicated history, and prepare a special coffee to 'purify' you after stepping on his 'cursed land'.

4 BELLAGIO

Most visitors are surprised that Bellagio (p146) is even more stunning in real life than it is on postcards. Aside from its glorious lakeside gardens, there's a great selection of shops, cafes and restaurants. Every Monday, local history buff Lucia Sala runs a guided tour exploring some of the 22 hamlets, and she'll even show you her wonderful local ethnographic collection. PromoBellagio (p146) can provide details.

115

Savour Da Vinci's Last Supper

You have to wonder whether it's worth making reservations weeks ahead to glimpse a mural. But even faded, Leonardo da Vinci's *Last Supper* (p127) makes the entire Renaissance perfectly clear. Instead of the usual medieval saints commanding the room like CEOs, Da Vinci shows them leaping from their chairs, shocked at Jesus' news that one of them would betray him. Damaged as they are, their humanity remains indelible.

④ Get Wowed atop Milan's Duomo

Parisians debate whether Milan's Duomo (cathedral; p143) is the ultimate example of International Gothic – and Milanese agree. With its teetering spires, the Duomo actually represents all 135 pinnacles of International Gothic. Topping those spires are 3200 statues of saints, even though no one but the bell-ringer could appreciate them. Now that the roof is open to visitors, Milanese can rest their case.

Live Bellagio's *Dolce Vita*

When most people imagine *la dolce vita* (the sweet life), their thoughts drift off to Italy – but when fashionable Italians do, odds are they're dreaming of Bellagio (p146). Beyond its speedboat-lined Lake Como shoreline, twisting stone staircases lead to villas with blooming gardens and gilded salons. Away from Milan's hubbub, songbirds twitter in the fountains and paparazzi cameras can hardly be bothered to click as another starlet breezes past.

Window-shop Milan's Quadrilatero d'Oro

International fashion trends are launched from the showcase windows of Milan's Quadrilatero d'Oro (p136) shopping district. With displays by top architects – and without models wobbling on impossibly high heels – the fashion looks better here than on runways. Price lists of featured items are included in window displays, so savvy fashionistas can cost-compare and admire budget-busters from a safe distance.

Eat All of Italy at Turin's Eataly

To sample Italy's best artisanal cheeses, you could spend a year grazing across the country, or you could spend an afternoon at Eataly (p150), Turin's Slow Food emporium. This gourmet wonderland features tastings and culinary workshops, in addition to Italy's largest selection of regional-specialty pastas, cured meats and wines – plus Willy Wonka–worthy quantities of chocolate.

Milan, the Lakes & Piedmont's Best…

Designer Dreams

◦ **Bulgari Spa** (p129) Perfumed massages and dips in the golden pool

◦ **3Rooms** (p131) Sleep in a Corso Como concept-store showcase

◦ **Il Salvagente** (p136) Discounts on hot-off-the-runway Milan fashion

◦ **Le Meridien Art+Tech** (p150) Crash in the Fiat 500 factory that houses this industrial-chic hotel

◦ **A. Picci** (p144) Score silks that shimmer like Lake Como

Romantic Interludes

◦ **Bellagio, Lago di Como** (p146) Mahogany boat sunsets make dates seem as dashing as George Clooney

◦ **Sentiero Azzuro, Cinque Terre** (p154) Cliff's-edge paths lead to breathtaking views in secluded coves

◦ **Teatro Alla Scala, Milan** (p126) Start dates on a high note: score box tickets to performances at Milan's legendary opera house

◦ **Isola Bella, Lago Maggiore** (p140) Sneak a smooch in palace rooms where Napoleon and Josephine would rendezvous

Gourmet Gifts

◦ **Peck, Milan** (p135) A sublime selection of jams, hams and 3200 cheeses – and that's just the Parmesans

◦ **Eataly, Turin** (p150) A temple of Slow Food treats with cured meats overhead, wines underfoot, and altars of truffles

◦ **Peyrano, Turin** (p152) The dastardly geniuses who thought of putting grappa inside dark chocolate

◦ **Alba** (p152) Precious white truffles and red-satin Barolo wine

Aperitivo Bars

○ **Rita's, Milan** (p113) Proof that fashion models do eat – fashionable yet friendly

○ **Living, Milan** (p134) Crafty cocktails and an urbane crowd

○ **Lobelix, Turin** (p151) A bountiful buffet that's the talk of Turin

○ **I Tre Galli, Turin** (p151) Gourmet bites and a spillover sidewalk scene

Need to Know

ADVANCE PLANNING

○ **Three months before** Book local accommodation during Milan's Salone del Mobile or Fashion Week, or during Turin's Salone Internazionale del Gusto

○ **Two months before** Book tickets to Teatro Alla Scala (p126) and Da Vinci's *The Last Supper* (p127), and accommodation during Aosta's winter ski season and Lake Como's summer season

○ **One week before** Scan www.easymilano.it and www.extratorino.it to see what's on in Milan and Turin. Book a table at Trattoria Abele la Temperanza (p132) or Elvezia (p141)

RESOURCES

○ **Milan Tourist Bureau** (www.provincia.milano.it/turismo)

○ **Lombardy Tourism Board** (www.turismo.regione.lombardia.it) Covers the entire Lombardy region

○ **Piedmont Tourism Board** (www.piemonteitalia.eu) Itineraries, accommodation and transport links

○ **Valle D'Aosta Tourist Board** (www.regione.vda.it/turismo)

GETTING AROUND

○ **Air** International connections to/from Milan and Turin

○ **Walk** Perfect for cities and towns, alpine trails and Cinque Terre

○ **Train** Good connections between major cities and towns. Metro services in Milan and Turin

○ **Boat** Handy for travel around and across the lakes

○ **Car** Convenient for exploring Piedmont's vineyards

○ **Bicycle** Ideal for alpine trails and Piedmont's wine region

BE FOREWARNED

○ **Museums** Most close Monday

○ **Restaurants** Many close in August; around the lakes and in Cinque Terre, many close November to March

○ **Accommodation** Book a month ahead if travelling to Milan or Turin, and three months in advance of international design and food fairs; reserve ahead for summer accommodation in Cinque Terre and the lakes

○ **Pickpockets** Operate in tourist areas and at fairs

Left: Black truffle appetiser, Piedmont (p147);
Above: Riomaggiore (p155), Cinque Terre

119

Milan, the Lakes & Piedmont Itineraries

Find out where Italy gets its hottest design ideas, from platform stilettos made for power-stomping Milan runways to the rocket-ship espresso machines fuelling Turin's creative reinvention.

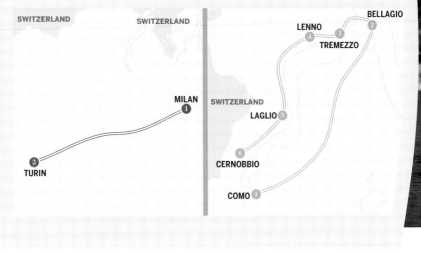

SWITZERLAND

SWITZERLAND

BELLAGIO **2**

LENNO **4**

TREMEZZO **3**

MILAN **1**

SWITZERLAND

LAGLIO **5**

TURIN **2**

CERNOBBIO **6**

COMO **7**

MILAN TO TURIN
Trend-Setting Cities

You don't have to wait for the next Salone del Mobile, Fashion Week or Salone del Gusto to see the upcoming big trends in **(1) Milan** and **(2) Turin**. Scan Milan's window displays of established designers like Prada and Alessi in Galleria Vittoria Emmanuele and Quadrilatero d'Oro, then head to the studios of emerging designers clustered around Porta Genova station in the Navigli neighbourhood. Ever wondered where Italian designers find inspiration for outrageous colour schemes and high-concept designs? Get answers along Parco Sempione at Living's street-fashion-wise happy hours and Triennale Design Museum, Milan's showcase of design objects and the experimental ideas that make them possible.

From fashion-forward Milan, hop on the fast train to Turin, where Napoleonic ambitions and post-war industry have been channelled into contemporary art and industrial chic. A castle was invaded by Arte Povera ('Poor Art') to form Museo d'Arte Contemporanea, and contemporary artists are taking over a baroque palace at Galleria Civica d'Arte Moderna e Contemporanea. Creative buzz is fuelled by locally-invented espresso machines at Turin's legendary cafes, where rapid-fire banter leads to ideas sketched on napkins.

4 DAYS

COMO TO CERNOBBIO
Lakeside Lounging

Drive or catch a train from Milan to spiffy **(1) Como**, where you can enjoy both glamorous getaways and serene retreats without ever losing sight of a dazzling shoreline. Take the vintage funicular, Funicolare Como-Brunate, to hilltop Brunate for splendid Como sunsets. After a night in art nouveau splendour at Albergo Terminus, retreat to villa-lined **(2) Bellagio** for a day of enchanted lakeside living at Albergo Silva. Nothing need interrupt your busy Bellagio schedule of sun-tanning, except perhaps a sunset cruises in Barindelli's mahogany boats or a reservation to sample Como's lavarello fish specialties at Itturismo Da Abate.

Rejuvenated, drive around the lake or hop on a ferry to **(3) Tremezzo** to see what is arguably the world's best wedding present, the Villa Carlotta, and to enjoy a leisurely lunch on the panoramic terrace of Al Veluu. Arrange an overnight stay here, and enjoy a lakeside drive or taxi-boat ride to famous locales along the western shore: Villa Balbianello, as seen in *Casino Royale*, in **(4) Lenno;** villa-lined **(5) Laglio**, home to actor/director/international playboy George Clooney; and picturesque *Oceans 12* location, **(6) Cernobbio**.

Lake Como (p141)

121

Discover Milan, the Lakes & Piedmont

At a Glance

○ **Milan** Runway fashion and Da Vinci masterpieces by day, cocktails and opera at night.

○ **The Lakes** (p138) Living large in movie-star villas, Como silks and lakeside resorts.

○ **Piedmont** (p147) Sleek design and modern art in Turin, vineyards and Slow Food in the hills.

Vineyard, Barolo (p152), Piedmont
ALAN BENSON/LONELY PLANET IMAGES ©

MILAN

POP 1.3 MILLION

Milan is Italy's city of the future, a fast-paced metropolis with New World qualities: ambition, aspiration and a highly individualistic, creative culture. In Milan appearances really do matter and materialism requires no apology. They love beautiful things, luxurious things, and it is for that reason perhaps that Italian fashion and design maintains its global position.

But beyond the designer surfaces there is a city of ancient roots and many treasures, that, unlike the rest of Italy, you will quite often get to experience without the queues or expectations. A warren of cobbled streets fans out from the Duomo while historic neighbourhoods like Brera and Navigli have character worthy of any tourist brochure. Join the Milanese for precision shopping, browsing edgy contemporary galleries or loading up a plate with local delicacies while downing an expertly mixed Negroni at *aperitivo* hour.

◎ Sights

MUSEO DEL NOVECENTO   Art Gallery
(☎ 02 79 48 89; www.museodel novecento.org; Piazza Duomo 12; adult/ reduced €5/3; ◷ 9.30am-7.30pm Tue-Sun, 2.30-7.30pm Mon) Overlooking the Piazza del Duomo, with fabulous views of the cathedral from its floor-to-ceiling windows, is Mussolini's **Arengario** from where he would harangue huge crowds in the glory days of his regime. Now it houses Milan's museum of 20th-century art.

DENNIS JOHNSON/LONELY PLANET IMAGES ©

Don't Miss **Duomo**

Milan's cathedral aptly reflects the city's creative brio and ambition. Begun by Gian Galeazzo Visconti in 1387, its design was originally considered unfeasible. Canals had to be dug to transport the vast quantities of marble to the centre of the city, and new technologies were invented to cater for the never-before-attempted scale. There was also that small matter of style. The Gothic lines went out of fashion – *c'e brutta!* (how hideous!) – and were considered 'too French', so it took on several styles as the years, then centuries, dragged on. Its slow construction became the byword for an impossible task (*fabrica del Dom* in the Milanese dialect).

But now its pearly white façade, rising like the filigree of a fairytale tiara, wows the crowds with extravagant detail. A veritable outdoor sculpture museum, its 135 spires showcase 3200 statues. The vast, echoing interior is no less impressive, with 146 stained-glass windows and intricately carved pillars and chapels. Although the ceiling also appears carved, it's a trompe l'oeil. High above the altar is a **nail** said to have been the one that impaled Christ's right hand on the cross. Predating the cathedral is the early Christian baptistry, the **Battistero di San Giovanni**, accessed via a stairwell next to the main entrance. The **crypt** (admission free) displays the remains of saintly San Carlo Borromeo, who died in 1584, in a glass casket.

By far the most interesting aspect is the view from the **roof**, from where you can gaze out over the city towards the Alps through a forest of spires and marble pinnacles. Crowning it all is a gilded copper statue of the **Madonnina** (Little Madonna), the city's traditional protector.

THINGS YOU NEED TO KNOW

Duomo (www.duomomilano.it; Piazza del Duomo); **Battistero di San Giovanni** (admission €4; ⊙9.30-5.15pm Tue-Sun); **roof** (stairs/lift €5/8; ⊙9am-5.30pm)

123

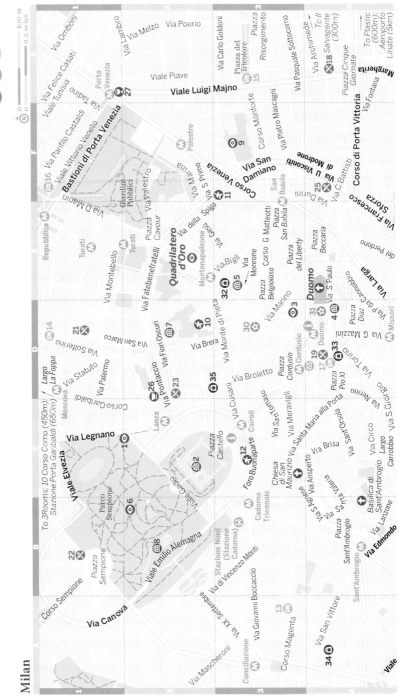

Built around a futuristic spiral ramp (an ode to the Guggenheim), the lower floors of the museum are cramped, but the heady collection, which includes the likes of Boccioni, Campigli, de Chirico, Fontana and Marinetti, is enough to distract.

Time your visit before lunch or dinner and end with a meal at the top-floor restaurant.

A smaller portion of the museum's collection is displayed at the **Casa Museo Boschi di Stefano** (☎02 2024 0568; www.fondazioneboschidistefano.it; Via Jan 15; admission free; ☉10am-6pm Tue-Sun).

PINACOTECA DI BRERA Art Gallery (☎02 9280 0361; www.brera.beniculturali.it; Via Brera 28; adult/reduced €9/6.50; ☉8.30am-7.15pm Tue-Sun) Located upstairs from the centuries-old Brera Academy (still one of Italy's most prestigious art schools) this gallery houses Milan's most impressive collection of old masters, much of the bounty 'lifted' from Venice by Napoleon. Rembrandt, Goya and van Dyck all have a place in the collection, but you're here to see the Italians: Titian, Tintoretto, glorious Veronese, a Caravaggio and the Bellini brothers. Much of the work has tremendous emotional clout, most notably Mantegna's brutal and unsentimental *Cristo morto nel Sepolcro e tre Dolenti* (Lamentation over the Dead Christ).

The number of treasures can be overwhelming, so take a break and join the students downstairs for a post-class Peroni.

CASTELLO SFORZESCO Castle, Museum (☎02 8846 3700; www.milanocastello.it; Piazza Castello; adult/reduced €7/3.50; ☉9am-5.30pm Tue-Sun) Originally a Visconti fortress, this immense red-brick castle was later home to the mighty Sforza dynasty that ruled Renaissance Milan. The castle's defences were designed by Leonardo da Vinci; Napoleon later drained the moat and removed the drawbridges. Today, it shelters a series of specialised museums, accessible on the same ticket.

Among the standouts are the **Museo d'Arte Antica**, containing Michelangelo's last, unfinished work, *Pietà Rondanini;*

Milan

the **Pinacoteca e Raccolte d'Arte**, which holds paintings by Bellini, Tiepolo, Mantegna, Titian and van Dyck; the **Museo della Preistoria** for local archaeological finds; and the **Museo degli Strumenti Musicali**, which has priceless early musical instruments.

PARCO SEMPIONE   Public Park
Sprawling over 47 hectares, Parco Sempione has everything you'd expect from a Milanese park: chic bars, a lovely, Liberty-style aquarium, **Acquario Civico**, and the Gió Ponti-designed steel tower, **Torre Branca** (☏ 02 331 41 20; lift €3; ⊙ 9.30am-midnight Tue-Fri, 10.30am-2pm & 2.30-7.30pm Sat & Sun May–mid-Oct, shorter hrs in winter), from the top of which you have a bird's-eye view of the city. Also here is the **Triennale di Milano** (☏ 02 72 43 41; www.triennaledesignmuseum.it; Viale Emilio Alemanga 6; adult/reduced €8/6.50; ⊙ 10.30am-8.30pm

Tue-Sun), a permanent museum dedicated to Italian design.

TEATRO ALLA SCALA   Opera House
(La Scala; www.teatroallascala.org; Via Filodrammatici) Despite technological renovations behind the scenes (superior acoustics and bilingual libretto screens on the backs of seats), the charm of the world's best-known opera house, Teatro alla Scala, remains resolutely of the 18th century.

Six stories of boxes and galleries are bedecked in gilt and lined in crimson, and, for evening performances at least, audiences are similarly turned out. If you miss out on a show, visit the **Museo Teatrale alla Scala** (La Scala Museum; ☏ 02 4335 3521; Piazza della Scala; adult/child €5/4; ⊙ 9am-12.30pm & 1.30-5.30pm). Your visit can include a glimpse of the theatre's interior from a box and a backstage tour if you don't clash with rehearsal time.

LEONARDO DA VINCI / THE BRIDGEMAN ART LIBRARY /GETTY IMAGES ©

Don't Miss **Da Vinci's Last Supper**

Leonardo Da Vinci's depiction of Christ informing his apostles that one of them will betray him in *The Last Supper* is one of the world's most iconic images. The restored mural is hidden away on one wall of the Cenacolo Vinciano, the refectory adjoining the **Chiesa di Santa Maria delle Grazie**. Admirers over the centuries claim to have read all kinds of signs in Da Vinci's faded, damaged but still arresting composition: mathematical symbols, musical notation, political commentary, even omens of the end of the world. Such is the power of this image that art historians and master painters dedicated 22 years to its painstaking restoration, completed in 1999.

See it now, while the apostles' facial expressions and Da Vinci's colours are still visible – despite the painstaking effort, nearly 80% of the original colour has been lost. Da Vinci himself is partly to blame: his experimental medium involves tempera applied on a dry gesso wall between 1495 and 1498, rather than on wet plaster over a week, as is typical of fresco techniques.

Reservations must be booked by phone or online a couple of weeks in advance to two months ahead in summer, or you can take a city tour that includes a visit. Once booked, you'll be allotted a visiting time and reservation number, which you present 30 minutes before your visit at the refectory ticket desk. If you show up late, your ticket will be resold. English-language guided tours (€3.25) take place at 9.30am and 3.30pm Tuesday to Sunday – again, you'll need to reserve ahead.

THINGS YOU NEED TO KNOW

Cenacolo Vinciano (📞 02 9280 0360; www.cenacolovinciano.net; adult/reduced €6.50/3.25, plus booking fee €1.50; 🕐 8.15am-7pm Tue-Sun; **Chiesa di Santa Maria delle Grazie** (Corso Magenta; 🕐 8.15am-7pm Tue-Sun)

MUSEO POLDI-PEZZOLI　　Museum
(☏ 02 79 48 89; www.museopoldipezzoli.it; Via
Alessandro Manzoni 12; adult/reduced €9/6;
🕙10am-6pm Wed-Mon) Botticelli's *Madonna
and Child* is the star attraction at the
Poldi-Pezzoli museum, once home to one
of Milan's wealthiest aristocratic families
and now the city's most important private
collection.

Inheriting his vast fortune at the age
of 24, Gian Giacomo also inherited his
mother's love of art and, during extensive
European travels, he became inspired by
the latest art-collecting trends and the
'house museum' that was later to become
London's V&A.

As his collection grew, Pezzoli had the
idea of transforming his apartments into
a series of historically themed rooms.
The staircase and the bedroom were
baroque in style, the Black Room was
inspired by the early Renaissance and the
Dante study by the early 14th-century.
Today the rooms, many of them works of
art in themselves, remain much as they
were during Pezzoli's lifetime and offer a

unique preserved-in-amber insight into
the heyday of 19th-century patronage.

NAVIGLI　　Neighbourhood
South of the city centre, the Navigli
neighbourhood is named after the canals
from which it got its name. The **Naviglio
Grande (Big Canal)** grew from an irrigation
ditch to one of the city's busiest thor-
oughfares lined with docks, laundries and
warehouses in the 1200s. Canals were the
motorways of medieval Milan, transport-
ing salt, oil, cheese, wine and marble for
the building of the cathedral to the centre
of the city. Later, with the advent of trains
and cars, many of them were filled in,
leaving the industrial warehouses to form
new art studios and galleries.

Nowadays, the area is home to some
of Milan's most lively bars. On the last
Sunday of every month more than 400
antique and secondhand traders set
up along a 2km stretch of the Naviglio
Grande for the **Mercatore Antiquario di
Navigli** (www.naviglilive.it), the city's largest
antique and flea market.

Left: Castello Sforzesco (p125) looks over Parco Sempione (p126);
Below: Wine racks, Sadler (p132)

(LEFT) PAOLO CORDELLI/LONELY PLANET IMAGES ©; (BELOW) MARTIN MOOS/LONELY PLANET IMAGES ©

VILLA NECCHI CAMPIGLIO Villa

(☎02 763 40 121; Via Mozart 14; adult/child €8/4; ☺10am-6pm Wed-Sun) On the outside, Milan's urban landscape may seem rigorous and austere, but behind the high walls hide some surprising homes and enchanted gardens. None more so than the restored 1930s Villa Necchi Campiglio designed by Piero Portaluppi for Pavian heiresses Nedda and Gigina Necchi, and Gigina's husband Angelo Campiglio.

Portaluppi's combining of rationalist and art deco styles perfectly symbolises the modernist imaginings of the era – the house had one of the only swimming pools in Milan as well as revolutionary electronic shuttering. Aside from the gorgeous architectural details, engaging quotidian details include a kitchen cupboard full of pressed linens, monogrammed hair brushes and silk evening frocks hanging ready for evenings at La Scala.

Activities

BULGARI SPA Spa

(☎02 805 80 51; www.bulgarihotel.com; Via Privata Fratelli Gabba 7/b) Milan's most luxurious spa, with its gold-tiled pool, is located in Antonio Cittero's lavishly designed Bulgari Hotel. Treatments from €65.

SPIGA 8 SPA AT HOTEL BAGLIONI Spa

(☎02 4547 3111; www.baglionihotels.com; Via della Spiga 8) This spa has a minimalist all-white aesthetic and a menu of treatments that seem good enough to eat, such as the chocolate facial. Treatments from €65.

Tours

AUTOSTRADALE Bus

(www.autostradale.it; €55) The tourist office sells tickets for these three-hour city bus tours including admission to *The Last*

129

Detour:
Certosa di Pavia

One of the Italian Renaissance's most glorious buildings is the **Certosa di Pavia** (Pavia Charterhouse; ✆ 0382 92 56 13; www.certosadipavia.com; Viale Monumento; admission by donation; ⏱ 9-11.30am & 2.30-5.30pm Tue-Sun). Gian Galeazzo Visconti of Milan founded the monastery in 1396 as a private chapel and mausoleum for the Visconti family. Construction proceeded in a stop-start fashion until well into the 16th century, making this a prime example of the transition from Gothic to Renaissance: inside it's mostly red-brick Gothic, while the exterior is a white-marble Renaissance splendour.

Walk through the spacious courtyard, through the **Small Cloister**, and into the elegant **Grand Cloister**. Under 123 arches there are 24 cells, each a self-contained living area for one monk. Several are open to the public, so you can see what it was like to live a life of singular purpose and devotion.

Starry skies are painted on vaulted ceilings inside the church, while walls are illuminated by masterpieces by Umbrian master, Il Perugino, and by frescoes showing the Madonna crowned between church patrons from the powerful Milanese Sforza family. Artists and scientists pay respects here at the tomb of Da Vinci's number one fan and champion, Beatrice d'Este, who is buried here with her husband, Duke of Milan Ludovico Sforza.

To reach Certosa di Pavia from Milan's Stazione Centrale, take **Sila** (www.sila.it) bus 175 (Pavia–Binasco–Milano), which takes about 35 minutes.

Supper, Castello Sforzesco and La Scala's museum. Tours depart from the taxi rank on the western side of Piazza del Duomo at 9.30am Tuesday to Sunday (except for a couple of weeks during August).

TRAM ATMOSFERA Tram, Food
(✆ 800 808 181; www.atm-mi.it; departs Piazza Castello; meal €65; ⏱ 1pm & 8pm Tue-Sun) This tram has been renovated to incorporate a restaurant where you can eat your way through a five-course menu as you tour the city. The food isn't stunning but the varnished teak walls, glass lanterns and upholstered benches are a treat.

🛏 Sleeping

Great value accommodation is hard to come by in Milan and downright impossible during the Salone del Mobile, Fashion Week and other large fairs. The tourist office distributes *Milano Hotels,* which lists over 350 options.

**OANTICA LOCANDA
SOLFERINO** Guesthouse €€€
(✆ 02 657 01 29; www.anticalocandasolferino.it; Via Castelfidardo 2; s €140-270; d €180-400; P ❄ 📶) This understated Brera beauty is a genuinely charming hideaway with 11 romantically retro rooms. Decorated with early 20th-century prints, *broderie anglais* curtains and antique furniture, it attracts a bohemian crowd of artists, writers and musicians. They also rent a two-person apartment kitted out in full 1960s style.

**HOTEL SPADARI
DUOMO** Design Hotel €€€
(✆ 02 7200 2371; www.spadarihotel.com; Via Spadari 11; d €185-345; ❄ 📶) Milan's original design hotel, the rooms at the Spadari are miniature galleries showcasing the work of emerging artists. The hotel itself is the creation of respected architect-engineers Urbano Pierini and Ugo La Pietra, who designed every inch of the 'look' down to the sinuous pale wood furniture.

FORESTERIA MONFORTE
B&B €€

(☎ 02 7631 8516; www.foresteriamonforte.
it; Piazza del Tricolore 2; d €150-250) With
Philippe Starck chairs, flat-screen TVs
and a communal kitchen, the three classy
rooms in this upmarket B&B are a short
walk from the Duomo. Breakfast is served
in your room.

3ROOMS
B&B €€€

(☎ 02 62 61 63; www.10corsocomo.com; Corso
Como 10; d €270-340; P ✳ @ 🛜) If you
can't drag yourself away from concept
store Corso Como, avail yourself of one of
the three keys to their luxurious palazzo
suites. Here you can sleep under Eames
bedspreads, sit in Arne Jacobsen chairs
and make tea with your Porsche kettle, all
of which are for sale upon check-out.

ANTICA LOCANDA
LEONARDO
Guesthouse €€

(☎ 02 4801 4197; www.anticalocandaleonardo.
com; Corso Magenta 78; s €120, d €165-245;
✳ 🛜) Rooms here exude homey comfort,
from the period furniture and parquet
floors to the plush drapes. Take breakfast
in the quiet, scented interior garden of
this 19th-century residence.

VIETNAMONAMOUR
B&B €€

(☎ 02 7063 4614; www.vietnamonamour.com;
Via Alessandro Pestalozza 7; s €80-100, d €100-
120; ✳ 🛜) Beautiful timber floors and
Vietnamese furnishings set the tone in
this 1903 residence-turned-B&B, with
four romantic rooms. Downstairs, the
Paris-born Vietnamese owner runs a
welcoming Vietnamese restaurant.

HOTEL CASA
MIA
Hotel €

(☎ 02 657 52 49; www.hotelcasamiamilano.it;
Viale Vittorio Veneto 30; s/d €62/85; ✳)
Cosying up to Piazza della Repubblica,
'My House' is a straightforward digs that
is handily placed about halfway between
Stazione Centrale and the Duomo, just
over the road from the Giardini Pubblici
gardens.

 Eating

CRACCO-PECK
Modern Italian €€€

(☎ 02 87 67 74; www.ristorantecracco.it; Via
Victor Hugo 4; meals €140; 🕙 Tue-Fri, dinner
Mon, lunch Sat) The gastronomic showcase
for Milan's premier delicatessen, Peck.

Certosa di Pavia (p130)

If You Like…
Italian Design

Between fall and spring fashion weeks and beyond the Quadrilatero d'Oro, Milan shows its avant-garde edge at these monuments to design:

1 **GALLERIA VITTORIO EMANUELE II** Neoclassical Galleria Vittorio Emanuele is a soaring iron-and-glass marvel that's remained Milan's most fashionable address for over a century. The Galleria is a marvel of 19th century engineering and marketing savvy: this elegant sheltered shortcut from Piazza di Duomo to La Scala is lined with high-fashion temptations, including the original Prada store. This showplace was designed by Giuseppe Mengoni, who tragically plummeted to his death from scaffolding just weeks before his 14-year effort was completed in 1877.

2 **FIERA MILANO** Milan has two trade fairgrounds, collectively known as **Fiera Milano** (www.fieramilano.it). Older **Fieramilanocity** is close to the centre (metro line 2, Lotto Fieramilanocity stop), but the showstopper showplace for the annual **Salone del Mobile** (Furniture Fair; www.cosmit.it) is the glass ship-shaped, Massimiliano Fuksas–designed **Fieramilano** in the western suburb of Rho (metro line 2, Rho Fiera stop).

3 **TRIENNALE DESIGN MUSEUM** (☎02 7243 41; www.triennaledesignmuseum. it; Viale Emilio Alemanga 6, Parco Sempione; adult/senior & student €8/6.50; ☉10.30am-8.30pm Tue-Sun) With a permanent collection covering Italian design's greatest hits, from Alessi teapots to Olivetti typewriters and international shows ranging from historic timepieces to experimental mass-luxury schemes, Triennale Design Museum is a temple for design pilgrims.

Carlo Cracco conjures up exemplary deconstructive *alta cucina* in a formal contemporary environment.

SADLER Modern Italian €€€ (☎02 876 730; www.sadler.it; Via Ascanio Sforza 77; meals €120; ☉Mon-Sat) On the Milanese

scene since 1995, Claudio Sadler's culinary wisdom remains undisputed. Try the pigeon ragout or the black cod with turnip greens, yoghurt and wasabi.

TRATTORIA ABELE LA TEMPERANZA Trattoria € (☎02 261 3855; Via Temperanza 5; meals €9; ☉8pm-1am Tue-Sun; ⊞) This traditional trattoria with its spartan decor, paper table mats and black-and-white photographs has dedicated itself to the pursuit of the perfect risotto. Here you can try over 100 different kinds of risotto alongside other traditional dishes such as *brasato* (braised stew). Go for the 'three rices', a selection of three different risottos, which change daily. Book ahead, don't be late and be prepared to wait 30 minutes for your meal, but rest assured, it's worth it.

OSTERIA DELLA LANTERNA Osteria €€ (☎02 5830 9604; Via Giuseppe Mercalli 14; meals €25-35; ☉Mon-Fri, dinner only Sat) This is one of the few genuine *osterie* left in Milan, hosted by the owner-cook who speaks to customers in Milanese dialect. Despite its unprepossessing appearance, reservations are essential if you want to try the homemade pastas and gnocchi with walnuts and gorgonzola.

GRAND HOTEL OSTERIA Osteria €€ (☎02 8951 1586; www.osteriagrandhotel.it; Via Cardinale Ascanio Sforza 75; meals €35-40; ☉dinner Mon-Fri, lunch & dinner Sat & Sun) In summer, dine beneath the flower-laden pergola at this traditional tavern overlooking the Naviglio Pavese. The owner is a wine expert (and an opera enthusiast) and the wine selection is exceptional. He sometimes runs wine, cheese and oil tastings.

AL BACCO Milanese €€ (☎02 5412 1637; Via Marcona 1; meals €25-30; ☉dinner Mon-Sat) An excellent palce to sample Milan's classic saffron risotto or veal cutlet. Otherwise, try the homemade

BLUE NOTE — Jazz Club

(📞02 6901 6888; www.bluenotemilano.com; Via Borsieri 37; tickets €25-30; 🕐Tue-Sun Sep-Jul) Top-class jazz acts perform here from around the world; get tickets by phone, online or at the door from 7.30pm. They also do a popular easy-listening Sunday brunch (€35 or €55 for two adults and two children).

Clubs

Clubs generally stay open until 3am or 4am Tuesday to Sunday; cover charges vary from €10 to upwards of €20. Door policies can be formidable as the night wears on.

PLASTIC — Club

(📞02 733 996; www.thisisplastic.com; Viale Umbria 120; 🕐Fri & Sat mid-Sep–Jun) Friday's London Loves takes no prisoners with an edgy, transgressive indie mix and Milan's coolest kids. If you're looking fab, club art director Nicola Guiducci's private Match à Paris on Sunday mashes French pop, indie and avant-garde sounds.

MAGAZZINI GENERALI — Club

(📞02 539 3948; www.magazzinigenerali.it; Via Pietrasanta 14; 🕐Wed-Sat Oct-May) When this former warehouse is full of people working up a sweat to an international indie act, there's no better place to be in Milan. Most gigs are under €20, and there's free entry on other nights when DJs get the party started.

Opera & Theatre

TEATRO ALLA SCALA — Opera House

(box office 📞02 07 75; www.teatroallascala. org; Via Filodramatio You'll need perseverance and luck to secure opera tickets at La Scala (€10 to €180; up to €2000 for opening night). About two months before the first performance, tickets can be bought by telephone and online. One month before the first performance, remaining tickets are sold at the **box office** (Galleria del Sagrato, Piazza del Duomo; 🕐noon-6pm). On performance days, 140 tickets for the gallery are sold two hours before the show (one ticket per customer). Queue early.

Sport

The city's two clubs are the 1899-established AC Milan, and the 1908-established FC Internazionale Milano (aka 'Inter'). They play on alternate Sundays during the season at the **San Siro stadium** (Stadio Giuseppe Meazza; 📞02 404 24 32; www.sansirotour.com; Via Piccolomini 5, museum & tours Gate 14; museum adult/reduced €7/5, incl guided tour €12.50/10; 🕐non-match days 10am-6pm). Guided tours of the stadium, built in the 1920s, take you behind the scenes to the players' locker rooms and include a visit to the Museo Inter e Milan museum, a shrine of memorabilia, papier-mâché caricatures of players and film footage.

Take tram 24, bus 95, 49 or 72, or the metro to the Lotto stop, from where a free bus shuttles to the stadium.

🔒 Shopping

PECK — Food, Wine

(📞02 802 31 61; www.peck.it; Via Spadari 7-9; 🕐3-7.30pm Mon, 8.45am-7.30pm Tue-Sat). This Milanese institution first opened its doors as a deli in 1883. Since then, it's expanded to a dining room bar upstairs and an *enoteca* (wine bar). The Aladdin's Cave–like food hall is the best in Milan, stocked with some 3200 variations of *parmigiano reggiano* (Parmesan) at its cheese counter, just for starters. Other treats include an exquisite array of chocolates, pralines and pastries; freshly made gelato; seafood; caviar; pâtés; fruit and vegetables; truffle products; olive oils and balsamic vinegar.

SPAZIO ROSSANA ORLANDI — Homeware, Design

(📞02 467 44 71; www.rossanorlandi.com; Via Matteo Bandello 14; 🕐Tue-Sat) Installed in a former tie factory in the Magenta district, finding this iconic interior design studio is a challenge in itself. Once inside though, you'll find it hard to leave this dreamlike treasure trove stacked with vintage and contemporary limited edition pieces from young and upcoming artists.

Don't Miss Quadrilatero d'Oro

For anyone interested in fashion, a stroll around the world's most fabled shopping district, **Quadrilatero d'Oro**, is a must. This quaintly cobbled quadrangle of streets may have always been synonymous with elegance and money (Via Monte Napoleone was where Napoleon's government managed loans), but the Quad's legendary fashion status belongs firmly to Milan's postwar reinvention. During the boom years of the 1950s, the city's fashion houses established ateliers in the area bounded by Via Monte Napoleone, Via Sant'Andrea, Via della Spiga and Via Alessandro Manzoni. By the 1960s, Milan had outflanked Florence and Rome to become the country's *haute couture* capital, with flagship showcases for Milan-based designers recognised worldwide by their namesake logos – including **Armani**, **Prada**, **Versace**, **Missoni** and **Dolce & Gabbana**.

Today, the world's top designers unveil their women's collections in Milan in February/March and September/October, while men's fashion hits the runways in January and June/July. Bargain alert: sales hit the racks in January and June, when designers clear their racks to make room for new collections.

MONICA CASTIGLIONI Jewellery
(☏02 8723 7979; www.monicacastiglioni.com; Via Pastrengo 4; ◷11am-8pm Thu-Sat) Located in the up and coming neighbourhood of Isola, Monica's studio turns out organic and industrial-style jewellery in bronze, silver and gold. Deeply rooted in Milan's modernist traditions, these are statement pieces and are well priced for the workmanship.

IL SALVAGENTE Fashion Outlet
(☏02 7611 0328; www.salvagentemilano.it; Via Fratelli Bronzetti 16; ◷Tue-Sat, 3-7pm Mon) The grim basement courtyard of Il Salvagente gives scant indication of the big brand names inside. Discounted Prada, D&G, Versace and Ferretti are just a few of the names on the tightly packed racks. Payment is in cash only.

Left: View over Lake Maggiore from Stresa;
Below: Statue at Palazzo Borromeo (p140), Isola Bella

Day passes are also available from €13. Services are drastically reduced in autumn and winter.

Bus

Buses leave from the waterfront at Stresa for destinations around the lake and elsewhere, including Milan.

SAF (☏0323 55 21 72; www.safduemila.com, in Italian) This daily Verbania Intra-Milan service links Stresa with Milan (1½ hours).

Train

Stresa is on the Domodossola-Milan train line. Tickets are available from the Navigazione Lago Maggiore ticket booths at each port.

Stresa

POP 5210

Since the 18th century, the town's easy accessibility from Milan has made it a favourite for artists and writers seeking inspiration. Hemingway was one of many; he arrived in Stresa in 1918 to convalesce from a war wound.

 Sights & Activities

People stream into Stresa to meander along its promenade, explore the hive of cobbled streets in its old centre and visit the Borromean islands.

FUNIVIA
STRESA-MOTTARONE   Cable Car

(☏0323 3 02 95; www.stresa-mottarone. it; Piazzale della Funivia; adult/child return €17.50/11; ⏱9.30am-5.30pm) Captivating views of the lake unfold during a 20-minute cable-car journey to the top of 1491m-high Monte Mottarone. Cars depart every 20 minutes in summer.

PARCO DELLA VILLA
PALLAVICINO   Animal Park

(☏0323 3 15 33; www.parcozoopallavicino. it; adult/child €9/6; ⏱9am-6pm Mar-Oct) Barely 1km southeast of Stresa along the SS33, exotic birds and animals roam relatively freely at the child-friendly

139

Villa Pallavicino. It is home to some 40 species of llama, Sardinian donkeys, flamingos and toucans.

📖 Sleeping & Eating

Seasonal closings (including hotels) are generally November to February, but this can vary, so it's always best to check ahead.

VILLA AMINTA   Hotel   €€€
(☎ 0323 93 38 18; www.villa-aminta.it; Via Sempione Nord 123; d €295-440; ❄ P 🛜 ⛵) Rooms decked out with Murano chandeliers, silk curtains and acres of gilt and velvet resemble the baroque opulence of the Borromeo Palace. The hotel also has its own private beach, heated pool, fitness centre and a regular shuttle service into Stresa.

HOTEL ELENA   Hotel   €
(☎ 0323 3 10 43; www.hotelelena.com; Piazza Cadorna 15; s/d €55/80; P) Adjoining a cafe, the old-fashioned Elena is situated slap-bang on Stresa's pedestrian central square. All of the comfortable rooms, with parquet floors, have a balcony, many overlooking the square. Wheelchair access is also possible.

Tremezzo (p145)

LA PIEMONTESE   Piedmontese   €€
(☎ 0323 3 03 99; Via Mazzini 25; meals €30; ⏰ Wed-Mon) This elegant wood-panelled dining room with its wisteria-covered internal courtyard serves Piedmontese cuisine, including specialities such as fried snails, duck confit and lake carp with a sweet-and-sour sauce.

ℹ️ Information

Tourist office (☎ 0323 3 13 08; www.stresaturismo.it; Piazza Marconi 16; ⏰ 10am-12.30pm & 3-6.30pm mid-Mar–mid-Oct, shorter weekend hr in winter).

Borromean Islands
Isola Bella

The **Palazzo Borromeo** (☎ 0323 3 05 56; www.borromeoturismo.it; adult/child €12.50/5.50; ⏰ 9am-5.30pm Apr–mid-Oct) is designed to look like a ship, this villa has gardens dripping down 10 tiered terraces. Well-known guests have included Napoleon and Josephine in 1797 (you can see the bed they slept in), and Prince Charles and Princess Di in 1985. A separate €4 ticket gives you access to the **Galleria dei Quadri** (Picture Gallery), a series of halls

covered from top to bottom with the Borromeo art collection. It includes several Old Masters including Rubens, Titian, Paolo Veronese and Andrea Mantegna. Elsewhere in the villa are other opulent works of art, such as priceless Flemish tapestries and sculptures by Antonio Canova.

A combined ticket covering admission to the Borromeo and Madre palaces costs €16.50/7.50 per adult/child.

Elvezia (☎ 0323 3 00 43; meals €30-35; ⊙ Tue-Sun Mar-Oct, Fri-Sun Nov-Feb) is the place for authentic family cooking. Book ahead.

Isola Madre

All of Isola Madre is taken up by the fabulous 16th- to 18th-century **Palazzo Madre** (☎ 0323 3 05 56; adult/child €10.50/5.50; ⊙ 9am-5.30pm Mar-Oct) and its gardens. The latter are more romantic and intimate than those of Palazzo Borromeo, brimming with azaleas, rhododendrons, camellias and hibiscus and home to white peacocks and vibrant-coloured Chinese pheasants. Palace highlights include a neoclassical puppet theatre designed by a scenographer from Milan's La Scala, and a 'horror' theatre with a cast of devilish marionettes.

Cannobio
POP 5,150

The medieval hamlet of Cannobio is the prettiest Italian town on the lake. The **tourist office** (☎ 0323 7 12 12; www.procannobio.it; Via Giovanola 25; ⊙ 9am-noon & 4-7pm Mon-Sat, 9am-noon Sun & holidays) is just inland off the main lakeside road.

Cannobio has an active sailing and windsurfing school, **Tomaso Surf & Sail** (☎ 0323 7 22 14; www.tomaso.com; Via Nazionale 7).

Sleeping & Eating

HOTEL PIRONI   Hotel €€
(☎ 0323 7 06 24; www.pironihotel.it; Via Marconi 35; s €100-120, d €130-180; **P**) Located in a 15th-century monastery, the restored rooms are filled with antiques, frescoed vaults and exposed timber beams.

LO SCALO   Modern Italian €€€
(☎ 0323 7 14 80; www.loscalo.com; Piazza Vittorio Emanuele III 32; meals €60; ⊙ Wed-Sun, dinner Tue) The setting is perfect and the cooking is sophisticated and clean, featuring dishes such as ribbon-thin tagliolini pasta with cuttlefish, zucchini and tomato and roast guinea fowl from the mountain valleys.

Lake Como

Shaped like an upside-down letter Y, Lake Como (Lago di Como) is lined with villages, including delightful Bellagio. The lake's main town, Como, sits where the southern and western shores converge.

ℹ Getting There & Around

Boat

Navigazione Lago di Como (☎ 800 55 18 01; www.navigazionelaghi.it) Ferries and hydrofoils criss-cross the lake, departing year-round from the jetty at the northern end of Piazza Cavour. For sightseeing, consider the one-day central lake ticket (€12).

Bus

ASF Autolinee (☎ 031 24 72 47; www.sptlinea. it) Operates regular buses around the lake, which depart from the bus station on Piazza Giacomo Matteotti. Key routes include Como-Bellagio (€2.80, one hour, 10 minutes, hourly).

Car

From Milan, take the A9 motorway and turn off at Monte Olimpino for Como. The SP342 leads east to Lecco and west to Varese. The roads around the lake are terribly scenic, but also windy, narrow and busy in summer.

Train

Trains from Milan's Stazione Centrale and Porta Garibaldi station (40 minutes to one hour) operate hourly services to the main Como San Giovanni station; some continue on to Switzerland. Trains from Milan's Stazione Nord use Como's lakeside Stazione FNM (listed on timetables as Como Nord Lago). If you're going to Bellagio, it is better to continue on the train to Varenna and make the short ferry crossing from there.

Como

POP 84,800

With its charming historic centre, 12th-century city walls and self-confident air, Como is an elegant and prosperous town. Built on the wealth of the silk industry, it remains Europe's most important producer of silk products; you can buy scarves and ties here for a fraction of the cost elsewhere.

Como

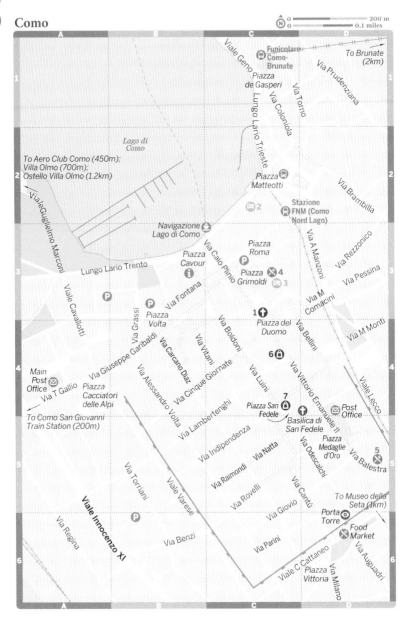

⊙ Sights & Activities

VILLA OLMO   Villa, Museum
(☑ 031 576 169; www.grandimostrecomo.it; Via
Cantoni 1; adult/reduced €10/8; ⊘9am-8pm
Tue-Thu, 9am-10pm Fri-Sun during exhibitions)
Set grandly facing the lake, the creamy
facade of neoclassical Villa Olmo is one
of Como's landmarks. If there is an art
exhibition inside, you'll get to admire the
sumptuous Liberty-style interiors. Otherwise, you can enjoy the Italianate and
English gardens, which are open all day.

During the summer, the **Lido di Villa
Olmo** (www.lidovillaolmo.it; Via Cernobbio 2;
adult/reduced €6/4 full day, €4.50/2.50 half-
day; ⊘9am-7pm mid-May–Sep), an open-air
swimming pool and lakeside bar, is open
to the public.

MUSEO DELLA SETA   Silk Museum
(☑ 031 30 31 80; www.museosetacomo.com; Via
Castelnuovo 9; adult/reduced €10/7; ⊘9am-
noon & 3-6pm Tue-Fri) Housed in the ugly
1970s buildings of the Instituto Tecnico
Industriale di Setificio textile school,
Como's Silk Museum unravels the town's
history, with early dyeing and printing
equipment on display.

**FUNICOLARE
COMO-BRUNATE**   Cable Car
(☑ 031 30 36 08; www.funicolarecomo.it;
Piazza de Gasperi 4; one-way/return €2.80/5.10;
⊘6am-midnight mid-Apr–mid-Sep, to 10.30pm
mid-Sep–mid-Apr) Northeast along the
waterfront, past Piazza Matteotti and the

Como

train station, is the Como-Brunate cable
car, which was built in 1894. It takes
seven minutes to reach hilltop **Brunate**
(720m), a quiet village offering splendid
views.

OAERO CLUB COMO   Seaplane Tours
(☑ 031 574 495; www.aeroclubcomo.com; Via
Masia 44) The 30-minute flight to Bellagio
costs €140 for two people.

FREE **DUOMO**   Cathedral
(Piazza del Duomo; ⊘8am-noon & 3-7pm)
Although largely Gothic, elements of
baroque, Romanesque and Renaissance
styles can be seen in Como's fancy,
marble-clad cathedral. Built between
the 14th and 18th centuries it is crowned
by a high octagonal dome. Next door is
the polychromatic **Broletto**, or medieval
town hall.

FREE **BASILICA DI
SANT'ABBONDIO**   Basilica
(Via Regina; ⊘8am-6pm Apr-Sep, to 4pm Oct-
Mar) About 500m south of the city walls
and just beyond Viale Innocenzo XI is this
remarkable 11th-century Romanesque
basilica. Aside from its proud, high structure and impressive apse with beautiful
geometric relief decoration around the
exterior windows, the highlight is the
fresco series inside the apse.

🛏 Sleeping

ALBERGO TERMINUS   Hotel €€€
(☑ 031 32 91 11; www.hotelterminus-como.it;
Lungo Lario Trieste 14; s €145-195, d €150-240;
P ❄ 🛜) Converted from a 19th-century
palazzo, the Terminus retains its turn-of-
the-century glamour with art nouveau
architectural details, damask upholstery
and grand tapestries and swagged
curtains.

LE STANZE DEL LAGO   Apartment €
(☑ 339 544 65 15; www.lestanzedellago.com;
Via Rodari 6; 2-/4-person apt €80/100; ❄ 🛗)
Five cosy apartments, nicely decked out
in a contemporary style with bright colour
schemes, make for a good-value deal in
the heart of Como.

Eating

TRATTORIA DEI
COMBATTENTI   Trattoria   €

(☎031 27 05 74; Via Balestra 5/9; meals €20; ☺Wed-Mon; 👪) Housed in the building of the Italian Retired Servicemen's association, this popular trattoria offers indoor seating at communal tables or outdoor seating in a sunny gravel yard. The cooking is simple and tasty, including grilled meats, salad and chunky seafood pasta.

RISTORANTE
SOCIALE   Traditional Italian   €€

(☎031 26 40 42; www.ristorantesociale.it; Via Rodari 6; meals €25-30; ☺Wed-Mon) Dine either downstairs in a brick-lined room or upstairs in the dining room with its outsized baroque fireplace and elaborate frescoes. The menu features favourites such as risotto with chicory.

🔒 Shopping

A craft and antiques market fills the piazza in front of the Basilica di San Fedele from 9am to 7pm every Saturday.

A. PICCI   Silk Shop

(☎031 26 13 69; Via Vittorio Emanuele II 54; ☺3-7.30pm Mon, 9am-12.30pm & 3-7.30pm Tue-Sat) Open since 1919, this is the last remaining silk shop in town dedicated to selling Como designed-and-made silk products such as ties, scarves, throws and sarongs. Products are grouped by price category (starting at €15 for a tie) reflecting the skill and workmanship involved in each piece.

Western Shore

Cernobbio to Lenno

Ocean's 11 may have been shot at Bellagio's Vegas namesake, but scenes from *Ocean's 12* were filmed in the Lake Como village of Cernobbio.

Left: Bellagio (p146) on Lake Como;
Below: Duomo (p143), Como
(LEFT) & (BELOW) JEAN-PIERRE LESCOURRET/LONELY PLANET IMAGES ©

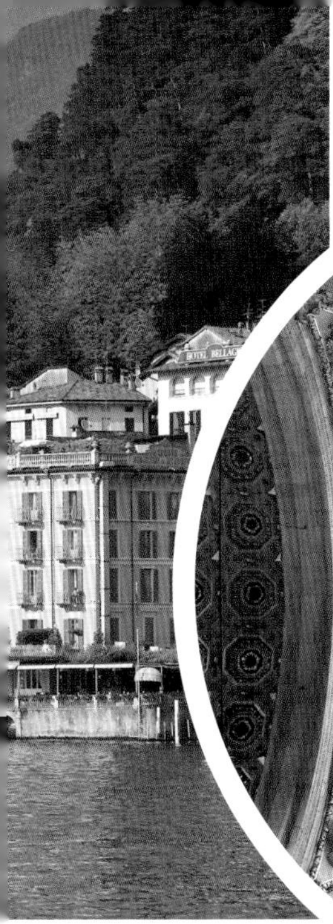

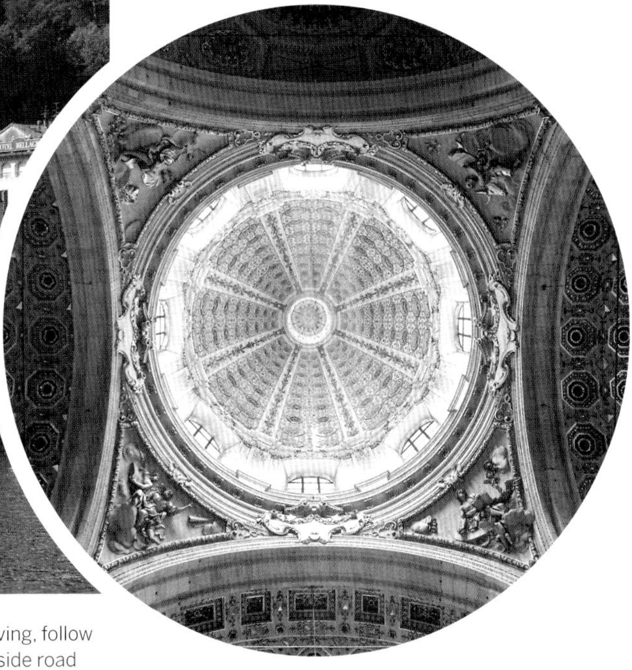

If you're driving, follow the lower lakeside road (Via Regina Vecchia) north from Cernobbio, which skirts the lake shore past a fabulous row of 19th-century villas (all private) around **Moltrasio**. A few kilometres north is the villa-lined hamlet of **Laglio**, home to *Ocean's* star George Clooney (he owns Villa Oleandra).

Finally, in Lenno, the **Villa Balbianello** (**☎0344 5 61 10; www.fondoambiente.it; Via Comoedia 5, Località Balbianello; villa & gardens adult/child €12/7, gardens only adult/child €6/3; ⏰10am-6pm Tue & Thu-Sun mid-Mar–mid-Nov)** takes the prize for the lake's most dramatically situated gardens, dripping down the sides of the high promontory like sauce off a melting ice-cream. Scenes from *Star Wars: Episode II* and 2006's James Bond remake, *Casino Royale,* were shot here. If you want to see inside, you must join a guided tour (generally in Italian) by 4.15pm. Visitors are only allowed to walk the 1km from the Lenno landing stage to the estate on Tuesday and at weekends; other days, you have to take a **taxi boat** (**☎333 410 38 54; return €6)** from Lenno.

Tremezzo

POP 1290

Tremezzo is high on everyone's list for a visit to the 17th-century **Villa Carlotta** (**☎0344 4 04 05; www.villacarlotta.it; Riva Garibaldi; adult/reduced €8.50/4.50; ⏰9am-6pm Easter-Sep, 10am-4pm mid-Mar–Easter & Oct–mid-Nov)**, whose botanic gardens are filled with orange trees knitted into pergolas and some of Europe's finest rhododendrons, azaleas and camellias. The villa, which is strung with paintings, alabaster-white sculptures (especially those by Antonio Canova) and tapestries, takes its name from the Prussian princess who was given the palace in 1847 as a wedding present from her mother.

Tremezzo's **tourist office** (**☎0344 4 04 93; Via Statale Regina; ⏰9am-noon & 3.30-6.30pm Wed-Mon Apr-Oct)** adjoins the jetty.

JEAN-PIERRE LESCOURRET/LONELY PLANET IMAGES ©

Don't Miss **Bellagio**

Picture-perfect Bellagio (population 3050) is even more charming in real life, with mahogany boats bobbing along the waterfront, a maze of stone staircases winding past green-shuttered, red-roofed houses and tall cypress trees and explosive pink rhododendron bushes adding exclamation marks to formal gardens. Guided tours lead visitors through splendid 20-hectare gardens at **Villa Serbelloni**. Tickets are sold 10 minutes in advance at **PromoBellagio**, housed in the basement of Bellagio's 11th-century watchtower.

Pose for your George Clooney glamour shot in a sleek mahogany boat on sunset tours around the Bellagio headlands arranged by **Barindelli**. For watersports, mountain biking and other lake activities, stop by Bellagio's **tourist office**, next to the boat landing.

Bellagio lives *la dolce vita* (the sweet life), and so can you at **Albergo Silvio** in contemporary lakefront rooms overlooking the 10th-century church of Santa Maria, villa gardens and Lake Como's western shore. Hotel guests have free use of Bellagio's Lido pool, complete with diving board over the lake. Day visitors can stop here to dine on the outdoor terrace, or hold out for traditional fish specialties 8km outside of Bellagio a **Ittiturismo Da Abate** – dishes include linguine and lake perch and black olives to Como's sweetwater *lavarello* fish in balsamic vinegar.

THINGS YOU NEED TO KNOW

Villa Serbelloni (☎031 95 15 55; Via Garibaldi 8; adult/child €8.50/4.50; ☺tours 11.30am & 3.30pm Tue-Sun Apr-Oct); **PromoBellagio** (☎031 95 15 55; www.bellagiolakecomo.com; Piazza della Chiesa 14; ☺9.30am-1pm Mon, 9.30am-12.30pm & 1.30-4pm Wed-Fri); **Barindelli** (☎338 211 0337; www.barindellitaxiboats.com; Piazza Mazzini; tour €130 for groups); **tourist office** (☎031 95 02 04; Piazza Mazzini; ☺9am-12.30pm & 1.30-6pm Mon-Sat, 10am-2pm Sun, shorter afternoon hrs in winter); **Albergo Silvio** (☎031 95 03 22; www.bellagiosilvio.com; Via Carcano 12; d €80-160; ☺Mar–mid-Nov & Christmas week; P❄🛜🏊); **Ittiturismo Da Abate** (☎338 584 3814; www.ittiturismodaabate.it; Frazione Villa 4, Lezzeno; meals €25-35; ☺dinner Tue-Sun, lunch Sun)

AL VELUU Restaurant, Hotel €€€
([phone]0344 4 05 10; alveluu.com; Via Rogaro 11;
meals €50-70; ⊙Wed-Mon; 🅿) The other
highlight of Tremezzo is this excellent
restaurant, serving wild asparagus and
polenta with panoramic views from its
hillside terrace. Upstairs there are two
equally comfortable suites (€130-200),
each sleeping up to four people. They
offer a pick-up from the dock.

PIEDMONT

POP 4.47 MILLION

Italy's second largest region arguably is
its most elegant; a purveyor of Slow Food
and fine wine, regal *palazzi* and an atmosphere that is superficially more *francais*
than *italiano*.

Most Piedmont journeys start in
grandiose Turin, famous for football
and Fiats. But beyond the car factories,
Piedmont is also notable for its food –
everything from arborio rice to white
truffles – and pastoral landscapes not
unlike nearby Tuscany.

Turin

POP 909,538 / ELEVATION 240M

There's a whiff of Paris in Turin's elegant
tree-lined boulevards and echoes of Vienna in its stately art nouveau cafes, but
make no mistake – this city is anything
but a copycat. The innovative Torinese
gave the world its first saleable hard chocolate and perpetuated one of its greatest
mysteries (the Holy Shroud).

 Sights

MOLE
ANTONELLIANA Landmark, Museum
(Via Montebello 20) The symbol of Turin, this
167m tower with its distinctive aluminium
spire appears on the Italian two-cent coin.
It was originally intended as a synagogue
when construction began in 1862, but
was never used as a place of worship. In
the mid 1990s, the tower became home
to the multifloored **Museo Nazionale del
Cinema** (www.museonazionaledelcinema.org;

adult/reduced €7/5; ⊙9am-8pm Tue-Fri & Sun,
to 11pm Sat), which takes you on a fantastic
tour through cinematic history, from the
earliest magic lanterns, stereoscopes
and other optical toys to the present day.
Movie memorabilia on display includes
Marilyn Monroe's black lace bustiere, Peter
O'Toole's robe from *Lawrence of Arabia* and
the coffin used by Bela Lugosi's Dracula.

The Mole's glass **panoramic lift** (lift
& museum ticket €9) whisks you 85m up
through the centre of the museum to the
roof terrace in 59 seconds.

MUSEO EGIZIO Museum
(Egyptian Museum; www.museoegizio.org;
Via Accademia delle Scienze 6; adult/reduced
€7.50/3.50; ⊙8.30am-7.30pm Tue-Sun) 'The
road through Memphis and Thebes
passes through Turin' trumpeted French
hieroglyphic decoder, Jean-François
Champollion in the early 19th century,
and he wasn't far wrong. Opened in 1824,
this legendary museum in the
Palazzo dell'Accademia delle Scienze
houses the most important collection of
Egyptian treasure outside Cairo. Two of
many highlights include a statue of Ram-
esses II (one of the world's most important
pieces of Egyptian art) and over 500 items
found in the tomb of Kha and Merit (from
1400 BC) in 1906. Though it remains open,
the museum is undergoing a five-year
refurbishment due for completion in 2013.

DUOMO DI SAN GIOVANNI Cathedral
(Piazza San Giovanni) Turin's cathedral
was built between 1491 and 1498 on
the site of three 14th-century basilicas
and, before that, a Roman theatre. Most
ignore the fairly plain interior and focus
on a far bigger myth: the church is home
to the famous **Shroud of Turin** (alleged
to be the burial cloth in which Jesus'
body was wrapped). A copy of the cloth
is on permanent display to the left of the
cathedral altar.

**GALLERIA CIVICA D'ARTE MODERNA E
CONTEMPORANEA** Art Gallery
(GAM; www.gamtorino.it; Via Magenta 31; adult/
reduced €7.50/6; ⊙10am-6pm Tue-Sun) Italy
can sometimes feel strangely light on
modern art, until you come to Turin. GAM

Turin

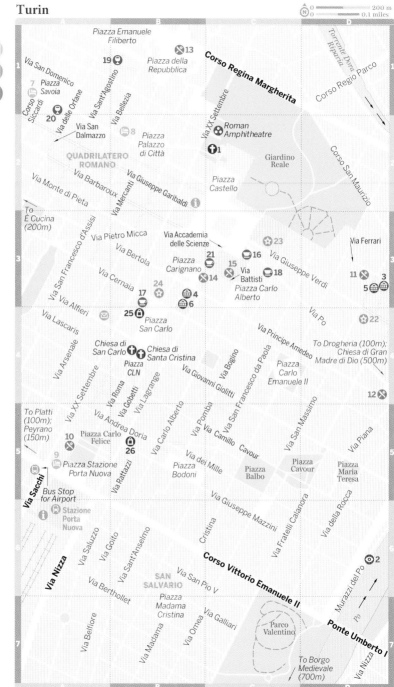

Piazza Emanuele Filiberto

Via San Domenico

7 Piazza Savoia

20

Corso Siccardi

Via delle Orfane

19

Via Sant'Agostino

Via Bellezia

Via San Dalmazzo

8

QUADRILATERO ROMANO

Via Barbaroux

Via Monte di Pieta

To È Cucina (200m)

Via Mercanti

Via Giuseppe Garibaldi

Piazza della Repubblica

13

Corso Regina Margherita

Via XX Settembre

Roman Amphitheatre

1

Piazza Palazzo di Città

Piazza Castello

Corso Regio Parco

Torrente Dora Riparia

Giardino Reale

Corso San Maurizio

Via Pietro Micca

Via Bertola

Via Cernaia

Via San Francesco d'Assisi

Via Accademia delle Scienze

21

Piazza Carignano

15

14

Via Battisti

16

23

Via Giuseppe Verdi

18

Via Ferrari

11

3

5

Via Alfieri

17

24

25

4

6

Piazza San Carlo

Piazza Carlo Alberto

Via Po

22

Via Lascaris

Via Arsenale

Chiesa di San Carlo

Chiesa di Santa Cristina

Piazza CLN

Via Roma

Via Gobetti

Via Lagrange

Via Giovanni Giolitti

Via Bogino

Via Principe Amedeo

Piazza Carlo Emanuele II

To Drogheria (100m); Chiesa di Gran Madre di Dio (500m)

12

Via San Francesco da Paola

To Platti (100m); Peyrano (150m)

Via XX Settembre

10

Piazza Carlo Felice

26

Via Andrea Doria

Via Carlo Alberto

Via Pomba

Via Camillo Cavour

Via Massimo

Piazza Cavour

Via Piana

9

Piazza Stazione Porta Nuova

Via Sacchi

Bus Stop for Airport

Stazione Porta Nuova

Via Rattazzi

Piazza Bodoni

Via dei Mille

Piazza Balbo

Piazza Maria Teresa

Via della Rocca

Via Nizza

Via Saluzzo

Via Goito

Via Sant'Anselmo

Cristina

Via Giuseppe Mazzini

Via Fratelli Calandra

Corso Vittorio Emanuele II

2

Via Belfiore

Via Berthollet

Via Madama

SAN SALVARIO

Via San Pio V

Piazza Madama Cristina

Via Galliari

Via Omea

Parco Valentino

Murazzi del Po

Po

Ponte Umberto I

Via Nizza

To Borgo Medievale (700m)

DISCOVER MILAN, THE LAKES & PIEDMONT TURIN

Turin

Sights
1 Duomo di San Giovanni........C2
2 Imbarco Murazzi........D6
3 Mole Antonelliana........D3
4 Museo Egizio........B3
5 Museo Nazionale del Cinema........D3
6 Palazzo dell'Accademia delle Scienze........B3

Sleeping
7 Ai Savoia........A1
8 Hotel Dogana Vecchia........B2
9 Hotel Roma e Rocca Cavour........A5

Eating
10 Grom........A5
11 Kuoki........D3
12 Porta di Savona........D4
13 Porta Palazzo........B1
14 Ristorante del Cambio........B3
15 Sfashion........C3

Drinking
16 Caffè Mulassano........C3
17 Caffè San Carlo........B3
18 Fiorio........C3
19 I Tre Galli........B1
20 Lobelix........A1
21 Mood........C3

Entertainment
22 Cinema Massimo........D4
23 Teatro Regio Torino........C3
24 Ticket office (football)........B3

Shopping
25 Paissa........B4
26 Pastificio Defilippis........B5

has an astounding 45,000 works in its vaults dedicated to 19th- and 20th-century artists, including de Chirico, Otto Dix and Klee.

MUSEO D'ARTE CONTEMPORANEA Art Gallery
(www.castellodirivoli.org; Piazza Mafalda di Savoia, Rivoli; adult/reduced €6.50/4.50; 10am-5pm Tue-Fri, 10am-7pm Sat & Sun) The Savoy family once resided in the 17th-century **Castello di Rivoli** where the cutting edge of Turin's contemporary art scene has been housed since 1984. The collection includes masterpieces of Turin's revolutionary 1960s-70s **Arte Povera** ('Poor Art') movement by Giuseppe Penone, Gilberto Zorio and Michelangelo Pistoletto, as well as commissions for the museum by international contemporary artists, including video-art pioneers Bill Viola, Pipilotti Rist and Yang Fudong. The castle is west of central Turin in the town of Rivoli. Take the metro to Paradiso station and then bus 36 to Rivoli bus station.

REGGIA DE VENARIA REALE Palazzo, Museum
(Piazza della Repubblica; www.lavenaria.it; adult/reduced €12/8, gardens €4/3; 9am-6pm Tue-Fri, 9am-9.30pm Sat, 9am-8pm Sun) Welcome to Turin's Versailles, a Unesco-listed palace complex built as a glorified hunting lodge by the frivolous Duke of Savoy Carlo Emanuele II in 1675. It is one of the biggest royal residences in the world and lengthy restoration works were concluded in late 2010. You can reach the palace complex on bus 11 from Porta Nuova station.

Sleeping

TOP CHOICE **HOTEL RESIDENCE TORINO CENTRO** Hotel €
(011 433 82 23; www.hoteltorinocentro.it; Corso Inghilterra 33; d/tr €77/90; P) The best new player in the field by a good stretch is this chic upgraded convent right behind the Porta Susa train station. Smart modern furnishings combine with old mosaic floors in huge rooms with all mod cons. Service is professional and efficient and there's a funky coffee bar (Coffee Lab Inghiliterra) downstairs in which to enjoy a complimentary breakfast.

AI SAVOIA Boutique Hotel €€
(339 1257711; www.aisavoia.it; Via del Carmine 1b; r €95-125; P) Occupying an 18th-century townhouse, this little treasure seems like something out of a small town rather than a big city. The classical decor of each of its

Don't Miss **Lingotto Fiere & Eataly**

With a twinkle in his eye and a rumble in his stomach, star architect **Renzo Piano** creatively repurposed Turin's former Fiat factory into **Lingotto Fiere**, home of **Salone Internazionale del Gusto** (www.salonedelgusto.it). This industrial-chic complex has it all: a rooftop art gallery studded with masterpieces by Canaletto, Renoir, Matisse and Picasso, the **Pinacoteca Giovanni e Marella Agnelli**; sleek **Le Meridien hotels**; and best of all, the gastronomical wonderland of **Eataly**.

The former factory is now a permanent showcase for Italy's best artisanal, sustainably produced food, with cured meats dangling like chandeliers, an entire truffle station and a dream wine cellar. The best time to visit is noon to 2.30pm, when each specialty food zone serves lunch. Stick around for sommelier-led wine tastings, seasonal food samples and cooking workshops (from €20). Lingotto is 3km south of the city centre, but easily accessible on Turin's new metro line.

THINGS YOU NEED TO KNOW

Lingotto Fiere (www.lingottofiere.it; Via Nizza 294); **Pinacoteca Giovanni e Marella Agnelli** (Via Nizza 230; admission €4; ☉10am-7pm Tue-Sun); **Eataly** (www.eatalytorino.it; Via Nizza 230; ☉10am-8pm Tue-Sun)

---

three rooms is ornate without being over-wrought, and staff are friendly and obliging.

LE MERIDIEN LINGOTTO & LE MERIDIEN ART + TECH Luxury Hotels €€€
(☎011 664 20 00; www.lemeridienlingotto.it; Via Nizza 262; Le Meridien Lingotto d €270-300, Le Meridien Art + Tech d €390-410; P ❋ ☎)

These twin hotels are both situated within the historic Fiat car factory, which was built in the 1920s and renovated by Renzo Piano in the late 1980s. Guests can jog around the former car-testing circuit on the roof, which was featured in the classic 1969 film *The Italian Job*.

HOTEL DOGANA VECCHIA   Hotel   €€

(011 436 67 52; www.hoteldoganavecchia.com; Via Corte d'Appello 4; s/d €90/110; P) Mozart, Verdi and Napoleon are among those who have stayed at this historic three-star inn. Recent renovations have fortunately preserved its old-world charm, and its location in the Quadrilatero Romano is hard to beat.

HOTEL ROMA E ROCCA CAVOUR   Hotel   €€

(011 561 27 72; www.romarocca.it; Piazza Carlo Felice 60; s €62.50-95.50, d €91-124; P ✳) If you've stayed in too many cramped hotel rooms, you'll love this c 1854 hotel opposite the Porta Nuova train station. Hallways are wide, ceilings are high and antique-furnished rooms are sumptuously proportioned, especially the 'comfort' rooms.

Eating

OSFASHION   Pizzeria   €

(Via Cesare Battisti 13; set menu €21, meals €7.50-14.50) Naples-thick and with wonderfully rustic ingredients (and not too much cheese) pizzas fly like hot bullets from the ovens of comic Torinese TV presenter Piero Chiamretti, surrounded by a funky postmodern interior.

È CUCINA   Fusion   €€

(www.cesaremarretti.com; Via Bertola 27a; meals €20-30) There is no printed menu; wait staff will merely tell you it's a *sorpesa* (surprise). You pay for the number of courses you consume. Bank on artichokes with prawns, eggplants overlaid with avocado cream, pears atop salmon, and plenty more.

KUOKI   Fusion   €

(011 839 78 65; Via Gaudenzio Ferrari 2h; set menus €9-25, meals €6-10; 11am-3pm & 6.30-11pm Mon-Sat) Head round the corner from the Mole Antonelliana to this intriguing spot run by Giorgio Armani's former personal chef, Toni Vitiello. At high communal tables, you can dine on Italian blackboard specials, or sushi bar twists such as a Kuoki roll (salmon or tuna with ricotta, olive oil and basil).

PORTA DI SAVONA   Trattoria   €€

(Piazza Vittoria Veneto 2; meals €25; lunch & dinner Wed-Sun, dinner Tue) An economical, unpretentious trattoria, it has a deserved reputation for superb *agnolotti al sugo arrosto* (Piedmontese ravioli in a meat gravy), and *gnocchi di patate al gorgonzola*.

RISTORANTE DEL CAMBIO   Gastronomic   €€€

(011 54 66 90; Piazza Carignano 2; set menus from €60; Mon-Sat) Crimson velvet, glittering chandeliers, baroque mirrors and a timeless air greet you at this grande dame of the Turin dining scene. It first opened its doors in 1757, and classic Piedmont cuisine still dominates the menu.

GROM   Gelateria   €

(www.grom.it; Piazza Paleocapa 1d; noon-midnight Mon-Thu, to 1am Fri & Sat, 11am-11pm Sun) The Slow Food–affiliated ice cream makers now have 37 outlets (including ones in New York, Tokyo and Paris), but the first ever Grom started here in 2003.

PORTA PALAZZO   Market   €

(Piazza della Repubblica; 8.30am-1.30pm Mon-Fri, to 6.30pm Sat) Europe's largest open-air food market has literally hundreds of food stalls. Pick up a picnic.

Drinking

I TRE GALLI   Wine Bar

(www.3galli.com; Via Sant'Agostino 25; noon-midnight) Spacious and rustic, this is a fabulous spot for a drink at any time, but most people come for the gourmet *aperitivi* snacks served on the buzzing pavement terrace.

MOOD   Cafe

(www.moodlibri.it; Via Battisti 3e; cafe 8am-9pm Mon-Sat, bookshop 10am-9pm Mon-Sat) Any mood suits this coffee shop/cocktail bar/bookshop combo, as long as you can find room among the shoppers and students flicking through Dante.

LOBELIX   Bar

(Via Corte d'Appello 15f; 7pm-3am Mon-Sat) Beneath the trees on Piazza Savoia, the

If You Like…
Slow Food

If you've got any room left after eating at Eataly (p150) try these Slow Food hotspots within an hour of Turin:

1 BRA

Not the undergarment, but the town where Carlo Petrini founded the Slow Food movement in 1987. Today Bra's baroque centre has family-run shops selling organic salami and handmade chocolates and, shutting twice weekly for a 'slowdown.' Get a liquid education with free library wine tastings at **Banca del Vino** (www.bancadelvino.it; Piazza Vittorio Emanuele II 13), advancing to ultralocal dinners upstairs from Slow Food headquarters at **Osteria del Boccondivino** (☏ 0172 42 56 74; www.boccondivinoslow.it; Via Mendicità Istruita 14, Bra; set menus €26-28; ✆ Tue-Sat). Trains link Bra with Turin (€3.50, one hour).

2 ALBA

Of 100 towers that once dotted medieval Alba's skyline, four remain. No matter: the towering achievements here are white truffles, dark chocolate and red wine. Alba's **tourist office** (www.langheroero.it; Piazza Risorgimento 2; ✆ 9am-6.30pm Mon-Fri, 10am-6.30pm Sat-Sun) organises September–October **truffle-hunting excursions** (price varies; two hours), September–November **winery tours** (€80-100; 3½ hrs), year-round **cooking courses** (half-/full-day €70/100) and **hot-air balloon flights** (incl transfers, wine & breakfast €220-250). Hourly trains connect Alba with Turin (€4.40 via Bra, 50 minutes).

3 BAROLO

For 400 years, the tiny village of Barolo southwest of Alba has bewitched drinkers with satiny, truffle-scented, food-loving Barolo. Winemaking secrets are spilled at **Museo del Vino a Barolo** (www.wimubarolo.it; adult/reduced €7/5; ✆ 10.30am-7pm Fri-Wed, closed Jan-Feb), housed in 10th-17th century **Castello Falletti** (www.baroloworld.it; Piazza Falletti). Don't miss the dungeons, where **Enoteca Regionale del Barolo** (✆ 10am-12.30pm & 3-6.30pm Fri-Wed) offers daily Barolo tastings (per taste/three tastes €2/5).

terrace here is a favourite place for an *aperitivo* – its buffet banquet is one of Turin's most extravagant.

Entertainment

TEATRO REGIO TORINO Theatre
(☏ 011 881 52 41; www.teatroregio.torino.it, in Italian; Piazza Castello 215; ✆ ticket office 10.30am-6pm Tue-Fri, to 4pm Sat & 1hr before performances) Sold-out performances can sometimes be watched free on live TV in the adjoining Teatro Piccolo Regio, where Puccini premiered *La bohème* in 1896. Tickets start at €48.

HIROSHIMA MON AMOUR Nightclub
(Via Bossoli 83; admission free-€15) This legendary dance club plays everything from folk and punk to tango and techno.

CINEMA MASSIMO Cinema
(Via Giuseppe Verdi 18; admission €7) Near the Mole Antonelliana, this cinema offers an eclectic mix of films, mainly in English or with subtitles.

Shopping

PEYRANO Chocolate
(www.peyrano.com; Corso Vittorio Emanuele II 76) Creator of *Dolci Momenti a Torino* (Sweet Moments in Turin) and *grappini* (chocolates filled with grappa), Peyrano has been in operation since 1912.

PASTIFICIO DEFILIPPIS Food
(Via Lagrange 39; ✆ 8.30am-1pm & 4-7.30pm Mon-Sat) Nose through the open doorway of this 1872 establishment to watch the family making dozens of varieties of pasta; you can buy it here fresh or dried.

PAISSA Food
(www.paissa.it; Piazza San Carlo 196) This wonderful old-fashioned emporium in Piazza San Carlo, complete with ladders

and a heavy wooden counter, is where you can buy everything Turin is famous for, including *grissini* (breadsticks), wine and chocolates.

ⓘ Information

Ospedale Mauriziano Umberto I (☎011 5 08 01; Largo Turati 62) Hospital.

Tourist office (☎011 535 181; Stazione Porta Nuova (🕓9.30am-7pm); Airport (🕓8am-11pm); Piazza Castello (🕓9am-7pm) Offers a free accommodation and restaurant booking service.

ⓘ Getting There & Away

Air

Turin airport (TRN; www.turin-airport.com), 16km northwest of the city centre in Caselle, has connections to European and national destinations, including service on budget airline.

Bus

Most international, national and regional buses terminate at the bus station (Corso Castelfidardo).

Train

Regular daily trains connect Turin's Stazione Porta Nuova (Piazza Carlo Felice) to the following destinations.

TO	FARE(€)	DURATION (HR)	FREQUENCY
Milan	9.55	1¾	28
Aosta	7.90	2	21
Venice	42	5	17
Rome	from 51.50	7	11

Most also stop at Stazione Porta Susa (Corso Inghilterra), which will gradually take over as the main station in the next few years.

ⓘ Getting Around

To/From the Airport

Sadem (www.sadem.it, in Italian) runs buses to the airport from Stazione Porta Nuova (40 minutes), also stopping at Stazione Porta Susa (30 minutes). Buses depart every 30 minutes between 5.15am and 10.30pm (6.30am and 11.30pm from the airport). Single tickets cost €5 from Confetteria

Detour:
Aosta

Jagged Alpine peaks rise like marble cathedrals above the town of Aosta (pop 35,078/elev 565m) – but before you hit those pristine slopes, take a moment to explore **Roman ruins** in the town centre, glimpse 10th-century frescoes under the roof of the still-active monastery at **Chiesa Di Sant'Orso** (Via Sant'Orso; ◷9am-7pm), and learn how Aosta's signature buttery **fontina cheese** is made 8.5 km outside of town at **Valpelline Visitors Centre** (www.fontinacoop.it; Frissonière; ◷8.30am-12.30pm & 2.30-6.30pm Mon-Fri, 9am-noon & 3-6pm Sat & Sun).

From Aosta, you can access Europe's best skiing: **Courmayeur** (www.courmayeur.com), alongside spectacular Mont Blanc; **Cervinia** (www.cervinia.it), near the Matterhorn; and **Monte Rosa** (www.monterosa-ski.com), with three valleys of challenging runs. For pass options, see www.skivallee.it. The best small ski resort is **Pila** (www.pila.it), accessible by cable car from Aosta.

In summer, Aosta offers mountain biking, Alpine hiking and wine-tasting. Stop by Aosta **tourism office** (www.regione.vda.it/turismo; Piazza Chanoux 2; ◷9am-6.30pm) for lists of guides, accommodation and wineries. West of the city centre, **Club Alpino Italiano** (www.caivda.it, in Italian; Corso Battaglione Aosta 81; ◷6.30-8pm Tue, 8-10pm Fri) organises hikes and climbs.

Unwind at **Hotel Milleluci** (☎0165 4 42 74; www.hotelmilleluci.com; Loc Porossan 15; s €110-130, d €130-240; P❄@≋), a converted hillside farmhouse with clawfoot baths, pools, sauna, balconies and sumptuous breakfasts. Don't miss local-specialty dinners at **Trattoria degli Artisti** (Via Maillet 5-7; meals €18-28; ◷Tue-Sat).

To reach Aosta, take the A5 highway from Turin, Turin-Aosta train (€7.55, two hours), or Savda (www.savda.it) bus from Milan (1½ to 3½ hours) or Courmayeur (€3.20, one hour).

Avvignano (**Piazza Carlo Felice 50**), opposite where the bus stops, or €5.50 if bought on the bus.

A taxi between the airport and the city centre will cost around €35 to €40.

Car & Motorcycle

Major car-rental agencies have offices at Stazione Porta Nuova and the airport.

Public Transport

Gruppo Torinese Trasporti (GTT; www.gtt.to.it, in Italian) has an information office (◷7am-9pm) at Stazione Porta Nuova. Buses and trams run from 6am to midnight and tickets cost €1 (€13.50 for a 15-ticket carnet and €3.50 for a one-day pass).

Turin's single-line metro (www.metrotorino.it) runs from Fermi to Lingotto.

Taxi

Call Centrale Radio (☎011 57 37) or Radio Taxi (☎011 57 30).

Cinque Terre

A Unesco World Heritage Site, Cinque Terre's winding walking paths meander along cliffsides, past tiny vineyards and lemon groves bursting from stone-walled terraces, to five seaside villages. Railway tunnels arrived in the 19th century and electricity in the 1990s, yet Monterosso, Vernazza, Corniglia, Manarola and Riomaggiore still recall their 1300s pirate's-cove heyday. An ancient mule path, **Sentiero Azzurro** (Blue Trail, marked No 2; admission with Cinque Terre card) reaches all five villages within 12km, with steep steps hewn into hillsides and end-of-the-world views. Get trail information and Cinque Terre walking/train passes at **Parco Nazionale offices** (www.parconazionale5terre.it; ◷7am-8pm) in Cinque Terre train stations. Trains link Turin and Cinque Terre via La Spezia (3 to 4½hrs, €25 to €35).

Monterosso

Monterosso, the westernmost village and most accessible by car, descends from lemon groves to a sandy beach. Pack a beach picnic of foccacia and Cinque Terre white wine at **Focacceria Enoteca Antonia** (Via Fegina 124; focaccia €2-3; ⊘9am-8pm Fri-Wed Mar-Oct).

Vernazza

Quaint cafes and artisans' studios line the cobbled street leading from the train station to the harbour, where **Gianni Franzi** (✆0187 82 10 03; www.giannifranzi.it; Piazza Matteotti 5; meals €22-30, s/d €70/100; ⊘mid-Mar–early Jan) offers seaside accommodation and local seafood, pesto ravioli and lemony anchovies.

Corniglia

Reaching this colourful village involves a 377-step climb from the train station, but there are sweeping vineyard views and detours to secluded, clothing-optional **Guvano Beach** – ask a local for directions through the abandoned railway tunnel. Reward yourself with pesto lasagna on Corniglia's piazza at **Caffe Matteo** (Piazza Taragio).

Manarola

Famous for rare **Sciacchetrà** dessert wine and medieval relics, Manarola offers promontory panoramas at **Punta Buonfiglio**.

Riomaggiore

With its ruined castle and pastel houses lining the harbour, Cinque Terre's easternmost village is also its unofficial HQ (the park office is here). Divers, snorklers and kayakers eyeing the crystalline, Unesco–protected waters can arrange outings at **Cooperative Sub 5 Terre** (✆0187 92 00 11; www.5terrediving.it; Via San Giacomo; ⊘vary seasonally).

Manarola

JOHN ELK III/LONELY PLANET IMAGES ©

Venice, Veneto & Bologna

The hype about this region is wrong – it's an understatement.

A habitual overachiever, Venice isn't only beautiful. Over the past millennium, the dazzling lagoon city has become musically gifted, exceptionally handy with molten glass and a single oar, and as you'll discover over Rialto happy-hour banter, wickedly funny. Logical types may initially resist Venetian charms, grousing about gondola rates and crooked *calli* (backstreets) – but then out comes the bubbly Prosecco and tasty *cicheti* (Venetian tapas), and suddenly newcomers are attempting toasts in Venetian dialect.

A silty lagoon may seem an inconvenient spot for a city of palaces, but it's ideally located for *la bella vita* (the beautiful life). Beaches line the Lido, vineyards just outside Verona supply exceptional wines, and Bologna awaits, a train ride away, a clever university town with the best-stocked delis on the planet.

Grand Canal (p176), Venice
GLENN BEANLAND/LONELY PLANET IMAGES ©

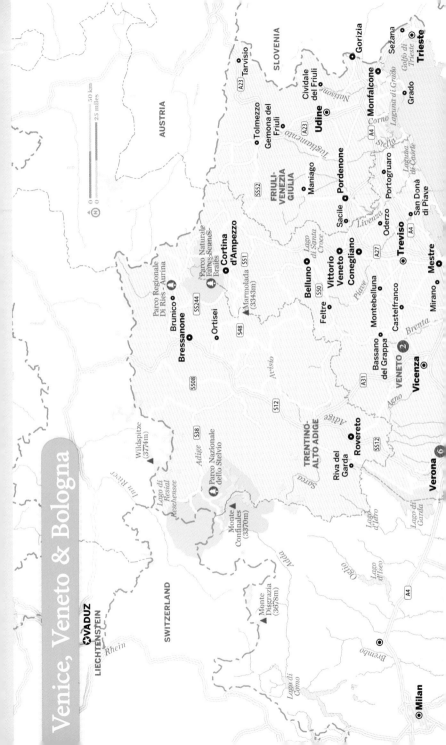

Venice, Veneto & Bologna

1 Legendary Venice
2 Culinary Bologna & Veneto
3 St Mark's Basilica, Venice
4 Ducal Palace, Venice
5 Venetian Masters
6 Roman Arena, Verona
7 Quadrilatero, Bologna

CROATIA

Adriatic Sea

Venice

Chioggia

Este

Rovigo

Ferrara

Comacchio

Argenta

Valle di Comacchio

Valle Bertuzzi

Po Delta

Stra

Villafranca

Mantua

Parma

Cremona

Reggio Emilia

Sassuolo

Maranello

San Giovanni in Persiceto

Bologna 2 7

Casalecchio di Reno

Pavullo nel Frignano

Sestola

Parco Nazionale dell'Appennino Tosco Emiliano

EMILIA-ROMAGNA

Fornovo di Taro

La Spezia

Imola

Faenza

Forlì

Ravenna

Cervia

Bellaria

Igea Marina

Rimini

SAN MARINO

SAN MARINO

Pesaro

UMBRIA

Arezzo

Florence

Arno

Tyrrhenian Sea

Lago di Massaciuccoli

Serchio

Reno

Panaro

Secchia

Enza

Taro

Parma

Chiese

Tyrrhenian Sea

Venice, Veneto & Bologna Highlights

① Legendary Venice

This lagoon city is anchored not just by thousands of poles under the paving stones, but by a thousand years of Venetian legends. Besides the obvious – Marco Polo's travels, Casanova's escapades, star-crossed romances that inspired Shakespeare – tales unfold around every canal bend. Gondola ride (p171); St Mark's Basilica (p185); Ducal Palace (p182)

Need to Know

CARNEVALE Costumed street theatre in February/March (www.carnevale.venezia.it) GRAND CANAL SIGHTSEEING Get a timed ticket for vaporetto (water-bus) line 1 See p170

Don't Miss List

BY ALESSANDRA SPISNI,
CHEF, COOKING TEACHER &
FOOD WRITER

1 LESSER-KNOWN LOCAL SPECIALITIES

Look out for highly prized Marroni di Castel Del Rio chestnuts and truffles from Savigno. In the artisan *salumerie* (delis) of Bologna (p209) and its province, don't pass up the chance to sample *salame rosa* (pink salami). It might look like mortadella, but it's actually prepared like regular salami then steam-cooked.

2 REGIONAL WINES

The vineyards around Modena, Reggio Emilia and Piacenza produce excellent Lambrusco, and much of Romagna is celebrated for its Sangiovese. The Colli Bolognesi (Bolognese Hills) produce wonderful merlot and my personal favourite, cabernet. The latter goes perfectly with our regional dishes, whether it's *brodo da tortellini* (broth with tortellini pasta), lasagne or a fragrant *arrosto* (roast). In neighbouring Veneto, fine wines include Amarone, Valpolicella red, the lemon-zesty Soave Classico and the nutty Recioto di Soave (the latter two are whites). Emilia-Romagna's wines tend to be lighter than their Veneto counterparts.

3 GASTRONOMIC TOWNS

Top of the list is Bologna (p210), not to mention Venice (p194), home to the wonderfully historic Pescaria and Rialto Market (p161), the latter operating in one form or another for 1000 years.

4 COOKING COURSES

One of the best ways to experience Italian culture is through food, and a cooking course (p210) offers both a fun window into the country and an investment in interesting future meals!

Glimpse Heaven Inside St Mark's Basilica

Excitement rises in multiple languages as the line of sightseers nears the Basilica's Egyptian purple-marble portals. But once you step over the threshold, the crowd hushes to a collective sigh: Oooooooooo. Millions of tiny, glittering mosaics turn the Basilica's domes into a billowing golden heaven, with hovering angels and skipping saints. A Unesco-certified wonder 800 years in the making, the Basilica (p185) is a uniquely uplifting experience.

4 Admire Propaganda at the Ducal Palace

Propaganda never looked as pretty as the gorgeous Gothic Ducal Palace (p182), covered floor to ceiling over three stories with testimonials to Venetian virtues by Titian, Veronese, Tiepolo and Tintoretto. For all its graces, this palace was a powerhouse. The doge (duke) lived downstairs and greeted ambassadors upstairs, while the secret service interrogated suspected traitors in the attic.

Meet the Venetian Masters

Despite complaints from Rome for depicting angels playing stringed instruments (too worldly!), apostles dining with Germans (too Protestant!) and Biblical scenes starring Venetian beauties (too alluring!), Venice kept right on painting. Hence the Gallerie dell'Accademia (p181). No ordinary museum, it is a parade of masterpieces by Venetian masters Titian, Bellini, Carpaccio, Tintoretto, Veronese and more. Don't miss the baroque portraits.

Clamour for More at Verona's Roman Arena

Big notes seem even bigger at Verona's pitch-perfect Roman Arena (p206), where A-list opera stars perform under the stars each summer on epic-scale sets (which have included the odd wild cat). Mortal combat is no longer on the bill at the 2000-year-old ampitheatre, but careers can still be made or killed here with an encore – luckily, Maria Callas and Placido Domingo didn't miss a note.

Eat Across Bologna's Quadrilatero

Ditch your diet on the train to Bologna (p207), Italy's most unabashedly food-loving city (and that's saying something). Lovingly nicknamed *la grassa* ('the fatty'), Bologna stocks Quadrilatero delis with celebrated local specialties, including syrupy *aceto balsamico di Modena* (aged balsamic vinegar from Modena). Walk it off with 40km of beautiful colonnaded sidewalks...or try dessert.

Venice, Veneto & Bologna's Best...

Worth-the-Trip Thrills

○ Glimpsing golden mosaic heavens inside **Basilica di San Marco** (p185)

○ Tangoing across Piazza San Marco during happy hour at **Caffè Florian** (p198)

○ Crossing the Grand Canal standing in a **traghetto** (p171)

○ Watching artisans breathe life into red-hot glass in **Murano** (p190)

○ Hiking in spring wildflower season through the **Dolomites** (p192)

Encore-Worthy Entertainment

○ **Roman Arena, Verona** (p206) Italy's most celebrated al fresco opera

○ **La Fenice, Venice** (p199) A tiny, incendiary stage with world-premiere credits from Verdi, Wagner and Britten

○ **Venice Biennale** (p191) Art events, plus top performing arts talents

○ **Interpreti Veneziani** (p200) Roaring revivals of baroque composers with Venetian talents rocking period instruments

○ **Cantina Bentivoglio** (p211) Lively jazz sessions in a Bologna wine cellar

Luxury Bargains

○ Tickets to red-carpet screenings at the **Venice Film Festival** (p191)

○ Private beach cabana rental on the **Lido** (p189)

○ Seafood *cicheti* along the Grand Canal at **Al Pesador** (p195)

○ Collectors' wines by the glass at **I Rusteghi** (p198)

○ Cappuccino inside an art installation at **Palazzo Grassi** (p184)

Need to Know

Unconventional Souvenirs

○ Murano glass soap-bubble necklaces from **Marina e Susanna Sent** (p200)

○ Handbag made of lagoon-swirled marble paper from **Cartè** (p200)

○ Balsalmic vinegar aged 40 years from Bologna's **Quadrilatero** (p209)

○ Poetry in Venetian dialect from **Old World Books** (p201)

○ Bar aprons silkscreened with the recipe for *spritz* from prison collective **Malefatte** (p201)

ADVANCE PLANNING

○ **Two months before** Reserve tickets to Venice's La Fenice (p199)

○ **One month before** Book your Itinerari Segreti tour at the Palazzo Ducal (p182), Row Venice lesson (p190) and Bologna cooking course (p210)

○ **One week before** Purchase tickets to Gallerie dell'Accademia (p181) online; reserve Laguna Eco Adventures sailing tours (p190) and meals at Venissa (p190)

RESOURCES

○ **Venice Tourist Board** (www.turismovenezia.it)

○ **Venice Connected** (www.veniceconnected.com) Official sales channel for tickets to major Venice events

○ **Veneto Tourist Board** (www.veneto.to)

○ **Venezia da Vivere** (www.veneziadavivere.com) Music performances, art openings and more

○ **Emilia Romagna Tourist Board** (www.emiliaromagnaturismo.it)

GETTING AROUND

○ **Air** Connections to/from Venice, Treviso, Verona and Bologna

○ **Train** Excellent connections between major cities and towns

○ **Walk** Perfect for Venice and smaller cities, towns and alpine trails

○ **Vaporetto** Public water-bus ply Venice's Grand Canal and connect central Venice with Marco Polo airport

○ **Gondola** Flat-bottom boats rowed with a single oar aren't just quaint: they're key to sightseeing

○ **Traghetto** Public gondola service for crossing Venice's Grand Canal between bridges

○ **Bus** Handy for Lido transport and inland towns not serviced by trains

○ **Bicycle** For small towns, the Lido and alpine trails

BE FOREWARNED

○ **Museums** Most close Monday

○ **Restaurants** Many close in August and January

○ **Accommodation** Book months ahead for Venice in February/March Carnevale (www.carnevale.venezia.it) or June-September Biennale (p191); Dolomites in winter ski season; and Bologna during spring and autumn trade fairs

Venice, Veneto & Bologna Itineraries

Whether you've got island fever or a powerful rumbling in the stomach, this region will cure what ails you with an astonishing variety of island adventures, deli delicacies, and – oh yes – phenomenal wines.

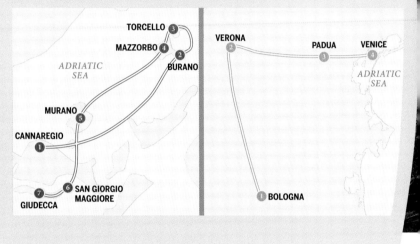

CANNAREGIO TO GIUDECCA

Venetian Island Adventure

Other islands in the Venetian lagoon have their own architectural styles and distinct cuisines. In the Venice neighbourhood of **(1) Cannaregio** at the Fondamenta Nuove stop, take the LP *vaporetto* (water-ferry) for a rejuvenating shock of colour on **(2) Burano**. Unlike Venice's genteel Gothic palaces, Burano's houses look like cartoons: bubble-gum-pink cottages squat comically next to lanky cobalt-blue townhouses.

The T-line ferry hops to bucolic, Byzantine **(3) Torcello**, where sheep bleat hello. Inside the 9th to 11th century Santa Maria Assunta Cathedral, sneaky devils tip the scales in the *Final Judgment* mosaic. Back in Burano,

cross the bridge to the garden island of **(4) Mazzorbo**, for a peaceful night and wildly creative, lagoon-inspired dinners at Venissa.

Catch an early LN *vaporetto* to **(5) Murano** to witness 500 years of glassblowing artistry at the Museum of Glass – and beat shoppers to the bargains at Murano-glass showrooms. The 42 *vaporetto* chugs from Murano to **(6) San Giorgio Maggiore**, where wcontemporary art fills the converted boat-shed behind Palladio's dazzling temple-inspired church. Hop the *vaporetto* one stop to **(7) Giudecca**, and end your adventure with spa treatments in the converted Palladian cloisters of Bauer Palladio & Spa.

BOLOGNA TO VENICE
Gourmet Treasure Hunt

Gourmet adventures abound in **(1) Bologna**, where the specialty in the delis of Il Quadrilatero isn't factory-processed lunch meat – it's artisan-cured *prosciutto* ham from nearby Parma. Climb the leaning Torre degli Asinelli to work up an appetite, and descend to dine on handmade tortellini at Drogheria della Rosa, a converted ancient pharmacy.

Make the most of a morning in Bologna with a cooking course, then catch the train to fair **(2) Verona**, where the scene has been set for happy hour at Piazza delle Erbe since it was a Roman forum. At Casa di Giulietta, you can post a note requesting Juliet's help to find your own Romeo or Juliet, but a surer bet is prized Amarone wine, which tastes like true love, with polenta and Venetian *sopressa* (soft salami) at Osteria del Bugiardo.

The next day, continue your train journey to **(3) Padua**. If you're not moved to tears by Giotto's tender frescoes in Padua's Scrovegni Chapel, the homemade pasta at Godenda might do the trick. Roll back onto the train and nap to **(4) Venice**, to reach the Rialto just as *cicheti* (Venetian tapas) appears at I Rusteghi, and corks pop on rare Ribolla Gialla white wine. Cin-cin!

Verona (p204)

Discover Venice, Veneto & Bologna

VENICE

POP 61,500 (CITY), 270,800 (TOTAL INCLUDING MAINLAND)

Imagine the audacity of people deciding to build a city of marble palaces on a lagoon. Instead of surrendering to *acqua alta* (high water) like reasonable folk might do, Venetians flooded the world with vivid painting, baroque music, modern opera, spice-route cuisine, bohemian-chic fashions and a Grand Canal's worth of *spritz:* the signature *prosecco*-aperol cocktail. Today, cutting-edge architects and billionaire benefactors are spicing up the art scene, musicians are rocking out 18th-century instruments and backstreet *osterie* are winning a Slow Food following. Your timing couldn't be better: the people who made walking on water look easy are well into their next act.

History

A malarial swamp seems like a strange place to found an empire, unless you consider the circumstances: from the 5th to 8th century AD, Huns, Goths and sundry barbarians repeatedly sacked Roman towns along Veneto's Adriatic coast. In AD 726 the people of Venice elected their first doge (duke), whose successors would lead the city for more than 1000 years.

Like its signature landmark, the Basilica di San Marco, the Venetian empire was dazzlingly cosmopolitan. Armenians, Turks, Greeks and Germans were neighbours along the Grand Canal, and Jewish communities persecuted elsewhere in Europe founded publishing houses, banks and medical practices in Venice.

Seafood platter, Venice
JULIET COOMBE/LONELY PLANET IMAGES ©

As the Age of Exploration began, Venice lost its monopoly over seafaring trade routes. Once it could no longer rule the seas, Venice changed tack and began conquering Europe by charm. By the end of the 16th century, Venice was known across Europe for its painting, catchy music and 12,000 registered prostitutes.

Venetian reputations did nothing to prevent Napoleon from claiming the city in 1797 and looting Venetian art. When Venice rallied to resist the Austrian occupation in 1848–49, a blockade left it wracked by cholera and short on food. Venetian rebels lost the fight but not the war: they became early martyrs to the cause of Italian independence, and in 1866 Venice joined the independent kingdom of Italy.

Italian partisans joined Allied troops to wrest Veneto from Fascist control, but the tragedy of war and mass deportation of Venice's historical Jewish population in 1942–44 shook Venice to its moorings. Post-war, many Venetians left for Milan and other centres of industry.

On 4 November 1966, disaster struck: record floods poured into 16,000 Venetian homes, stranding residents in the wreckage of 1200 years of civilisation. But Venice's cosmopolitan charm was a saving grace: assistance from admirers poured in (from Mexico to Australia, millionaires to pensioners) and Unesco coordinated some 27 international charities to redress the ravages of the flood.

Defying centuries of dire predictions, Venice has not yet become a Carnevale-masked parody of itself or a lost Atlantis. The city remains relevant and realistic, a global launching pad for daring art and film, ingenious craftsmanship, opera premieres and music revivals, even as it seeks sustainable solutions to rising water levels.

Sights

Piazza San Marco & Around
MUSEO CORRER Museum
(Map p178; 041 240 52 11; www.museicivici veneziani.it; Piazza San Marco 52; adult/reduced incl Palazzo Ducale €14/8, or Museum Pass; 10am-7pm Apr-Oct, to 5pm Nov-Mar) Napoleon filled his royal digs over Piazza San Marco with the riches of the doges, and took some of Venice's finest heirlooms to France as trophies. But the biggest treasure here couldn't be lifted: Jacopo Sansovino's 16th-century **Libreria Nazionale Marciana**, covered with larger-than-life philosophers by Veronese, Titian and Tintoretto and miniature back-flipping sea-creatures.

In the **Pinacoteca** (Picture Gallery) don't miss Paolo Veneziano's 14th-century sad-eyed saints (Room 25); Lo Schiavone's Madonna with a bouncing baby Jesus,

Gondolas

A gondola ride is anything but pedestrian, with glimpses into *palazzi* courtyards and hidden canals. Official daytime rates are €80 for 40 minutes (six passengers maximum) or €100 from 7pm to 8am, not including songs (negotiated separately) or tips. Additional time is charged in 20-minute increments (day/night €40/50). Agree on a price, time limit and singing in advance to avoid surcharges. Gondole cluster at *stazi* (stops) along the **Grand Canal**, at the train station (041 71 85 43), the Rialto (041 522 49 04) and near major monuments, but you can also book a pickup at a canal near you (041 528 50 75).

For a brief, bargain gondola ride, try a *traghetto*, the gondola service locals use to cross the Grand Canal. *Traghetti* rides cost just €0.50 and typically operate from 9am to 6pm, for major *traghetto* crossings.

Venice

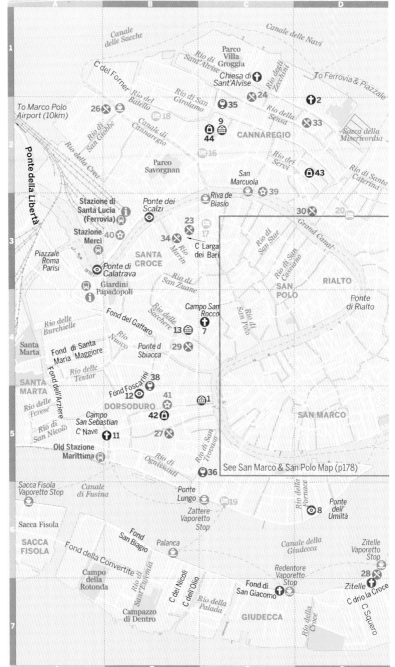

Canale delle Sacche

Canale delle Navi

C del Forner

Parco Villa Groggia

Rio di Sant'Alvise

Chiesa di Sant'Alvise

Rio degli Zecchini

To Ferrovia & Piazzale

26

Rio del Bateilo

Rio di San Girolamo

35

24

Rio della Sensa

2

To Marco Polo Airport (10km)

Rio di San Giobbe

Canale di Cannaregio

18

33

Rio della Crea

9

44

CANNAREGIO

Sacca della Misericordia

Ponte della Libertà

Parco Savorgnan

16

Rio dei Serví

43

Rio di Santa Caterina

San Marcuola

Stazione di Santa Lucia (Ferrovia)

Ponte dei Scalzi

Riva de Biasio

39

30

20

Stazione Merci

40

23

Rio di San Stae

Grand Canal

Piazzale Roma Parisi

Ponte di Calatrava

34

Rio Marin

17

SANTA CROCE

C Larga dei Bari

Rio di San Cassiano

SAN POLO

RIALTO

Giardini Papadopoli

Rio di San Zuane

Campo San Rocco

Rio di San Polo

Ponte di Rialto

Rio delle Burchielle

Fond del Gaffaro

Rio delle Sacchere

13

7

Santa Marta

Fond di Santa Maria Maggiore

Rio Nuovo

Ponte d Sbiacca

29

SANTA MARTA

Fond dell'Arzere

Rio delle Tentor

38

Rio delle Terese

Fond Foscarini

12

41

1

Rio di San Nicolò

Campo San Sebastian

DORSODURO

42

SAN MARCO

C Nave

11

27

Old Stazione Marittima

Rio di Sant'Trovaso

Rio di Ognissanti

36

See San Marco & San Polo Map (p178)

Sacca Fisola Vaporetto Stop

Canale di Fusina

Ponte Lungo

19

Rio della Fornace

8

Ponte dell' Umiltà

Sacca Fisola

Zattere Vaporetto Stop

SACCA FISOLA

Fond San Biagio

Palanca

Canale della Giudecca

Zitelle Vaporetto Stop

Fond della Convertite

C dei Nicolò

C dell'Olio

Rio della Palada

Redentore Vaporetto Stop

28

Zitelle

Campo della Rotonda

Rio di Sant'Eufemia

Fond di San Giacomo

C drio la Croce C Squero

Campazzo di Dentro

GIUDECCA

Rio della Croce

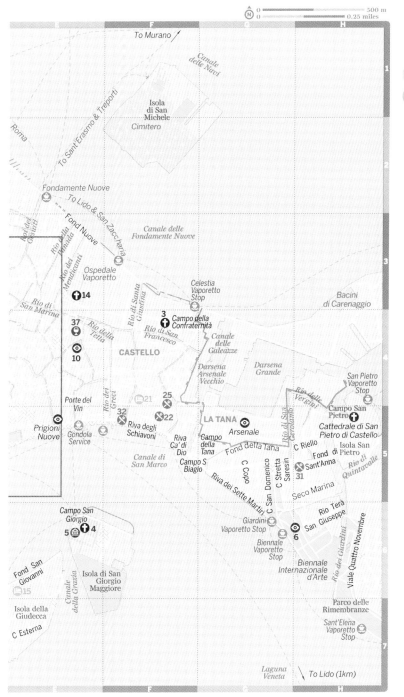

To Murano

Canale delle Navi

Isola di San Michele
Cimitero

Roma

To Sant'Erasmo & Treporti

To Lido & San Zaccaria

Fondamente Nuove

Fond Nuove

Canale delle Fondamente Nuove

Rio dei Gesuiti

Rio della Sensa

Rio dei Mendicanti

Ospedale Vaporetto

14

Rio di San Marina

37

10

Rio della Tetta

Rio di Santa Giustina

CASTELLO

Celestia Vaporetto Stop

3 Campo della Confraternità

Rio di San Francesco

Canale delle Galeazze

Darsena Arsenale Vecchio

Darsena Grande

Bacini di Carenaggio

San Pietro Vaporetto Stop

Rio delle Vergini

Porte del Vin

Rio dei Greci

21

32

25

22

Riva degli Schiavoni

LA TANA

Arsenale

Rio di San Gerolamo

Campo San Pietro

Cattedrale di San Pietro di Castello

Prigioni Nuove

Gondola Service

Riva Ca' di Dio

Riva degli Schiavoni

Riva Ca' di Dio

Campo della Tana

Fond della Tana

C Riello

Fond di Pietro

Isola San Pietro

Rio di Quintavalle

31 Sant'Anna

Canale di San Marco

Campo S Biagio

Riva dei Sette Martiri

C Copo

C San Domenico

C Stretta Saresin

Seco Marina

Campo San Giorgio

5 **4**

Giardini Vaporetto Stop

Biennale Vaporetto Stop

Rio Terà San Giuseppe

6

Biennale Internazionale d'Arte

Rio dei Giardini

Viale Quattro Novembre

Fond San Giovanni

15

Isola di San Giorgio Maggiore

Canale della Grazia

Isola della Giudecca

C Esterna

Parco delle Rimembranze

Sant'Elena Vaporetto Stop

Laguna Veneta

To Lido (1km)

Venice

wearing a coral good-luck charm (Room 31); Jacopo di Barbari's minutely detailed woodblock perspective view of Venice (Room 32); an entire room of bright-eyed, peach-cheeked Bellini saints (Room 36); and a wonderful anonymous 1784 portrait of champion rower Maria Boscola, five-time regatta winner (Room 47).

TORRE DELL'OROLOGIO Landmark

(Clock Tower; Map p178; ☏ 041 4273 0892; www.museiciviciveneziani.it; Piazza San Marco; adult/reduced €12/7, or Museum Pass; ☉tours in English 10am & 11am Mon-Wed, 2pm & 3pm Thu-Sat, in Italian noon & 4pm daily, in French 2pm & 3pm Mon-Wed, 10am & 11am Thu-Sun) Legend has it that the inventors of this 1497 gold-leafed timepiece (which tracks lunar phases) were assassinated so that no other city could boast a comparable engineering marvel. Moving barrels indicate minutes and hour on the clock face; 132-stroke chimes keep the time; Do Mori (Two Moors) bronze statues strike the hour on a bell atop the tower; and wooden statues of Three Kings and the Angel emerge to wild cheers on Epiphany and the Feast of the Ascension. Tours climb the steep, claustrophobia-inducing spiral staircase behind the clock to the terrace for giddy, close-up views of the Moors in action.

NEGOZIO OLIVETTI Notable Building

(Olivetti Store; Map p178; ☏ 041 522 83 87; www.fondoambiente.it; Piazza San Marco 101, Procuratie Vecchie; audiotours adult/reduced €5/3; ☉10am-7pm Apr-Oct, to 5pm Nov-Mar) Like a revolver pulled from a petticoat, starkly modern Negozio Olivetti was an outright provocation when it first appeared under the frilly arcades of Piazza San Marco in 1957. High-tech pioneer Olivetti commissioned Venetian architect Carlo Scarpa to transform a narrow, dim souvenir shop into a showcase for its sleek typewriters and 'computing machines' (several 1948–54 models are displayed). Visitors cross floors of Murano glass tile in appealing primary colours, scale a floating white marble stairway, pass satiny Venetian plaster walls, and stroll an indoor balcony sheathed in warm teak wood.

MUSEO FORTUNY Museum
(Map p178; [☎]041 4273 0892; www.museicivici veneziani.it; Campo San Beneto 3758; adult/reduced €9/6 or Museum Pass; [☉]10am-6pm Wed-Mon) Find design inspiration at the home studio of Venetian-Spanish designer Mariano Fortuny y Madrazo, whose shockingly uncorseted Delphi goddess frocks for Isadora Duncan set global Bohemian-chic standards. The salons showcase original Fortuny dresses alongside more recent avant-garde fashion, such as Roberta di Camerino's trompe l'oeil maxidresses. Large-scale art installations in the attic warehouse are often overshadowed by the striking architecture, but the downstairs gallery hosts fascinating rotating shows on Venetian themes, such as Paolo Ventu-

ri's moving photos of hand-built dioramas representing the Venice Ghetto c 1942.

Dorsoduro
PEGGY GUGGENHEIM COLLECTION Art Gallery
(Map p178; [☎]041 240 54 11; www.guggenheim -venice.it; Palazzo Venier dei Leoni 704; adult/ reduced €12/7; [☉]10am-6pm Wed-Mon) After tragically losing her father on the *Titanic*, heiress Peggy Guggenheim befriended Dadaists, dodged Nazis and amassed avant-garde works by 200 modern artists at her palatial home on the Grand Canal. Peggy collected according to her own convictions rather than for prestige or style, so her collection includes folk art and lesser-known artists alongside Kandinsky, Picasso, Man Ray, Calder, Joseph Cornell and Dali. Wander past bronzes by Moore, Giacometti and Brancusci, Yoko Ono's *Wish Tree* and a shiny black granite lump by Anish Kapoor in the sculpture garden, where the city of Venice granted Peggy honorary dispensation to be buried alongside her pet dogs in 1979.

Making the Most of Your Euro

These passes can help you save admission costs on Venetian sights.

◦ **Museum Pass** (Musei Civici Pass; www.museicivicivenezizani.it; adult/child €18/12) Valid for single entry to 10 civic museums for six months, or just the five museums around Piazza San Marco (adult/child €14/8). Purchase online or at participating museums, including Palazzo Ducale, Museo Correr, Museo Fortuny and Ca' Rezzonico.

◦ **Chorus Pass** (www.chorusvenezia.org; adult/reduced €10/7; [☉]visits 10am-5pm Mon-Fri) Offers single entry to 16 Venice churches; sold at participating churches.

◦ **Venice Card** ([☎]041 2424; www.hellovenezia.com; adult/reduced €40/30; [☉]call centre 8am-7.30pm) Combines the Museum Pass and Chorus Pass and includes reduced entry to the Biennale, two public bathroom entries and discounts on concerts, temporary exhibits and parking. Purchase at tourist offices and at HelloVenezia booths at *vaporetto* stops.

◦ **Rolling Venice** (ages 14-29 €4) Entitles young visitors to discounted access to monuments and cultural events, plus eligibility for a 72-hour public transport pass for just €18 rather than the regular price of €33. Identification is required for purchase at tourism offices or HelloVenezia booths.

Grand Canal

The 3.5km route of vaporetto (passenger ferry) No 1, which passes some 50 palazzi (mansions), six churches and scene-stealing backdrops featured in four James Bond films, is public transport at its most glamorous.

The Grand Canal starts with controversy: **Ponte di Calatrava** ❶ a luminous glass-and-steel bridge that cost triple the original €4 million estimate. Ahead are castle-like **Fondaco dei Turchi** ❷, the historic Turkish trading-house; Renaissance **Palazzo Vendramin** ❸, housing the city's casino; and double-arcaded **Ca' Pesaro** ❹. Don't miss **Ca' d'Oro** ❺, a 1430 filigree Gothic marvel.

Points of Venetian pride include the **Pescaria** ❻, built in 1907 on the site where fishmongers have been slinging lagoon crab for 600 years, and neighbouring **Rialto Market** ❼ stalls, overflowing with island-grown produce. Cost overruns for 1592 **Ponte di Rialto** ❽ rival Calatrava's, but its marble splendour stands the test of time.

The next two canal bends could cause architectural whiplash, with Sanmicheli-designed Renaissance **Palazzo Grimani** ❾ and Mauro Codussi's **Palazzo Corner-Spinelli** ❿ followed by Giorgio Masari-designed **Palazzo Grassi** ⓫ and Baldassare Longhena's baroque jewel box, **Ca' Rezzonico** ⓬.

Wooden **Ponte dell'Accademia** ⓭, was built in 1930 as a temporary bridge, but the beloved landmark was recently reinforced. Stone lions flank **Peggy Guggenheim Collection** ⓮, where the American heiress collected ideas, lovers and art. You can't miss the dramatic dome of Longhena's **Chiesa di Santa Maria della Salute** ⓯, or **Punta della Dogana** ⓰, Venice's triangular customs warehouse reinvented as a contemporary art showcase. The Grand Canal's grand finale is pink Gothic **Palazzo Ducale** ⓱ and its adjoining **Ponte dei Sospiri** ⓲, currently draped in advertising.

Palazzo Grassi
French magnate François Pinault scandalised Paris when he relocated his contemporary art collection here, with galleries designed by Gae Aulenti and Tadao Ando.

Ca' Rezzonico
See how Venice lived in baroque splendour at this 18th-century art museum with Tiepolo ceilings, silk-swagged boudoirs and even an in-house pharmacy.

Ponte dell'Accademia

Peggy Guggenheim Collection

Chiesa di Santa Maria delle Salute

Punta della Dogana
Minimalist architect Tadao Ando creatively repurposed abandoned warehouses as galleries, which now host contemporary art installations from François Pinault's collection.

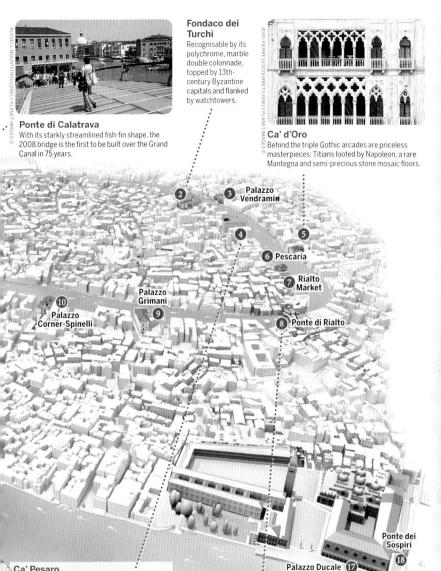

Fondaco dei Turchi
Recognisable by its polychrome, marble double colonnade, topped by 13th-century Byzantine capitals and flanked by watchtowers.

Ponte di Calatrava
With its starkly streamlined fish-fin shape, the 2008 bridge is the first to be built over the Grand Canal in 75 years.

Ca' d'Oro
Behind the triple Gothic arcades are priceless masterpieces: Titians looted by Napoleon, a rare Mantegna and semi-precious stone mosaic floors.

Palazzo Vendramin

Pescaria

Rialto Market

Palazzo Grimani

Palazzo Corner-Spinelli

Ponte di Rialto

Ponte dei Sospiri

Palazzo Ducale

Ca' Pesaro
Originally designed by Baldassare Longhena, this palazzo was bequeathed to the city in 1898 to house the Galleria d'Arte Moderna and Museo d'Arte Orientale.

Ponte di Rialto
Antonio da Ponte beat out Palladio for the commission of this bridge, but construction costs spiralled to 250,000 Venetian ducats – about €19 million today.

San Marco & San Polo

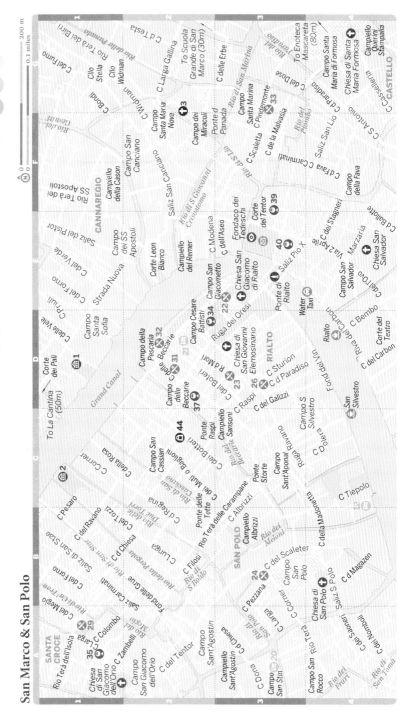

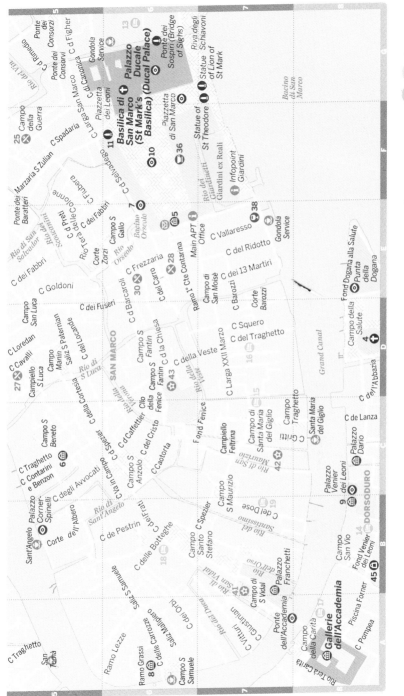

San Marco & San Polo

CA' REZZONICO   Museum
(Museum of the 18th Century; Map p172;
☏ 041 241 01 00; www.museicivicivenezieni.
it; Fondamenta Rezzonico 3136; adult/reduced
€8/5.50, or Museum Pass; ⊙10am-6pm
Wed-Mon Apr-Oct, to 5pm Wed-Mon Nov-Mar)
Baldassare Longhena's luminous baroque
palace on the Grand Canal celebrates
18th-century decadence in lavish music
salons, sumptuous boudoirs and even an
attic pharmacy with medicinal scorpions. Giambattista Tieopolo's Throne
Room ceiling is a masterpiece of elegant
social climbing, showing gorgeous Merit
ascending to the Temple of Glory clutch-
ing the Golden Book of Venetian nobles'
names – including Tiepolo's patrons, the
Rezzonico family.

Collection highlights include the
Pietro Longhi Salon of socialite satires,
Rosalba Carriera's wry society portraits,
Giandomenico Tiepolo's swinging court
jesters in reassembled Zianigo Villa
bedroom frescoes, and Emma Ciardi's
moody Venice views on the top floor. Last
entry is an hour before closing; check the
schedule downstairs for concerts in the
trompe l'oeil frescoed ballroom.

SAN SEBASTIANO   Church
**(Map p172; www.chorusvenezia.org; Campo San
Sebastiano 1687; admission €3, or Chorus Pass;
⊙10am-5pm Mon-Sat)** Over three decades,
the modest parish church of San Sebastiano was covered by Paolo Veronese with
floor-to-ceiling masterpieces. Veronese's
horses rear over the frames of the coffered ceiling; the organ doors are covered

© JEAN-PIERRE LESCOURRET/CORBIS

Don't Miss **Gallerie dell'Accademia**

Don't be fooled by the serene Palladian exterior of this former convent: Gallerie dell'Accademia contains more murderous intrigue and forbidden romance than the most outrageous Venetian parties. For sheer, shimmering gore, there's no topping Carpaccio's *Crucifixion and Glorification of the Ten Thousand Martyrs of Mount Ararat* (room two). In rooms three to five, Andrea Mantegna's 1466 haughtily handsome *St George* and Giovanni Bellini's *Madonna and Child* amid neon-red cherubs highlight Venice's twin artistic tendencies: high drama and vivid colour.

Visits advance rapidly through the Renaissance, including Tintoretto's *Creation of the Animals,* a fantastical bestiary that suggests that God put forth his best efforts inventing Venetian seafood (no arguments here). Restoration illuminates possibly Titian's last work: a 1576 *Pietà*, with paint Titian applied with bare hands.

Artistic triumph over censorship dominates room 10. Paolo Veronese's controversial *Feast in the House of Levi* was originally called *Last Supper* until church Inquisition leaders condemned Veronese for showing dogs, drunkards, dwarfs, even Reformation-minded Germans cavorting amid the apostles. Veronese would only change the title, and Venice stood by this act of artistic defiance.

Baroque portrait galleries can scarcely contain the larger-than-life Venetian personalities: Lorenzo Lotto's 1525 soul-searching *Portrait of a Young Scholar;* Rosalba Carriera's brutally honest self-portrait c 1730; Pietro Longhi's stern chaperone in *The Dance Lesson*; and Giambattista Piazzetta's saucy socialite in his 1740 *Fortune-Teller.*

The newly restored **Sala dell'Albergo** is fronted by Antonio Vivarini's giant 1446 triptych and Titian's 1534–9 *Presentation of the Virgin,* with the young Madonna trudging up an intimidating staircase as onlookers point to her example.

THINGS YOU NEED TO KNOW

Map p178; 041 520 03 45; www.gallerieaccademia.org; Campo della Carità 1050; adult/reduced €6.50/3.25; 8.15am-2pm Mon, to 7.15pm Tue-Sun, last entry 1hr before closing

GLENN BEANLAND/LONELY PLANET IMAGES ©

Don't Miss Ducal Palace

Underneath that lacy pink Gothic exterior, Venice's Ducal Palace (Palazzo Ducale) flexes serious muscle. Enter the courtyard, where Sansovino's brawny statues of Apollo and Neptune flank Antonio Rizzo's recently restored **Scala dei Giganti** (Giants' Staircase). Climb the **Scala dei Censori** (Stairs of the Censors) to the **Doges' Apartments**, where Venice's doge (duke) lived, with a short commute to work up a secret staircase capped with Titian's *St Christopher*. **Sala del Scudo** (Shield Room) is covered with 1483–1762 **world maps** that reveal the extents of Venetian power.

Head up Sansovino's 24-karat gilt stuccowork **Scala d'Oro** (Golden Staircase), and enter **Sala delle Quattro Porte** (Hall of the Four Doors), covered with gorgeous propaganda: a Palladio-designed ceiling fresco by Tintoretto shows Justice presenting sword and scales to Doge Girolamo Priuli, near Titian's 1576 *Doge Antonio Grimani Kneeling before Faith*.

Delegations waited in the **Anticollegio** (College Antechamber) under Veronese's 1577 *Venice Distributing Honors* ceiling, faced with a vivid reminder of diplomatic behaviour to avoid: Veronese's *Rape of Europe*. Few were granted audience in the Palladio-designed **Collegio** (Council Room), where Veronese's 1578–82 *Virtues of the Republic* ceiling shows Venice as a bewitching blonde.

Politics wasn't pretty: under Veronese's *St Mark in Glory* ceiling in **Sala della Bussola** (Compass Room; Room 21) is a slot for anonymous accusations of treason. Note the black space in the frieze depicting 76 Venetian doges in the **Sala del Maggior Consiglio** (Grand Council Hall). From here, follow the footsteps of condemned prisoners across the **Bridge of Sighs** into Venice's 16th-century **Priggione Nove** (New Prisons).

THINGS YOU NEED TO KNOW

Map p178; 041 271 59 11; www.museiciviveneziani.it; Piazzetta San Marco 52; adult/reduced incl Museo Correr €14/8, or Museum Pass, Itinerari Segreti tour adult/reduced €18/12; 8.30am-7pm Apr-Oct, to 5.30pm Nov-Mar, Itinerari Segreti English tours 9.55am, 10.45am & 11.35am) with vivid Veronese masterworks; and in Veronese's *Martyrdom of Saint Sebastian* near the altar, the bound saint defiantly stares down his tormentors amid a Venetian crowd of socialites, turbaned traders and Veronese's signature frisky spaniel.

CHIESA DI SANTA MARIA DELLA SALUTE
Church

(Map p178; www.seminariovenezia.it, in Italian; Campo della Salute 1b; ⌚9am-noon & 3-5.30pm) The equivalent of a monumental sigh of relief, this church was built in 1631 by survivors of Venice's 1630 plague as thanks for their salvation. Baldassare Longhena's unusual octagonal church is an inspired design that architectural scholars have compared to Graeco-Roman temples and Jewish Kabbala diagrams, and it remains the site of Festa Della Madonna Della Salute (Venetians' annual pilgrimage to pray for health). Extensive interior restorations may limit access to Tintoretto's surprisingly upbeat *The Wedding Feast of Cana* and 12 key works by Titian in the **sacristy** (admission €2), including a vivid self-portrait in the guise of St Matthew and his earliest known work, *Saint Mark on the Throne* from 1510.

SCUOLA GRANDE DEI CARMINI
Notable Building

(Map p172; ☎041 528 94 20; www.scuola grandecarmini.it; Campo Santa Margherita 2617; adult/reduced €5/4; ⌚11am-5pm) If a time machine could return you to Venice 300 years ago, you could stay in this refuge run by Carmelite nuns and lavishly appointed by Giambattista Tiepolo and Baldessare Longhena. Longhena designed the stucco-frosted and gold-leafed stairway to heaven, which is glimpsed upstairs in Tiepolo's nine-panel ceiling of a resplendent *Virgin in Glory*. Ask about concerts by **Musica in Maschera** (Musical Masquerade; www.musicainmaschera.it), performed here in 1700s costume.

San Polo & Santa Croce

BASILICA DI SANTA MARIA GLORIOSA DEI FRARI
Church

(Map p172; www.chorusvenezia.org; Campo dei Frari 3004; admission €3 or Chorus Pass; ⌚9am-6pm Mon-Sat, 1-6pm Sun) This soaring Italian-brick Gothic church features marquetry choir stalls, Canova's pyramid mausoleum, Bellini's achingly sweet *Madonna with Child* triptych in the sacristy, and Longhena's creepy Doge Pesaro funereal monument hoisted by burly slaves bursting from ragged clothes like Invisible Hulks – yet visitors are inevitably drawn to the small altarpiece. This is Titian's 1518 *Ascension,* in which a radiant Madonna in a Titian-red cloak reaches heavenward, steps onto a cloud and escapes this mortal coil.

St Mark's Basilica (p185).

If You Like…
Contemporary Art

Miss the Venice Biennale? Never fear: there's more cutting-edge, controversial art inside Venice's newest contemporary art showcases, housed in creatively repurposed historic buildings.

1 PUNTA DELLA DOGANA
(Map p178; ☎199 13 91 39; www.palazzograssi. it; admission adult/reduced €15/10, combined ticket with Palazzo Grassi €20/15; ⏰10am-7pm Wed-Mon) **Fortuna**, the weather vane atop Punta della Dogana, swung Venice's way in 2009, when minimalist architect Tadao Ando converted Venice's abandoned **customs warehouse** into a showcase for billionaire François Pinault's collection of oversized, outrageous artworks.

2 PALAZZO GRASSI
(Map p178; ☎044 535 70 99; www. palazzograssi.it; Campo San Samuele 3231; admission adult/reduced €15/10, combined ticket with Punta della Dogana €20/15; ⏰10am-7pm Wed-Mon) Rounding a Grand Canal bend, gondola riders gasp with the shock of the new: installations by contemporary shock-artists like Jeff Koons and Richard Prince, docked at Giorgio Masari's 1749 neoclassical palace. In galleries designed by postmodernist Gae Aulenti and Tadao Ando, featured works collected by François Pinault range from Takashi Murakami's superflat daisies to Barbara Kruger's non-commercial slogans.

3 MAGAZZINI DEL SALE
(Map p172; www.fondazionevedova.org; Zattere 266; donation suggested; ⏰during shows 10.30am-6pm Wed-Mon) A recent retrofit designed by Pritzker Prize–winning architect Renzo Piano transformed Venice's historic **salt warehouses**. Alongside a public art gallery is **Fondazione Vedova** (www.fondazionevedova.org), dedicated to pioneering Venetian abstract painter Emilio Vedova. Shows here are literally moving: powered by renewable energy sources, 10 robotic arms designed by Vedova and Piano rotate artworks in and out of storage slots.

SCUOLA GRANDE DI SAN ROCCO   Museum
(Map p172; ☎041 523 48 64; www.scuola grandesanrocco.it; Campo San Rocco 3052; adult/reduced €7/5; ⏰9.30am-5.30pm) Everyone wanted the commission to paint this building dedicated to the patron saint of the plague-stricken, so Tintoretto cheated: instead of producing sketches like rival Veronese, he gifted a splendid ceiling panel of patron St Roch, knowing it couldn't be refused or matched by other artists. Old Testament scenes Tintoretto painted from 1575 to 1587 for the Sala Grande Superiore ceiling upstairs read like a modern graphic novel: you can almost hear the *swoop!* overhead as an angel dives down to feed ailing Elijah. In the assembly hall, Tintoretto tells Mary's life story, starting on the left wall with *Annunciation* and ending with dark and cataclysmic *Ascension* opposite. Gregorian chant concerts are occasionally performed here (ask at the counter), and you can practically hear their echoes in Tintoretto's haunting paintings.

CA' PESARO   Art Gallery
(Map p178; ☎041 72 11 27; www.museici vicineziani.it; Fondamenta de Ca' Pesaro 2070; adult/reduced €8/5, or Museum Pass; ⏰10am-6pm Tue-Sun Apr-Oct, to 5pm Nov-Mar) Three storeys of Venetian modern art history begin with flag-waving early Biennales, showcasing Venetian landscapes and Venetian socialites by Venetian painters (notably Giacomo Favretto and Guglielmo Ciardi). The savvy Biennale organisers soon diversified, showcasing Gustav Klimt's 1909 *Judith II (Salome)* and Marc Chagall's *Rabbi of Vitebsk* (1914–22). Climb the creaky attic stairs past a phalanx of samurai warriors, girded for battle: this marks the beginning of an epic 1887–89 souvenir-shopping spree across Asia that Prince Enrico di Borbone preserved for posterity. Edo-era netsukes, screens and a lacquerware palanquin are standouts in his collection of 30,000 *objets d'art*.

WIBOWO RUSLI/LONELY PLANET IMAGES ©

Don't Miss St Mark's Basilica

Creating Venice's magnificent St Mark's Basilica (Basilica di San Marco) took nearly 800 years of painstaking labor and one saintly barrel of lard. Legend holds that in AD 828, wily Venetian merchants smuggled St Mark's corpse out of Egypt in a barrel of pork fat to avoid inspection by Muslim customs authorities. So proud was Venice of its master-thief merchants that their story was captured in **lunette mosaics** on the front of St Mark's, over the left-most portal (c1270) and second portal from the right (c 1660).

Inside the Basilica are **8500 sq m of mosaics**, many made with 24-karat gold to represent divine light. The atrium's **Dome of Genesis** depicts the separation of sky and water, while **Last Judgment** mosaics cover the atrium vault and the **Apocalypse** looms large in vault mosaics over the gallery. In the central 13th-century **Cupola of the Ascension**, angels swirl overhead while dreamy-eyed St Mark rests on the pendentive. St Mark's life story unfolds around the **Dome of the Prophets**, over the main altar.

Behind the main altar containing **St Mark's sarcophagus** is the **Pala d'Oro**, studded with 2000 gemstones and bright-eyed **biblical figures** in vibrant cloisonnè. Crusades loot filling the **Tesoro** includes St Roch's femur and the arm St George used to slay the dragon.

Upstairs in the **Museo** are **gilt bronze horses** looted from Constantinople and nicked by Napoleon until repossessed by Venice.

THINGS YOU NEED TO KNOW

Map p178; ☏041 241 38 17; www.basilicasanmarco.it, advance booking at www.venetoinside.com; Piazza San Marco; basilica entry free; ◷9.45am-5pm Mon-Sat, 2-4pm Sun & holidays; modest dress required and mandatory free baggage storage); **Pala d'Oro** (admission €2; ◷9.45am-4pm Mon-Sat & 2-4pm Sun); **Tesoro** (Treasury; admission €3; ◷9.45am-4pm Mon-Sat, 2-4pm Sun); **Museo** (admission adult €4; ◷9.45am-4pm Mon-Sat, 2-4pm Sun)

Cannaregio

CHIESA DELLA MADONNA DELL'ORTO
Cathedral

(Map p172; Campo della Madonna dell'Orto 3520; admission €3 or Chorus Pass; ☺10am-5pm Mon-Sat) This elegant 1365 brick Gothic cathedral dedicated to the patron saint of travellers remains one of Venice's best-kept secrets. This was the parish church of Venetian Renaissance master Tintoretto, who is buried here in the corner chapel and saved two of his finest works for the apse: *Presentation of the Virgin in the Temple,* with throngs of starstruck angels and mortals vying for a glimpse of Mary, and his 1546 *Last Judgment,* where lost souls attempt to hold back a teal tidal wave while an angel rescues one last person from the ultimate *acqua alta.*

CHIESA DI SANTA MARIA DEI MIRACOLI
Church

(Map p178; Campo dei Miracoli 6074; admission €3 or Chorus Pass; ☺10am-5pm Mon-Sat) A minor *miracolo* (miracle) of early Renaissance architecture, Pietro Lombardo's little marble chapel, **Chiesa di Santa Maria dei Miracoli**, was ahead of its time, dropping Gothic grandiosity for human-scale classical architecture. By pooling resources and scavenging multicoloured marble from San Marco slag heaps, the neighbourhood commissioned this church to house Niccolò di Pietro's Madonna icon when it miraculously started weeping in c 1480. Completing this monument to community spirit, Pier Maria Pennacchi filled 50 ceiling panels with portraits of prophets dressed as Venetians.

MUSEO EBRAICO
Museum

(Map p172; ☏041 71 53 59; www.museoebraico.it; Campo del Ghetto Nuovo 2902b; adult/reduced €3/2, tours incl admission €8.50/7; ☺10am-7pm Sun-Fri except Jewish holidays Jun-Sep, to 6pm Oct-May) At the heart of the Ghetto, this museum explores the history of Venice's Jewish community and its pivotal contributions to the worlds of science, literature, fashion, religion, philosophy and commerce. Hour-long English-language tours leave from the museum four times daily starting at 10.30am, and lead inside three of the Ghetto's seven tiny synagogues.

Chiesa di San Rocco and Scuola Grande di San Rocco (p184)

DISCOVER VENICE, VENETO & BOLOGNA VENICE

The Original Ghetto

In medieval times, this Cannaregio outpost housed a *getto* (foundry). But it was as the designated Jewish quarter from the 16th to 18th centuries that this area gave the word a whole new meaning. In accordance with the Venetian Republic's 1516 decree, Jewish lenders, doctors and clothing merchants were allowed to attend to Venice's commercial interests by day, while at night and on Christian holidays most were restricted to the gated island of Ghetto Nuovo. Unlike most European cities at the time, pragmatic Venice granted Jewish doctors dispensation for consultations. In fact, Venice's Jewish and Muslim physicians are credited with helping establish the quarantine on incoming ships that spared Venice the worst ravages of the plague.

When Jewish merchants fled the Spanish Inquisition for Venice in 1541, there was no place to go in the Ghetto but up. Around Campo del Ghetto Nuovo, upper storeys housed new arrivals, synagogues and publishing houses. Despite a 10-year censorship order issued by the church in Rome in 1553, Jewish Venetian publishers contributed hundreds of titles popularising new Renaissance ideas on religion, humanist philosophy and medicine. By the 17th century, Ghetto literary salons organised by philosopher Sara Copio Sullam, Rabbi Leon da Modena and others brought leading thinkers of all faiths to the Ghetto.

After Napoleon lifted restrictions in 1797, some 1626 Ghetto residents gained standing as Venetian citizens. However, Mussolini's 1938 race laws were throwbacks to the 16th century, and in 1943 most Jewish Venetians were rounded up and sent to concentration camps; only 37 returned. Today few of Venice's 400-strong Jewish community actually live in the Ghetto, but their children come to Campo del Ghetto Nuovo to play, surrounded by the Ghetto's living legacy of bookshops, art galleries and religious institutions.

CA' D'ORO   Museum

(House of Gold; Map p178; ☏ 041 520 03 45; www.cadoro.org; Calle di Ca' d'Oro 3932; adult/reduced €6/3; ☾ 8.15am-2pm Mon, to 7.15pm Tue-Sun) Even without the original gold-leaf details that gave the palace its name, this 15th-century Gothic palace is rivalled only by its own shimmering reflection in the Grand Canal. The lacy Gothic arcade framing the two-tier balcony makes for Venice's most irresistible photo-ops, and the intricate semi-precious stone mosaics paving the water door entry make a grander entrance than any red carpet. Collection highlights include Andrea Mantegna's teeth-bearing, arrow-riddled *Saint Sebastian*, Pietro Lombardo's tender *Madonna and Child* in glistening Carrara marble, and Titian fresco fragments rescued after Venice's 1967 flood.

Castello

ZANIPOLO   Church

(Chiesa dei SS Giovanni e Paolo; Map p172; ☏ 041 523 59 13; Campo SS Giovanni e Paolo; admission €2.50; ☾ 9am-6pm Mon-Sat, noon-6pm Sun) Built by Dominicans to rival the Franciscans' I Frari, this 14th-century church lacks I Frari's soaring grace but makes up the difference with the sheer scale and variety of its masterpieces. In the Cappella del Rosario, Paolo Veronese's ceiling depicts a rosy Virgin ascending a staggering staircase. The chapel dome on the southwest end of the nave boasts Giambattista Lorenzetti's *Jesus the Navigator,* with Jesus scaning the heavens like a Venetian sea captain. The church is also a kind of pantheon, with 25 doges' tombs by such notable sculptors as Nicolo Pisano and Tullio Lombardo,

187

and a 15th-century Murano stained-glass window in the south transept that has been gorgeously restored.

PALAZZO GRIMANI — Museum

(Map p172; ☏ 041 520 03 45; www.palazzo grimani.org; Ramo Grimani 4858; adult/student & senior €9/7; ⏰9am-7pm) Just south of Campo Santa Maria Formosa, this light-filled palazzo has finally reopened to the public after nearly three decades. Built in the 1500s by Doge Antonio Grimani to house his remarkable collection of Graeco-Roman antiquities (most of which are now in Museo Correr), the lovingly restored palazzo houses high-calibre temporary exhibitions.

CHIESA DI SAN FRANCESCO DELLA VIGNA — Church

(Map p172; ☏ 041 520 61 02; Campo San Francesco della Vigna 2786; ⏰9.30am-12.30pm & 3-6pm Mon-Sat, 3-6pm Sun) Designed and built by Jacopo Sansovino with a facade by Palladio, this is one of Venice's most underrated attractions. Madonna positively glows in Bellini's 1507 *Madonna and Saints* in the Capella Santa off the cloisters; swimming angels and strutting birds steal the scene in Antonio da Negroponte's c 1460–70 *Virgin Enthroned;* and Pietro Lombardo's lifelike lions seem ready to pounce right out of the 15th-century marble reliefs in the Capella Giustiniani, to the left of the altar.

GIARDINI PUBBLICI — Park

(Map p172) Begun under Napoleon as the city's first green space, a large portion of these leafy public gardens serve as the main home of the Biennale, with curators and curiosity-seekers swarming the pavilions, from Carlo Scarpa's daring 1954 raw-concrete-and-glass Venezuelan Pavilion to Peter Cox's awkward 1988 Australian Pavilion, which is frequently mistaken for a shed. Part of the gardens is open to the public all year round; sometimes during off years you can wander among the pavilions and admire the facades.

Left: Ponte di Rialto, Grand Canal (p176);
Below: Carnevale (p42)

Isola di San Giorgio Maggiore

CHIESA DI SAN GIORGIO MAGGIORE
Church

(Map p172; ☎ 041 522 78 27; Isola di San Giorgio Maggiore; ⏱9.30am-12.30pm & 2.30-6.30pm Mon-Sat May-Sep, 9.30am-12.30pm & 2.30-4.30pm Oct-Apr) Solar eclipses are only marginally more dazzling than Palladio's white Istrian marble facade. Two of Tintoretto's masterworks flank the altar, and a lift whisks visitors up the 60m-high **bell tower** (€3) for stirring Ventian panoramas – it is a great alternative to long lines at San Marco's campanile.

Behind the church, a defunct naval academy has been converted into a shipshape gallery by the **Fondazione Giorgio Cini** (Map p172; ☎ 041 220 12 15; www.cini.it; Isola di San Giorgio Maggiore; adult/reduced €12/10; ⏱guided tours in English & French 11am, 1pm, 3pm, 5pm Sat & Sun, in Italian 10am, noon, 2pm & 4pm Sat & Sun). After escaping the Dachau internment camp with his son Giorgio,

Vittorio Cini returned to Venice on a mission to save San Giorgio Maggiore, which was a ramshackle mess in 1949. Cini's foundation restored the island into a cultural centre. In addition to its permanent collection of Old Masters and modern art, the gallery hosts important contemporary works, from Peter Greenaway to Anish Kapoor.

The Lido

(off Map p172) Only 15 minutes by *vaporetti* 1, 51, 52, 61, 62, 82 and N from San Marco, this barrier island has brought glamour to beach-going since the late 19th century, when Venetians began to flee muggy Venetian summers for the Lido's breezy, Liberty-style villas. **Lido beaches** (deposit/chair/hut/umbrella & chair/€5/6/11/17; ⏱9.30am-7pm May-Sep) remain a major draw. But to avoid the crowds, rent a bicycle by the *vaporetto* stop at **Lido on Bike** (☎ 041 526 80 19;

189

If You Like...
Island Getaways

Serene San Giorgio Maggiore and the beachy Lido make great escapes – but don't stop there. Hop the *vaporetto* (ferry) for chandelier shopping, extreme colour schemes and golden treasure on a near-deserted island.

1 MURANO
Venetians have created glass marvels since the 10th century, but due to fire hazards, glass-blowing was moved to Murano (off Map p172). Trade secrets were so jealously guarded that any glass-worker who left the city was accused of treason and subject to assassination. Today, a 10-minute ride on the 42 *vaporetto* lets you watch glass artisans at work in Murano's studio showrooms, and discover 1500 years of top-secret techniques at Murano's **Museum of Glass** (Museo del Vetro; ☑041 73 95 86; www.museiciviciveneziani.it; Fondamenta Giustinian 8; adult/reduced €8/5.50 or Museum Pass; ☉10am-6pm Thu-Tue Apr-Oct, to 5pm Nov-Mar).

2 BURANO
Ready for a shock of colour? Pink and blue houses admire their own reflections in the canals of Burano (off Map p172), a colourful island fishing village 50 minutes from Venice's Fondamenta Nuove via Laguna Nord (LN) ferry. Book ahead for wildly creative, lagoon-fresh seafood at **Venissa** (☑041 527 22 81; www.venissa.it; Fondamenta Santa Caterina 3, Mazzorbo/Burano;meals from €60; ☉noon-3pm & 7-9.30pm Tue-Sun).

3 TORCELLO
In the wilderness of Torcello (off Map p172), a three-minute T-line ferry-hop from Burano, sheep outnumber humans. It's hard to believe this was a Byzantine metropolis of 20,000 – until you see the golden mosaic Madonna inside medieval **Santa Maria Assunta Cathedral** (Piazza Torcello; admission & audioguide cathedral €6, incl museum €8; ☉10.30am-6pm Mar-Oct, 10am-5pm Nov-Feb).

The biggest event on the Lido social calendar is September's Venice International Film Festival, when starlets and socialites blind paparazzi with Italian couture. Major events are held at the 1930s **Palazzo del Cinema**, which looks like a Fascist airport without a red carpet.

 ## Tours

April to October, APT tourist offices (see p201) offer guided tours ranging from the classic gondola circuit (€40 per person) to a penetrating look at Basilica di San Marco (€18 per person).

LAGUNA ECO ADVENTURES Boat
(☑329 722 62 89; www.lagunaeco adventures.com; 2½-8hr trips per person €40-150) Explore the far reaches of the lagoon by day or hidden Venetian canals by night in a traditional *sampi-erota,* a narrow twin-sailed boat. Reserve ahead and note that trips are subject to weather conditions.

ROW VENICE Boat
(☑345 241 52 66; www.rowvenice.com; 2hr lessons from €40) The next best thing to walking on water: rowing a *sandolo* (Venetian boat) standing up like gondolieri do with Australian-Venetian rowing coach Jane Caporal.

TERRA E ACQUA Boat
(☑347 420 50 04; www.terraeacqua.com; day trips per person incl lunch from €70) Spot rare lagoon wildlife, admire architectural gems of Burano and Torcello, and moor for a tasty fish-stew lunch, all via *bragosso* (Venetian barge).

Sleeping

Many Venetians open their historical homes as B&Bs, and hundreds are listed at **APT tourist board** (www.turismovenezia.it), **Lonely Planet** (www.lonelyplanet.com), **A Guest in Venice** (www.unospitedivenezia.it) and **Venice Hoteliers Association** (www.veneziasi.it).

www.lidoonbike.it; Gran Viale 21b; bikes per 90min/day €5/9; ☉9am-7pm Apr-Sep) and head south to **Alberoni** and other pristine, windswept beaches.

Piazza San Marco & Around

NOVECENTO Boutique Hotel €€
(Map p178; ☎ 041 241 37 65; www.novecento.
biz; Calle del Dose 2683/84; d €130-260; ❊ 🛜)
World travellers put down roots in nine
bohemian-chic rooms with Turkish kilim
pillows, Fortuny draperies and 19th-
century scallop-shell carved bedsteads.
Linger over breakfast in the garden under
an Indian sun parasol, meet the artists at
hotel-organised art exhibitions, go for a
massage at sister property Hotel Flora or
mingle around the honesty bar.

GIO' & GIO' B&B €€
(Map p178; ☎ 347 366 50 16; www.giogiovenice.
com; Calle delle Ostreghe 2439; d €90-150; ❊ 🛜)
Restrained baroque sounds like an oxy-
moron, but here you have it: polished wood
floors, pearl-grey walls, bronze silk curtains,
burl-wood dressers and spotlit art.

HOTEL FLORA Hotel €€€
(Map p178; ☎ 041 520 58 44; www.hotelflora.it;
Calle Bergamaschi 2283a; d €150-290; ❊ 🛜 👪)
Down a lane from glitzy Calle Larga XXII
Marzo, this ivy-covered garden retreat
quietly outclasses its brash top-end neighbours with its plush rooms, delightful
tearoom and gym offering shiatsu massage. Guestrooms feature antique carved
beds piled with soft mattresses and
fluffy duvets; ask for opulent gilded
No 3 or No 32, which opens onto
the garden.

**LOCANDA ART
DECO** B&B €€
(Map p178; ☎ 041 277 05
58; www.locandaartdeco.
com; Calle delle Botteghe
2966; d incl breakfast
€80-170; ❊) Rakishly
handsome, cream-
coloured guestrooms
have parquet floors
and comfy beds in
custom wrought-iron
bedsteads. Helpful
hotel staff arrange
in-room massages

Venice Biennale & Venice International Film Festival

Venice's signature cultural event,
the **Biennale** (www.labiennale.org),
is something of a misnomer. The
city-run Biennale organises cultural
events every year, with avant-garde
dance, theatre, cinema and music
programs throughout the city. In
odd years the Art Biennale runs
from June to October in Giardini
Pubblici pavilions, while in even
years the Architecture Biennale
runs from September to November
in the Arsenale. The Biennale also
organises the annual **Venice Film
Festival** (www.labiennale.org/en/cinema).
The world's oldest film festival
remains the most glamorous, with
Italian-desigener-clad stars studding
the red carpet on the Lido.

Burano (p190)
EMILY RIDDELL/LONELY PLANET IMAGES ©

Detour:
The Dolomites

For skiing, Unesco–protected mountain biking and wildflower hikes, head to Italy's alpine mountains: the **Dolomites** (www.infodolomiti.it), three hours from Venice by train or car.

Renaissance-era mountain hamlet **Belluno** (pop 36,600/390m) is backed by **Parco Nazionale delle Dolomiti Bellunesi** (www.dolomitipark.it), a Unesco World Heritage site. From June to September, rare flora thrive along its **Alte Vie delle Dolomiti** (high-altitude walking trails). After your walk, don't miss dinner at **Al Borgo** (☎ 0437 92 67 55; www.alborgo.to; Via Anconetta 8; meals €35; ☺ lunch Mon, lunch & dinner Wed-Sun), an 18th-century villa 3km south of Belluno serving homemade salami, roast lamb and decadent Schiz (semi-soft cow's milk cheese). Enthusiastic, English-speaking hosts welcome you to **Azienda Agrituristica Sant'Anna** (☎ 0437 274 91; www.aziendasantanna.it; Via Pedecastello 27, Castion; d per night/ week €50-80/330-460), a charming stone farmhouse inn 4km outside Belluno.

The Italian supermodel of ski resorts, **Cortina d'Ampezzo** (pop 6100/elev 1224m) is fashionable, icy and gorgeous, with church spires framed by the Alps. Get the Dolomiti Superski pass from Cortina's **ski pass office** (☎ 0436 86 21 71; Via G Marconi 15; 1-/2-/3-day/week pass €46/91/132/247; ☺ vary) to access 12 runs from December to April. **Gruppo Guide Alpine Cortina** (☎ 0436 86 85 05; www.guidecortina.com; Corso Italia 69a) runs summertime rock-climbing courses (three-day course including gear €260), mountain-climbing and guided nature hikes (prices vary). Reserve meals and stays at **Baita Fraina** (☎ 0436 36 34; www. baitafraina.it; d summer/winter €50/65, Jan-Nov €60-100, Dec €100-140; P), an Alpine inn with knotty pine rooms and hearty, mountain-inspired cuisine.

By car, take the A27 from Venice/Mestre. Trains from Venice (€6, 2½ hours) run to Belluno. Dolomiti Bus (www.dolomitibus.it) departs to Cortina from Belluno's train station.

and boattours with Venice's pioneering woman gondolier.

Dorsoduro

CHARMING HOUSE DD.724   B&B €€€
(Map p178; ☎ 041 277 02 62; www.thecharming house.com; Ramo de Mula 724; d incl breakfast €99-400; ✳ @ ☎) Guestrooms are designer yet cosy, and the superior double has a bathtub and balcony overlooking Peggy Guggenheim's garden. Babysitting, massages and guided tours available on request.

LA CALCINA   Inn €€
(Map p172; ☎ 041 520 64 66; www.lacalcina.com; Fondamenta Zattere ai Gesuati 780; s €80-150, d €110-310; ✳ ☎) An idyllic seaside getaway, it has breakfasts on the roof terrace, an elegant canalside restaurant and 29 airy,

parquet-floored guestrooms, several facing the Giudecca Canal and Palladio's Redentore church.

HOTEL GALLERIA   Inn €€
(Map p178; ☎ 041 523 24 89; www.hotelgalleria. it; Campo della Carità 878a; s €70-120, d €100-200, all incl breakfast) Smack on the Grand Canal at the Ponte dell'Accademia, this converted 17th-century mansion offers small doubles overlooking the Grand Canal (Nos 7, 8 and 9). Most rooms share updated bathrooms; two rooms accommodate larger families.

San Polo & Santa Croce

OLTRE IL GIARDINO   B&B €€€
(Map p178; ☎ 041 275 00 15; www.oltreilgiardino -venezia.com; Fondamenta Contarini 2542; d €150-350; ✳ @) Live the designer dream

in one of these six guestrooms brimming with historical charm and modern comforts: marquetry composer's desks, flat-screen TVs, candelabra, Bulgari bath products, 19th-century poker chairs and babysitting services.

PENSIONE GUERRATO   Pensione   €€
(Map p178; ☏ 041 528 59 27; www.pensione guerrato.it; Ruga due Mori 240a; d incl breakfast €95-140; ❄️) In a 1227 landmark that once sheltered knights heading off on the Third Crusade, updated guestrooms haven't lost their sense of history – ask for one with frescoes or glimpses of the Grand Canal, or the newly restored apartment.

CA' ANGELI   B&B   €€
(Map p178; ☏ 041 523 24 80; www.caangeli.it; Calle del Traghetto della Madonnetta 1434; d €80-250; ❄️ @) Brothers Giorgio and Matteo inherited this Grand Canal mansion and converted it into an antique showplace, with original Murano glass chandeliers, namesake angels from the 16th century and a restored Louis XIV sofa in the canalside reading room.

DOMINA HOME
CA' ZUSTO   Boutique Hotel   €€
(Map p172; www.dominavacanze.it; Campo Rielo 1358; d incl breakfast €118-225; ❄️ 📶) With a wink at the nearby Fondaco dei Turchi, the historical Turkish trading house, strikingly modern guestrooms are named after Turkish women and decked out in harem stripes and silk brocade, with plush beds fit for pashas.

Cannaregio
PALAZZO
ABADESSA   Boutique Hotel   €€€
(Map p172; ☏ 041 241 37 84; www.abadessa.com; Calle Priuli 4011; d €125-345; ❄️ 📶) Sumptuous guestrooms feature plush beds, silk-damask walls and 18th-century vanities; go baroque and request a larger room with ceiling frescoes, Murano chandeliers and canal or garden views.

DOMUS ORSONI   B&B   €€
(Map p172; ☏ 041 275 95 38; www.domusorsoni. it; Corte Vedei 1045; s incl breakfast s €80-150, d €100-250; ❄️ @) Surprise: along a tranquil back lane near the Ghetto are five of Venice's most stylish guestrooms. In summer breakfast is served in the garden by Orsoni mosaic works, located here since 1885 – hence the mosaic fantasias glittering across walls, headboards and bathrooms.

CA' POZZO   Inn   €€
(Map p172; ☏ 041 524 05 04; www.capozzo venice.com; Sotoportego Ca' Pozzo 1279; d €80-170; ❄️ 📶) Biennale-bound travellers find a home away from home in this minimalist-chic hotel near the Ghetto. Several guestrooms have balconies, two accommodate disabled guests and spacious No 208 could house a Damien Hirst entourage.

Castello
CA' DEI DOGI   Boutique Hotel   €€
(Map p178; ☏ 041 241 37 51; www.cadeidogi.it; Corte Santa Scolastica 4242; d €100-140; ❄️ 📶) Streamlined modern rooms look like ships' cabins, with wood-beamed ceilings, dressers resembling steamer trunks, and compact mosaic-covered bathrooms.

PALAZZO SODERINI   B&B   €€
(Map p172; ☏ 041 296 08 23; www.palazzo soderini.it; Campo di Bandiera e Mori 3611; d €150-200; ❄️ 📶) This tranquil, all-white retreat with a lily pond in the garden offers a welcome reprieve from Venice's visual onslaught. There are only three rooms; book ahead.

Giudecca
BAUER PALLADIO &
SPA   Luxury Hotel   €€€
(Map p172; ☏ 041 520 70 22; www.palladiohotel spa.com; Fondamenta della Croce 33; d from €590; ❄️ 📶) Splash out in a serene, Palladio-designed former cloister with San Marco views, private solar-powered boat service and a superb spa. Once home to nuns and orphans, this converted monastery now offers heavenly comfort in rosy, serenely demure guestrooms, many with garden terraces or water views.

 Eating

Piazza San Marco & Around

ENOTECA AL VOLTO   Venetian **€**
(Map p178; ☑041 522 89 45; Calle Cavalli 4081;
cicheti €2-4, mains €7-18; ⊙9.30am-3pm &
5.30-10pm Mon-Sat) Join the bar crowd
working its way through the vast selection
of wine and *cicheti,* or come early for a
table outdoors (in summer) or inside the
snug backroom for the seaworthy bowls
of pasta with bottarga (dried fish roe) or
housemade ravioli. Cash only.

**OSTERIA
SAN MARCO**   Modern Italian **€€**
(Map p178; ☑041 528 52 42; www.osteriasan
marco.it; Frezzeria 1610; mains €20-30;
⊙12.30-11pm Mon-Sat) Romance is in the
air here – but the top-notch wines lining
the exposed brick walls surely help. Under
strategic spotlights, dishes seem to arrive
with a halo, especially heavenly lagoon
clams with squid ink linguine.

OSTERIA DA CARLA   Osteria **€**
(Map p178; ☑041 523 78 55; Frezzeria 1535;
mains €8-13; ⊙10am-9pm Mon-Sat) For the
price of a Piazza San Marco hot chocolate, diners in the know duck into this
hidden courtyard to feast on ravioli with
poppy seed, pear and sheep's cheese.

CAVATAPPI   Osteria **€**
(Map p178; ☑041 296 02 52; Campo della Guerra
525/526; cicheti €2-4, mains €8-13; ⊙10am-9pm
Tue-Thu & Sun, 10am-11pm Fri & Sat) This casual
charmer offers *cicheti,* DOC bubbly by the
glass and that rarest of San Marco finds:
a tasty sit-down meal under €20. Get the
risotto of the day and sheep's cheese drizzled with wildflower honey for dessert.

Dorsoduro

TRATTORIA LA BITTA   Trattoria **€€**
(☑041 523 05 31; Calle Lunga San Barnaba 2753a;
meals €35-40; ⊙7-10pm Mon-Sat) The daily
menu is presented on a miniature artist's
easel, while the rustic fare looks like a still
life and tastes like a dream: gnocchi is
graced with pumpkin and herbs, and roast

rabbit arrives on a bed of marinated rocket.

ENOTECA AI ARTISTI
Traditional Italian €
(Map p172; ☎041 523 89 44; www.enoteca artisti.com; Fondamenta della Toletta 1169a; mains €9-23; ⏱noon-4pm & 6.30-10pm Mon-Sat) Heart-warming pasta and inspired cheeses are paired with exceptional wines (by the glass) by your oenophile hosts.

AVOGARIA
Modern Italian €€
(☎041 296 04 91; Calle Dell'Avogaria 1629; cicheti €1.5-4, mains €10-22; ⏱noon-3pm & 6-11pm Wed-Sun) Dates begin casually enough in this exposed-brick, wood-beamed restaurant, with happy-hour *cicheti* and *spritz* at the sleek glass bar, but a bite of Venetian *crudi* (sushi) laced with fresh herbs leads to seafood risotto for two...and by the time the tiramisu arrives, you'll be swooning.

IMPRONTA CAFÉ
Traditional Italian €
(Map p172; ☎041 275 03 86; Calle Crosera 3815; meals €8-15; ⏱11am-1am Mon-Sat) Join Venice's value-minded jet set for prosecco and bargain polenta-salami combos, surrounded by witty diagrams of cooking pots.

San Polo & Santa Croce

ALL'ARCO
Venetian €
(Map p178; ☎041 520 56 66; Calle dell'Arco 436; cicheti €1.50-4; ⏱noon-8.30pm Mon-Sat Apr-Jun & Sep, to 3.30pm Oct-Mar, closed Jul-Aug) On Mondays when the Pescaria is closed, Francesco might wrap wild asparagus in rare roast beef with grainy mustard; when Saturday's seafood haul arrives, Matteo might create Sicilian tuna tartare with mint, Dolomite strawberries and aged balsamic. Even with copious *prosecco*, hardly any meal here tops €20 or falls short of five stars.

TOP CHOICE AL PESADOR
Modern Italian €€
(Map p178; ☎041 523 94 92; www.alpesador .it; Campo San Giacometo; mains €15-30; ⏱noon-3pm & 7-11pm Mon-Sat) Pesador offers a Grand Canal setting and culinary

finesse: *cicheti* feature a terrine of tiny lagoon clams topped with lemon gelée, while *primi* (mains) include red-footed scallops kicking wild herbs across squid-ink gnocchi.

PRONTO PESCE PRONTO Seafood €
(Map p178; ☎041 822 02 98; Rialto Pescheria 319; cicheti €3-8; ⊙noon-2.45pm Tue-Sat) Grab a stool and a (unfortunately) plastic glass of DOC Soave to have with your *folpetti* (baby octopus) salad and plump prawn *crudi* (Venetian sushi), or enjoy yours dockside along the Grand Canal.

DAI ZEMEI Venetian €
(Map p178; ☎041 520 8546; www.osteriadai zemei.it; Ruga Vecchia San Giovanni 1045; cicheti €2-5; ⊙9am-8pm Wed-Mon) Small meals with oversized imagination: octopus salad with marinated rocket, duck breast drizzled with truffle oil, or *crostini* (toast) loaded with velvety tuna mousse.

🍃ALASKA Ice Cream
(Map p172; ☎041 71 52 11; Calle Larga dei Bari, Santa Croce 1159; gelato €1.50-2; ⊙noon-8pm) Outlandish organic gelato: enjoy a Slow Food scoop of house-roasted local pistachio, or two of tangy Sicilian lemon with vaguely minty *carciofi* (artichoke).

TEAROOM CAFFÉ ORIENTALE Vegetarian €
(Map p178; ☎041 520 17 89; Rio Marin 888; meals €6-12; ⊙noon-9pm Fri-Wed) Detour from tourist-trail espresso bars and seafood restaurants to this art-filled canalside tearoom; it offers vegetarian delights from asparagus-studded quiches to hearty bean soups.

OSTERIA LA ZUCCA Modern Italian €
(Map p178; ☎041 524 15 70; www.lazucca. it; Calle del Tentor 1762; small plates €5-12; ⊙12.30-2.30pm & 7-10.30pm Mon-Sat) Vego-centric seasonal small plates bring spice-trade influences to local produce: zucchini with ginger zing, cinnamon-tinged pumpkin flan and raspberry spice cake.

ANTICA BIRRERIA DELLA CORTE Pizzeria €
(Map p178; ☎041 275 05 70; Campo San Polo 2168; pizzas €8-13; ⊙noon-11pm Mon-Fri) Standouts include wood-fired bresaola, and rocket and buffalo mozzarella, washed down with beer – German on tap, Italian artisan in bottles.

Cannaregio

ANICE STELLATO Venetian €€
(Map p172; ☎041 72 07 44; Fondamenta della Sensa 3272; meals €25-40; ⊙noon-2pm & 7.30-11pm Wed-Sun) If finding this obscure corner of Cannaregio seems like an adventure, wait until dinner arrives: herb-encrusted lamb chops, housemade ravioli and lightly fried *moeche* (soft-shelled crab) gobbled whole. Book ahead.

DALLA MARISA Venetian €€
(Map p172; ☎041 720 211; Fondamenta San Giobbe 652b; set menu €30-35; ⊙11am-3pm & 7-11pm Tue & Thu-Sat) Like a friend of the family, you'll be seated where there's room and get no menu. You'll have whatever Marisa's cooking, but you will be informed whether the menu is meat- or fish-based when you book; house wine is included in the price.

OSTERIA L'ORTO DEI MORI Modern Italian €€
(Map p172; ☎041 524 36 77; Campo dei Mori 3386; meals €20-40; ⊙12.30-3.30pm & 7.30-midnight Wed-Mon) Sicilian chef Lorenzo makes fresh pasta daily, including squid atop spinach tagliolini and bow-tie pasta with sausage and *raddichio di Treviso* (red rocket). Upbeat staff and fish-shaped lamps add a playful air to evenings here, and you'll be handed *prosecco* to endure the wait for tables (book ahead).

LA CANTINA Venetian €€
(Map p172; ☎041 522 82 58; Campo San Felice 3689; cicheti €3-6, mains €15-30; ⊙11am-11pm Mon-Sat) Talk about Slow Food: grab a stool and local Morgana beer while you await seasonal bruschetta made to order and hearty bean soups.

bar crammed with *cicheti* and 60 different wines, including top-notch *prosecco* and DOC wines by the glass (€2 to €3.50).

⊘ **ENOTECA MASCARETA** Wine Bar
(Map p172; ☏041 523 07 44; Calle Lunga Santa Maria Formosa 5138; meals €30-45; ☺7pm-2am Fri-Tue) Oenophiles keep this atmospheric place packed year-round, thanks to brilliantly curated local meats, cheeses and above all wines – including cloudily organic *prosecco*.

HARRY'S BAR Bar
(Map p178; ☏041 528 57 77; www.cipriano.com; Calle Vallaresso, San Marco 1323; ☺10.30-11pm) Aspiring auteurs throng the bar frequented by Ernest Hemingway, Charlie Chaplin, Truman Capote, Orson Welles and others, enjoying a signature €15 Bellini (fresh peach juice and *prosecco*) with a side of reflected glory.

CANTINA DO SPADE Bar
(Map p178; ☏041 521 05 83; www.cantina dospade.it; Calle delle Do Spade, San Polo 860; ☺10am-3pm & 6-10pm Mon-Sat) Since 1488 this bar has kept Venice in good spirits, and friendly young management extend warm welcomes to spritz-sipping Venetian regulars and visiting connois-seurs here for double malt Dolomite beer and bargain Venetian DOC Cab Franc.

OSTERIA ALLA BIFORA Wine Bar
(☏041 523 61 19; Campo Santa Margherita, Dorsoduro 2930; ☺noon-3pm & 6pm-midnight) Other bars around this *campo* cater to spritz-pounding students, but this converted medieval winecellar caters to dreamers who flirt over glasses of big-hearted Veneto merlot and shareable plates of cold cuts in the flattering glow of five chandeliers.

OSTERIA ALL'ALBA Wine Bar
(Map p178; ☏340 124 56 34; Ramo del Fontego dei Tedeschi 5370; ☺7-1pm) That roar behind the Rialto means the DJ's funk set is kick-ing in at All'Alba. Squeeze inside to order salami sandwiches (€1 to €2.50) and DOC Veneto wines (€5 to €6), and check out walls festooned with vintage LPS and 'hanks scrawled in 12 languages.

⭐ **Entertainment**

For blockbuster events like the Biennale or La Fenice operas, you'll need to book ahead online at the appropriate website or www.veniceconnected.com. Otherwise, event tickets are sold at **helloVenezia ticket outlets** (☏041 24 24; www.hellovenezia .com), located near key vaporetto stops (p172). To find out what's on the calendar in Venice during your visit, drop by the APT tourism office (p201), click on the Calendar button at www.comune.venezia or visit these sites:

A Guest in Venice (www.aguestinvenice.com) Hotelier association that provides information on upcoming exhibits, events and lectures.

Venezia da Vivere (www.veneziadavivere. com) The creative guide to Venice, featuring music performances, art openings, nightlife and design events.

Venezia Si (www.veneziasi.it) Online booking service with calendar listings for Venice venues and festivals.

Casinos

CASINÒ DI VENEZIA Casino
(Map p172; ☏041 529 71 11; www.casinovenezia. it; Palazzo Vendramin 2040; admission €5 or free with €10 gaming token purchase; ☺11am-2.30am Sun-Thu, 11am-3am Fri & Sat) No opera can match the dramas at Venice's palatial gambling house since the 16th century: Richard Wagner survived the 20-year effort of composing his stormy *Ring* cycle only to expire here in 1883. Slots open at 11am; to take on the gam-ing tables, arrive after 3.30pm wearing your best jacket and poker face.

Opera & Classical Music

TEATRO LA FENICE Opera House
(Map p178; ☏041 78 66 11; www.teatrolafenice.it; Campo San Fantin 1965; tickets €40-120) Tours are possible with advance booking (☏041 24 24), but the best way to see La Fenice is with the *loggione* – opera buffs who pass judgment from the top-tier cheap seats. When the opera is in recess, look for sym-phonies and chamber-music concerts.

, VENEZIANI Live Music

(☑041 277 05 61; www.interpreti
om; Chiesa San Vidal 2862; adult/
⌀25/20; ◷doors open 8.30pm) Every-
you knew of Vivaldi from lift music
mobile ring tones is proved wrong by
erpreti Veneziani, who play Vivaldi on
18th-century instruments as a dramatic
soundtrack for Venice – you'll never listen
to *The Four Seasons* again without hearing
summer storms erupting over the lagoon,
or muffled footsteps hurrying across
footbridges in winter night's intrigue.

MUSICA A PALAZZO Live Music
(Map p178; ☑340 971 72 72; www.musicapalazzo
.com; Palazzo Barbarigo-Minotto, Fondamenta
Barbarigo o Duodo 2504; tickets €50; ◷doors
open 8pm) In salons overlooking the Grand
Canal with splendid Tiepolo ceilings, the
soprano's high notes might make you fear
for your wineglass. During 1½ to two hours
of selected arias, 70 guests trail singers
in modern dress from receiving-room
overtures to heartbreaking finales in the
bedroom.

Live Music

B.EACH Nightclub
(☑041 526 80 13; Lungomare D'Annunzio 20x;
◷9am-2am May-Sep) Days flow into nights
at this Lido beach venue with four-poster
sun beds, sports and chill-out zones for
daytime use, plus cocktails, occasional
live music and DJs after dark.

VENICE JAZZ CLUB Live Music
(Map p172; ☑041 523 20 56; www.venicejazzclub.
com; Ponte dei Pugni, Dorsoduro 3102; tickets incl
drink €20; ◷doors open 7pm) Resident Venice
Jazz Club Quartet swings to Miles Davis
and Charles Mingus and grooves on Italian
jazz standards.

🔒 Shopping

CARTÈ Artisanal, Gifts
(Map p178; ☑320 024 87 76; www.cartevenezia.
it; Calle di Cristi 1731; ◷10am-6.30pm Mon-Sat)
This is the cupboard-sized studio of Rosanna Corró, a former book restorer who
learned the ancient art of *carta marmoriz-
zata* (marbled paper) and began creating
bookish beauties: marbled cocktail
rings, mesmerising statement necklaces
and surreal book-bound handbags in
woodgrain patterns.

**MARINA E SUSANNA
SENT** Artisanal, Glass
(Map p178; ☑041 520 81 36; www.
marinaesusannasent.com; Campo
San Vio 669; ◷10am-1pm &
3-6.30pm Tue-Sat, 3-6.30pm
Mon) Having trained as an
architect and a jeweller,
respectively, these
sisters from Murano
were told that women
couldn't handle working
in molten glass. They
have gone on to create
Murano's bestselling line
of colourfully minimal-
ist, hand-blown glass
jewellery.

Murano glass, Murano (p190)
HOLGER LEUE/LONELY PLANET IMAGES ©

Detour:
Padua

Just 37km west of Venice, **Padua** (www.turismopadova.it) looks more like Milan, with medieval piazzas, a vibrant university scene and broad boulevards lined with elegant Liberty edifices, sinister Fascist facades and postwar cereal-box architecture. To pack in the sights, buy a **PadovaCard** (www.padovacard.it; per 48/72hr €16/21), a public transport/monument pass.

Almost 200 years before Michelangelo's Sistine Chapel came Padua's Renaissance breakthrough: Giotto's moving 1303–05 frescoes for **Scrovegni Chapel** (049 201 00 20; www.cappelladegliscrovegni.it; Giardini dell'Arena; adult/reduced €13/8, admission with PadovaCard free; by advance reservation only 9am-7pm, to 10pm summer). Medieval churchgoers were accustomed to blank stares from two-dimensional saints, but Giotto depicted biblical figures as relatable characters. Fresco fans shouldn't miss Padua's 13th-century **Baptistry** (Piazza del Duomo; adult/reduced €2.80/ 1.80, with PadovaCard free; 10am-6pm), which Giusto de' Menabuoi lined with saints.

Basilica di Sant'Antonio (www.basilicadelsanto.org; Piazza del Santo; 6.30am-7.45pm, until 6.45pm Nov-Mar) is the final resting place of St Anthony of Padua (1193–1231). Across the square, **Oratorio di San Giorgio** (Piazza del Santo; admission €4; 9am-12.30pm & 2.30-5pm, until 7pm Apr-Sep) is awash in jewel-like 1378 frescoes.

Reserve ahead at **Godenda** (049 877 41 92; www.godenda.it; Via Squarcione 4/6; meals €30-50; 10am-3pm, 7pm-1am Mon-Sat, closed Aug), with creative takes on Venetian classics, like house-made pasta with jerked horsemeat.

Trains connect Padua with Venice (€3 to €15, 25 to 50 minutes, three per hour). By car, take the A4 (Turin–Milan–Venice–Trieste).

MALEFATTE Artisanal, Gifts
(Map p172; 041 521 02 72; www.rioteradeipens ieri.org; Calle Zancani 2433; 10am-1pm & 3-6pm Tue-Sat) Make up for any past gift-giving *malefatte* (misdeeds) while giving a second chance to Giudecca prison in-mates, who run this nonprofit vocational training project and craft one-of-a-kind wallets and man-bags from recycled Ven-ice museum vinyl banners. Also organic botanical skincare products.

LAURETTA VISTOSI Artisanal, Accessories
(Map p172; 041 528 65 30; www.laurettavistosi .org; Calle Lunga San Barnaba 2866B; 10am-1pm & 3-7pm Tue-Sat) A Murano-born Renaissance artisan, she handcrafted shoes, stationery and dresses before inventing an entirely new craft: ultramod-ern handstitched handbags, totes and journals, emblazoned with Murano-glass bullseye buttons.

OLD WORLD BOOKS Bookstore
(Map p172; 041 275 94 56; Punto del Ghetto Vecchio 282; 10am-1pm & 4-7pm Mon Fri) Rare books and speciality titles for Venice obsessives (*Chimney Pots of Venice*).

Information

Medical Services

Ospedale Civile (041 529 41 11; Campo SS Giovanni e Paolo 6777) Venice's main hospital; for emergency care and dental treatment, ask for the *pronto soccorso* (ER).

Tourist Information

Azienda di Promozione Turistica (APT; info line 041 529 87 11; www.turismovenezia.it) Marco Polo airport (arrivals hall; 9.30am-7.30pm); Piazzale Roma (Map p172; 9.30am-4.30pm); Piazza San Marco (Map p172; Piazza San Marco 71f; 9am-3.30pm Mon-Sat); Stazione di Santa Lucia (Map p172; 8am-6.30pm)

201

ⓘ Getting There & Away

Air

Most flights arrive and depart from Marco Polo airport (VCE; ☎ 041 260 92 60; www.veniceairport.it), 12km outside Venice, east of Mestre. Ryanair also uses San Giuseppe airport (TSF; ☎ 0422 31 51 11; www.trevisoairport.it), about 5km southwest of Treviso and a 30km, one-hour drive from Venice. For details on getting to and from the airport, see Getting Around.

Car & Motorcycle

The congested Trieste-Turin A4 passes through Mestre. From Mestre, take the Venezia exit. Once over the Ponte della Libertà bridge from Mestre, cars must be left at the car park at Piazzale Roma or Tronchetto; expect to pay €20 or more for every 24 hours. The car-rental companies listed here all have offices on Piazzale Roma and at Marco Polo airport.

Avis (Map p172; ☎ 041 523 73 77)

Europcar (Map p172; ☎ 041 523 86 16)

Hertz (Map p172; ☎ 041 528 40 91)

Train

Trains run to Venice's Stazione di Santa Lucia (signed as Ferrovia within Venice). Local trains that link Venice to the Veneto are frequent, reliable and inexpensive, including Padua (€3, 30-50 minutes, three to four per hour), Verona (€6.35, 1¾ hours, three to four each hour), and points in between.

There is also a direct, intercity service to most major Italian cities, including Milan (€15 to €32, 2½ to 3½ hours), Florence (€24 to €43, 2-3 hours), Rome (€45 to €75, 3½-6 hours) and Naples (€49 to €121, 5½ to 9 hours), plus major points in France, Germany, Austria, Switzerland, Slovenia and Croatia.

ⓘ Getting Around

To/From the Airport

Alilaguna (☎ 041 240 17 01; www.alilaguna.com) operates several lines that link the airport with various parts of Venice. Boats to Venice cost €13 and leave from the airport ferry dock (an eight-minute walk from the terminal).

ATVO (☎ 041 520 55 30; www.atvo.it) buses run to the airport from Piazzale Roma (€5, one hour, every 30 minutes 8am to midnight).

Left: Cyclists pass the Dolomites (p192);
Below: Moored gondolas, Venice
(LEFT) JOHN ELK III/LONELY PLANET IMAGES ©; (BELOW) KRZYSZTOF DYDYNSKI/LONELY PLANET IMAGES ©

Boat

The city's main mode of public transport is *vaporetto* – Venice's distinctive water buses. Tickets can be purchased from the HelloVenezia ticket booths (www.hellovenezia. com) at most landing stations. Instead of spending €6.50 for a one-way ticket, consider a VENICECard, a timed pass for unlimited travel within a set period (beginning at first validation). Passes for 12/24/36/48/72 hours are €16/18/23/28/33.

Vaporetto stops can be confusing, so check the signs at the landing dock to make sure you're at the right stop for the *vaporetto* line and direction you want. Here are key *vaporetto* lines and major stops, subject to seasonal change:

1 Piazzale Roma-Ferrovia-Grand Canal (all stops)-Lido and back.

2 Circular line: San Zaccaria-Redentore-Zattere-Tronchetto-Ferrovia-Rialto-Accademia-San Marco.

41/42 Circular line: Murano-Fondamente Nuove-Ferrovia-Piazzale Roma-Redentore-San Zaccaria- Fondamente Nuove-San Michele-Murano.

51/52 Circular line: Lido-Fondamente Nuove-Ferrovia-Piazzale Roma-Zattere-San Zaccaria-Giardini-Lido.

N All-stops night circuit: Lido-Giardini-San Zaccaria-Grand Canal (all stops)-Ferrovia-Piazzale Roma-Tronchetto-Zattere-Redentore-San Giorgio-San Zaccaria (starts around 11.30pm; last service around 5am).

T Torcello-Burano (half-hourly service) and back (7am to 8.30pm).

Water Taxis

The standard water taxi (☎ 041 522 23 03, 041 240 67 11; www.venicewatertaxi.com) between Marco Polo airport and Venice costs €90 to €100 for up to four people. Official rates start at €8.90 plus €1.80 per minute, plus €6 if they're called to your hotel and more for night trips, luggage and large groups.

Verona

POP 264,500

Shakespeare placed star-crossed Romeo Montague and Juliet Capulet in Verona for good reason: romance, drama and fatal family feuds have been the city's hallmark for centuries. Lombard king Alboin, who conquered Verona in AD 569, was murdered by his wife three years later. After Mastino della Scala (aka Scaligeri) lost re-election to Verona's commune in 1262, he claimed absolute control, until murdered by his rivals. Mastino's son Cangrande I (1308–28) went on to conquer Padua and Vicenza, with Dante, Petrarch and Giotto benefitting from the city's patronage. But the fratricidal rage of Cangrande II (1351–59) complicated matters, and the Scaligeri were run out of town in 1387.

Today, as the city grapples with its changing identity as an Italian, European and international commercial centre, it has become a Lega Nord (Northern League) stronghold. Yet the city is a Unesco World Heritage Site and a cosmopolitan crossroads, especially in summer when the 2000-year-old arena hosts opera's biggest names, and each April during **VinItaly** (www.vintialy.com), Italy's premier wine showcase.

Sights

Available at tourist sights as well as tobacconists, **VeronaCard** (www.veronacard.it; 2/5 days €15/20) grants access to most major monuments and churches (included all listed in this book), plus unlimited use of town buses

CASTELVECCHIO   Museum
(☑ 045 806 26 11; Corso Castelvecchio 2; adult/reduced €6/4.50 or Verona Card; ☉8.30am-7.30pm Tue-Sun, 1.30-7.30pm Mon) Built by tyrannical Cangrande II to guard the river Adige, this 1350s fortress was severely damaged by Napoleon's troops and WWII bombings. Architect Carlo Scarpa reinvented the building in the 1960s, placing bridges over exposed foundations, covering bomb blasts with glass panels, and balancing a statue of Cangrande I above the courtyard on a concrete gangplank. Now Verona's main museum, it houses a collection ranging from medieval artefacts to works by Giovanni Bellini, Tiepolo, Carpaccio and Veronese, plus often-excellent temporary shows.

BASILICA DI SAN ZENO
MAGGIORE   Church
(www.chieseverona.it; Piazza San Zeno; admission €2.50, combined Verona church ticket €6 or Verona Card; ☉8.30am-6pm Tue-Sat, 12.30-6pm Sun Mar-Oct, 10am-1pm & 1.30-5pm Tue-Sat, 12.30-5pm Sun Nov-Feb) Construction began on this masterpiece of Romanesque architecture in the 12th century to honour the city's patron saint. Its vast nave is lined with 12th- to 15th-century frescoes, including Mary Magdalene modestly covered in a curtain of her own hair and St George casually slaying a dragon atop a startled horse. Mantegna's 1457–59 altarpiece proffers such convincing perspective and textures that you'd swear there were real garlands behind the Virgin's throne.

CASA DI GIULIETTA   Museum
(Juliet's House; ☑ 045 803 43 03; Via Cappello 23; adult/reduced €6/4.50 or free with Verona Card; ☉8.30am-7.30pm Tue-Sun, 1.30-7.30pm Mon) Never mind that Romeo and Juliet were completely fictional characters, and that there's hardly room for two on the narrow stone balcony: romantics flock to this 14th-century house to add their love-lorn pleas to the graffiti on the courtyard causeway.

PIAZZA DELLE ERBE & PIAZZA DEI
SIGNORI   Historical Buildings
Originally a Roman forum, Piazza delle Erbe is ringed with buzzing cafes and seperated from Piazza dei Signori by the monumental gate known as **Arco della Costa**, hung with a whale's rib that, according to legend, will fall on the first just person to walk beneath it. So far, it remains intact, despite visits by popes and kings. Through the archway at the far end of the piazza are the open-air **Arche Scaligere** – the elaborate Gothic tombs

Verona

Verona

◎ Top Sights
Roman Arena B4

◎ Sights
1 Arche Scaligere C1
2 Arco della Costa C2
3 Casa di Giulietta................................... C2
4 Piazza dei Signori C1
5 Piazza delle Erbe C2
6 Scavi Scaligeri...................................... C2
7 Torre dei Lamberti................................ C2

🛏 Sleeping
8 Anfitheatro B&B B3

9 Hotel Gabbia d'Oro................................ B1

✖ Eating
10 Pintxos Bistrot...................................... D2
11 Pizzeria Du de Cope.............................. B2

🍷 Drinking
12 Antica Bottega del Vino C3
13 Osteria del Bugiardo B2

🎭 Entertainment
14 Ente Lirico Arena di Verona.................. B4
15 Roman Arena.. B4
Roman Arena Ticket Office ....(see 14)

of the Scaligeri family where murderers are interred next to the relatives they killed. Situated between the two piazzas, the towering striped **Torre dei Lamberti** (☎045 927 30 27; adult/reduced €6/4.50; ⊗8.30am-7.30pm, to 8.30pm Jun-Sep) rises up to a neck-craning 85m.

MARTIN HUGHES/LONELY PLANET IMAGES ©

Don't Miss **Verona's Roman Arena**

The symbol of Verona, this pink marble **amphitheatre** was built by Romans in the 1st century AD and survived a 12th-century earthquake to become Verona's legendary open-air opera house, seating 30,000 people. This is where Placido Domingo made his debut, and the annual June–August opera season includes legendary performances. In winter, classical concerts are held at the 18th-century **Ente Lirico Arena di Verona**.

THINGS YOU NEED TO KNOW

Ente Lirico Arena di Verona (045 800 51 51; www.arena.it; Piazza Brà, tickets at Ente Lirico Arena di Verona, Via Dietro Anfiteatro 6b; adult/reduced €6/4.50 or free with Verona Card, tickets €15-150; opera season Jun-Aug, visits 8.30am-7.30pm Tue-Sun, 1.30-7.30pm Mon, last admission 6.30pm).

Sleeping

For more options, **Cooperativa Albergatori Veronesi** (045 800 98 44; www.veronapass.com) offers a no-fee booking service for two-star hotels.

ANFITHEATRO B&B B&B €€
(347 248 84 62; www.anfiteatro-bedandbreakfast.com; Via Alberto Mario 5; s €60-90, d €80-130, tr €100-150) This recently restored 19th-century townhouse offers spacious guestrooms with high wood-beamed ceilings, antique armoires and divans for swooning after shows at the nearby Roman Arena.

HOTEL GABBIA D'ORO Hotel €€€
(045 59 02 93; www.hotelgabbiadoro.it; Corso Porta Borsari 4a; d from €220; P ❄ @ ⓢ) One of the city's top addresses and one of its most romantic, the Gabbia d'Oro features luxe rooms inside an 18th-century palazzo that manages to be both elegant and cosy.

Eating

PINTXOS BISTROT   Gastronomic   €€€
(☏045 59 42 87; www.ristorantealcristo.it; Piazzetta Pescheria 6; meals €40-60; ☉lunch & dinner Tue-Sun) This airy bistro offers an excitingly eclectic menu mixing Italian pasta, Catalan cheeses and hams, and small plate dishes perfumed with exotic ingredients like lemon grass and tamarind.

PIZZERIA DU DE COPE   Pizzeria   €
(☏045 59 55 62; www.pizzeriadudecope.it; Galleria Pellicciai 10; pizza €6-12; ☉noon-2pm & 7-11pm) This fashion-forward pizzeria manages to blend refinement with a relaxed ease in its airy and vividly coloured dining space. Wood-fired pizzas from the wood-burning oven are excellent.

Drinking

ANTICA BOTTEGA DEL VINO   Wine Bar
(☏045 800 45 35; www.bottegavini.it; Vicolo Scudo di Francia 3; ☉lunch & dinner Wed-Mon) Wine is the primary consideration at this historical *enoteca* with beautiful wood panelling, backlit bottles of Valpolicella and fine spirits.

OSTERIA DEL BUGIARDO   Wine Bar
(☏045 59 18 69; Corso Portoni Borsari 17a; ☉11am-11pm, to midnight Fri & Sat) On busy Corso Portoni Borsari, traffic converges at Bugiardo for glasses of upstanding Valpolicella bottled specifically for the *osteria*. Polenta and *sopressa* make worthy bar snacks for the powerhouse Amarone.

ℹ Information

Tourist offices (www.tourism.verona.it) Verona-Villafranca airport (☏045 861 91 63; ☉10am-3pm Mon-Sat); Via degli Alpini (☏045 806 86 80; Via degli Alpini 9; ☉10am-1pm & 2-6pm Mon-Tue, 9am-6pm Wed-Sat, 10am-4pm Sun, shorter hours Jan & Feb)

ℹ Getting There & Away

AIR Verona-Villafranca airport (VRN; ☏045 809 56 66; www.aeroportoverona.it) is 12km outside town and accessible by ATV Aerobus to/from the train station (€5, 15 minutes, every 20 minutes 6.30am to 11.30pm).

CAR & MOTORCYCLE Verona is at the intersection of the A4 (Turin-Trieste) and A22 motorways.

TRAIN There are at least three trains hourly to Venice (€6.35 to €20, 1¼ to 2½ hours) and Padua (€5.10 to €16, 40 to 90 minutes) and Vicenza (€4 to €14, 30 minutes to one hour).

ℹ Getting Around

AVT (www.atv.verona.it) city buses 11, 12, 13 and 14 (bus 91 or 92 on Sunday and holidays) connect the train station with Piazza Brà. Tickets can be purchased from newsagents and tobacconists before you board the bus (tickets one hour/day €1.20/3.50).

BOLOGNA

POP 372,000

Forget Ferraris: most travellers come to the province of Emilia-Romagna not for its famous fast cars, but for its slow food. Emilia-Romagna's capital of Bologna is nicknamed *La Grassa* ('the fat one'), celebrating a rich food legacy (*ragú* or Bolognese sauce was first concocted here). Bologna is also known as *La Dotta* ('the learned one') for the city university – the world's oldest, founded in 1088 – and *La Rossa* ('the red one') for its terracotta medieval buildings as well as the city's longstanding penchant for left-wing politics. Sure, there are plenty of zealous churches and musty museums to contemplate, but save some time to uncover the real highlight – the city's intriguing split personality.

Sights

Piazza Maggiore & Around

FREE **PALAZZO COMUNALE**   Art Gallery
(Piazza Maggiore) Home to Bologna city council since 1336, with a statue of Pope Gregory XIII, the Bolognese prelate responsible for the Gregorian calendar, placed above the main portal in 1580. Inside,

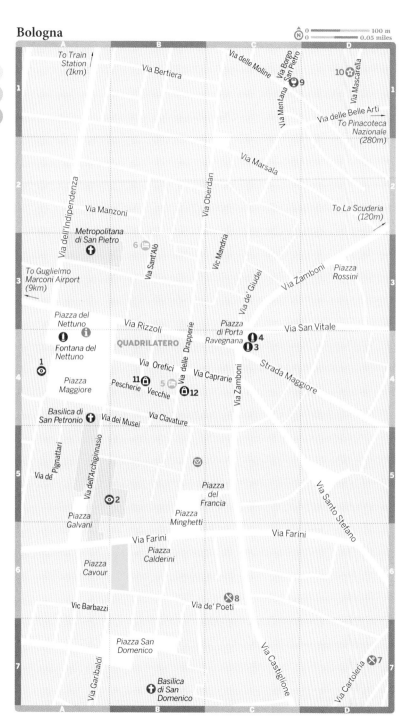

DISCOVER VENICE, VENETO & BOLOGNA   BOLOGNA

0   100 m
0   0.05 miles

To Train
Station
(1km)

Via Bertiera

Via delle Moline

Via Borgo
San Pietro

9

10

Via Mascarella

Via Mentana

Via delle Belle Arti

To Pinacoteca
Nazionale
(280m)

Via Marsala

Via Manzoni

Via Oberdan

To La Scuderia
(120m)

Via dell'Indipendenza

Metropolitana
di San Pietro

6

Via Sant'Alò

Vic Mandria

Via de' Giudei

Via Zamboni

Piazza
Rossini

To Guglielmo
Marconi Airport
(9km)

Piazza del
Nettuno

Via Rizzoli

Via delle Drapperie

Piazza
di Porta
Ravegnana

Via San Vitale

Fontana del
Nettuno

QUADRILATERO

Via Orefici

4

3

1

Piazza
Maggiore

Pescherie
Vecchie

11

5

12

Via Caprarie

Via Zamboni

Strada Maggiore

Basilica di
San Petronio

Via dei Musei

Via Clavature

Via de' Pignattari

Via dell'Archiginnasio

2

Piazza
del
Francia

Via Santo Stefano

Piazza
Galvani

Piazza
Minghetti

Via Farini

Via Farini

Piazza
Cavour

Piazza
Calderini

Vic Barbazzi

Via de' Poeti

8

Piazza San
Domenico

Via Garibaldi

Basilica
di San
Domenico

Via Castiglione

Via Cartoleria

7

Bologna

Donato Bramante's 16th-century staircase was designed to allow horse-drawn carriages to ride directly up to the 1st floor.

On the 2nd floor you'll find the *palazzo's* two **art galleries** (⊙9am-6.30pm Tue-Fri, 10am-6.30pm Sat & Sun): the **Collezioni Comunali d'Arte**, with its interesting collection of 13th- to 19th-century paintings, sculpture and furniture, and the **Museo Morandi**, dedicated to the trademark still-life paintings of Bolognese artist Giorgio Morandi.

Outside the *palazzo*, three large panels bear photos of hundreds of partisans killed in the resistance to German occupation, many on this very spot.

THE QUADRILATERO   Historic Centre
To the east of Piazza Maggiore, the grid of streets around Via Clavature (Street of Locksmiths) sits on what was once Roman Bologna. Known as the Quadrilatero, this compact district is ringed with old-style delis selling Emilia-Romagna's world-famous produce: *prosciutto di Parma* (Parma's thin-sliced ham), *aceto balsamico di Modena* (Modena's aged balsamic vinegar), and *parmigiano reggiano* (aged parmesan cheese).Leaders in local gastronomy are **Paolo Atti** (Via Drapperie 6; ⊙7.30am-1.30pm & 4-7.15pm Mon-Sat) and **La Baita** (Via Pescheria Vecchie 3; ⊙8am-8pm, closed Sun Jun-Aug).

FREE **PALAZZO DELL'
ARCHIGINNASIO**   Palazzo, Museum
(Piazza Galvani 1)Seat of the city university from 1563 to 1805, this palace houses the 700,000-volume **Biblioteca Comunale** (Municipal Library) and the fascinating 17th-century **Teatro Anatomico** (⊙9am-6.45pm Mon-Fri, to 1.45pm Sat) where public body dissections were held under the sinister gaze of an Inquisition priest, ready to intervene if proceedings became too spiritually compromising. The canopy above the lecturer's chair is supported by two skinless figures carved into the wood.

University Quarter

LE DUE TORRI   Towers
Standing sentinel over Piazza di Porta Ravegnana, Bologna's two leaning towers are the city's main symbol. The taller of the two, the 97.6m-high 1109–19 **Torre degli Asinelli** (admission €3; ⊙9am-6pm, to 5pm Oct-May) is open to the public, although it's not advisable for vertigo-sufferers or owners of arthritic knees (there are 498 steps up a semi-exposed wooden staircase). Superstitious students also boycott it. Local lore says if you climb the tower you'll never graduate.

PINACOTECA NAZIONALE   Art Gallery
(Via delle Belle Arti 56; admission €4; ⊙9am-7pm Tue-Sun) The city's main art gallery has a powerful collection of works by Bolognese artists from the 14th century onwards, including a number of important canvases by the late-16th-century Carracci cousins Ludovico, Agostino and Annibale. Works to look out for include Ludovico's *Madonna Bargellini*, the *Comunione di San Girolamo* (Communion of St Jerome)

by Agostino and the *Madonna di San Ludovico* by Annibale. Elsewhere in the gallery you'll find several works by Giotto, as well as Raphael's *Estasi di Santa Cecilia* (Ecstasy of St Cecilia).

MAMBO Art Gallery
(Museo d'Arte Moderna di Bologna; Via Don Minzoni 14; adult/reduced €6/4; ⊙12pm-6pm Tue, Wed & Fri, to 10pm Thu, to 8pm Sat & Sun) Avant-gardes, atheists, and people who've had their fill of dark religious art can seek solace in Bologna's newest museum (opened 2007), housed in a cavernous former municipal bakery. Its permanent and rotating exhibits showcase the work of up-and-coming Italian artists. Entrance to the permanent collection is free on Wednesday.

Courses

LA VECCHIA SCUOLA BOLOGNESE Cooking
(www.lavecchiascuola.com; Via Malvasia 49) It stands to reason; Bologna is also a good place to learn to cook and this is one of several schools that offer courses for English speakers. Prices range from €80 for a single four-hour course to €210 for three days.

Sleeping

PRENDIPARTE B&B B&B €€€
(☎051 58 90 23; www.prendiparte.it; Via Sant'Alò 7; r €250-300) You don't just get a room here, you get an entire 900-year-old tower (Bologna's second tallest). The living area (bedroom, kitchen and lounge) is spread over three floors and there are nine more levels to explore, with a 17th-century prison halfway up and outstanding views from the terrace up top.

ALBERGO DELLE DRAPPERIE Hotel €
(☎051 22 39 55; www.albergodrapperie.com; Via delle Drapperie 5; s €60-70, d €75-85; ✳) Buzz-in at ground level and climb the

stairs to discover 21 attractive rooms with wood-beamed ceilings, the occasional brick arch and colourful ceiling frescoes. Breakfast is €5 extra.

Eating

DROGHERIA DELLA ROSA Trattoria €€
(☎051 22 25 29; www.drogheriadellarosa.it; Via Cartoleria 10; meals €35-40; ⊙lunch & dinner) With its wooden shelves, apothecaries' jars and bottles, it's not difficult to picture this place as the pharmacy that it once was. Nowadays it's a charming, high-end trattoria, run by a congenial owner who seems to find time to get round every table and explain the day's short, sweet menu. Expect superbly prepared versions of Bolognese classics such as tortellini or steak with balsamic vinegar.

OSTERIA DE' POETI Osteria €€
(www.osteriadepoeti.com; Via de' Poeti 1b; meals €30-40; ⊙closed Mon Oct-May, Sun Jun-Aug) In the wine cellar of a 14th-century *palazzo*, this historic eatery is an atmospheric place to enjoy hearty local fare. Evenings feature frequent live music.

Drinking

LE STANZE Wine Bar
(www.lestanzecafe.com; Via Borgo San Pietro 1; ⊙11am-3am Mon-Sat) If La Scuderia reeks of undergraduate days you'd rather forget, hit the more chic Le Stanze, a former chapel where each of the four interior rooms have their own design concept. The aperitif buffet is top-notch here with paellas, pastas and chicken drumsticks to accompany your wine/cocktail.

LA SCUDERIA Bar, Cafe
(www.lascuderia.bo.it; Piazza Verdi 2; ⊙8am-1am Mon-Sat; 📶) The bar occupies the Bentivoglio family's former stables and features towering columns, vaulted ceilings and arty photos.

Palazzo Comunale (p207), Bologna

RUSSELL MOUNTFORD/LONELY PLANET IMAGES ©

 Entertainment

CANTINA BENTIVOGLIO Live Music
(www.cantinabentivoglio.it; Via Mascarella 4b;
☺8pm-2am) Bologna's top jazz joint is part
wine bar and part restaurant (the daily
prix-fixe menu costs €28).

CASSERO Nightclub
(www.cassero.it; Via Don Minzoni 18; ☺9.30pm-
5am Sat, to 2am Wed-Fri, to midnight Sun-Tue)
Saturday and Wednesday are the big
nights at this legendary gay and lesbian
(but not exclusively) club, home of Italy's
Arcigay organisation.

ℹ **Information**

Tourist office (www.bolognaturismo.info; Piazza
Maggiore 1e; ☺9am-7pm) Also has offices in the
airport and train station.

ℹ **Getting There & Away**

Air

Bologna's Guglielmo Marconi airport (BLQ;
www.bologna-airport.it) is 8km northwest of
the city.

Car & Motorcycle
The A13 heads directly to Padua and Venice.

Train
Bologna connects to Venice (€16.50 to €29, 1¼
to 2¼hrs); Rome (€25.50 to €59, 21/4-5hrs);
and Milan (€13.60 to €42, one to 2¼hrs); and the
new high-speed train to Florence (€25) takes 37
minutes.

ℹ **Getting Around**

Car
Much of the city centre is off-limits to vehicles. If
you're staying downtown, your hotel can provide a
ticket (€7 per day) that entitles you to enter the ZTL
(Zona a Traffico Limitato), park in designated spaces
and make unlimited trips on city buses for 24 hours.

Public Transport
ATC (www.atc.bo.it) buses 25 and 30 connect
the train station with the city centre, and aerobus
shuttles (€5) connect the station and Guglielmo
Marconi airport every 15 to 30 minutes between
5.30am and 11.10pm.

Florence, Tuscany & Umbria

When ears hear 'Italy', the mind ditches work and heads to Tuscany. Leaning towers, Michelangelo's stark-naked David, and – oh yes – Florentine steak on the bone, washed down with some unattainable, unforgettable red while debating Dante. Fair enough: human imaginations have been captivated for centuries by Tuscany's Renaissance masterminds, who established an Italian and international ideal with sublime architectural proportions, radical notions we now call science, and art that raises eyebrows and empties tear ducts. Amazingly, this idealistic outlook was achieved not on a sunny day in Chianti, but through generations of plague and turf warfare.

Happily, the region's city-states recovered and quit fighting – now they just compete for your attention. If your perfect dreamscape involves Spoleto performance poetry instead of Florentine sculpture, Umbrian truffles instead of steak, and Orvieto white wine instead of Tuscan reds, Umbria awaits next door to Tuscany. Michelangelo won't take it personally.

Duomo (p226), Florence

Florence, Tuscany & Umbria

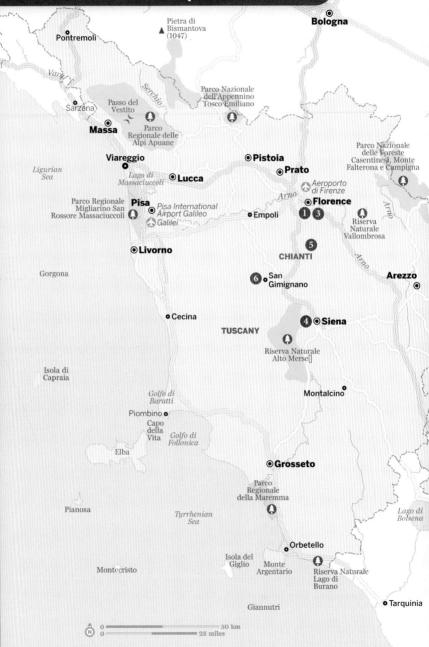

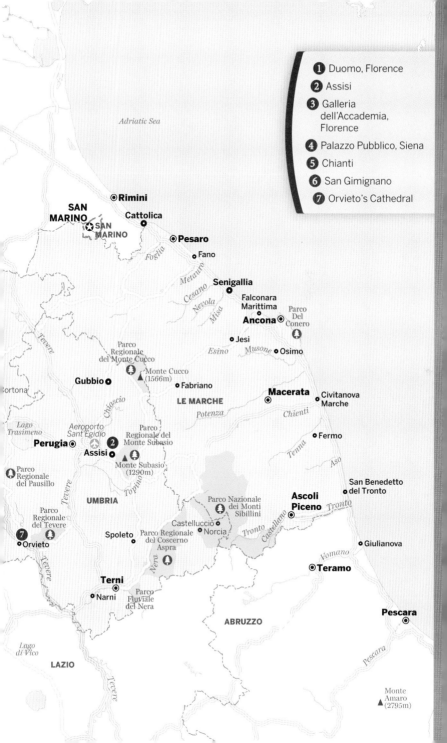

Florence, Tuscany & Umbria Highlights

1

Duomo, Florence

More than simply a monumental spiritual centrepiece, the Duomo symbolises the city's economic wealth between the years 1300 and 1500, and the incredible artistic and cultural explosion that it spurred. The building still dominates Florence, like a mountain of marble topped by a giant ruby.

Need to Know
FEWER CROWDS
November to March
MAGICAL MOMENT Walk
the Duomo's piazza early in
the morning BEST PHOTO
From the back of the nave
See our review
on p226.

Duomo
Don't Miss List

BY PATRIZIO OSTICRESI,
OPERA DI SANTA MARIA DEL FIORE
(OPERA DEL DUOMO) ADMINISTRATOR

1 PRICELESS ARTWORK

The Duomo heaves with beautiful art and craftsmanship. Particularly famous is Domenico di Michelino's 1465 painting *La Divina Commedia Illumina Firenze* (Dante Explaining the Divine Comedy). Recently restored, the 15th-century stained-glass windows at the base of the dome are the work of Donatello, Lorenzo Ghiberti, Paolo Uccello and Andrea del Castagno. Above them are the wonderful *Last Judgment* dome frescoes by Giorgio Vasari and Federico Zuccari.

2 VIEWS FROM THE DOME

The panoramas are reason enough to head to the top of Brunelleschi's dome, but other incentives include a fine view of the interior's inlaid marble floors and the chance to get closer to the *Last Judgment* frescoes adorning the dome.

3 BAPTISTRY

Both the exterior and the interior of the 11th-century baptistry are feasts for the eyes, and examples of architectural and artistic genius. Especially beautiful are the 13th-century ceiling mosaics, the inlaid marble pavement, the bronze doors and the Cossa funerary monument, created by Donatello and Michelozzo in 1428.

4 MUSEO DELL'OPERA DEL DUOMO

Many precious works of art removed from the piazza's monuments are held at the Museo dell'Opera del Duomo in order to better preserve them. Highlights include Donatello's *Maddalena* statue, the original baptistry doors by Lorenzo Ghiberti, original panels from Giotto's *campanile* (bell tower) and Michelangelo's *Pietà,* which he sculpted for his own tomb but was intensely unsatisfied with.

Sacred Assisi

Through the life and good deeds of St Francis, patron saint of animals and the environment, Assisi has undergone a transformation from a sleepy Umbrian hill town to spiritual centre that's nothing short of miraculous. A short walk across this medieval town covers holy sites and artistic marvels that provide tangible links to the distant past, and to generations of devoted pilgrims.

Need to Know

BEST TIME TO VISIT Weekdays, and outside the summer months and holiday periods **APPROPRIATE ATTIRE** Wear clothing that covers shoulders and knees **For more, see p263.**

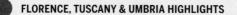

Sacred Assisi Don't Miss List

BY FRA MIRKO, FRANCISCAN MONK

1 BASILICA DI SAN FRANCESCO

Built soon after St Francis' death to house and venerate his body, the basilica (p263) is of major artistic importance. The upper church is most famous for its Giotto frescoes, while the lower church has works by Cimabue, Lorenzetti and Simone Martini. Personally, I think the lower church is the more atmospheric of the two. The crypt of St Francis is especially spiritual. Assisi is where I live and where I had my conversion several years ago.

2 SANTUARIO DI SAN DAMIANO

This **convent** (⊙10am-noon & 2-6pm summer, to 4.30pm winter), just outside the old city walls, has beautiful views over the Valley of Spoleto. The site itself is wonderfully silent and visually arresting. Keep an eye out for the verdant, flower-filled Giardino del Cantico, where St Francis wrote his *Cantico di Frate Sole* in approximately 1225.

3 EREMO DELLE CARCERI

These **caves** (⊙6.30am-7pm Easter-Oct, to sunset Oct-Easter) 4km east of Assisi are a fine example of a Franciscan hermitage. It's where St Francis himself would head for silent contemplation, and its location high above the town adds to the sense of isolation. It's particularly striking because it has changed very little since St Francis' time.

4 BASILICA DI SANTA CHIARA

The final resting place of St Clare, this basilica (p264) is also home to the Byzantine crucifix that spoke to St Francis at the Santuario di San Damiano. The reliquary in the crypt holds some important objects, including garments and other belongings of the saint and her contemporary, St Francis.

5 BASILICA DI SANTA MARIA DEGLI ANGELI

This great 16th-century **basilica** (near the train station; ⊙6.15am-12.50pm & 2.30-7.30pm summer) actually encases the tiny 10th-century Porziuncola chapel. It was on this site that St Francis lived with the original members of his order, and it was at the site of the Cappella del Transito that he passed into eternal ʼ on 3 October 1226.

Develop a Celebrity Crush at the Accademia

You may not have met him personally, but this guy is everywhere, and usually naked. Like most superstars, he goes by a single name: *David*. Before his sculpted abs appeared on fridge magnets and souvenir aprons, *David* was discovered by Michelangelo in a block of Carrara marble. Now people wait for hours to see him at Florence's Galleria dell'Accademia (p231) – though you can get a backstage pass with advance tickets.

3

4 Actually Enjoy Politics at Palazzo Pubblico

While its neighbours were squabbling violently over borders, medieval Siena put itself on the map with a rudimentary representative government, wall-to-wall public artwork, and one really tall tower. Siena's Palazzo Pubblico (Town Hall; p252) is a monument to civic spirit and far-sightedness, with frescoes that helpfully remind voters how to tell good government from bad (hint: one has fewer devils).

Drink in the Chianti Landscape (5)

With its gentle green hills, olive groves and stone farmhouse-villas, Chianti (p255) is bound to make you wax poetic – or maybe that's the wine talking. Gone are the days when any old basket-clad red could pass itself off as Chianti: now this historic growing region's Chianti Classico has won Italy's highest DOCG quality status. Bike or drive through Chianti countryside, but always brake for reds.

(6) Feel Small in San Gimignano

One-upmanship reached its height in medieval San Gimignano (p256), where neighbourly competition to build the biggest tower turned this small hill town into a mini-Manhattan. Of the original 72, eleven structures have stood the test of time. Standing in the long shadow of these towering achievements will leave you with an entirely fresh perspective on the Dark Ages – and might inspire you to redesign your own backyard shed.

(7) Survive the *End of the World* inside Orvieto's Cathedral

From the front, Orvieto's Cathedral (p266) looks like a gorgeous Gothic wedding cake, but inside, happily ever after doesn't look likely in Signorelli's frescoes. Signorelli had survived plague, book-burnings, earthquakes and witch-hunts when he started *End of the World* in 1500, and never has apocalypse been so vividly pictured. Five hundred years later it's a testament to what humans can survive, sometimes with flying colours.

Florence, Tuscany & Umbria's Best...

Wining & Dining

○ Tackling a three-fingers-thick *bistecca alla fiorentina* (Florentine steak) at Florence's **Trattoria Mario** (p239)

○ Raising Tuscan–toasts to Tuscany's celebrity butcher at Chianti's **Solociccia** (p255)

○ Pairing local saffron ravioli with Vernaccia wine at San Gimignano's **Perucá** (p256)

○ Enjoying raucous, tasty dinner theatre at Florence's **Teatro del Sale** (p239)

○ Mastering regional cooking (and drinking) with **Strada del Vino di Montepulciano** (p236) classes

World Heritage Treasures

○ **Florence** (p226) A-list museums, architectural wonders and killer shopping

○ **Basilica di San Francesco** (p263) Earthquake-shattered frescoes, miraculously restored and profoundly moving

○ **Siena** (p250) This model medieval government ended gang warfare with public art and horse races

○ **San Gimignano** (p256) Towering ambition put this medieval hill town on the map

○ **Urbino** (p263) Fifteenth-century town designed by a Renaissance brain trust

Breathtaking Views

○ Moonlit climbs up 294 tilting steps up Pisa's **Leaning Tower** (p244)

○ Michelangelo's ageless, studly David at Florence's **Galleria dell'Accademia** (p231)

○ Drinking in the landscape – literally – in **Chianti** (p255)

○ *The End of the World*, foretold in Signorelli fresco at Orvieto's **Cathedral** (p266)

○ Sunsets over the Arno at Florence's **Ponte Vecchio** (p235)

Souvenirs That Don't Feature David

◦ Heavenly perfume blended from monastery-grown flowers at **Officina Profumo-Farmaceutica di Santa Maria Novella** (p230)

◦ Rare Brunello vintages you won't find outside the cellars of **Montalcino** (p254)

◦ Glamorous Italian fashion at **Mrs Macis** (p242)

◦ Handmade marble-paper stationery from **Guilo Giannini e Figlio** (p242)

◦ Ribbon-wrapped artisanal chocolate truffles from Perugia's **Sandri** (p260)

Left: Leaning Tower of Pisa (p244);
Above: Vineyards, Chianti (p255)

Need to Know

ADVANCE PLANNING

◦ **Three months before** Book accommodation and tickets to Spoleto's summer festival (p266)

◦ **One to two months before** Book high-season accommodation in Assisi (p265), and Florence (p237)

◦ **Two weeks before** Book online for Pisa's Leaning Tower (p244), as well as for Florence's Uffizi (p227) and Galleria dell'Accademia (p231)

◦ **One day before** Book your tour of Florence's Palazzo Vecchio (p227), Cappella Brancacci (p235), and dinner in Florence (p238)

RESOURCES

◦ **APT Firenze** (www.firenzeturismo.it) Official Florence tourism website

◦ **Firenze Musei** (www.firenzemusei.it) Booking for Florentine museums

◦ **Tuscany Tourist Board** (www.turismo.intoscana.it) Interest-based itineraries

◦ **InfoUmbria** (www.infoumbria.com) Umbria travel resource with *agriturismi* (farm-stay accommodation) listings

GETTING AROUND

◦ **Air** Routes service Pisa and, to a lesser extent, Florence and Perugia

◦ **Walk** The best way to get around historic town centres, and the traditional way to reach pilgrimage sites like Assisi

◦ **Train** Good connections between major cities, with connecting buses to towns.

◦ **Bus** Best for reaching Siena and San Gimignano

◦ **Bicycle** The scenic way to cover Chianti; handy for Florence

◦ **Car** Convenient for reaching hill towns, *agriturismi* and wineries

BE FOREWARNED

◦ **Museums** Many close Monday

◦ **Restaurants** Many close in August; some also close in January

◦ **Accommodation** Book months ahead, especially if travelling on holiday weekends, in summer or during local festivals

◦ **Wine-tasting** Vineyard visits are often free but require reservations, which can usually be booked through local information offices

Florence, Tuscany & Umbria Itineraries

So you've seen the Leaning Tower and David – two masterpieces down, untold wonders to go. Where to begin? Wander Tuscan wine country to reach spiritual enlightenment, or uncover splendours in Umbria's hill towns.

3 DAYS

FLORENCE TO MONTALCINO
Tuscan Vineyards

Sun-washed vineyards, country roads flanked by olive groves and frequent, tasty pitstops make this a mellow, indulgent road trip. From **(1) Florence**, head south on the SS222 to **(2) Greve in Chianti**, the epicentre of the historic Chianti wine region. Drop by Castello di Verrazzano to wine-taste in a castle, and browse gourmet treats like local honey and *vin santo*. Enjoy a suitably heavenly lunch and wine-tasting at nearby La Bottega, located at a medieval abbey, then unwind poolside at Fattoria di Rigana, a luxury farmstead guesthouse. Take your sweet time the next day heading south along SS2 to **(3) Siena**, where you'll

find gourmet picnic supplies at Morbidi for lunch in the medieval Campo. Continue south on SS2 through Brunello wine country 10.5km past Montalcino, reaching **(4) Abbazia di Sant'Antimo** just in time for sunset Gregorian chants in the Romanesque church. Backtrack to **(5) Montalcino** for a Brunello tasting and dinner at Osticcio, then retreat to your rustic-chic guestroom in Hotel Vecchia Oliviera, a converted olive mill. Before you return to Siena or Florence, stop by Montalcino's *fortezza*, a fort with a wine cellar where you can get Brunello packaged to stash in your suitcase.

ORVIETO TO SPOLETO

Umbrian Hill Towns

5 DAYS

Secretive Umbria hides its splendours on hilltops behind ancient stone walls. Though these medieval hill towns seem far removed from the modern world, they're surprisingly accessible by train and elevators running through subterranean tunnels.

The adventure begins with a cliffhanger: **(1) Orvieto**, where Signorelli's frescoed handsome devils star in the shimmering pink Gothic cathedral. Spelunk through secret passageways with Orvieto Underground, then come up for air and seasonal daily specials at Trattoria dell'Orso. After a night in frescoed 1500s Villa Mercedes, hop the train to heady, chocoholic **(2) Perugia**. Check

into Etruscan Chocohotel, enjoy desserts at historic Sandri, and let that sugar buzz carry you through Galleria Nazionale dell'Umbria.

Devote two days to **(3) Assisi**, for quiet contemplation of Giotto's moving frescoes in Basilica di San Francesco and Umbrian cooking classes at *agriturismo* (farm-stay accommodation) Alla Madonna del Piatto. Artistic inspiration awaits in **(4) Spoleto**, which hosts Italy's landmark summer arts festival in its Roman ampitheatre and draws creative types year-round to novel-worthy Hotel Charleston.

Wine bar, Montalcino (p254)

Discover Florence, Tuscany & Umbria

At a Glance

o **Florence** (p226) Towering Renaissance achievements and priceless art treasures.

o **Siena** (p250) Florence's historic rival took an early lead with democracy, frescoes and fanfare.

o **Chianti** (p255) Super-Tuscan wines in a superlative castle-dotted landscape.

o **Umbria** (p258) Walled medieval hill towns hold treasures of frescoes, truffles and chocolate.

Bottles of Chianti on display, Tuscany
ROCCO FASANO/LONELY PLANET IMAGES ©

FLORENCE

POP 368,900

Cradle of the Renaissance and home of Machiavelli, Michelangelo and the Medici, Florence (Firenze) is magnetic, romantic, unrivalled and – above all – busy.

Yet there's more to this intensely absorbing place than priceless masterpieces. Towers and palaces evoke a thousand tales of its medieval past; designer boutiques and artisan workshops stud its streets; there's a buzzing cafe and bar scene; and – when the summer heat simply gets too stifling – vine-laden hills and terrace restaurants are only a short drive away.

◉ Sights

Piazza del Duomo

DUOMO   Duomo

(Cattedrale di Santa Maria del Fiore or St Mary of the Flower; www.duomofirenze.it; ⊙10am-5pm Mon-Wed & Fri, to 3.30pm Thu, to 4.45pm Sat, to 3.30pm 1st Sat of month, 1.30-4.45pm Sun, mass in English 5pm Sat) The city's most iconic landmark with its famous red-tiled dome, graceful bell tower and breathtaking pink, white and green marble facade has wow factor in spades. Begun in 1296 by Sienese architect Arnolfo di Cambio, the cathedral took almost 150 years to complete. Scaling the 463 steep stone steps up to the **dome** (admission €8; ⊙8.30am-7pm Mon-Fri, to 5.40pm Sat) is a must. No supporting frame was used in its construction – it's actually two concentric domes built from red brick to designs by Filippo Brunelleschi.

Equally physical is the 414-step climb up the neighbouring 82m-high **campanile** (adult/child €6/free; ☺8.30am-7.30pm daily).

BATTISTERO Baptistry
(Piazza di San Giovanni; admission €4; ☺12.15-7pm Mon-Sat, 8.30am-2pm 1st Sat of the month & Sun) Lorenzo Ghiberti designed the famous gilded bronze bas-reliefs adorning the eastern doors of Florence's 11th-century Romanesque baptistery, an octagonal striped structure of white and green marble.

Piazza della Signoria
PALAZZO VECCHIO Palazzo
(www.palazzovecchio-museoragazzi.it; Piazza della Signoria; adult/reduced €6/4.50; ☺9am-7pm Mon-Wed & Fri-Sun, 9am-2pm Thu) Built by Arnolfo di Cambio between 1298 and 1314 for the Signoria, the highest level of Florentine republican government, the palace became the residence of Cosimo I in the 16th century. Sheer size aside, what impresses most are the swirling, floor-to-ceiling battle scenes by Vasari glorifying Florentine victories by Cosimo I over arch rivals Pisa and Siena; unlike the Sienese, the Pisans are depicted bare of armour (play 'Spot the Leaning Tower'). To top off this unabashed celebration of his own power, Cosimo had himself portrayed as a god in the centre of the exquisite panelled ceiling – but not before commissioning Vasari to raise the original ceiling 7m in height.

The best way to see this building is by **guided tour** (obligatory reservations ☎055 276 82 24; info.museoragazzi@comune.fi.it).

GALLERIA DEGLI UFFIZI Art Gallery
(www.uffizi.firenze.it; Piazza degli Uffizi 6; adult/reduced €6.50/3.25, with temporary exhibition €11/5.50; ☺8.15am-6.50pm Tue-Sun) Housed inside Palazzo degli Uffizi, built between 1560 and 1580 as a government office building, this world-class art museum safeguards the Medici family's private art collection. It is bequeathed to the city in 1743 on the condition that it never leaves Florence.

An ongoing and vastly overdue €65 million refurbishment and redevelopment project will see the addition of a new exit

Museum Passes

The all-new **Firenze Card** (www.firenzecard.it; €50) is valid for 72 hours and covers admission to 33 museums (it covers all the biggies), villas and gardens in Florence as well as unlimited use of public transport. Buy it online (and collect upon arrival in Florence) or in Florence at tourist offices or ticketing desks of the Uffizi (Entrance 2), Palazzo Pitti, Palazzo Vecchio, Cappella Brancacci and Museo di Santa Maria Novella.

loggia designed by Japanese architect Arato Isozaki and the doubling of exhibition space.

The world-famous collection spans the gamut of art history from ancient Greek sculpture to 18th-century Venetian paintings, arranged in chronological order by school. But its core is the masterpiece-rich Renaissance collection.

Visits are best kept to three or four hours max. When it all gets too much, head to the rooftop cafe (aka the terraced hanging garden where the Medici clan listened to performances on the square below) for fresh air and fabulous views.

Around Piazza della Repubblica
MUSEO DEL BARGELLO Art Gallery
(Via del Proconsolo 4; adult/reduced €7/3.50; ☺8.15am-5pm Tue-Sun & 1st & 3rd Mon of month) It was behind the stark exterior of Palazzo del Bargello, Florence's earliest public building, that the *podestà* (council) meted out justice from the late 13th century until 1502.

Michelangelo was just 21 when a cardinal commissioned him to create the drunken, grape-adorned *Bacchus* (1496-97) displayed here. Other Michelangelo works to look out for include the marble bust of *Brutus* (c 1539–40), the *David/Apollo* from 1530–32 and the large,

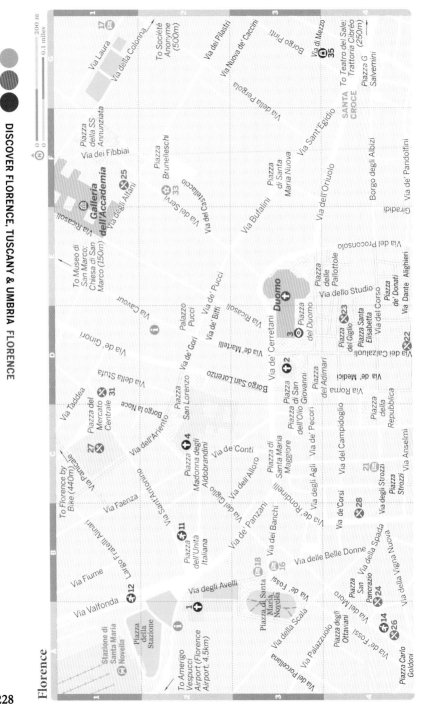

Florence

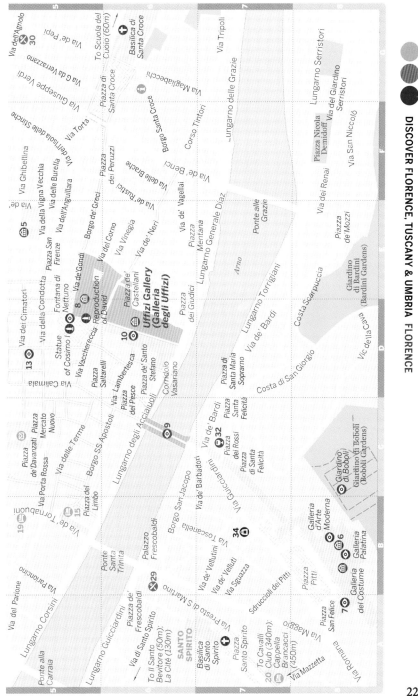

229

Florence

uncompleted roundel of the *Madonna and Child with the Infant St John* (1503–05, aka the *Tondo Pitti*).

On the 1st floor, to the right of the staircase, is the Sala di Donatello where Donatello's two versions of *David* fascinate: Donatello fashioned his slender, youthful, dressed image in marble in 1408 and his fabled bronze between 1440 and 1450. The latter is extraordinary – the more so when you consider it was the first freestanding naked statue to be sculpted since classical times.

Santa Maria Novella Area

BASILICA DI SANTA MARIA NOVELLA   Church

(Piazza di Santa Maria Novella; admission €3.50; ◷9am-5.50pm Mon-Thu, 11am-5.30pm Fri, 9am-5pm Sat, 1-5pm Sun) Just south of the central train station, this church was begun in the mid-13th century as the Dominican order's Florentine base. The highlight of the

Gothic interior, halfway along the north aisle, is Masaccio's superb fresco *Trinity* (1424–25), one of the first artworks to use the then newly discovered techniques of perspective and proportion.

FREE OFFICINA PROFUMO-
FARMACEUTICA DI SANTA MARIA
NOVELLA   Pharmacy
(www.santamarianovella.com.br; Via della Scala 16; ◷9.30am-7.30pm Mon-Sat, 10.30am-8.30pm Sun, museum 10am-5.30pm Mon-Fri) In business since 1612, this perfumery-pharmacy is famed for the remedies and sweet-smelling unguents it concocts using medicinal herbs cultivated in the monastery garden. After a day battling crowds at the Uffizi or Accademia, you may want to come here to source some Aqua di Santa Maria Novella, said to cure hysterics.

The Genius of Botticelli
Room 10–14

The miniature form of *The Discovery of the Body of Holofernes* (c 1470) makes Botticelli's early Renaissance masterpiece all the more impressive. Don't miss the artist watching you in *Adoration of the Magi* (1475), left of the exit.

View of the Arno

Indulge in intoxicating city views from this short glassed-in corridor – an architectural masterpiece. Near the top of the hill, spot one of 73 outer towers built to defend Florence and its 15 city gates below.

Second Corridor

Tribuna

First Corridor

Arno River

Portrait of Pope Leo X
Room 26

Stare into the eyes of the trio in this Raphael masterpiece (1518) and work out what the devil they're thinking – a perfect portrayal of High Renaissance intrigue.

Entrance to Vasari Corridor

Third Corridor

Matter of Fact

The Uffizi collection spans the 13th to 18th centuries, but its 15th- and 16th-century Renaissance works are second to none.

Doni Tondo
Room 25

David's creator, Michelangelo, was essentially a sculptor and no painting expresses this better than *Doni Tondo* (1506–08). Mary's muscular arms against a backdrop of curvaceous nudes are practically 3D in their shapeliness.

Annunciation
Room 15

Admire the exquisite portrayal of the Tuscan landscape in this painting (c 1475–80), one of few by Leonardo da Vinci to remain in Florence.

Value Lunchbox

Try the Uffizi rooftop cafe or – better value – gourmet *panini* at 'Ino (www.ino-firenze.com; Via dei Georgofili 3-7r).

San Lorenzo Area

CAPPELLE MEDICEE Mausoleum
(Piazza Madonna degli Aldobrandini; adult/
reduced €6/3; ☉8.15am-4.50pm Tue-Sat & 1st,
3rd Sun & 2nd, 4th Mon of month) Principal
burial place of the Medici rulers, this
mausoleum is sumptuously adorned with
granite, the most precious marble, semi-
precious stones and some of Michelangelo's most beautiful sculptures. A corridor
leads to the stark but graceful **Sagrestia
Nuova** (New Sacristy), Michelangelo's
first architectural work and showcase for
three of his most haunting sculptures:
Dawn and Dusk, Night and Day and *Madonna and Child*.

CENTRAL MARKET Food Market
(Piazza del Mercato Centrale; ☉7am-2pm Mon-
Fri, to 5pm Sat) Housed in a 19th-century
iron-and-glass structure, Florence's
oldest and largest food market is noisy,
smelly and full of wonderful fresh produce
to cook and eat.

San Marco Area

MUSEO DI SAN MARCO Museum
(Piazza San Marco 1; adult/reduced €4/2;
☉8.15am-1.50pm Mon-Fri, 8.15am-4.50pm Sat &
Sun, closed 1st, 3rd & 5th Sun of month, 2nd & 4th
Mon) At the heart of Florence's university
area sits the **Chiesa di San Marco** and
adjoining 15th-century Dominican monastery where gifted painter Fra' Angelico (c
1400–55) and sharp-tongued Savonarola
piously served God. Today, the monastery
showcases the work of Fra' Angelico. It is
one of Florence's most spiritually uplifting
museums.

On the 1st floor is Fra' Angelico's most
famous work, *Annunciation* (c 1440),
and cells frescoed between 1440 and
1441 to guide the meditation of his fellow
friars. Quite a few frescoes are extremely
gruesome – check out the cell of San
Antonino Arcivescovo, which features
a depiction of Jesus pushing open the
door of his sepulchre, squashing a nasty-
looking devil in the process.

The Oltrarno

PONTE VECCHIO   Landmark

Florence's iconic bridge has twinkled with the glittering wares of jewellers since the 16th century when Ferdinando I de' Medici ordered them here to replace the often malodorous presence of the town butchers, who were wont to toss unwanted leftovers into the river.

The bridge as it stands was built in 1345 and was the only one in Florence saved from destruction by the retreating Germans in 1944.

PALAZZO PITTI   Palazzo, Museum
(Piazza de' Pitti 1; adult €7-12, 3-day ticket valid when no temporary exhibition €11.50) This vast palace was begun in 1458 for the Pitti family, rivals of the Medici.

Raphaels and Rubens vie for centre stage in the enviable collection of 16th- to 18th-century art amassed by the Medici and Lorraine dukes in the 1st-floor **Galleria Palatina** (⊙8.15am-6.50pm Tue-Sun). Don't miss the **Sala di Saturno**, full of magnificent works by Raphael.

The sentimental favourite, Tiberio Titi's charming portrait of the young Prince Leopoldo de' Medici, hangs in the Sala di Apollo and the Sala di Venere shines with Titian's *Portrait of a Lady* (c 1536).

CAPPELLA BRANCACCI   Church
(Piazza del Carmine; ☎advance reservations 055 276 82 24; admission €4; ⊙10am-5pm Wed-Fri & Sat, 1-5pm Sun) The 13th-century **Basilica di Santa Maria del Carmine** might have been all but destroyed by fire in the late 18th century, but the magnificent frescoes in its chapel were not. Masaccio painted them in his early 20s but interrupted the task to go to Rome, where he died aged only 28. Filippino Lippi completed the cycle some 60 years later. Masaccio's contribution includes the *Expulsion of Adam and Eve from Paradise* and *The Tribute Money* on the chapel's upper left wall.

Visits to the chapel are by guided tour which must be booked in advance.

If You Like…
Cooking Classes

Once you've covered *bistecca fiorentina* (steak Florentine) and other Florentine cuisine basics, branch out with these tasty lessons covering the best of regional cuisine:

1 MONTEPULCIANO
There's more to this Tuscan hilltop town than its namesake red 'noble wine' – you can discover the bounty of these rolling hillsides by taking an official Montepulciano-region Slow Food tour (€100 to €155) or enrolling in a regional cooking course (€60 to €180) or Tuscan wine-tasting/ wine-pairing lessons (€37 to €60). You can organise your bookings through the **Strada del Vino Nobile di Montepulciano information office** (☏0578 71 74 84; www.stradavinonobile.it; Piazza Grande 7; ⏰10am-1pm & 3-6pm Mon-Fri). For more information about Montepulciano wine, see p259.

2 LUCCA
Lucchese are known for their glorious peasant cuisine, working culinary wonders with bread, beans, vegetables and legendary local olive oil. Rent a Lucca apartment or villa with equipped kitchen through **2italia** (2-night minimum; ☏3355 208 251; www.2italia.com; Via della Anfiteatro74; apt for 2 adults & up to 4 kids €150-170; 🛜👪) and ask English/Norwegian owners Kristen and Kaare to organise hands-on Lucchese cooking courses at your apartment. For more information on Lucca, see p247.

3 ASSISI
St Francis of Assisi fasted for 40 days at a stretch to reach higher spiritual ground – but with black Norcia truffles, sheep's milk cheeses and handmade pasta, Umbrian cuisine seems to be the obvious shortcut to heaven. From her Assisi *agriturismo* (farm-stay accommodation) aptly named **Alla Madonna del Piatto** (The Madonna of the Plate; p265), owner Letizia runs cooking classes that start off shopping in local markets and end with creating a feast of your own in a location overlooking St Francis' basilica.

Courses

SCUOLA DEL CUOIO — Leather-working
(☏055 24 45 34; www.scuoladelcuoio.com; Via San Giuseppe 5r) Held here are leather-working courses in a leather school created by Franciscan friars after WWII.

FOOD & WINE ACADEMY — Cooking
(☏055 012 39 94; www.florencecooking classes.com; Via de' Lamberti 1; one-day classes with lunch €79) Shop at the market with charismatic chef Giovanni, learn how to cook what you've bought, then eat it.

LA CUCINA DEL GARGA — Cooking
(☏055 21 13 96; www.divinacucina.com; Via del Moro 48r; one-day classes with lunch €155) Delve into the secrets of Florentine trattoria cuisine with American-born Sharon Oddson.

Tours

Bus

CAF TOURS — Coach
(☏055 21 06 12; www.caftours.com; Via Sant'Antonino 6r) Half- and full-day city coach tours (€45 to €190), including designer-outlet shopping tours (€35, six hours).

CITY SIGHTSEEING FIRENZE — Bus
(☏055 29 04 51; www.firenze.city-sight seeing.it; Piazza Stazione 1; tickets incl audioguide adult/5-15yr €22/11) Explore Florence by red, open-top bus, hopping on and off at 15 bus stops around the city. Tickets, sold by the driver, are valid for 24 hours.

I BIKE FLORENCE — Bike
(☏055 012 39 94; www.ibikeflorence.com; Via de' Lamberti 1) Guided history tours of Florence by bike (€29, two hours) and guided day trips to Chianti (€80 including lunch and wine tasting).

🛌 Sleeping

Piazza del Duomo & Piazza della Signoria

HOTEL SCOTI   Hotel €

(☎055 29 21 28; www.hotelscoti.com; Via de' Tornabuoni 7; s €29-75, d €45-125, tr €75-150, q €85-175; 🔊 ⚊) Wedged between Prada and McQueen, this *pensione* is a splendid mix of old-fashioned charm and value for money. Its 16 rooms are clean and comfortable, but the star of the show is the frescoed living room (1780). Breakfast costs €5.

HOTEL CESTELLI   Boutique Hotel €

(☎055 21 42 13; www.hotelcestelli.com; Borgo SS Apostoli 25; s with shared bathroom €40-60, d €50-100; ☉closed 4 weeks Jan-Feb, 3 weeks Aug) Located a stiletto hop and a skip from the Arno and fashionable Via de' Tornabuoni, this eight-room hotel is a gem. Before stepping out quiz Italian photographer Alessio and Japanese wife Asumi on the latest best addresses to drink, dine and shop. No breakfast.

PALAZZO VECCHIETTI   Historic Hotel €€€

(☎055 230 28 02; www.palazzovecchietti.com; Via degli Strozzi 4; d €284-734; ⚊ @ 🔊 ⚊) Wow, and wow again! This *residenza d'epoca* (historic residence) with 14 hopelessly romantic rooms and loggia in a 15th-century *palazzo* is a buzzword for hotel chic. No surprise: this is the handiwork of Florentine interior designer Michele Bönan.

Santa Maria Novella Area

TOP CHOICE HOTEL L'OROLOGIO   Design Hotel €€€

(☎055 27 73 80; www.hotelorologioflorence. com; Piazza di Santa Maria Novella 24; d €178-450; ⚊ ⚊ @ 🔊) Designed to be something of a showcase for the (very wealthy) owner's (exceedingly expensive) luxury wristwatch collection, the hotel has four stars, five floors and 54 rooms named after watches and clocks pretty much everywhere you look. Room 501 has a perfect balcony view of the Duomo.

HOTEL ROSSO 23   Boutique Hotel €€

(☎055 27 73 00; www.hotelrosso23.com; Piazza di Santa Maria Novella 23; s €79-100, d €85-195; ⚊ @ 🔊) The entrance to this hotel is so discrete you might well walk straight pass this stylish townhouse with a beautiful facade and smart, oyster-grey and red interior colour scheme. Rooms, all 42 of them, are thoroughly modern and breakfast is served in a bijou interior courtyard.

San Lorenzo Area

JOHANNA & JOHLEA   B&B €€

(☎055 463 32 92, 055 48 18 96; www.johanna.it; s €50-90, d €70-170; ⚊ 🔊) One of the most established B&Bs in town, J&J has more than a dozen tasteful, impeccable, individually decorated rooms split between five historic residences, some with wi-fi connections.

San Marco Area

HOTEL MORANDI ALLA CROCETTA   Hotel €€

(☎055 234 47 47; www.hotelmorandi.it; Via Laura 50; s €70-140, d €110-220, tr €130-195; q €150-370; P ⚊ 🔊) This medieval convent-turned-hotel away from the madding crowd is a stunner. A couple of rooms have handkerchief-sized gardens to laze in, but the pièce de résistance is frescoed No 29, the former chapel.

PALAZZO GUADAGNI HOTEL   Hotel

(☎055 265 83 76; www.palazzoguadagni.com; Piazza Santo Spirito 9; d €100-150, f per person €35; ⚊ 🔊) This hotel, with impossibly romantic loggia, is legendary – Zefferelli shot several scenes of *Tea with Mussolini* here. The Renaissance 16th-century palace has been brought back to life – in the most fabulous of manners – by local Florentines Laura and Ferdinando. Spacious rooms contain a tasteful mix of old and new, and that loggia terrace with wicker garden furniture is, well, dreamy....

Eating

Piazza del Duomo & Piazza della Signoria

TOP CHOICE OBIKÀ   Cheese bar €€

(☎ 055 277 35 26; www.obika.it; Via de' Tornabuoni 16; 3/5 mozzarellas €19.50/30, pizza €9-14.50; ⏰lunch & dinner Mon-Sat, 10am-11pm Sun) Taste different mozzarella cheeses with basil, organic veg or sun-dried tomatoes in the cathedral-like interior or snuggle beneath heaters in the star-topped courtyard.

CANTINETTA DEI
VERRAZZANO   Wine Cellar, Bakery €

(Via dei Tavolini 18-20; platters €4.50-12, focaccia €3-3.50, panini €2.50-4; ⏰noon-9pm Mon-Sat) The focaccia, perhaps topped with cara-melised radicchio or porcini mushrooms, is a must – as is a mixed cold-meat platter (try to ignore the bristly boar legs strung in the small open kitchen).

Coquinarius   Wine Bar €

(☎ 055 230 21 53; www.coquinarius.com; Via delle Oche 15r; meals €35; ⏰noon-10.30pm)

Olio e Convivium (p239)

Nestled within the shadow of the Duomo, this *enoteca* (wine bar) is extremely popular with tourists – try the justly famous ravioli with cheese and pear. Bookings essential.

Santa Maria Novella

L'OSTERIA DI GIOVANNI   Tuscan €€

(☎ 055 28 48 97; www.osteriadigiovanni.it; Via del Moro 22; meals €45; ⏰lunch & dinner Fri-Mon, dinner Tue-Thu) The cuisine here is staunchly Tuscan and stunningly creative. Think chickpea soup with octopus or pear-and-ricotta-stuffed *tortelli* (ravioli) bathed in a leek and almond cream. Throw the complimentary glass of *prosecco* as aperitif and subsequent *vin santo* (with homemade *cantuccini* – crunchy, almond-studded biscuits – to dunk in) at the end of the meal and you'll return time and again.

Il Latini   Trattoria €€

(☎ 055 21 09 16; www.illatini.com; Via dei Palchetti 6r; meals €40; ⏰lunch & dinner Tue-Sun) Melt-in-your-mouth *crostini,* Tuscan meats, fine pasta and roasted meats served at shared tables. There are two dinner seatings (7.30pm and 9pm); bookings are mandatory.

GIORGIO COSULICH/LONELY PLANET IMAGES ®

DISCOVER FLORENCE, TUSCANY & UMBRIA   FLORENCE

San Lorenzo & San Marco

TRATTORIA MARIO   Trattoria €
(www.trattoriamario.com; Via Rosina 2; meals €15-25; ⏲noon-3.30pm Mon-Sat, closed 3 weeks Aug) Arrive at noon to ensure a stool around a shared table at this busy trattoria. Monday and Thursday is tripe, Friday fish and Saturday the day locals flock here for a brilliantly blue *bistecca alla fiorentina* (€35/kg). No advance reservations, no credit cards.

LA MESCITA   Wine Bar €
(Via degli Alfani 70r; mains €5-10; ⏲10.30am-4pm Mon-Sat, closed Aug) Conveniently close to *David* and the Galleria dell'Accademia, this part *enoteca* part *fiaschetteria* (wine seller) is an unapologetically old-fashioned place from 1927. It serves Tuscan specialities such as *maccheroni* with sausage and *insalata di farro* (farro salad), and has a great marble-topped bar propped up by noontime tipplers.

TEATRO DEL SALE   Traditional Italian €€
(☎055 200 14 92; www.teatrodelsale.com; Via dei Macci 111r; breakfast/lunch/dinner €7/20/30; ⏲9-11am, 12.30-2.30pm & 7-11pm Tue-Sat Sep-Jul) Aptly set in an old Florentine theatre, this members-only club is the brainchild of larger-than-life Florentine chef Fabio Picchi. Teatro del Sale serves breakfast, lunch and dinner, culminating at 9.30pm in a live performance of drama, music or comedy arranged by artistic director and famous comic actress (and Picchi's wife) Maria Cassi. Dinners are hectic affairs and advance reservations are essential: grab a chair, serve yourself water, wine and antipasti and wait for Picchi to yell out what's just about to be served before queuing at the glass hatch for your *primo* (first course) and *secondo* (second course). Dessert and coffee are laid out buffet-style just prior to the performance.

TRATTORIA CIBRÈO   Trattoria €€
(Via dei Macci 122r; meals €35; ⏲12.50-2.30pm & 6.50-11.15pm Tue-Sat Sep-Jul) Dine here and you'll instantly understand why a queue gathers outside before it opens. Once in, revel in top-notch Tuscan cuisine: perhaps ricotta and potato flan with a rich meat sauce, puddle of olive oil and grated parmesan (divine!) or a simple plate of polenta, followed by homemade sausages, beans in a spicy tomato sauce and braised celery. No advance reservations, no credit cards, no coffee and arrive early to snag a table.

PIZZAMAN   Pizza €
(Via dell'Agnolo 79; ⏲noon-2.30pm & 6.30pm-midnight Mon-Fri, 6.30pm-midnight Sat & Sun) This cheap and cheerful pizzeria with booth-style seating gets rave reviews for its Naples-style pizza (baked in a wood-burning oven).

The Oltrarno

IL SANTO BEVITORE   Modern Tuscan €€
(☎055 21 12 64; www.ilsantobevitore.com; Via di Santo Spirito 64-66r; meals €35; ⏲lunch & dinner Sep-Jul) The menu is a creative reinvention of seasonal classics, and different for lunch and dinner: hand-chopped beef tartare, chestnut millefeuille and lentils, pureed purple cabbage soup with mozzarella cream and anchovy syrup, acacia honey *bavarese* (type of firm, creamy mousse) with *vin santo*-marinated dried fruits ...

OLIO & CONVIVIUM   Tuscan €€
(☎055 265 81 98; Via di Santo Spirito 4; meals €40; ⏲lunch & dinner Tue-Sat, lunch Mon) A key address on any gastronomy agenda: your tastebuds will tingle at the sight of the legs of ham, conserved truffles, wheels of cheese, artisan-made bread and other delectable delicatessen products sold in this shop. Dine out the back.

 **Drinking**

LE VOLPI E L'UVA   Wine Bar
(www.levolpieluva.com; Piazza dei Rossi 1; ⏲11am-9pm Mon-Sat) The city's best *enoteca con degustazione* (wine bar with tasting) bar none: this intimate address chalks up an impressive list of wines by the glass (€3.50 to €8).

SKY LOUNGE CONTINENTALE — Bar

(www.continentale.it; Vicolo dell Oro 6r; ⏲2.30-11.30pm Apr-Sep) This rooftop bar with wooden-decking terrace accessible from the 5th floor of the Ferragamo-owned Hotel Continentale is as chic as one would expect of a fashion-house hotel. Dress the part or feel out of place.

LOCHNESS LOUNGE — Bar

(www.lochnessfirenze.com; Via de' Benci 19r; ⏲7pm-2am) Lochness is a sassy, vintage-cool music and cocktail venue with an Andy Warhol twist to its bold interior. Drinks cost €5 during the daily 7pm to 10pm 'happy hour'; check Facebook for the week's line-up.

Sei Divino — Wine Bar

(Borgo Ognissanti 42r; ⏲daily) This stylish 'wine gallery' hosts one of Florence's most happening *aperitivo* scenes, complete with music, the odd exhibition and plenty of pavement action.

⭐ Entertainment

To find out what's on when, check **Firenze Spettacolo** (www.firenzespettacolo.it), **The Florentine** (www.theflorentine.net) and **Notte Fiorentina** (www.nottefiorentina.it).

Nightclubs

CENTRAL PARK — Nightclub

(Via Fosso Macinante 1; ⏲11pm-4am Wed-Sat) Flit between a handful of different dance floors at this mainstream club in city park Parco delle Cascine where everything from Latin to pop, house to drum-and-bass plays. From May the dance floor moves outside beneath the stars.

CAVALLI CLUB — Nightclub

(www.cavalliclub.com; Piazza del Carmine 8r; ⏲7.30pm-2.30am Tue-Sun) Incongruously wedged beside 13th-century Basilica di Santa Maria del Carmine, designer Robert Cavalli's club – in a deconsecrated

Left: Ponte Vecchio (p235) over the Arno River, Florence;
Below: Fresh pasta for sale, Lucca (p247)
(LEFT) JOHN ELK III/LONELY PLANET IMAGES ©; (BELOW) RACHEL LEWIS/LONELY PLANET IMAGES ©

church, look for the shiny red door – is glitzy, glam, wildly theatrical and over-the-top.

Cargo Club   Nightclub
(http://cargoclub.wordpress.com; Via dell'Erta Canina 12r; ☾11pm-4am Wed-Sat) This club prides itself on being a tad underground; DJs spin all sounds.

Live Music

LA CITÉ   Live Music
(www.lacitelibreria.info; Borgo San Frediano 20r; ☾10am-1am Mon-Sat, 4pm-1am Sun; 🛜) By night, the intimate bookshelf-lined space morphs into a vibrant live-music space: think swing, fusion, jam-session jazz. The staircase next to the bar hooks up with mezzanine seating up top.

JAZZ CLUB   Jazz Club
(www.jazzclubfirenze.com; Via Nuovo de' Caccini 3; ☾9pm-2am Tue-Sat, closed Jul & Aug) Catch salsa, blues, Dixieland and world music as well as jazz at Florence's top jazz venue.

BE BOP MUSIC CLUB   Live Music
(Via dei Servi 76r; admission free; ☾8pm-2am) Inspired by the Swinging Sixties, this beloved retro venue features everything from Led Zeppelin and Beatles cover bands to swing jazz and 1970s funk.

Theatre, Classical Music & Ballet

TEATRO DEL MAGGIO MUSICALE FIORENTINO   Theatre
(☎055 287 222; www.maggiofiorentino.com; Corso Italia 16) The curtain rises on opera, classical concerts and ballet at this lovely theatre, host to summertime music festivals.

 **Shopping**

Visit www.florenceartfashion.com, an authoritative guide to the city's fashion studios and workshops. Themed itineraries walk you through small ateliers and

241

boutiques that design and craft footwear, women's fashion, jewellery, and so on; and you can also sign up for an on-the-ground guided fashion tour.

MRS MACIS
Fashion

(Borgo Pinti 38r; ☺3-7.30pm Mon-Sat) Workshop and showroom of the talented Carla Macis, this eye-catching boutique – dollhouse-like in design – specialises in very feminine 1950s, '60s and '70s clothes and jewellery made from new and recycled fabrics.

ANTICO SETIFICO FIORENTINO
Artisanal

(www.anticosetificiofiorentino.com; Via Bartoini 4; ☺9am-1pm & 2-5pm Mon-Fri) Precious silks, velvets and other luxurious fabrics are woven on 18th- and 19th-century looms at this world-famous fabric house where opulent damasks and brocades in Renaissance styles have been made since 1786.

GUILO GIANNINI E FIGLIO
Artisanal

(www.guilogiannini.it; Piazza Pitti) One of Florence's oldest artisan families, the Gianninis – bookbinders by trade – make and sell marbled paper, beautifully bound

books, stationery and so on. Don't miss the workshop upstairs.

SOCIÉTÉ ANONYME
Fashion

(www.societeanonyme.it; Via Niccolini 3f) Near Sant' Ambrogio food market, this urban concept store turns to London's Brick Lane, Berlin's Mitte and other hip neighbourhoods for inspiration. Look for its list of brands chalked on the board outside (and the Shared Platform design gallery next door).

❶ Information

Tourist Information

Amerigo Vespucci airport (☎055 31 58 74; ☺8.30am-8.30pm)

Train station (☎055 21 22 45; Piazza della Stazione 4; ☺8.30am-7pm Mon-Sat, 8.30am-2pm Sun) Baby-changing facilities.

Santa Croce (☎055 234 04 44; www.comune. fi.it, in Italian; Borgo Santa Croce 29r; ☺9am-7pm Mon-Sat, 9am-2pm Sun)

San Lorenzo (☎055 29 08 32; www. firenzeturismo.it; Via Cavour 1r; ☺8.30am-6.30pm Mon-Sat)

Leaning Tower of Pisa (p244)

Getting There & Away

Air

Florence Airport (FLR; www.aeroporto.firenze.it) Also known as Amerigo Vespucci or Peretola airport, 5km northwest of the city centre; domestic and a handful of European flights.

Pisa Airport (PSA; www.pisa-airport.com) Tuscany's main international airport named after Galileo Galilei is nearer Pisa, but well linked with Florence by public transport.

Bus

Services from the SITA bus station (www.sitabus.it; Via Santa Caterina da Siena 17r; ⊙information office 8.30am-12.30pm & 3-6pm Mon-Fri, 8.30am-12.30pm Sat), just west of Piazza della Stazione, go to the following towns:

Siena (€7.10, 1¼ hours, at least hourly)

San Gimignano via Poggibonsi (€6.25, 50 minutes, at least hourly).

Greve in Chianti (€3.30, one hour, hourly)

Car & Motorcycle

Florence is connected by the A1 northwards to Bologna and Milan, and southwards to Rome and Naples. The S2 links Florence with Siena.

Train

Florence's central train station is Stazione di Santa Maria Novella (Piazza della Stazione).
Services include the following:

Lucca (€5.10, 1½ hours to 1¾ hours, half-hourly)

Pisa (€5.80, 45 minutes to one hour, half-hourly)

Pistoia (€3.10, 45 minutes to one hour, half-hourly)

Rome (€17.25, 1¾ hours to 4¼ hours)

Bologna (€10.50 to €25, one hour to 1¾ hours)

Milan (€29.50 to €53, 2¼ hours to 3½ hours)

Venice (€24 to €43, 2¾ hours to 4½ hours)

Getting Around

To/From the Airport

BUS A shuttle (single/return €5/8, 25 minutes) runs between Florence Airport and Florence's Stazione di Santa Maria Novella train station every 30 minutes between 6am and 11.30pm.
Terravision (www.terravision.eu) runs daily services (single/return €10/16, 1¼ hours, 13 daily) between the bus stop outside Florence's Stazione di Santa Maria Novella on Via Alamanni and Pisa's Galileo Galilei airport – buy tickets online, on board or from the Terravision desk (Via Alamanni 9r; ⊙6am-7pm) inside the Deanna Bar.
TRAIN Trains link Florence's Stazione di Santa Maria Novella with Pisa's Galileo Galilei airport (€5.80, 1½ hours, hourly from 4.30am to 10.25pm).
TAXI A taxi between Florence Airport and town costs a flat rate of €20, plus surcharges of €2 on Sunday and holidays, €3 between 10pm and 6am and €1 per bag. Exit the terminal building, bear right and you'll come to the taxi rank.

Car & Motorcycle

Most traffic is banned from the historic centre and motorists risk a hefty fine if they breach the rules.
Many hotels arrange parking for guests.

Public Transport

Buses and electric *bussini* (minibuses) run by ATAF (☎800 42 45 00; from mobiles ☎199 10 42 45; www.ataf.net, in Italian) serve the city.
Tickets valid for 90 minutes (no return journeys) cost €1.20 (€2 on board) and are sold at kiosks, tobacconists and the ATAF ticket & information office (⊙7.30am-7.30pm) adjoining the train station.
A carnet of 10 tickets costs €10, a handy *biglietto multiplo* (four-journey ticket) is €4.70 and a travel pass valid for 1/3/7 days is €5/12/18.

Taxi

☎055 42 42
☎055 43 90

NORTHERN & WESTERN TUSCANY

Pisa

POP 87,440

Once a maritime power to rival Genoa and Venice, Pisa now draws its fame from an architectural project gone terribly wrong. But the world-famous Leaning Tower is just one of many noteworthy sights in this compact and compelling city.

Save the Leaning Tower and its miraculous square for the latter part of the day – or, better still, an enchanting visit after dark (mid-June to August) when the night casts a certain magic on the glistening white monuments and the tour buses have long gone. Enjoy low-key architectural and art genius at the Chiesa di Santa Maria della Spina and Palazzo Blu, and lunch with locals at Sottobosco.

👁 Sights

Along the Arno

CHIESA DI SANTA MARIA DELLA SPINA   Church

(Lungarno Gambacorti; adult/reduced €2/1.50; ⏱11am-12.45pm & 3-5.45pm Tue-Fri, 11am-12.45pm & 3-6.45pm Sat & Sun) This now-deconsecrated church, built between 1230 and 1223 to house a reliquary of a *spina* (thorn) from Christ's crown, is refreshingly intimate. Its ornate, triple-spired exterior is encrusted with tabernacles and statues. The focal point inside is Andrea and Nino Pisano's *Madonna and Child* (aka Madonna of the Rose; 1345–48), a masterpiece of Gothic sculpture that still bears traces of its original colours and gilding.

FREE PALAZZO BLU   Art Gallery

(www.palazzoblu.it; Lungarno Gambacorti 9; ⏱10am-7pm Tue-Fri, 10am-8pm Sat & Sun) Facing the river is this magnificently re-stored, 14th-century building with striking dusty-blue facade. Inside, its over-the-top 19th-century interior decoration is the perfect backdrop for the Foundation Cari-Pisa's art collection – Pisan works from the 14th to the 20th century, plus various temporary exhibitions.

Piazza Dei Miracoli

LEANING TOWER   Landmark

(Torre Pendente; www.opapisa.it; admission ticket office/online €15/17; ⏱8.30am-8.30pm Apr–mid-Jun & Sep, 8.30am-11pm mid-Jun–Aug, 9am-7.30pm Oct, 9.30am-6pm Nov & Feb-Mar, 10am-5pm Dec-Jan) In 1160 Pisa boasted 10,000-odd towers – but no bell tower for its cathedral. Loyal Pisan Berta di Bernardo righted this in 1172 when she died, leaving a legacy of 60 soldi in her will to the city to get cracking on a *campanile*. Construction work started in 1173 but ground to a halt a decade later when the structure's first three tiers started tilting. In 1272 work started again, with artisans and masons attempting to bolster the foundations but failing miserably.

By 1993 it was 4.47m out of plumb, more than five degrees from the vertical.

Access to the Leaning Tower is limited to 40 people at one time – children under eight are not admitted. Visits last 30 minutes and involve a steep climb up 294 occasionally slippy steps. All bags, handbags included, must be deposited at the free left-luggage desk next to the central ticket office – cameras are about the only thing you can take up.

Reserve and buy tickets for the Leaning Tower from one of two well-signposted **ticket offices** (www.opapisa.it; Piazza dei Miracoli; ⏱8am-7.30pm Apr-Sep, 8.30am-7pm Oct, 9am-5pm Nov & Feb, 9.30am-4.30pm Dec-Jan, 8.30am-6pm Mar): the main ticket office behind the tower or the smaller office inside Museo delle Sinópie. To guarantee your visit to the tower, book tickets via the website at least 15 days in advance. The ticket offices also sell combination tickets covering the Baptistry and Museo dell'Opera del Duomo (ticket covering one/two/five attractions adult €5/6/10, reduced €2/3/5).

DUOMO   Duomo

(Piazza dei Miracoli; adult/reduced €2/1, free Nov-Mar & Sun year-round; ⏱10am-8pm mid-Mar–Sep, 10am-7pm Oct, 10am-1pm & 2-5pm Nov-Feb, 10am-6pm or 7pm early–mid-Mar) Pisa's cathedral was paid for with spoils brought home after Pisans attacked an Arab fleet entering Palermo in 1063. Its main facade – not completed until the 13th century – has four exquisite tiers of columns diminishing skywards, while the vast interior is propped up by 68 hefty granite columns in classical style. The wooden ceiling decorated with 24-carat gold is a legacy from the period of Medici rule.

Inside, don't miss the extraordinary early-14th-century octagonal **pulpit** in the north aisle. Sculpted from Carrara marble by Giovanni Pisano and featuring nude and heroic figures, its depth of detail and heightening of feeling brought a new pictorial expressionism and life to Gothic sculpture.

BAPTISTRY   Baptistery
(Piazza dei Miracoli; adult/reduced €5/2; ⊗8am-8pm Apr-Sep, 9am-7pm Oct, 10am-5pm Nov-Feb, 9am-6pm Mar) This unusual round Baptistry has one dome piled on top of another. The lower level of arcades is styled in Pisan-Romanesque; the pinnacled upper section and dome are Gothic.

Inside, the beautiful hexagonal marble **pulpit** carved by Nicola Pisano between 1259 and 1260 is the undisputed highlight. Inspired by the Roman sarcophagi in the Camposanto, Pisano used powerful classical models to enact scenes from biblical legend.

Don't leave the baptistery without (a) admiring the Islamic floor (b) climbing up to the gallery for a stunning overview (c) risking a whisper and listening to it resound.

**MUSEO DELL'OPERA
DEL DUOMO**   Museum
(Piazza dei Miracoli; adult/reduced €5/2; ⊗8am-8pm Apr-Sep, 9am-7pm Oct, 9am-5pm Nov-Feb, 9am-6pm Mar) Highlights of this museum include Giovanni Pisano's ivory carving of the *Madonna and Child* (1299), made for the cathedral's high altar, and his mid-13th-century *Madonna del colloquio*, originally from a gate of the Duomo. Legendary booty includes various pieces of Islamic art including the griffin that once topped the cathedral and a 10th-century Moorish hippogriff.

Sleeping

TOP CHOICE **ROYAL VICTORIA HOTEL** Hotel €
(☎050 94 01 11; www.royalvictoria.it; Lungarno Pacinotti 12; s with shared bathroom €30-45, d with shared bathroom €40-55, d €65-80, tr €80-120, q €120-175; P ✳ ⊚ ♿) This doyen of Pisan hotels has been run with pride by the Piegaja family since 1837, with a shabby-chic mix of Grand Tour antique and modern-day comfort.

Baptistry, Piazza dei Miracoli, Pisa

Hotel Relais dell'Orologio Hotel €€€
(050 83 03 61; www.hotelrelaisorologio.com;
Via della Faggiola 12-14; d €200-800; P ❄ 📶)
Something of a honeymoon venue, Pisa's
dreamy five-star hotel occupies a tastefully
restored 14th-century fortified tower house in a
quiet street.

 Eating

IL MONTINO Pizzeria
(Vicolo del Monte 1; pizza €4.20-7.50;
🕐10.30am-3pm & 5-10pm Mon-Sat) Order
pizza to take away or grab one of a
handful of tightly packed tables, inside
or out, and munch on house specialities
like *cecina* (chickpea pizza), *castagnacci*
(chestnut cake) and *spuma* (sweet, non-
alcoholic drink).

IL COLONNINO Osteria €€
(050 313 84 30; Via Sant'Andrea 37-41;
meals €30; 🕐lunch & dinner Tue-Sun) Go for
spaghetti-like *tagliolini* sprinkled with San
Miniato truffles, pork fillet in a balsamic
and pink peppercorn sauce or – for the
springtime veggie in you – white asparagus with boiled egg sauce. The fixed €25
menu is excellent value.

BIOSTERIA 050 Organic, Tuscan €
(050 54 31 06; www.zerocinquanta.com; Via
San Francesco 36; meals €25; 🕐12.30-2.30pm
& 7.45-10.30pm Mon & Wed-Sat, 7.45-10.30pm
Sun;) Seasonal Tuscan dishes here
are strictly local and organic. Try black
cabbage, nut and gorgonzola risotto,
rabbit with sweet mustard or one of
the excellent-value daily lunch specials
chalked on the board outside.

**OSTERIA DEL PORTON
ROSSO** Osteria €€
(050 58 05 66; Vicolo del Porton Rosso 11;
meals €35; 🕐lunch & dinner Mon-Sat) Pisan
specialities such as ravioli with salted
cod and chickpeas happily coexist with
Tuscan classics such as grilled fillet steak.

ⓘ Information

Tourist Information

Tourist office (www.pisaunicaterra.it); airport
(050 50 25 18; 🕐9.30am-11.30pm); train
station (050 4 22 91; Piazza Vittorio Emanuele
II 13; 🕐9am-7pm Mon-Sat, 9am-4pm Sun);
town centre (050 91 03 50; tourist-
point@comune.pisa.it; Piazza XX
Settembre; 🕐8.30-12.30pm)

ⓘ Getting There & Away

AIR Galileo Galilei Airport
(PSA; www.pisa-airport.
com) Tuscany's main
international airport, 2km
south of town; flights to
most major European cities.
CAR Pisa is close to the A11
and A12.
TRAIN Florence (€5.80, 1¼
hours, frequent)

Palazzo Pfanner (p247), Lucca

Lucca (€2.40, 30 minutes, every 30 minutes)

Rome (€16.85, 2½ to four hours, 16 daily)

Getting Around

To/From the Airport

BUS The LAM Rossa (red) bus line (€1.10, 10 minutes, every 10 to 20 minutes) passes through the city centre and the train station en route to/ from the airport.

TAXI A taxi between the airport and city centre costs around €10. To book, call Radio Taxi Pisa (☑050 54 16 00; www.cotapi.it).

TRAIN Services run to/from Stazione Pisa Centrale (€1.10, five minutes, 33 per day); be sure to purchase and validate your ticket before you get on the train.

Car & Motorcycle

There's a free car park outside the zone on Lungarno Guadalongo near the Fortezza di San Gallo on the south side of the Arno.

Lucca

POP 84,640

Hidden behind imposing Renaissance walls, Lucca has a rich history, excellent restaurants and a musical **Summer Festival** (www.summer-festival.com) that draws top talent.

Founded by the Etruscans, Lucca became a Roman colony in 180 BC and a free *comune* (self-governing city) during the 12th century, when it enjoyed a period of prosperity based on the silk trade.

Napoleon ended all this in 1805, when he created the principality of Lucca and placed his sister Elisa in control. Lucca miraculously escaped being bombed during WWII, so the fabric of the historic centre has remained unchanged for centuries.

Sights

CITY WALLS Landmark

Lucca's monumental **mura** (walls), built around the old city in the 16th and 17th centuries and defended by 126 canons, remain in almost perfect condition. Twelve metres high and 4km in length, the ramparts are crowned with a tree-lined footpath that looks down on the old town and out towards the Apuane Alps.

FREE CATTEDRALE DI SAN MARTINO Cathedral

(Piazza San Martino; ⊙9.30am-5.45pm Mon-Fri, 9.30am-6.45pm Sat, 9.30-10.45am & noon-6pm Sun) Lucca's predominantly Romanesque cathedral dates to the start of the 11th century.

The interior was rebuilt in the 14th and 15th centuries with a Gothic flourish.

The cathedral's many works of art include a magnificent *Last Supper* by Tintoretto above the third altar of the south aisle and Domenico Ghirlandaio's 1479 *Madonna Enthroned with Saints* in the **sacristy** (adult/reduced €2/1.50).

LUCCA CENTER OF CONTEMPORARY ART Art Gallery

(☑0583 57 17 12; www.luccamuseum.com; Via della Fratta 36; adult/reduced €7/5; ⊙10am-7pm Tue-Sun) A refreshing change from the historic Tuscan norm, Lucca's contemporary art museum hosts some riveting temporary exhibitions.

PALAZZO PFANNER Palazzo

(www.palazzopfanner.it; Via degli Asili 33; palace or garden adult/reduced €4/3.50, both €5.50/4.50; ⊙10am-6pm Apr-Oct) Felix Pfanner, may God rest his soul, was an Austrian émigré who first brought beer to Italy – and brewed it in this mansion's cellars. Take the outdoor staircase to the frescoed and furnished *piano nobile* (main reception room), then visit the ornate, statue-studded 18th-century garden. August to October, watch out for the lovely chamber-music concerts Palazzo Pfanner hosts.

Sleeping

Tourist offices have accommodation lists and, if you visit in person, can make reservations for you (free of charge); pay 10% of the room price as on-the-spot deposit and the remainder at the hotel.

PICCOLO HOTEL PUCCINI   Hotel €
(☎0583 55 42 1; www.hotelpuccini.com; Via di Poggio 9; d €75-95, tr €95-120, q €120-140; ❄ 🛜) This elegant address is an ode to Puccini. The decor is an unobtrusive mix of some period furnishings and historic collectables.

LA BOHEME   B&B €€
(☎0583 46 24 04; www.boheme.it; Via del Moro 2; d €90-140; ❄ @) Rooms here are furnished in antique Tuscan style; some have breathtaking high ceilings and all have decent-sized bathrooms. Breakfast is generous.

ALLA CORTE DEGLI ANGELI   Boutique Hotel €€
(☎0583 46 92 04; www.allacortedegliangeli. com; Via degli Angeli 23; s €80-110, d €110-160; ❄ @ 🛜) Occupying three floors of a 15th-century townhouse, this four-star boutique hotel with 10 rooms and an old-fashioned rocking horse in its wood-beamed lounge oozes charm.

Eating

TOP CHOICE DA FELICE   Pizzeria €
(www.pizzeriadafelice.com; Via Buia 12; focaccia €1-3.50, pizza slice €1.30; ⏱10am-8.30pm Mon-Sat) *Cecina,* a salted chickpea pizza served piping-hot from the oven, and *castagnacci* (chestnut cakes) are Felice's raison d'être.

PECORA NERA   Trattoria €
(☎0583 46 97 38; www.lapecoraneralucca.it; Piazza San Francesco 4; pizza €5-9, meals €20; ⏱Wed-Sat, lunch Sun) The only Lucca restaurant recommended by the Slow Food Movement – scores extra brownie points for social responsibility (its profits fund workshops for young people with Down syndrome). Thirty-odd different pizza types and a handful of Tuscan classics is what's cooking in the kitchen.

TRATTORIA CANULEIA   Tuscan €€
(☎0583 46 74 70; Via Canuleia 14; meals €40; ⏱lunch & dinner Mon-Sat) What makes this

dining address stand out from the crowd is its secret walled garden out back – the perfect spot to escape the tourist hordes and listen to birds tweet over partridge risotto, artichoke and shrimp spaghetti or a traditional *peposa* (beef and pepper stew).

OSTERIA BARALLA Osteria €€
(☏ 0583 44 02 40; www.osteriabaralla.it; Via Anfiteatro 5; meals €32; ☺ lunch & dinner Mon-Sat)
Feast on local specialities beneath huge red-brick vaults at this busy *osteria* from 1860. Thursday is *bolito misto* (mixed boiled meat) day, Saturday roast pork.

 **Drinking**

CAFFÈ DI SIMO Cafe
(Via Fillungo 58; ☺ 9am-8pm & 8.30pm-1am) For a respite from the sun's glare, immerse yourself in the chic Liberty (art nouveau) interior of Lucca's famous coffee shop. Its cakes are masterpieces.

ENOTECA CALASTO Wine bar
(www.lucca-wine-treasures.com; Piazza San Giovanni 5; ☺ 11am-11pm) A Brit and a Dane are the creative duo behind this *enoteca* with a terracotta-pot terrace. Its wine list only features local Lucchesi production and Thursday evening ushers in wine tasting (€5) with a local producer.

ⓘ Information

Tourist office (www.luccatourist.it) Piazza Santa Maria 35 (☏ 0583 91 99 31; ☺ 9am-7pm daily); Piazzale Verdi (☏ 0583 58 31 50; ☺ 9am-7pm daily Apr-Sep, to 5pm Oct-Mar); Via Elisa 67 (☺ 9am-1pm & 2-6pm Wed-Mon Apr-Sep)

ⓘ Getting There & Away

BUS Vaibus (www.vaibus.it) runs services throughout the region.
Pisa airport (€3.20, 45 minutes to one hour, 30 daily).

CAR & MOTORCYCLE The A11 runs westwards to Pisa and eastwards to Florence.

TRAIN

Florence (€5.30, 1¼ to 1¾ hours, hourly)

Pisa (€2.40, 30 minutes, every 30 minutes)

ℹ Getting Around

BICYCLE Rent regular wheels (€2.50/12 per hour/day; ID required) from the Piazzale Verdi tourist office or a city/mountain bike (€3/4 per hour), racer (€5 per hour) or tandem (€6.50 per hour).

Cicli Bizzarri (☎ 0583 49 66 82; www.ciclibizzarri.net, in Italian; Piazza Santa Maria 32; ⏱ 9am-7pm daily)

CENTRAL TUSCANY
Siena
POP 54,414

The rivalry between historic adversaries Siena and Florence continues to this day, and participation isn't limited to the locals – most travellers tend to develop a strong preference for one over the other. These allegiances often boil down to aesthetic preference: while Florence saw its greatest flourishing during the Renaissance, Siena's enduring artistic glories are largely Gothic.

History

A plague outbreak in 1348 killed two-thirds of Siena's 100,000 inhabitants and led to a period of decline that culminated in the city being handed over to Cosimo I de' Medici, who barred the inhabitants from operating banks and thus severely curtailed its power.

Today Siena is a Unesco World Heritage Site as the living embodiment of a medieval city.

Sights

IL CAMPO Piazza
This sloping piazza has been Siena's civic and social centre for nearly 600 years.

Il Campo is the undoubted heart of the city. It's also the site of the annual Palio, the dangerous, costumed bareback horse race held at 7.45pm in July and 7pm in August.

DUOMO Duomo
Siena's *duomo* is one of Italy's greatest Gothic churches, and is the focal point of this important group of **ecclesiastical buildings** (www.operaduomo.siena.it; Piazza del Duomo).

Construction of the **duomo** (admission €3, audioguide adult/child €5/3; ⏱ 10.30am-8pm Mon-Sat, 1.30-6pm Sun Jun-Aug, shorter hrs rest of year) started in 1215 and work continued well into the 14th century. The magnificent facade of white, green and red polychrome marble was designed by Giovanni Pisano (the statues of philosophers and prophets are copies; you'll find Pisano's originals in the Museo dell'Opera Metropolitana).

The interior features a magnificent inlaid marble floor decorated with 56 panels depicting historical and biblical subjects. The most valuable are kept covered and are revealed only from late August to late October each year (admission is €6 during this period).

Through a door from the north aisle is the enchanting **Libreria Piccolomini**, built to house the books of Enea Silvio Piccolomini, better known as Pius II. The walls of the small hall are decorated with vividly coloured narrative frescoes (1502–07) painted by Bernardino Pinturicchio.

On the right-hand (eastern) side of the *duomo* is the **Museo dell'Opera** (admission €6; ⏱ 9.30am-7pm Mar-May & Sep-Oct, to 8pm Jun-Aug, 10am-7pm Nov-Feb). Its highlight is Duccio di Buoninsegna's striking *Maestà* (1311), which was painted on both sides as a screen for the *duomo*'s high altar. The main painting portrays the Virgin surrounded by angels, saints and prominent Sienese citizens of the period; the rear panels (sadly incomplete) portray scenes from the Passion of Christ.

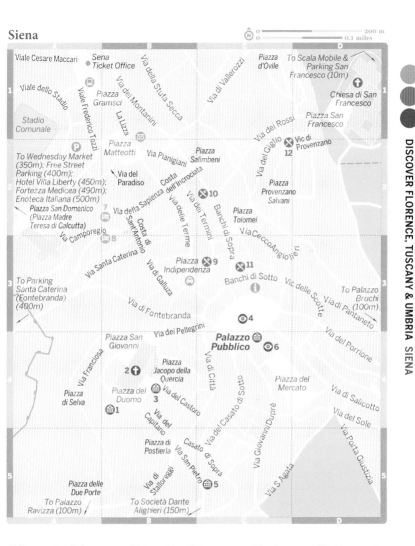

Siena

Siena

Don't Miss **Palazzo Pubblico**

Siena's 14th-century Palazzo Pubblico (also known as Palazzo Communale or Town Hall) offers sweeping views from its 120m 14th-century tower, **Torre del Mangia**, and far-sighted visions in its frescoed council chamber, **Sala della Pace** (Room of Peace). Unlike medieval paintings that show heaven as a golden haze, Ambrogio Lorenzetti pictured paradise on earth here in Siena in his c1338–40 fresco *Allegory of Good Government*. Merchants haggle pleasantly in a tidy marketplace, neighbours join in public wedding celebrations and the grey-bearded figure of Legitimate Authority is flanked by gorgeous women representing the virtues. Sadly, Lorenzetti was lost to the plague before seeing his painting finished – and despite politicians' promises, his vision has yet to be realised.

Many visitors enter the courtyard of the Palazzo Comunale and climb the Torre del Mangia without realising that Siena's most towering achievements can be glimpsed on the 1st floor, behind closed council chamber doors. Though Siena lost battles to Florence and the plague, its groundbreaking representative government had many triumphs: the city redirected bloody family feuds into a horserace, the annual Palio; collected fines for cursing, in the world's first communal swear jar; and in good economic times and crises, the city reserved public funds for the arts. Besides Lorenzetti, another key beneficiary was the great Sienese painter Simone Martini, whose glowing, expressive *Maestà* (Virgin Mary in Majesty; 1315) fresco in the Palazzo Pubblico Museum is a missing link between Byzantine idealism and Renaissance realism.

THINGS YOU NEED TO KNOW

Courtyard entry free, tower admission €8, museum admission adult/reduced €8/4.50; ⏰10am-7pm Mar-Oct, tower to 4pm mid-Oct–Feb, museum to 6pm Nov–mid-Mar

COMPLESSO MUSEALE SANTA MARIA DELLA SCALA
Cultural Centre

(www.santamariadellascala.com; Piazza del Duomo 1; adult/reduced €6/3.50; ⏱10.30am-6.30pm) This former hospital, parts of which date to the 13th century, was built as a hospice for pilgrims travelling the Via Francigena, but soon expanded its remit to shelter abandoned children and care for the poor. The **Pellegrinaio** (Pilgrim's Hall) has 15th-century frescoes by Lorenzo Vecchietta, Priamo della Quercia and Domenico di Bartolo lauding the good works of the hospital and its patrons.

PINACOTECA NAZIONALE
Art Gallery

(Via San Pietro 29; adult/reduced €4/2; ⏱8.15am-7.15pm Tue-Sat, 9am-1pm Sun & Mon) The highlights here are all on the second floor: Room 3 has Duccio's polyptych *Madonna col Bambino e I Santi* (Madonna with Child and Saints, 1305) and Simone Martini's *Madonna col Bambino* (Madonna with Child, c1321); Room 5 has Martini's *Il Beato Agostino* altarpiece (The Blessed Agostino, 1324); Room 7 houses Ambrogio Lorenzetti's luminous *Annunciazione* (Annunciation, 1343–44); and Room 11 has Taddeo di Bartolo's *Annunciazione di Maria Vergine* (The Annunciation of the Virgin Mary, 1409).

 Sleeping

CAMPO REGIO RELAIS
Boutique Hotel €€€

(🕿 0577 22 20 73; www.camporegio.com; Via della Sapienza 25; s €150-220, d €190-250, ste €250-450; ❄@🛜) Siena's most charming hotel has only six rooms, all of which are individually decorated and luxuriously equipped. Breakfast is served in the sumptuously decorated lounge or on the terrace, which has a sensational view of the *duomo* and Torre del Mangia.

PALAZZO RAVIZZA
Hotel €€

(🕿 0577 28 04 62; www.palazzoravizza.com; Pian dei Mantellini 34; r €75-230, ste €150-320; P❄@🛜) Occupying a Renaissance-era *palazzo* located in a quiet but convenient

corner of the city, this impressive hotel offers rooms with frescoed ceilings, huge beds and small but well-equipped bathrooms.

HOTEL ALMA DOMUS
Hotel €

(🕿 0577 4 41 77; www.hotelalmadomus.it; Via Camporegio 37; s €40-45, d €65-75; ❄@🛜) Owned by the Catholic diocese and still home to eight Dominican nuns who act as guardians at the Casa Santuario di Santa Caterina (located in the same complex), this convent is now privately operated as a budget hotel. Most of the simple but spotlessly clean rooms have views over the narrow green Fontebranda Valley across to the *duomo*. There's a 1am curfew.

PALAZZO BRUCHI
B&B €€

(🕿 0577 28 73 42; www.palazzobruchi.it; Via di Pantaneto 105; s €80-90, d €90-150; @🛜) Host Camilla Masignani goes out of her way to make guests feel at home at her six-roomed B&B in a 17th-century *palazzo* close to Il Campo. It's one of the few places in Siena where one wakes up to church bells and chirping birds rather than street noise (rooms overlook the Fontebranda Valley).

 Eating & Drinking

TOP CHOICE ENOTECA I TERZI
Modern Italian €€

(🕿 0577 4 43 29; www.enotecaiterzi.it; Via dei Termini 7; meals €39; ⏱11am-1am Mon-Sat) Close to Il Campo but off the well-beaten tourist trail, this classy modern *enoteca* is a favourite with bankers from the nearby headquarters of the Monte dei Paschi di Siena bank, who love to linger over their working lunches of light-as-air fried *bacalà* (cod), handmade pasta, flavoursome risotto and succulent grilled meats.

TRE CRISTI
Seafood €€

(🕿 0577 28 06 08; www.trecristi.com; Vicola di Provenzano 1-7; 4-course tasting menus €35-40, 6-course menu €60; ⏱closed Sun) The menu here is as elegant as the decor, and added touches such as a complimentary glass of *prosecco* at the start of the meal add to the experience. Dishes are delicate and delicious, and the tasting menus offer excellent value.

MORBIDI
Deli €

(Via Banchi di Sopra 75; ⊙9am-8pm Mon-Sat) Local gastronomes shop here, as the range of cheese, cured meats and imported delicacies is the best in Siena. If you are self-catering you can join them, but make sure you also investigate the downstairs **lunch buffet (€12;** ⊙12.30-2.30pm), which offers fantastic value.

ENOTECA ITALIANA
Wine Bar €€

(www.enoteca-italiana.it; Fortezza Medicea; ⊙noon-1am Mon-Sat Apr-Sep, till midnight Oct-Mar) The former munitions cellar and dungeon of this Medici fortress has been artfully transformed into a classy *enoteca* that carries over 1500 Italian labels. You can take a bottle with you, ship a case home or enjoy a glass or two in the attractive courtyard or atmospheric vaulted interior.

Pasticceria Nannini
Cafe €

(24 Via Banchi di Sopra; ⊙7.30am-11pm) Come here for the finest *cenci* (fried sweet pastry), panforte (a rich cake of almonds, honey and candied fruit) and *ricciarelli* (almond biscuits) in town, enjoyed with a coffee.

🔒 Shopping

WEDNESDAY MARKET
Market

(⊙7.30am-1pm) Spreading around Fortezza Medicea and towards the Stadio Comunale, this is one of Tuscany's largest markets and is great for foodstuffs and cheap clothing.

ⓘ Information

Tourist office (☎0577 28 05 51; www. terresiena.it; Piazza del Campo 56; ⊙9am-7pm) Reserves accommodation, sells a map of Siena (€0.50), organises car and scooter hire, and sells train tickets.

ⓘ Getting There & Away

Bus

Siena Mobilità (☎800 570530; www. sienamobilita.it) runs frequent 'Corse Rapide' (Express) buses to Florence (€7.10, 1¼ hours), San Gimignano (€5.50, one to 1½ hours, 10 daily either direct or changing in Poggibonsi), Montalcino (€3.65, 1½ hours, six daily) and Arezzo (€5.40, 1½ hours, eight daily).

Sena (☎861 1991900; www.sena.it) buses run to/from Rome (€21, 3½ hours, eight daily), Milan (€35, 4¼ hours, four daily), Venice (€28, 5¼ hours, two daily) and Perugia (€12, 90 minutes, one daily). Its ticket office (⊙8.30am-7.45pm Mon-Sat) is also underneath the bus station.

Car & Motorcycle

For Florence, take the RA3 Siena–Florence *superstrada* (expressway) or the SR222.

ⓘ Getting Around

TO/FROM THE AIRPORT A Siena Mobilità bus travels between Pisa airport and Siena (one-way/return, €14/26, two hours), leaving Siena at 7.10am and Pisa at 1pm. Tickets should be purchased at least one day in advance from the bus station or online.

My Tour (☎0577 23 63 30; www.mytours.it) operates a shuttle service between Florence airport and Siena twice daily (one-way/return, €30/50, two hours). Tickets can be booked through the tourist office.

BUS Siena Mobilità operates city bus services (€1 per 90 minutes). Buses 9 and 10 run between the train station and Piazza Gramsci.

CAR & MOTORCYCLE There are large, conveniently located car parks at the Stadio Comunale and around the Fortezza Medicea, both just north of Piazza San Domenico.

Montalcino
POP 5278

This placid medieval hill town is known throughout the world for its coveted wine, Brunello. In February each year, the new vintage is celebrated at **Benvenuto Brunello**, a weekend of tastings and award presentations organised by the Consorzio del Vino Brunello di Montalcino

(www.consorziobrunellodimontalcino.it), the association of local producers.

◎ Sights

Within the 14th-century **fortezza** (courtyard free, ramparts adult/child under 12 €4/2; ⊙9am-8pm Apr-Oct, 9am-6pm Nov-Mar) is an *enoteca* where you can sample and buy local wines.

The beautiful **Abbazia di Sant'Antimo** (www.antimo.it; Castelnuovo dell'Abate; admission free; ⊙10.30am-12.30pm & 3-6.30pm Mon-Sat, 9.15-10.45am & 3-6pm Sun) lies in an isolated valley just below the village of Castelnuovo dell'Abate, 10.5km from Montalcino. Its Romanesque exterior, built in pale travertine stone, features stone carvings set in the bell tower and apsidal chapels. Monks perform Gregorian chants in the abbey during daily services – check times on the website.

It's a two-hour walk from Montalcino to the abbey. The route starts next to the police station near the main roundabout in town; many visitors choose to walk there and return by bus – check the timetable with the tourist office.

🛏 Sleeping

HOTEL VECCHIA OLIVIERA Hotel €€
(☎0577 84 60 28; www.vecchiaoliviera.com; Via Landi 1; s €70-85, d €120-190; ⊙closed Dec–mid-Feb; P✴🛜🛥) Just beside the Porta Cerbaia, this former olive mill has been tastefully restored and converted into a stylish hotel with 11 individually decorated rooms. The garden terrace has a spectacular view.

HOTEL IL GIGLIO Hotel €€
(☎0577 84 81 67; www.gigliohotel.com; Via Soccorso Saloni 5; s €88, d €130-140, annex s/d €60/95, apt €100-140; P🛜) The comfortable wrought-iron beds here are each gilded with a painted *giglio* (lily), and all doubles have panoramic views. Room 1 has a private terrace with a fantastic view, and the small single is very attractive.

✕ Eating & Drinking

For a quick and delicious snack, head to **Pizzeria La Torre** (€1 per slice; ⊙11am-9pm Tue-Sun) on Piazza del Popolo. The best cafe in town, **Alle Logge di Piazza** (⊙7am-1am Thu-Tue; 🛜), is on the opposite side of the piazza.

The **Friday market** on and around Via della Libertà sells fresh local produce.

OSTICCIO Osteria €€
(www.osticcio.it; Via Matteoti 23; antipasto plate €10, meals €36; ⊙11am-11pm Fri-Wed) A huge selection of Brunello and its more modest – but still very palatable – sibling Rosso di Montalcino joins dozens of bottles of wine from around the world at this excellent *enoteca/osteria*. After browsing the selection downstairs, claim a table in the upstairs dining room for a glass of wine accompanied by a antipasto plate or a full meal. You can also enjoy a tasting session here (three Brunello €14.50, one Rosso and one Brunello €8).

RISTORANTE DI POGGIO ANTICO Modern Italian €€
(☎0577 84 92 00; www.poggioantico.com; meals €48, 6-/7-course tasting menu €50/70; ⊙lunch & dinner Tue-Sun Apr-Oct, lunch Tue-Sun Nov-Mar) Located 4.5km outside town on the road to Grosseto, Poggio Antico makes award-winning wines (try its Brunello or Madre IGT), conducts tours of the winery (free), offers paid tastings (€22 for five wines) and has one of the area's best restaurants.

❶ Information

The tourist office (☎0577 84 93 31; www.prolocomontalcino.it, in Italian; Costa del Municipio 1; ⊙10am-1pm & 2-5.50pm daily Apr-Oct, closed Mon Nov-Mar) is just off the main square. It can supply information about vineyard visits and book accommodation.

❶ Getting There & Away

BUS Regular Siena Mobilità buses (€3.65, 1½ hours, six daily) run to/from Siena.
CAR & MOTORCYCLE From Siena, take the SR2 (Via Cassia) and exit onto the SP14 at Lama. There's free parking next to the *fortezza*.

UMBRIA
Perugia
POP 166,667

A large, well-preserved Etruscan-medieval hill town, Perugia has a strong artistic tradition. In the 15th century it was home to fresco painters Bernardino Pinturicchio and his master Pietro Vannucci (known as Perugino), who would later teach Raphael. Toay Perugia is also known for students and chocolate, thanks to University of Perugia, the famous Università per Stranieri (University for Foreigners) and the annual nine-day educational binge each October know as **Eurochocolate** (📞075 502 58 80; www.eurochocolate.com).

Sights

Savings can be made on most of the attractions listed below by purchasing a **Perugia Città Museo Card** (€10), which provides admission to five museums of your choice. It's available at all the participating sights and the tourist office.

PALAZZO DEI PRIORI Palazzo

The palace houses some of the best museums in Perugia, including Umbria's foremost art gallery, the stunning **Galleria Nazionale dell'Umbria** (📞800 69 76 16; Palazzo dei Priori, Corso Vannucci 19; adult/reduced €6.50/3.25; ⊙8.30am-7.30pm Tue-Sun), Entered via Corso Vannucci, it's an art historian's dream, with 30 rooms of works featuring everything from Byzantine art from the 13th century to the 16th-century creations of hometown heroes Pinturicchio and Perugino.

The same building also holds what some consider the most beautiful bank in the world, the **Nobile Collegio del Cambio** (Exchange Hall; 📞075 572 85 99; Corso Vannucci 25; adult/reduced €4.50/2.60; ⊙9am-12.30pm & 2.30-5.30pm Mon-Sat, 9am-1pm Sun, closed Mon afternoon winter), whose rooms have 17th-century wooden stalls carved by Giampiero Zuccari and frescoes by Perugino.

CASA MUSEO DI PALAZZO SORBELLO Museum

(📞075 573 27 75; Piazza Piccinino 9; adult €5; ⊙noon-1.30pm Mon, 11am-1.30pm Tue-Sun) This grand city-centre mansion, once

Perugia

owned by the noble Sorbello family, has recently been restored to its frescoed, gilt-clad, 18th-century prime. Guided tours (in Italian) let you admire the family's almost ludicrously opulent collection of art, porcelain and manuscripts.

CAPELLA DI SAN SEVERO   Church
(📞075 573 38 64; Piazza Raffaello, Porta Sole; adult/reduced €3/2; ⊙10am-1.30pm & 2.30-6pm Tue-Sun May-July & Sep-Oct, 10.30am-1.30pm & 2.30-5pm Tue-Sun Nov-Mar, 10am-1.30pm & 2.30-6pm daily Apr & Aug) Illuminating this tiny chapel is Raphael's lush *Trinity with Saints* (thought by many to be his first fresco), painted during the artist's residence in Perugia (1505–08).

 **Sleeping**

TORRE COLOMBAIA   Agriturismo €
(📞075 878 73 41; www.torrecolombaia.it; San Biagio delle Valle; per person incl breakfast €40, apt €85-135, dinner €23; ⊙dinner Fri-Sun; **P** 🐾) Just 15 minutes from downtown Perugia, this former hunting farm now offers well-equipped antique-strewn rooms, an organic restaurant (supplied by the first organic farm in Umbria), a meditation room and plentiful wildlife-spotting opportunities in the surrounding woodland.

HOTEL BRUFANI PALACE   Luxury Hotel €€€
(📞075 573 25 41; www.sinahotels.com; Piazza Italia 12; s/d €99/205, ste €105-260; **P** ❄ @ 🛜 🏊) One of Umbria's few five-star hotels and a truly spectacular experience, the palace's special touches include frescoed public rooms, impeccably decorated bedrooms, a garden terrace for summer dining, and helpful trilingual staff. Swim over Etruscan ruins in the subterranean fitness centre.

ETRUSCAN CHOCOHOTEL   Hotel €€
(📞075 583 73 14; www.chocohotel.it; Via Campo di Marte 134; s €54-73, d €88-140; **P** ❄ @ 🛜 🏊) It's hard to believe, but this is the

❤ **If You Like…**
Wine

Three superb regional wines have less international name recognition, with good reason: the best vintages are such excellent values that they're snapped up locally and rarely exported. To taste these wines, head straight to their namesake regions.

1   **VERNACCIA DI SAN GIMIGNANO**
(p256) This crisp, elegant white is one of the most ancient wines still in production, and the first awarded Italy's DOC quality status (since upgraded to DOCG). Discover why Dante's *Divine Comedy* blames Vernaccia for inciting gluttony at San Gimignano's **Museo del Vino** (Wine Museum; Parco della Rocca; ⊙11.30am-6.30pm), where you can see Vernaccia memorabilia and enjoy tastings (four wines/six wines €6/10) on a panoramic terrace.

2   **VINO NOBILE DI MONTEPULCIANO**
Montepulciano has produced noteworthy wines since Etruscan times, and its namesake DOCG Sangiovese blend is aged in oak barrels for two years to reveal its velvety, spicy character. Enjoy Montepulciano's 'noble wine' in a proper palace: **Palazzo Ricci** (www.palazzoricci.com; Via Ricci 9-11) offers tastings in its historic wine cellar, **Cantina del Redi** (www.vecchiacantinadimontepulciano.com; admission free, paid tastings; ⊙10.30am-1.30pm & 3-7.30pm mid-Mar–early Jan, Sat & Sun only early Jan–mid Mar).

3   **ORVIETO CLASSICO**
Medieval peasant life hardly seems enviable, until you try Orvieto's satiny, grassy, medieval white wine. Compare celebrated DOCG and experimental IGT versions at Orvieto's **Palazzo del Gusto** (📞0763 34 18 18; www.ilpalazzodelgusto.it; Via Ripa Serancia I 16; tastings €5-30; ⊙11am-1pm & 3-5pm winter, 11am-1pm & 5-7pm Mon-Fri summer).

world's only chocolate-themed hotel. Once you've unpacked in your (brown, obviously) room, you can gorge on items from the restaurant's 'chocomenu', shop at the 'chocostore' or swim in the rooftop pool (sadly, filled with water).

 Eating

SANDRI Pastries & Cakes **€**

(☎ 075 572 41 12; Corso Vannucci 32; ☺ 10am-8pm Tue-Sun) When you enter into your third century of business, you must be doing something right. This place is known for delectable chocolate cakes, candied fruit, espresso and pastries. Staff wrap all take-home purchases, no matter how small, in beautiful red paper with a ribbon bow.

CAFFÈ DI PERUGIA Cafe **€**

(☎ 075 573 18 63; Via Mazzini 10; mains €14-20; ☺ noon-3pm & 7pm-midnight Wed-Mon) The fanciest sit-down cafe in town, its desserts are worth the high prices. It also serves a fine choice of basic pasta and meat dishes and offers outdoor seating in summer.

AL MANGIAR BENE Pizzeria **€**

(☎ 075 573 10 47; Via della Luna 21; pizzas €5-8) Proudly flying the organic flag in Perugia,

this subterranean restaurant at the end of a narrow alley sources nearly all its ingredients locally from organic suppliers. Pizzas and calzones are baked in a hearth-like brick oven. Even the beer and wines are organic.

IL GUFO Traditional Italian **€€**

(☎ 075 573 41 26; Via della Viola 18; meals €29; ☺ 8pm-1am Tue-Sat) The owner-chef gathers ingredients from local markets and cooks up whatever is fresh and in season. Try dishes such as wild boar with fennel (€12.50) or pappardelle with rabbit *ragù* (€9). A two-course set menu is €15. No credit cards.

**RISTORANTE DAL
MI'COCCO** Traditional Italian **€**

(☎ 075 573 25 11; Corso Garibaldi 12; set meals €13; ☺ Tue-Sun) Don't ask for a menu because there isn't one at this most traditional Perugian restaurant. Diners get a set menu of a starter, main course, side dish and dessert. You may receive asparagus risotto in May or *tagliatelle* with

Left: Chocolate pastries at Sandri (p260), Perugia;
Below: Fresco, Assisi (p263)

(LEFT) FRANK WING/LONELY PLANET IMAGES ©. (BELOW) DIANA MAYFIELD/LONELY PLANET IMAGES ©

peas and ham in November. Extremely popular with students, it's best to call ahead.

 Drinking

CAFFÈ MORLACCHI Cafe €
(☎ 075 572 17 60; Piazza Morlacchi 6/8; ☺ 8am-1am Mon-Sat) Bring your bongo drums and leftist rhetoric to this most hip of establishments. Students, professors and expats nosh on international fare, sipping tea or hot chocolate during the day and cocktails at night.

BOTTEGA DEL VINO Wine Bar
(Via del Sole 1; ☺ 7pm-1am Mon-Sat) A fire or candles burn romantically on the terrace, while inside live jazz and hundreds of bottles of wine lining the walls add to the romance of the setting. You can taste dozens of Umbrian wines, which you can purchase with the help of sommelier-like experts.

⭐ Entertainment

CINEMA TEATRO DEL PAVONE Cinema
(☎ 075 572 49 11; www.teatrodelpavone.it; Corso Vannucci 67) Dating back to 1717, the grand theatre plays host to not only films but also musical performances and special events.

ⓘ Information

InfoUmbria (☎ 075 57 57; www.infoumbria.com, in Italian; Piazza Partigiani Intercity bus station, Largo Cacciatori delle Alpi 3; ☺ 9am-1pm & 2.30-6.30pm Mon-Fri, 9am-1pm Sat) Also known as InfoTourist, it offers information on all of Umbria, and is a fantastic resource for *agriturismi*.

Tourist office (☎ 075 573 64 58; info@iat.perugia.it; Piazza Matteotti 18; ☺ 8.30am-6.30pm) Plenty of maps and tourist pamphlets for hotels, activities, events etc. Also has the most up-to-date bus and train timetables.

ⓘ Getting There & Away

Air

Aeroporto Sant'Egidio (PEG; ☎ 075 59 21 41; www.airport.umbria.it), 13km east of the city, offers at least three daily **Alitalia** (www.alitalia.it) flights to Milan, plus a **Ryanair** (www.ryanair.co.uk) service to London Stansted thrice weekly.

Bus

Intercity buses leave from Piazza Partigiani; for Florence (€10.50, 2½ hours) – take the escalators from Piazza Italia.

Most routes within Umbria are operated by **APM** (☎ 800 512141; www.apmperugia.it) in the north and **SSIT** (☎ 0743 21 22 11; www.spoletina.com) or **ATC Terni** (☎ 0744 40 94 57; www.atcterni.it) in the south.

Car & Motorcycle

From Rome, leave the A1 at the Orte exit and follow the signs for Terni. Once there, take the SS3bis/E45 for Perugia. From the north, exit the A1 at Valdichiana and take dual carriageway SS75 for Perugia. The SS75 to the east connects the city with Assisi.

Train

Trains run to the following destinations:

TO	FARE (€)	DURATION (HR)	FREQUENCY
Assisi	2.50	½	hourly
Florence	11-16	2	8 daily
Orvieto	7	1¼	every 2 hours
Rome	11-35	2¼-3	15 daily

ⓘ Getting Around

To/From the Airport

A white shuttle-bus (€3.50) leaves from Piazza Italia for the airport about two hours before each flight, stopping at the train station.

Bus

It's a steep 1.5km climb uphill from Perugia's train station, so a bus is highly recommended (and essential for those with luggage). The bus takes

Outdoor cafe, Urbino (p263)

FRANK WING/LONELY PLANET IMAGES ©

Detour: Urbino

This small walled hill town in Le Marche is a showplace of big ideas, and a Unesco World Heritage site. In the 15th century, Urbino's Duke Federico da Montefeltro gathered great artists, architects and scholars to form a Renaissance think-tank. Today Urbino embodies their best ideas, with a vibrant university and Renaissance masterpieces.

First stop is the duke's own tower-flanked Renaissance palace, **Palazzo Ducale** (☏0722 2 76 01; Piazza Duca Federico; adult/reduced €5/2.50; ⊙8.30am-7.15pm Tue-Sun, 8.30am-2pm Mon). A monumental staircase (one of Italy's first) leads to the Ducal Apartments, featuring works by Piero della Francesca in the library and showcasing works by Raphael, Titian and Signorelli.

Another 15th-century landmark is **Casa Natale di Raffaello** (☏0722 30 92 70; Via Valerio 1; adult/reduced €2/1; ⊙9am-1pm & 3-7pm daily Mar-Oct, 9am-2pm Mon-Sat, 9am-2pm Sun Nov-Feb), the house where Raphael was born and lived for 16 years, featuring a tender Madonna with child that may be Raphael's first fresco. You can see where Renaissance artists found inspiration at colourfully frescoed, 14th-century **Oratorio di San Giovanni** (☏347 6711181; Via Barocci; admission €2.50; ⊙10am-12.30pm & 3-5.30pm Mon-Sat, 10am-12.30pm Sun).

Urbino cuisine gets inventive at **La Trattoria del Leone** (☏0722 32 98 94; Via Cesare Battisti 5; meals €20-24; ⊙dinner nightly, lunch Sat & Sun) including ravioli with Casciotta d'Urbino cheese or baked rabbit with olives, bacon and sausage. Stay behind the Palazzo Ducale in well-designed modern comfort at **Albergo Italia** (☏0722 27 01; www.albergo-italia-urbino.it; Corso Garibaldi 32; s €50-70, d €80-120, all incl breakfast; ✱ @).

The S73B connects Urbino with the SS3 heading for Rome. Cars are banned from the walled city; park outside city gates.

---

you to Piazza Italia. Tickets cost €1.50 from the train station kiosk or €2 on board.

Car & Motorcycle

Perugia has several fee-charging car parks (€0.80 to €1.60 per hour, 24 hours a day). There's also a free car park at Piazza Cupa.

Minimetrò

These single-car people-movers traverse between the train station and Pincetto (just off Piazza Matteotti) every minute. The same €1.50 tickets work for the bus and Minimetrò.

Taxi

☏075 500 48 88

Assisi

POP 27,740

The spiritual capital of Umbria is Assisi, a town tied to its most famous son – St Francis of Assisi was born here in 1181 and preached his message throughout Umbria until his death in 1226.

The city's main annual event is the saint's holiday **Festa di San Francesco**, which falls on 3 and 4 October.

 Sights

BASILICA DI SAN FRANCESCO Church
(☏075 81 90 01; Piazza di San Francesco) The **upper church** (⊙8.30am-6.45pm Easter-Oct, to 6pm Oct-Easter) was built just after the

lower church, between 1230 and 1253, and is a terribly grand place. Circling the inner walls is one of the most famous pieces of art in the world, a giant multi-part fresco usually attributed to Giotto (though there is some debate within the art-historian community) depicting 28 scenes from St Francis's life below corresponding images from the Old and New Testaments. It revolutionised art in the Western world, with the standard gold leaf and flat iconic images of the Byzantine and Romanesque periods eschewed for natural backgrounds and a human, suffering Jesus.

The **lower church** (⏾6am-6.45pm Easter-Oct, to 6pm Oct-Easter) was built between 1228 and 1230. Lorenzetti's triptych in the left transept ends with his famous and controversial *Madonna Who Celebrates Francis*. Mary is seen holding the baby Jesus and indicating with her thumb towards St Francis. On the other side of Mary is the Apostle John, whom we assume is being unfavourably compared with Francis. In 1234 Pope Gregory IX

decided that the image was not heretical because John had written the gospel, but Francis had lived it. Cimabue was the most historically important painter who worked in this church because he was the only artist to get a first-hand account from St Francis' two nephews, who had personally known the saint. In the *Madonna in Majesty*, in the right transept, Cimabue's depiction of St Francis is considered the most accurate.

Downstairs from the lower church is the **Tomb of St Francis**, where the saint's body has been laid to rest, and the **Reliquary Chapel** (⏾9am-6pm daily, 1-4.30pm holidays), which contains items from St Francis' life, including his simple, much patched tunic and fragments of his celebrated *Canticle of the Creatures*.

BASILICA DI SANTA CHIARA   Church
(☏075 81 22 82; Piazza Santa Chiara; ⏾6.30am-noon & 2-7pm summer, to 6pm winter) Built in the 13th century in a Romanesque style, with steep ramparts and a striking white and pink facade,

Left: Stone house, Assisi (p263);
Below: Plum tree, Orvieto (p267)

the basilica was raised in honour of St Clare, a spiritual contemporary of St Francis and founder of the Sorelle Povere di Santa Chiara (Order of the Poor Ladies), now known as the Poor Clares. She is buried in the church's crypt. The Byzantine cross that is said to have spoken to St Francis is also housed here.

Sleeping

The tourist office has a complete list of private rooms, religious institutions (of which there are 17), flats and *agriturismi* options in and around Assisi.

NUN ASSISI　　　Luxury Hotel　**€€€**
(075 815 51 50; www.nunassisi.com; Via Eremo delle Carceri 1a; s €180-325, d €220-480, all incl breakfast; P @ ≋) An elegant restored former convent, this has just enough of the original features to be charming, and just the right level of mod-cons to be luxurious. The rooms are beautiful, the restaurant a cut above and the spa is set within 1st-century Roman ruins (and it's not every spa that can say that).

**ALLA MADONNA
DEL PIATTO**　　　Agriturismo　**€€**
(075 819 90 50; www.incampagna.com; Via Petrata 37, Pieve San Nicolo; d incl breakfast €85-105; Mar–mid-Nov; P) As beautiful as it is seemingly isolated, this *agriturismo* is less than 15 minutes from the basilica. Each of the six Moroccan- or Indian-themed guest chambers is truly a room with a view. But the real reason to stay here is the intimate cooking classes Letizia runs (in Italian or English). Two-night minimum.

HOTEL SAN RUFINO　　　Hotel　**€**
(075 81 28 03; www.hotelsanrufino.it; Via Porta Perlici 7; s €42-50, d €52-65, breakfast €4-5; P) With rooms in two locations (those at the **Albergo Il Duomo** round the corner are slightly smaller), this hotel

Detour:
Spoleto

This sleepy Umbian hill town became a world stage in 1958 when Italian American composer Gian Carlo Menotti founded Festival dei Due Mondi, better known today as the **Spoleto Festival** (✆box office 800 565600; www.festivaldispoleto. it; performance tickets €5-200, most €20-30; ☺June-July). Ever since, the annual festival has given exceptional talents their big break in dance, spoken word, theatre, music and opera in the town's 1st-century **Teatro Romano** (Roman Ampitheatre).

Atmospheric Spoleto (www.visitspoleto.it) provides year-round inspiration for artistic breakthroughs. Roman ruins served as building blocks for Spoleto's 11th-century **cathedral** (✆0743 4 43 07; Piazza Duomo; ☺8.30am-12.30pm & 3.30-7pm summer, to 5.30pm winter), with frescoes by Fra' Filippo Lippi completed posthumously by his illegitimate son, Renaissance master Filippino. Cross **Ponte delle Torri**, a medieval bridge built atop a Roman aqueduct, to 13th-century **Chiesa di San Pietro** (✆0743 44 882; Loc San Pietro; ☺9am-6.30pm summer; 9am-noon & 3.30-5pm winter), where fanciful carved animals frolic across the facade.

Artists have no fear of starving in Spoleto, where **Osteria del Trivio** (✆0743 44 349; Via del Trivio 16; meals €28; ☺Wed-Mon, closed Jan) dishes heaps of local *strangozzi alla spoletina* (local pasta in a tangy tomato sauce). Named after Spoleto's sister city in South Carolina, **Hotel Charleston** (✆0743 220 052; www.hotelcharleston.it; Piazza Collicola 10; s/d incl breakfast from €59/79; ✳@☎) is a 17th-century artist's retreat with inspired upgrades: sauna, fireplace, parquet floors and designer furniture.

Spoleto is on the E45 road. Trains connect Spoleto with Rome (€8 to €12.30, 1½ hours, hourly), Perugia (€4.80, one hour, nine daily) and Assisi (€3.24, 40 minutes, hourly). From the station, take bus A, B or C to Spoleto's centre (Centro).

is as quiet as it is comfortable. Stairs to the hotel can be tricky, but once you arrive at the San Rufino, there's a handy lift. Sweetly decorated rooms all come with private bathrooms and TVs.

Eating

MEDIO EVO Traditional Italian €€
(✆075 81 30 68; Via Arco dei Priori 4; meals €33; ☺Thu-Tue) Traditional Umbrian dishes are served in fabulous vaulted 13th-century surroundings, including lamb stew with artichokes (€13.50) and truffle omelettes (€11).

GRAN CAFFÈ Cakes & Pastries €
(✆075 815 51 44; Corso Mazzini 16; ☺8am-midnight) This elegant place has the most fabulous gelati, mouth-watering pastries and cakes, and a great selection of drinks. Try the *tè freddo alla pesca* (iced tea with peach) on a hot day, or choose from a selection of delicious hot chocolates and coffee when the weather is cool. Remember it costs much more to sit.

POZZO DELLA MENSA Osteria €€
(✆075 815 52 36; Via del Pozzo della Mensa; meals €30; ☺Fri-Wed) Just far enough off the main sightseeing routes to be more of a local than a tourist restaurant, this is presided over by two friends who serve up a small menu of regional favourites, such as *torta al testa* (try the sausage and wild greens), *crostini misti* and ravioli with white truffle sauce. A roof terrace opens in summer.

Orvieto

artists such as Simone Martini and the three Pisanos: Andrea, Nino and Giovanni.

ORVIETO
UNDERGROUND Historical Site
(📞 0763 34 48 91; www.orvietounderground.it; Parco delle Grotte; adult/reduced €5.50/4.50; 🕑 tours 11am, 12.15pm, 4pm & 5.15pm daily Mar-Jan, Sat & Sun Feb) The coolest place in Orvieto – literally – this series of 440 caves has been used for millennia by locals for various purposes, including as WWII bomb shelters, refrigerators, wells and, during many a pesky Roman or barbarian siege, as dovecotes to trap the usual one-course dinner: pigeon (still seen on local restaurant menus as *palombo*). Tours (with English-speaking guides) leave from in front of the tourist office.

MUSEO CLAUDIO FAINA
E CIVICO Museum
(📞 0763 34 15 11; www.museofaina.it; Piazza Duomo 29; adult/reduced €8/5; 🕑 9.30am-6pm Apr-Sep, 10am-5pm Tue-Sun Oct-Mar) This fantastic museum opposite the cathedral houses one of Italy's most important collections of Etruscan archaeological

artefacts, as well as some significant Greek ceramic works.

TORRE DEL MORO Historical Building
(Moor's Tower; 📞 0763 34 45 67; Corso Cavour 87; adult/reduced €2.80/2; 🕑 10am-8pm May-Aug, 10am-7pm Mar, Apr, Sep & Oct, 10.30am-1pm & 2.30-5pm Nov-Feb) Climb all 250 steps for sweeping views of the city.

Sleeping

HOTEL MAITANI Hotel €€
(📞 0763 34 20 11; www.hotelmaitani.com; Via Lorenzo Maitani 5; s/d €77/126, breakfast €10; **P 🛜**) Every detail is covered, from a travel-sized toothbrush and toothpaste in each room to chocolates (Perugino, of course) on your pillow. Several rooms have cathedral or countryside views. Rooms are pin-drop quiet, as they come with not one but two double-glazed windows.

B&B LA MAGNOLIA B&B €
(📞 0763 34 28 08, 338 9027400; www.bbla magnolia.it; Via del Duomo 29; r €65-75, apt for 2 people €75) In the centre of Orvieto, next to a small cafe north of the duomo (the sign is small and easy to miss), this light-filled historic residence has six delightful

---

Making the Most of your Euro

The **Orvieto Unica Card** (adult/reduced valid 1 year €18/15) permits to the town's nine main attractions (including the Cappella di San Brizio in the cathedral, Museo Claudio Faina e Civico, Orvieto Underground, Torre del Moro, Museo dell'Opera del Duomo) and a round trip on the funicular and city buses. It can be purchased at many of the attractions, the tourist office, the Piazza Cahen tourist office and the railway station.

Don't Miss **Orvieto's Cathedral**

Rounding tight corners along Orvieto's medieval cobblestone streets, you're suddenly faced with the impossible: the giant Gothic **Duomo** (cathedral), blushing pink under golden **mosaics**, tiers of saintly statuary and a lacy **rosette window** on its 1290–1607 facade. The cathedral is no less striking from its striped marble sides, and beyond those mighty **bronze portals** is a masterpiece studied by Michelangelo and Sigmund Freud for psychological insight and still scanned for apocalyptic omens: Luca Signorelli's *Last Judgement*.

In **Cappella di San Brizio**, angelic frescoes were begun by Fra Angelico in 1447 and resumed by Signorelli in 1500 – only this time, with apocalyptic visions from Dante's *Divine Comedy*. In his archway fresco, **The End of the World** is both vividly colourful and psychologically dark. Cities collapse overhead; people tumble screaming down arch supports; mothers clutch babies as devils swoop down to claim souls.

If his muscular devils seem uncannily realistic and their judgment furious, perhaps that's because Signorelli was working from recent memory: after persecuting Renaissance thinkers and burning their humanist paintings and books, Florentine friar-turned-tyrant Savonarola was executed in 1498 for heresy. In **The Preaching of the Antichrist**, Signorelli shows a man dressed as a saint listening to the devil, surrounded by crowds that include Renaissance luminaries Dante, Raphael, Boccacio, and the artist himself, standing next to Fra Angelico.

While such violence may make viewers flinch, the underlying pathos of Signorelli's scenes make it hard to look away. While Signorelli worked on Orvieto frescoes, he lost his son to plague. Vasari recalls grieving Signorelli sketching his son, including his final portrait as Christ in the **Pieta' Alcove**.

THINGS YOU NEED TO KNOW

📞0763 34 11 67; www.opsm.it; Piazza Duomo; admission €3; 🕒9.30am-7.30pm Apr-Oct, 9.30am-1pm & 2.30-5pm Nov-Mar, chapel closed during mass

rooms, an English-speaking owner and a large shared kitchen.

VILLA MERCEDE B&B €

(0763 34 17 66; www.argoweb.it/casareligiosa _villamercede; Via Soliana 2; s/d incl breakfast €50/70; P) Heavenly close to the Duomo, with 23 rooms there's space for a gaggle of pilgrims. The building dates back to the 1500s, so the requisite frescoes adorn several rooms. High ceilings, a quiet garden and free parking seal the deal.

Eating & Drinking

TRATTORIA DELL'ORSO Trattoria €€

(0763 34 16 42; Via della Misericordia 18; meals €32; Wed-Sun) As the owner of Orvieto's oldest restaurant, Gabriele sees no need for such modern fancies as written menus, instead reeling off the day's dishes at you as you walk in the door (in either Italian or English, depending on how bemused you look). Go with his recommendations – perhaps the *zuppa di farro* followed by fettuccine with porcini – as he knows what he's talking about. And be prepared to take your time.

RISTORANTE I SETTE CONSOLI Modern Italian €€€

(0763 34 39 11; Piazza Sant'Angelo 1/a; meals €45; Thu-Tue) The inventive, artfully presented dishes here, such as guinea fowl stuffed with chestnuts, get foodies flocking in all the way from Rome and Milan.

CANTINA FORESI Enoteca €

(/fax 0763 34 16 11; Piazza Duomo 2; snacks from €4.50; 9.30am-7.30pm) This family-run *enoteca* and cafe serves up *panini* and sausages, washed down with dozens of local wines from the ancient cellar.

VINOSUS Wine Bar

(Piazza Duomo 15; meals €35; Tue-Sun) In photo-op range of the cathedral's north-west wall is this wine bar and eatery. Try the cheese platter with local honey and pears (€8) for an elegant addition to wine. Open until the wee hours.

Entertainment

TEATRO MANCINELLI Theatre

(0763 34 04 22; Corso Cavour 122; adult/ reduced €2/1, tickets €15-60; 10am-1pm & 4-7pm Mon-Sat, 4-8pm Sun) The theatre plays host to Umbria Jazz Winter but offers everything from ballet and opera to folk music and Pink Floyd tributes throughout the year. If you're not able to catch a performance, it's worth a visit to see the allegorical frescoes and tufa walls.

Information

Tourist office (0763 34 17 72; info@iat. orvieto.tr.it; Piazza Duomo 24; 8.15am-1.50pm & 4-7pm Mon-Fri, 10am-1pm & 3-6pm Sat, Sun & holidays)

Getting There & Away

BUS Bargagli (057 778 62 23) runs a daily bus service to Rome's Tiburtina station (€8, one hour and 20 minutes, 8.10am and 7.10pm on Sunday).

CAR & MOTORCYCLE Orvieto is on the Rome–Florence A1. There's plenty of metered parking on Piazza Cahen.

TRAIN Connections include Rome (€7.10 to €14.50, 1¼ hours, hourly), Florence (€11.20 to €19, 1½ to 2½ hours, hourly) and Perugia (€7, 1¼ hours, every two hours).

Getting Around

CABLE CAR A century-old cable car (€1.80; every 10min 7.05am-8.25pm Mon-Fri, every 15min 8.15am-8pm Sat & Sun) connects Piazza Cahen with the train station west of the centre. The fare includes a bus ride from Piazza Cahen to Piazza Duomo.

BUS Bus 1 runs up to the old town from the train station (€1), ATC bus A connects Piazza Cahen with Piazza Duomo and bus B runs to Piazza della Repubblica.

TAXI 0763 30 19 03 or 0763 34 26 13.

Naples, Pompeii & the Amalfi Coast

Inspiring, historic, swoon-worthy – and we're not only talking about the pizza. You may have already unconsciously developed a craving for Naples from its most famous dish, but nothing prepares you for the vibrant, complex flavour of this city. The street theatre over a tomato purchase in Naples' historic markets rivals performances at its groundbreaking opera house, while ancient Roman bakeries lurk underneath baroque Neapolitan church floors.

Though Mt Vesuvius hasn't even dusted a local pizza with ash since 1944, the volcano that buried Pompeii still looms on the local horizon. Consider this your reminder that life is short, and there's no time like the present to unwind on the beach-blessed isle of Capri, or make your romantic getaway to the Amalfi Coast. Then you'll comprehend the secret to Neapolitan pizza: it's the spice of life.

Positano (p305)

273

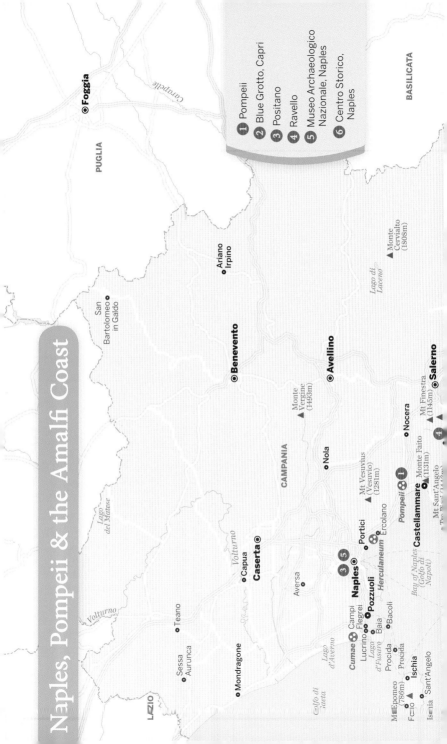

Naples, Pompeii & the Amalfi Coast

1. Pompeii
2. Blue Grotto, Capri
3. Positano
4. Ravello
5. Museo Archaeologico Nazionale, Naples
6. Centro Storico, Naples

Ruins of Pompeii

The standard first impression heard from visitors to Pompeii is 'Amazing!'. Many are surprised by the area's vastness and assume a somewhat faraway look, as if they've been transported to another dimension. The fascination lies in the fact that each stone speaks of life and love, of stories suspended for an eternity.

Need to Know

GUIDES Official guides outside the entrances allow visitors to form groups to cut tour costs **PHOTOS** Flash photography damages the frescoes **See our author's review on p298**

Pompeii Don't Miss List

BY VALENTINA VELLUSI,
TOUR GUIDE

1 CASA DEL FAUNO

Pompeii's greatest mosaics were uncovered at the House of the Faun, including one of Alexander the Great. The original is in Naples' Museo Archaeologico Nazionale (p289), but there's a faithful copy on site. With a sophisticated use of perspective and colour, it captures the last moments of the Battle of Issos.

2 IL FORO

The Forum was the city's main piazza – a huge rectangle flanked by limestone columns. To the north stands the Tempio di Giove (Temple of Jupiter) and the Grano del Foro (Forum Granary). The Foro is particularly beautiful in the late afternoon sun, when exhausted visitors sit down and open up to the spirit of the place.

3 LA FULLONICA DI STEPHANUS

This house represents Pompeii's final period, between the earthquake of AD 63 and AD 79 Vesuvius' eruption. Transformed into a washhouse, you can still see the vats used to wash, rinse and dye clothes. Urine was commonly used to bleach clothes and assist in the dyeing process – opposite the entrance is the phallic-shaped spot where people were encouraged to relieve themselves to contribute to supplies.

4 ORTO DEI FUGGIASCHI

The plaster casts here capture the final moments of two family groups trying to flee the eruption: the screams, the hopeless attempt to shield themselves from the falling lapilli (burning pumice stone). The very moment of their demise has been frozen forever.

Sing in the Blue Grotto

The Blue Grotto (p301) is exactly the kind of place you expect to find mermaids singing, with magical blue light glowing through the cave's narrow opening and an eerie echo. On recent inspection, there weren't any hanging around, though there is an ancient Roman shrine to the local water nymph. Sing a line from *The Little Mermaid* and see if you can bring any out of hiding.

Get a Positive Outlook in Positano

Is this heaven? No, but with any luck it looks like Positano (p305), with angels in the architecture, divine seafood feasts, and everlasting cliff's-edge sunsets over cobalt-blue waters. The cove may be crowded with umbrellas, but this affordable, relentlessly cheerful Amalfi Coast beach town is bound to leave the most jaded recluse in an upbeat, sociable mood.

Become Speechless in Ravello ④

Entire operas have been written here, but you might find yourself at a loss for words upon arrival in the Amalfi Coast hilltop town of Ravello (p306). Gardens dangle from bluffs over glittering seas, and a medieval cathedral tower punctuates the scene like an exclamation mark. Choose your words carefully, or at least your travelling partner – you wouldn't be the first Ravello visitor to blurt out 'Marry me.'

Turn Back Time at Museo Archaeologico Nazionale ⑤

By the 18th century, Pompeii and Herculaneum were already thoroughly looted – luckily, the most priceless booty only made it as far as Naples' royal palace, which now houses the Museo Archaeologico Nazionale (p289). The Bourbon king of Naples had exceptional taste in stolen goods – from heroic Pompeii mosaics to Roman pornography – so the museum gives a rare, intimate glimpse into Roman life.

Make a Meal of the Centro Storico ⑥

A fierce Rome/Naples pizza rivalry has raged for a century, and only you can resolve this thin/puffy crust food-fight. Head to the place where even Romans concede pizza originated: Naples' Centro Storico (p291). Eat your way around the historic Mercato di Porta Nolana as Neopolitans do – puffy crusts first. Just you try to leave room for Rome...

Naples, Pompeii & the Amalfi Coast's Best...

Gourmet Landmarks

○ **Pizzeria Gino Sorbillo** (p291) Epic Neapolitan pizzas

○ **President** (p299) For modern feasts worthy of ancient Pompeii

○ **Mercato di Porta Nolana** (p291) For Naples' best ingredients

○ **La Stanza del Gusto** (p291) Wine pairings with legendary Neapolitan cheese

○ **Caffè Mexico** (p292) For Naples' mightiest espresso

○ **Da Vincenzo** (p305) Fresh, simple seafood with an Amalfi lemon squeeze

Places to Whisper 'Ti Amo'

○ On the terrace at Ravello's **Villa Rufolo** (p306)

○ Before the end of the third act at **Teatro San Carlo** (p292) in Naples

○ Inside the **Blue Grotto** (p301) on Capri

○ Over a castle-top dinner at **Albergo Il Monastero** (p304) on the island of Ischia

○ On a chartered yacht off the coast of **Procida** (p304)

Baroque Beauties

○ **Duomo** (p284) Naples' never-shy cathedral, studded with silver busts and capped with glowing frescoes

○ **Museo Nazionale di San Martino** (p285) The least modest monastery ever, covered with frescoes

○ **Palazzo Reale di Capodimonte** (p288) A 160-room palace is barely big enough to contain this many baroque painting masterpieces

○ **Cattedrale di Sant'Andrea** (p307) The sweeping staircase makes every entrance to Amalfi's cathedral grand

Need to Know

Affordable Luxuries

o Ferry to island beach getaways on **Procida** (p304)

o Hot springs in the secluded cove of **Il Sorgeto** on the island of Ischia (p304)

o Candles scented with wild carnations at **Carthusia I Profumi di Capri** (p304)

o Silk sheets on baroque beds at **Parteno** (p291)

o Seggiovia chairlift joy-rides on Capri with the **Unico Capri pass** (p293)

ADVANCE PLANNING

o **Three months before** Book accommodation, especially if hitting the islands of Capri, Ischia or Procida or the Amalfi Coast between June and mid-September

o **One to two months before** Book tickets to the Ravello Festival (p306) and tickets to opera opening nights at Naples' Teatro San Carlo (p292)

o **One week before** Reserve a table at Palazzo Petrucci (p291) in Naples; book an urban spelunking tour in Naples with Napoli Sotteranea (p299)

RESOURCES

o **Naples Tourist Board** (www.inaples.it)

o **Pompeii Sites** (www.pompeiisites.org) Covers Pompeii and Herculaneum

o **Capri** (www.capri.net) Listings, itineraries and ferry schedules

GETTING AROUND

o **Air** International and domestic flights service Naples' Capodichino airport

o **Walk** Ideal in Naples, on island beaches, in smaller towns and along coastal trails

o **Train** Naples is a major rail hub, with frequent connections between Naples, Pompeii, Ercolano (Herculaneum) and Sorrento

o **Bus** Regular services between Naples and the Amalfi Coast

o **Ferries & Hydrofoils** Regular summer services between Naples, Capri, Ischia and Procida, as well as to/from Sorrento and the Amalfi Coast. Reduced winter services

BE FOREWARNED

o **Museums** Many close Monday or Tuesday

o **Restaurants** In Naples, many close in August. On Capri and the Amalfi Coast, many close November to March

o **Accommodation** Many hotels close November to March on Capri and along the Amalfi Coast

o **Pickpockets and bag snatchers** Active in Naples and Pompeii after sunset

281

Naples, Pompeii & the Amalfi Coast Itineraries

Magic potions and time machines aren't strictly necessary in this lucky landscape, where you'll find short-cuts to romance through blue grottos and ancient Roman cities trapped in time under a still-active volcano.

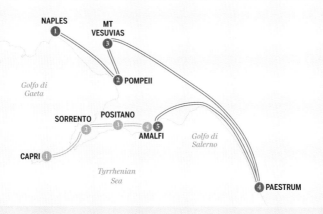

NAPLES TO AMALFI

Time-Travel Trip

In **(1) Naples**, begin your time travels underground, exploring Roman secret passages by candlelight with Napoli Sotterranea and peeking under church floors into ancient laundries at Chiesa e Scavi di San Lorenzo Maggiore. Emerge blinking into daylight and wander into the future at Madre, Naples' cutting-edge contemporary art showcase. Wake up and wonder what century you're in at Hotel Piazza Bellini, a new art hotel in a 16th-century palace.

Exquisite mosaics and ancient erotica take you back a couple millennia at Museo Archaeologico Nazionale, but don't dawdle too long: you've got a date with destiny c 79AD at **(2) Pompeii**. A volcano eruption trapped the ancient Roman town under a layer of volcanic ash, but in the 21st century, you can hop on a bus right to the source of the Pompeii's troubles: the still-active cone of **(3) Mt Vesuvius**. The next day, hurtle onward along the coast and backward in time by car (or more gradually by train and bus) to the breathtaking 6th century BC Greek temples of **(4) Paestum**. Afterwards, rejoin the modern world at your leisure on the beaches of **(5) Amalfi**.

CAPRI TO RAVELLO
Amalfi Affair

4-5 DAYS

Romance is ready when you are, just south of Naples. Catch the ferry to **(1) Capri**, where you can take a boat into the mermaid-worthy Blue Grotto or a chairlift to mesmerising views atop Monte Solaro – but no one could blame you if you didn't budge from these sandy beach coves.

After a night or two at Hotel Villa Sarah amid balmy, lemon-scented breezes, hop the ferry to **(2) Sorrento**, where you'll become besotted with the region's legendary buffalo-milk mozzarella at Inn Bufalito. Take a bus to **(3) Positano**, where you can wander boutique-laced lanes and sleep like royalty at Hotel

Palazzo Murat, a Napoleonic palace turned luxury love-nest.

Take the scenic route by boat to **(4) Amalfi**, and dive into another enchanted sea-cave, though this one's emerald-green: Grotta dello Smeraldo. Let the Museo della Carta inspire your own medieval love-letters, or settle in at Ristorante La Caravella to work your way through the 1,750-wine menu. Retreat to lofty **(5) Ravello** for sigh-worthy views from Villa Cimbrone's Infinity Terrace, and script your own Shakespeare-worthy balcony scenes at Hotel Villa Amore.

Ravello (p306)

Discover Naples, Pompeii & the Amalfi Coast

Market stalls, Naples
RICHARD I'ANSON/LONELY PLANET IMAGES ©

NAPLES

POP 3,079,000

Italy's most misunderstood city is also one of its finest – an exhilarating mess of bombastic baroque churches, bellowing baristas and electrifying street life. First stop for many is the Unesco World Heritage-listed *centro storico* (historic city centre). It's here, under the washing lines, that you'll find Naples' arabesque street life – cocky kids playing football in noisy piazzas, overloaded Vespas hurtling through cobbled alleyways and clued-up *casalinghe* (homemakers) bullying market vendors.

If you plan to blitz the sights, **Campania Artecard** (☑ 800 600601; www.campania rtecard.it) covers museum admission and transport, from €12-30, covering Naples only or including sites in Pompeii and Paestum.

 Sights

Centro Storico

DUOMO   Duomo, Museum
(☑ 081 44 90 97; Via Duomo;
⊙ 8.30am-1.30pm & 2.30-8pm Mon-Sat, 8.30am-1.30pm & 4.30-8pm Sun) Naples' 13th to 17th century spiritual centrepiece sits on the site of earlier churches and a temple to the god Neptune. The 17th-century baroque **Cappella di San Gennaro** (Chapel of St Januarius, also known as the Chapel of the Treasury; ⊙ 8.30am-12.30pm & 4.30-6.30pm Mon-Sat, 8.30am-1pm & 5-7pm Sun) features a fiery painting by Giuseppe Ribera and a bevy of silver busts and bronze statues. Above them, a heavenly dome glows with frescoes by Giovanni Lanfranco. The **baptistry** (admission €1.50; ⊙ 8.30am-12.30pm & 4.30-7pm Mon-Sat, 8.30am-1.30pm Sun) is the

oldest in western Europe, with remarkably fresh 4th-century mosaics.

At the Duomo's southern end, the **Museo del Tesoro di San Gennaro** (☎081 29 49 80; Via Duomo 149; admission €6; ☷10am-5pm Thu-Tue) glimmers with gifts made to Naples' patron saint St Januarius over the centuries.

BASILICA DI SANTA CHIARA
Church, Museum

(☎081 551 66 73; www.monasterodisantachiara.eu; Via Benedetto Croce; ☷7.30am-1pm & 4.30-8pm) The real attraction here is the adjacent **nuns' cloisters** (adult/reduced €5/3.50; ☷9.30am-5.30pm Mon-Sat, 10am-2.30pm Sun, last entry 30mins before closing), a long parapet lavished with decorative ceramic tiles depicting scenes of rural life, from hunting to posing peasants. Adjacent to the cloisters, an elegant **museum** of mostly ecclesiastical props also features the excavated ruins of a 1st-century spa complex.

MADRE
Museum

(Museo d'Arte Contemporanea Donnaregina; ☎081 1931 3016; www.museomadre.it; Via Settembrini 79; admission €7, Mon free; ☷10.30am-2.30pm Wed-Mon) Naples' top contemporary museum includes Jeff Koons' uberkitsch *Wild Boy and Puppy*, Rebecca Horn's eerie *Spirits,* and a perspective-warping installation by Anish Kapoor.

Vomero

MUSEO NAZIONALE DI SAN MARTINO
Monastery, Museum

(☎848 80 02 88; Largo San Martino 5; admission €6; ☷8.30am-7.30pm Thu-Tue, last entry 6.30pm) The high point (quite literally) of Neapolitan baroque, this stunning charterhouse-turned-museum was founded as a Carthusian monastery in the 14th century. The **church** contains a feast of frescoes and paintings by Naples' greatest 17th-century artists – Francesco Solimena, Massimo Stanzione, Giuseppe de Ribera and Battista Caracciolo.

Adjacent to the church, the elegant **Chiostro dei Procuratori** leads to the larger **Chiostro Grande**, designed by Giovanni Antonio Dosio in the late 16th century with white Tuscan-Doric porticoes. The skulls mounted on the balustrade were a light-hearted reminder to the monks of their own mortality. To the north of the Chiostro Grande, the

Capella di San Gennaro (p284), Duomo, Naples

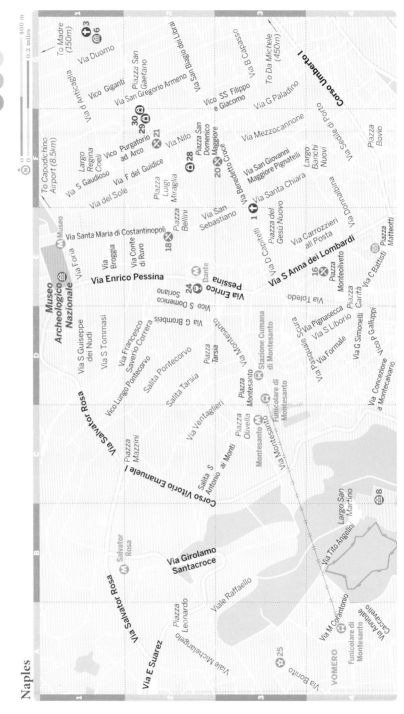

Naples

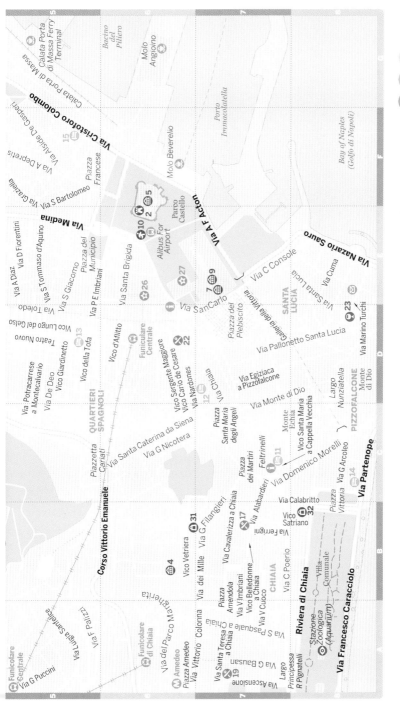

Naples

Sezione Presepiale houses a whimsical collection of rare Neapolitan *presepi* (nativity scenes) carved in the 18th and 19th centuries.

Santa Lucia & Chiaia

CASTEL NUOVO　　Castle, Museum
(☎081 795 58 77; admission €5; ⊙9am-7pm Mon-Sat) This crenellated 13th-century castle is a strapping Neapolitan landmark, with fragments of the original Giotto frescoes alongside the Gothic windows of **Cappella Palatina**. Today, the **Museo Civico** spreads across several halls on three floors, with 14th- and 15th-century frescoes and sculptures on the ground floor and Guglielmo Monaco's 15th-century bronze door with a cannonball embedded in it.

ISI ARTI ASSOCIATE　　Art Gallery
(☎081 658 63 81; www.isiartiassociate.net; Vico del Vasto a Chiaia 47; ⊙during exhibitions check website) This hip art space exhibits anything from contemporary painting and photography, to sculpture and multimedia installations from Italy and abroad. Check the website for DJ sessions, live music, performance art and themed culinary tastings.

Capodimonte

PALAZZO REALE DI CAPODIMONTE　　Palazzo, Museum, Park
Originally intended as a hunting lodge for Charles VII of Bourbon in 1738, this monumental *palazzo* houses the art collection Charles inherited from his mother Elisabetta Farnese. **Museo di Capodimonte** (☎081 749 91 11; www.museo-capodimonte.it; Parco di Capodimonte; admission €7.50; ⊙8.30am-7.30pm Thu-Tue, last entry 90min before closing) is spread over three floors and 160 rooms. Highlights are numerous, but look out for Masaccio's *Crocifissione* (Crucifixion), Bellini's *Trasfigurazione* (Transfiguration), Parmigianino's *Antea,* Caravaggio's *Flagellazione* (Flagellation) and Andy Warhol's poptastic *Mt Vesuvius.*

GREG ELMS/LONELY PLANET IMAGES ©

Don't Miss **Museo Archaeologico Nazionale**

Talk about a decor upgrade: a former cavalry barracks that served as the seat of the city's university became arguably the world's finest antiquities museum in the late 18th century, when Bourbon king Charles VII redecorated the place with antiquities he had inherited from his mother, Elisabetta Farnese, plus treasures looted from Pompeii and Herculaneum.

The impressive **Borgia collection** of Egyptian and Etruscan relics has been bumped to the basement, saving pride of place on the ground floor to showcase the **Farnese collection** of Greek and Roman sculpture – including the 3rd century *Toro Farnese* (Farnese Bull), discovered in Rome in 1545 and restored by Michelangelo before being shipped to Naples in 1787. On the mezzanine is a small but stunning collection of mosaics from Pompeii, notably Casa del Fauno's action-packed *La Battaglia di Alessandro Contro Dario* (The Battle of Alexander against Darius).

Beyond the mosaics is the **Gabinetto Segreto** (Secret Room), home to the museum's ancient pornography collection. The climax, so to speak, is an intriguing statue of Pan servicing a nanny goat, originally found in Herculaneum. The erotic paintings depicting sexual positions once served as a menu for brothel clients.

Upstairs, the vast **Sala Meridiana** contains the *Farnese Atlante,* a statue of Atlas carrying a globe on his shoulders. To make sure you don't miss highlights or get lost in rambling galleries numbered in Roman numerals, it's worth investing in the National Archaeological Museum of Naples guide (€7.50) or an English audioguide (€5) and – given recent staff shortages – calling ahead to ensure the galleries you want to see are open.

THINGS YOU NEED TO KNOW

📞081 44 01 66; Piazza Museo Nazionale 19; admission €6.50; ⏰9am-7.30pm Wed-Mon

CATACOMBE DI SAN GENNARO
Catacomb

(☎ 081 744 37 14; www.catacombedinapoli.it; Via di Capodimonte 13; admission €8; ⏱1hr tours every hr 10am-5pm Mon-Sat, to 1pm Sun) The oldest and most famous of Naples' ancient catacombs date to the 2nd century. Spread over two levels and decorated with early Christian frescoes, they contain a mix of tombs, corridors and broad vestibules held up by columns and arches.

 Tours

CITY SIGHTSEEING NAPOLI
Bus

(☎ 081 551 72 79; www.napoli.city-sightseeing.it; adult/child €22/11) Operates a hop-on, hop-off bus service with four routes across the city. All depart from Piazza del Municipio Parco Castello; tickets are valid for 24 hours for each of route. Tour commentaries are provided in English.

🛌 Sleeping

HOTEL PIAZZA BELLINI
Boutique Hotel €€

(☎ 081 45 17 32; www.hotelpiazzabellini.com; Via Costantinopoli 101; s €70-125, d €80-150, tr €100-170; ❄ @ 🛜 👪) Naples' newest art hotel inhabits a 16th-century *palazzo*, its cool white spaces spiked with original majolica tiles and the work of emerging artists. Rooms offer pared-back cool, with designer fittings, chic bathrooms and mirror frames drawn straight on the wall.

ROMEO HOTEL
Design Hotel €€€

(☎ 081 017 50 01; www.romeohotel.it; Via Cristoforo Colombo 45; r €165-330; ❄ @ 🛜) Naples' top design hotel combines Artesia stone with A-list art and furniture, a fabulous rooftop restaurant, and super sleek spa centre. 'Classic' category rooms are small but luxe, with DeLonghi espresso machines and sleek bathrooms.

HOTEL IL CONVENTO
Hotel €€

(☎ 081 40 39 77; www.hotelilconvento.com; Via Speranzella 137a; s €55-90, d €65-160; ❄ 🛜) Taking its name from the neighbouring convent, this lovely hotel blends antique Tuscan furniture, erudite book collections and candlelit stairs. Rooms are cosy and elegant, with creamy tones, dark woods and patches of 16th-century brickwork.

CHIAJA HOTEL DE CHARME
Boutique Hotel €€

(☎ 081 41 55 55; www.hotelchiaia.it; Via Chiaia 216; s €95-105, d €99-145, superior d €140-165; ❄ @ 🛜) Encompassing a former brothel and an aristocratic town house, this refined, peaceful hotel lives up to its name. The look is effortlessly noble – think gilt-framed portraits on pale lemon walls, opulent table lamps and heavy fabrics.

Pasta shop, Naples
ROCCO FASANO/LONELY PLANET IMAGES ®

Grazing Across the Centro Storico

Even more so than soccer, eating is Naples' favorite sport – and nowhere is the action hotter or tastier than in Centro Storico. Great Neopolitan meals start with ingredients fresh from **Mercato di Porta Nolana** (☉8am-6pm Mon-Sat, to 2pm Sun), where you'll hear sing-song fishmongers and get whiffs of fragrant bakeries for blocks around. Pizza isn't a snack but a quasi-religious experience in the Centro Storico, where **Pizzeria Gino Sorbillo** (Via dei Tribunali 32; pizzas from €2.30; ☉Mon-Sat) follows heavenly pies hot from the wood-fired oven with cloud-like *torroncino semifreddo* (almond nougat chilled dessert). Pizza purists observe time-honoured rituals at **Da Michele** (Via Cesare Sersale 1; pizzas from €4; ☉Mon-Sat): grab a ticket, get in line and choose between classic *marinara* (tomatoes, garlic and oregano) and Naples' venerable *margherita* (tomato, basil and mozzarella).

Neopolitan pizza-makers have an unfair advantage: fresh local mozzarella. But there's more fantastic *formaggi* (cheese) in store at **La Stanza del Gusto** (☏081 40 15 78; www.lastanzadelgusto.com, in Italian; Via Costantinopoli 100; lunch special €13, 5/7 course tasting menu €45/65; ☉cheese bar 3.30pm-midnight Mon, 11am-midnight Tue-Sat, restaurant dinner Mon-Sat), with a casual ground floor 'cheese bar' offering wine pairings and modern taste sensations like almond and saffron soup.

Diners get creative at **Palazzo Petrucci** (☏081 552 40 68; www.palazzopetrucci.it, in Italian; Piazza San Domenico Maggiore 4; 5-course degustation menu €50; ☉Mon-Sat), where clever twists are added to classic dishes: layers of raw prawn and mozzarella become 'lasagna,' and the poached-egg onion soup is positively un-French.

For dessert and delectable souvenirs, head to **Limonè** (Piazza San Gaetano 72) for organic *limoncello* (lemon liqueur) and pasta made with heady, aromatic Amalfi lemons.

B&B CAPPELLA VECCHIA   B&B €

(☏081 240 51 17; www.cappellavecchia11.it; Vico Santa Maria a Cappella Vecchia 11; s €50-70, d €75-100; ✳@☎) Run by a super helpful young couple, this B&B has six simple, witty rooms with funky bathrooms and different Neapolitan themes, from *mal'occhio* (evil eye) to *peperoncino* (chilli) There's a spacious communal area for breakfast, and free internet available 24/7.

PARTENO   B&B €€

(☏081 245 20 95; www.parteno.it; Via Partenope 1; s €80-99, d €100-125; ✳@☎) Six chic rooms are exquisitely decorated with period furniture, vintage Neapolitan prints and silk bedding. The azalea room (€130 to €165) steals the show with its seamless view of sea, sky and Capri.

Eating

TRATTORIA SAN FERDINANDO   Trattoria €€

(Via Nardones 117; meals €30; ☉lunch Mon-Sat, dinner Wed-Fri) For a Neapolitan taste trip, ask for a rundown of the day's antipasti and choose your favourites for an *antipasto misto*. Seafood standouts include a delicate *seppia ripieno* (stuffed squid), while the homemade desserts make for a satisfying dénouement.

IL GARUM   Traditonal Italian €€

(Piazza Monteoliveto 2A; meals €39) In the soft glow of wrought-iron lanterns, regulars tuck into rigatoni with mussels and shredded zucchini, and exquisite grilled calamari stuffed with vegetables, cherry tomatoes and parmesan. All the desserts are made on-site.

LA TRATTORIA DELL'OCA   Trattoria €€
(Via Santa Teresa a Chiaia 11; meals €35;
⊙closed dinner Sun Oct-May, closed all day Sun
Jun-Sep) Refined yet relaxed, this softly lit
trattoria celebrates beautifully cooked
classics, which may include *gnocchi al
ragù* or a superb *baccalà* (salted cod)
cooked with succulent cherry tomatoes,
capers and olives.

LA FOCACCIA   Pizza by Slice €
(Vico Belledonne a Chiaia 31; focaccia from €1.50;
⊙11am-late Mon-Sat, 5pm-late Sun) Head to
this funky, no-fuss bolthole for fat focaccia squares stacked with combos like
artichokes and *provola,* or eggplant with
pecorino cheese and smoked ham.

Drinking

PENGUIN CAFÉ   Wine Bar
(Via Santa Lucia 88; ⊙7.30pm-late) Not just
a snug wine bar, Penguin sells cinema-
themed books, hosts literary events, and
offers live music Thursday to Saturday.
The 100-plus wine list includes six fine
drops by the glass, perfectly paired with
quality cheeses, *salumi* (charcuterie),

Teatro San Carlo

salads and a handful of heartier, seasonal
dishes.

CAFFÈ MEXICO   Cafe
(Piazza Dante 86; ⊙7am-8.30pm Mon-Sat)
Make a beeline for Naples' best-loved
espresso bar, where old-school baristas
serve up the city's mightiest espresso.

 **Entertainment**

For cultural listings, check www.incampa
nia.it; for the latest club news, check out
the free minimag *Zero* (www.zero.eu, in
Italian), available from many bars.

Opera & Ballet

Teatro San Carlo (☎081 797 23 31, guided
tours 081 553 45 65; www.teatrosancarlo.it; Via
San Carlo 98; tours €5, performance tickets
€50-140; ⊙box office 10am-7pm Tue-Sat,
10am-3.30pm Sun) Famed for its perfect
acoustics, Italy's largest opera house was
built in 1737, predating its northern rival,
Milan's La Scala, by 41 years. The theatre
stages a standout year-round programme
of opera, ballet and concerts; book ahead.

Tickets Please

Tickets for public transport in Naples and the surrounding Campania region are managed by **Unico Campania** (www.unicocampania.it) and sold at stations, ANM booths and tobacconists. The following ticket options are available:

○ **Unico Napoli** (90-minutes €1.20, 24-hours weekdays €3.60, weekends €3) Unlimited travel by bus, tram, funicular, metro, Ferrovia Cumana or Circumflegrea.

○ **Unico 3T** (72-hours €20) Unlimited travel throughout Campania, including the Alibus, EAV buses to Mt Vesuvius and transport on the islands of Ischia and Procida.

○ **Unico Ischia** (90-minutes €1.20, 24-hours €4) Unlimited bus travel on Ischia.

○ **Unico Capri** (60-minutes €2.20, 24-hours €6.90) Unlimited bus travel on Capri. The 60-minute ticket covers a single trip on the funicular connecting Marina Grande to Capri Town; the daily ticket covers two funicular trips.

○ **Unico Costiera** (45-minutes €2.40, 90-minutes €3.60, 24-hours €7.20, 72-hours €18) The 24- and 72-hour tickets also cover the City Sightseeing tourist bus between Amalfi and Ravello, which runs from April to October.

Nightclubs & Live Music

ARENILE RELOAD Live Music, Club
(www.arenilereload.com, in Italian; Via Coroglio 14, Bagnoli) The biggest of Naples' beach-side clubs, head in for poolside cocktails, see-and-be-seen aperitivo sessions, live bands and dancing under the stars. The club is a short walk south of Bagnoli station on the Cumana rail line.

AROUND MIDNIGHT Live Music
(🕿 081 742 32 78; www.aroundmidnight.it, in Italian; Via Bonito 32A; 🕒 Tue-Sun Sep-Jun) One of Naples' oldest and most famous jazz clubs, this tiny swinging bolthole features mostly home-grown live gigs, with the occasional blues band putting in a performance.

 **Shopping**

For organic, handmade soaps and beauty products, try **Kiphy** (www.kiphy.it, in Italian; Vico San Domenico Maggiore 3), while those after quality, handcrafted nativity scene figurines shouldn't miss **La Scarabattola** (www.lascarabattola.it; Via dei Tribunali 50). The chic neighborhood of Chiaia has several legendary Neapolitan tailors, including **Mariano Rubinacci** (www.marianorubinacci.net; Via Filangeri 26) and **Marinella** (www.marinellanapoli.it; Via Riviera di Chiaia 287).

ℹ Information

Dangers & Annoyances

Petty crime can be a problem in Naples, so be smart: leave valuables in your hotel room and never leave bags unattended. Be careful if walking alone late at night, particularly near Stazione Centrale.

Medical Services

Ospedale Loreto-Mare (🕿 081 20 10 33; Via Amerigo Vespucci 26)

Tourist Information

Tourist Information Office Piazza del Gesù Nuovo 7 (🕒 9am-7pm Mon-Sat, 9am-2pm Sun); Stazione Centrale (🕒 9am-8pm Mon-Sat, to 6pm Sun); Via San Carlo 9 (🕒 9.30am-1.30pm & 2.30-6.30pm Mon-Sat, 9am-1.30pm Sun)

Detour:
Mt Vesuvius

Towering darkly over Naples and its environs, Mt Vesuvius (Vesuvio; 1281m) is the only active volcano on the European mainland. Now a nature preserve, **Parco Nazionale del Vesuvio** (www.parconazionaledelvesuvio.it) lets visitors tempt fate and explore the volcano's turbulent geology, conditions permitting. From a car park at the summit, an 860m path leads up to the volcano's **crater** (admission incl tour €8; ⏱9am-6pm Jul & Aug, to 5pm Apr-Jun & Sep, to 4pm Mar & Oct, to 3pm Nov-Feb, ticket office closes 1hr before closing). About halfway up the hill, the **Museo dell'Osservatorio Vesuviano** (Museum of the Vesuvian Observatory; ☎081 610 84 83; www.ov.ingv.it; admission free; ⏱10am-2pm Sat & Sun) covers 2000 years of Mt Vesuvius and its 30 eruptions, from the AD63 eruption that buried Pompeii to the most recent eruption in 1944.

EAV Bus (☎800 053 939; www.eavbus.it) runs two daily services from Naples to Vesuvius (€14.60 return, 90 minutes), stopping at Piazza Garibaldi at 9.25am and 10.40am; return services depart Vesuvius at 12.30pm and 2pm. It also runs eight to 10 daily buses to Vesuvius from Piazza Anfiteatro in Pompeii (€10, one hour). By car, exit the A3 at Ercolano Portico and follow signs for the Parco Nazionale del Vesuvio.

❶ Getting There & Away

Air

Capodichino airport (NAP; ☎081 751 54 71; www.gesac.it), 7km northeast of the city centre, is southern Italy's main airport, linking Naples with most Italian and several major European cities, as well as New York.

Boat

Catch fast ferries and hydrofoils for Capri, Sorrento, Ischia (both Ischia Porto and Forio) and Procida from Molo Beverello in front of Castel Nuovo; hydrofoils for Capri, Ischia and Procida also sail from Mergellina.

Major high-season services include:

Caremar (☎081 551 38 82; www.caremar.it, in Italian) Services to Capri (€16, 50min), Ischia (€16, 50min) and Procida (€13, 40min).

Gescab-Alilauro (☎081 497 22 22; www.alilauro.it) Services to Ishcia (€17, 50-65min) and Sorrento (€11, 35min).

Gescab-Navigazione Libera del Golfo (NLG; ☎081 552 07 63; www.navlib.it, in Italian) Services to Capri (€17, 40min).

Gescab-SNAV (☎081 428 55 55; www.snav.it)

Bus

Most national and international buses leave from Piazza Garibaldi.

Regional bus services are operated by SITA (☎199 730 749; www.sitabus.it, in Italian) and include the following:

Amalfi (€4, 2hrs, five daily Mon-Sat)

Pompeii (€2.80, 30min, half-hourly)

Positano (€4, 2hr, one daily Mon-Sat)

You can buy SITA tickets and catch buses either from Porto Immacolatella, near Molo Angioino, or from Via Galileo Ferraris, near Stazione Centrale.

Car & Motorcycle

Car and motorcycle theft is rife, so think twice before bringing a vehicle into town and never leave anything in your car. Naples is on the A1 (north to Rome and Milan) and the A3 (south to Salerno and Reggio di Calabria).

Train

Most national trains arrive at or depart from Stazione Centrale or, underneath the main station, Stazione Garibaldi. Some services also stop at Mergellina station. There are up to 42 trains daily to Rome, including Frecciarossa (High Velocity; 2nd class €45; 70 minutes) and ES (Eurostar; 2nd class €36; 1¾ hours).

Stazione Circumvesuviana (☎081 772 24 44; www.vesuviana.it; Corso Garibaldi) connects Naples to Sorrento (€4, 65 minutes), with stops at Ercolano/Herculaneum (€2.10, 15 minutes) and Pompeii (€2.80, 35 minutes).

❶ Getting Around

To/From the Airport

Airport buses include ANM (☎800 639525; www.unicocampania.it) bus 3S (€1.20, 45 minutes, every 20 minutes) from Piazza Garibaldi or the Alibus (☎800 639525) airport shuttle (€3, 45 minutes, every 20 minutes) from Piazza del Municipio or Piazza Garibaldi.

Official taxi fares to the airport are as follows: €23 from a seafront hotel or from the Mergellina hydrofoil terminal; €19 from Piazza del Municipio; and €15.50 from Stazione Centrale.

Bus

Most ANM buses pass through Piazza Garibaldi, the city's chaotic transport hub.

Car & Motorcycle

Vehicle theft and anarchic traffic make driving in Naples a bad option. Officially, much of the city centre is closed to nonresident traffic for much of the day.

Funicular

Funicolare Centrale Ascends from Via Toledo to Piazza Fuga.
Funicolare di Chiaia From Via del Parco Margherita to Via Domenico Cimarosa.
Funicolare di Montesanto From Piazza Montesanto to Via Raffaele Morghen.

Metro

Metropolitana (☎800 568866; www.metro.na.it) Naples' metro system is covered by Unico Napoli tickets (see boxed text, p293).

Taxi

Use only marked, official white taxis and ensure the meter is running. There are taxi stands at most of the city's main piazzas or you can call one of the five taxi cooperatives: Napoli (☎081 556 44 44), Consortaxi (☎081 22 22), Cotana (☎081 570 70 70), Free (☎081 551 51 51) or Partenope (☎081 556 02 02).

Marina in Naples, looking out to Mt Vesuvius

RICHARD I'ANSON/LONELY PLANET IMAGES ©

Tragedy in Pompeii

24 August AD 79

8am Buildings including the **Terme Suburbane** ❶ and the **foro** ❷ are still undergoing repair after an earthquake in AD 63 caused significant damage to the city. Despite violent earth tremors overnight, residents have little idea of the catastrophe that lies ahead.

Midday Peckish locals pour into the **Thermopolium di Vetutius Placidus** ❸. The lustful slip into the **Lupanare** ❹, and gladiators practise for the evening's planned games at the **anfiteatro** ❺. A massive boom heralds the eruption. Shocked onlookers witness a dark cloud of volcanic matter shoot some 14km above the crater.

3pm–5pm Lapilli (burning pumice stone) rains down on Pompeii. Terrified locals begin to flee; others take shelter. Within two hours, the plume is 25km high and the sky has darkened. Roofs collapse under the weight of the debris, burying those inside.

25 August AD 79

Midnight Mudflows bury the town of Herculaneum. Lapilli and ash continue to rain down on Pompeii, bursting through buildings and suffocating those taking refuge within.

4am–8am Ash and gas avalanches hit Herculaneum. Subsequent surges smother Pompeii, killing all remaining residents, including those in the **Orto dei Fuggiaschi** ❻. The volcanic 'blanket' will safeguard frescoed treasures like the **Casa del Menandro** ❼ and **Villa dei Misteri** ❽ for almost two millennia.

TOP TIPS

Visit in the afternoon

Allow three hours

Wear comfortable shoes and a hat

Bring drinking water

Don't use flash photography

Terme Suburbane
The *laconicum* (sauna), *caldarium* (hot bath) and large, heated swimming pool weren't the only sources of heat here; scan the walls of this suburban bathhouse for some of the city's raunchiest frescoes.

Villa di Diomede

Casa dei Vettii

Casa del Poeta Tragico

Porta Ercolano

Casa del Fauno

Basilica

Tempio di Apollo

Porta Marina

Terme del Foro

Macellum

Teatro Grande

Quadriportico dei Teatri

Porta di Stabia

Teatro Piccolo

Foro
An ancient Times Square of sorts, the forum sits at the intersection of Pompeii's main streets and was closed to traffic in the 1st century AD. The plinths on the southern edge featured statues of the imperial family.

Villa dei Misteri
Home to the world-famous *Dionysiac Frieze* fresco. Other highlights at this villa include *trompe l'oeil* wall decorations in the *cubiculum* (bedroom) and Egyptian-themed artwork in the *tablinum* (reception).

Lupanare
The prostitutes at this brothel were often slaves of Greek or Asian origin. Mattresses once covered the stone beds and the names engraved in the walls are possibly those of the workers and their clients.

Thermopolium di Vetutius Placidus
The counter at this ancient snack bar once held urns filled with hot food. The *lararium* (household shrine) on the back wall depicts Dionysus (the god of wine) and Mercury (the god of profit and commerce).

Eyewitness Account
Pliny the Younger (AD 61– c 112) gives a gripping, first-hand account of the catastrophe in his letters to Tacitus (AD 56–117).

Porta del Vesuvio

Porta di Nola

Casa della Venere in Conchiglia

Porta di Sarno

Grande Palestra

Tempio di Iside

③

⑦

⑥

⑤

Casa del Menandro
This dwelling most likely belonged to the family of Poppaea Sabina, Nero's second wife. A room to the left of the atrium features Trojan War paintings and a polychrome mosaic of pygmies rowing down the Nile.

Orto dei Fuggiaschi
The Garden of the Fugitives showcases the plaster moulds of thirteen locals seeking refuge during Vesuvius' eruption – the largest number of victims found in any one area. The huddled bodies make for a moving scene.

Anfiteatro
Magistrates, local senators and the games' sponsors and organisers enjoyed front-row seating at this veteran amphitheatre, home to gladiatorial battles and the odd riot. The parapet circling the stadium featured paintings of combat, victory celebrations and hunting scenes.

JEAN-BERNARD CARILLET/LONELY PLANET IMAGES ©

SOUTH OF NAPLES

Pompeii

POP 25,760

A stark reminder of the malign forces that lie deep inside Vesuvius, Pompeii (Pompei in Italian) is Europe's most compelling archaeological site. In AD 63, a massive earthquake hit the city, causing widespread damage and the evacuation of much of the 20,000-strong population. Many had not returned when Vesuvius blew its top on 24 August AD 79, burying the city under a layer of *lapilli* (hot pumice) and killing some 2000 men, women and children.

 Sights

RUINS OF POMPEII   Roman Ruins
(☏ 081 861 90 03; www.pompeiisites.org; entrances at Porta Marina & Piazza Anfiteatro; adult/EU national 18yr-25yr/EU national under 18yr & over 65yr €11/5.50/free, combined ticket incl Herculaneum, Oplontis, Stabiae & Boscoreale & 3 minor sites €20/10/free; ☺8.30am-7.30pm

Apr-Oct, 8.30am-5pm Nov-Mar, last entry 90min before closing) Of Pompeii's original 66 hectares, 44 have now been excavated; for highlights, see p296. Audioguides (€6.50) are a sensible investment, as is a hat and sunscreen. The **Museo Vesuviano** (☏ 081 850 72 55; Via Bartolomeo 12; admission free; ☺9am-1pm Mon-Fri), southeast of the excavations, contains an interesting array of artefacts. The ruins are best visited on a day trip from Naples or Sorrento, as once the excavations close for the day, the area around the site becomes decidedly seedy.

 Tours

Authorised guides wear identification tags, and you can expect to pay between €100 and €120 for a two-hour tour, whether you're alone or in a group. Reputable tour operators include **Yellow Sudmarine** (☏ 081 362 52 28; www.yellow sudmarine.com), **Torres Travel** (☏ 081 856 78 02; www.torrestravel.it) and **Pompeii Cast** (☏ 081 850 49 12; www.pompeiicast.it).

Eating

TOP CHOICE PRESIDENT   Modern Italian €€
(☎081 850 72 45; Piazza Schettini 12; meals €40; ⌚closed Mon & dinner Sun Nov-Mar, closed 2 weeks Jan) Under dripping chandeliers, regional produce is celebrated in brilliant creations like *millefoglie* (flaky puff pastry) with Cetara anchovies, *mozzarella filante* (melted mozzarella) and grated *tarallo* (savoury almond biscuit). The degustation menus (€40 to €70) are a gourmand's delight.

ℹ Information

Tourist office Porta Marina (☎081 536 32 93; www.pompeiturismo.it; Piazza Porta Marina Inferiore 12; ⌚8am-3.45pm Mon-Sat); Pompeii town (☎081 850 72 55; Via Sacra 1; ⌚8am-3.30pm Mon-Fri, to 1.30pm Sat)

ℹ Getting There & Away

Frequent Circumvesuviana trains run from Pompeii-Scavi-Villa dei Misteri station to Naples (€2.80, 35min) and Sorrento (€2.10, 30min). SITA (☎199 730749; www.sitabus.it, in Italian) operates buses half-hourly to/from Naples (€2.80, 30min).

To get here by car, take the A3 from Naples. Use the Pompeii exit and follow signs to Pompeii Scavi.

Sorrento

POP 16,610

Cliff-straddling Sorrento has laid-back southern Italian charm resisting all attempts to swamp it in graceless development. The bad news: Sorrento does not have great beaches. The good news: Bagni Regina Giovanna, a rocky beach set among the ruins of the Roman Villa Pollio Felix, is much nicer; walk or take the SITA bus or the EAV bus (Linea A) for Massalubrense.

The narrow streets of *centro storico* are thronged on summer evenings, with a holiday atmosphere around souvenir stores, cafes, churches and restaurants.

If You Like...
Buried Roman Cities

Anyone fascinated by Pompeii and unearthed Roman artefacts at Museo Archaeologico Nazionale shouldn't miss these ancient sites:

1 HERCULANEUM
(☎081 732 43 38; Corso Resina 6; adult €11, combined ticket incl Pompeii €20; ⌚8.30am-7.30pm Apr-Oct, to 5pm Nov-Mar, last entry 90min before closing) The Roman seaport of Herculaneum was still recovering from an AD63 earthquake when it was submerged under 16m of mud by the same volcanic eruption that buried Pompeii. Furniture, clothing and fleeing crowds were essentially fossilised. Today visitors can explore Herculaneum's remarkably preserved ruins. Reach Herculaneum by Circumvesuviana train (get off at Ercolano-Scavi) to/from Naples (€2.10), Pompeii (€1.50) and Sorrento (€2.10).

2 NAPOLI SOTTERRANEA
(☎081 29 69 44; www.napolisotterranea.org; Piazza San Gaetano 68; tours €9; ⌚tours noon, 2pm & 4pm Mon-Fri, 10am & 6pm Sat & Sun, 9pm Thu) 'Underground Naples' tours lead 40m below the city, into creepy ancient Roman passages and caves that served as air-raid shelters in WWII. Spooky candlelit portions of the tour lead through passages that are scarcely shoulder width – not for claustrophobes.

3 CHIESA E SCAVI DI SAN LORENZO MAGGIORE
(☎081 211 08 60; Via dei Tribunali 316; church admission free, excavations & museum adult/reduced €9/6; ⌚9.30am-5.30pm Mon-Sat, to 1.30pm Sun) Hidden in the basement of Naples' 13th century Gothic church are some remarkable *scavi* (excavations) of the original Graeco-Roman city, with ancient bakeries, wineries and communal laundries.

Join the crowds at Slow Food mozzarella bar-restaurant **Inn Bufalito** (Via Fuoro 21; meals €30; ⌚Apr-Oct) for Sorrento-style cheese fondue, buffalo-meat carpaccio and *salsiccia* (local sausage) with broccoli, and occasionally live music. To sightsee in Sorrento, consult online

Sorrento Tour (www.sorrentotour.it) or **Sorrento tourist office** (Via Luigi De Maio 35; 🕗8.30am-4.15pm Mon-Fri).

🛈 Getting There & Away

Boat

Sorrento is the main jumping-off point for Capri and also has excellent ferry connections to Naples, Ischia and Amalfi coastal resorts. Alilauro (☎081 878 14 30; www.alilauro.it) runs up to five daily hydrofoils between Naples and Sorrento (€9, 35min). Gescab-Linee Marittime Partenopee (☎081 704 19 11; www.consorziolmp.it) runs hydrofoils from Sorrento to Capri from April to November (€15, 20min, 15 daily). All ferries and hydrofoils depart from the port at Marina Piccola, where you buy your tickets.

Train

Circumvesuviana (☎081 772 24 44; www.vesuviana.it) trains run every half-hour between Sorrento and Naples (€4), via Pompeii (€2.10) and Ercolano (€2.10).

Bus

SITA (☎199 730749; www.sitabus.it, in Italian) buses serve the Amalfi Coast between Sorrento and Amalfi (€2.40, 1¾ hours), looping around Positano (€2.40, 1 hour). Change at Amalfi for Ravello.

Capri
POP 14,050

A stark mass of limestone rock rising through impossibly blue water, Capri (pronounced *ca*-pri) epitomises Mediterranean appeal: chichi piazzas and cool cafes, Roman ruins and rugged seascapes. With it's whitewashed stone buildings and tiny car-free streets, Capri Town feels like a film set. Central to the action is **Piazza Umberto I** (aka the Piazzetta), the showy, open-air salon where tanned tourists pay eye-watering prices to sip at one of four squareside cafes.

◎ Sights

To the east of the Piazzetta, Via Vittorio Emanuele and its continuation, Via Serena, lead down to the picturesque **Certosa di San Giacomo** (Charterhouse of San Giacomo; ☎081 837 62 18; Viale Certosa 40; admission free; 🕗9am-2pm Tue-Sun), a 14th-century monastery with two cloisters and some fine 17th-century frescoes in the chapel. From the *certosa* (charterhouse), Via Matteotti leads down to the colourful **Giardini di Augusto** (Gardens of Augustus; 🕗dawn-dusk), founded by the Emperor Augustus.

Outside Capri Town

Capri's hinterland retains an unspoiled rural charm with grand villas, overgrown vegetable plots and banks of brilliantly coloured

Monte Solaro (p302), Capri

DISCOVER NAPLES, POMPEII & THE AMALFI COAST CAPRI

LOOK DIE BILDAGENTUR DER FOTOGRAFEN GMBH / ALAMY ©

Don't Miss **Blue Grotto**

A stunning sea cave aglow with iridescent blue light, the Grotta Azzurra (Blue Grotto) creates a mesmerising optical effect as sunlight bounces off the sides of the 1.3m-high entrance and reflects off the grotto's white-sand bottom. At the back of the cave, you'll notice a Roman landing stage built by Emperor Tiberius around AD 30, complete with a shrine to the water nymph.

The easiest way to visit is to take a boat tour from **Marina Grande** (return trip €23.50, one hour), which includes a motorboat trip from the marina, cave admission fee, rowboat ride into the cave and singing boat captains (tip optional). Check at the Marina about conditions, because the grotto closes when the water is too choppy.

THINGS YOU NEED TO KNOW

Blue Grotto (admission €2; ☻9am to 1hr before sunset) From Anacapri bus terminal, **Staiano Autotrasporti** (www.staiano-capri.com, in Italian) buses serve the Grotta Azzurra. From Punta Carena, you also can walk up the **Sentiero dei Fortin**i (Path of the Small Forts) to the Grotto.

bougainvillea. East of Capri Town, a comfortable 2km walk along Via Tiberio, are the romantic ruins of **Villa Jovis** (Jupiter's Villa; ☏081 837 06 34; Via Tiberio; admission €2; ☻9am to 1hr before sunset). Standing 354m above sea level, this was the largest and most sumptuous of the island's 12 Roman villas, and Tiberius' main Capri residence. The stairway behind the villa leads to the 330m-high **Salto di Tiberio** (Tiberius' Leap), a sheer cliff from where

Tiberius had out-of-favour subjects hurled into the sea.

Coming up from Capri Town, the bus drops you at Piazza Victoria, a short walk from Roman-sculpture-filled **Villa San Michele di Axel Munthe** (☏081 837 14 01; www.villasanmichele.eu; Via Axel Munthe; admission €6; ☻9am-6pm May-Sep, 9am-3.30pm Nov-Feb, 9am-4.30pm Mar, 9am-5pm Apr & Oct) and its beautifully preserved gardens, where classical concerts

take place from July to August. From Piazza Vittoria, hop onto the **Seggiovia** (081 837 14 28; Piazza Vittoria; single/ return €7.50/10; 9.30am-4.30pm Apr-Oct, 9.30am-3.30pm Nov-Mar) chairlift to reach the summit of **Monte Solaro** (589m), Capri's highest point.

Activities

Marina Grande is the hub of Capri's thriving water-sports business. **Sercomar** (081 837 87 81; www.caprisub.com, in Italian; Via Colombo 64; closed Nov) offers various diving packages, costing from €100 for a single dive to €350 for a four-session beginners course.

Top swimming spots include Punta Carena's **public beach** and **Lido del Faro**, where €20 will get you access to the private beach, complete with swimming pool and a pricey but fabulous restaurant. To get here, catch the bus to Faro.

Sleeping

TOP CHOICE **CASA MARIANTONIA**　　　Boutique Hotel €€
(081 837 29 23; www.casamariantonia.com; Via G Orlandi 80, Anacapri; r €100-260, ste €180-400; P ☀ 🛜 ☷) With past guests including Jean-Paul Sartre and Alberto Moravia, you might just find your own muse by the pool at this gorgeous boutique retreat. Rooms deliver restrained elegance in soothing hues, as well as a private terrace with garden views.

RELAIS MARESCA　　　　　　　　Hotel €€
(081 837 96 19; www.relaismaresca.it; Via Marina Grande 284, Marina Grande; r incl breakfast €130-250; Apr-Oct; ☀ 🛜) A delightful four-star, this is the top choice in Marina Grande, with acres of gleaming ceramic in turquoise, blue and yellow. There's a range of rooms (and corresponding prices); the best have balconies and

GLENN BEANLAND/LONELY PLANET IM

Don't Miss **Positano**

A pearl in the rugged Amalfi coastline, Positano is the coast's most photogenic town. As visitor John Steinbeck wrote in 1953: 'Positano bites deep. It is a dream place that isn't quite real when you are there and becomes beckoningly real after you have gone.'

The loft, ceramic-tiled dome of **Chiesa di Santa Maria Assunta** is Positano's most fam sight, with cherubs peeking above every arch indoors. With greyish sand polk-dotted w colourful umbrella's, Positano's **Spiaggia Grande** is more family-friendly than romanti

Climb to panoramic **Ristorante Bruno** for swoon-worthy Positano panoramas an orange-marinated fish. But even for sunsets, you might not want to look up from p sensational grilled octopus with fried artichokes at **Da Vincenzo**.

THINGS YOU NEED TO KNOW

For rental rooms or apartments, ask at the **tourist office** (www.aziendaturismopositano.it; V sl Saracino 4; 8.30am-7.30pm Mon-Sat Apr-Oct, to 4.30pm Mon-Fri Nov-Mar). Between April a October, ferries link Positano with Amalfi, Sorrento, Salerno and Capri. **Ristorante Bruno** (Via Col o 157; meals €40; closed Nov-Jan); **Da Vincenzo** (089 87 51 28; Via Pasitea 172-178; m ℃40; dinner daily, lunch Wed-Mon Apr-Nov)

Getting There & Away

Boat

Boat service to Amalfi Coast towns are generally limited to the period between April and October, including twice-daily Gescab-Alicost (089

87 14 83; www.alicost.it, in Italian) servic m Amalfi and Positano to Capri.

Bus

SITA (199 730749; www.sitabus.it, i)
operates a frequent, year-round servic the SS163 between Sorrento and Salerno via Amalfi.

GLENN BEANLAND/LONELY PLANET IMAGES ©

Don't Miss **Ravello**

High in the hills above Amalfi, refined Ravello has inspired artists from opera composer Richard Wagner to novelist Virginia Woolf. Former resident Gore Vidal considered Ravello's sweeping coastal panoramas the world's finest, and it's hard to argue otherwise at sunset on the Infinity Terrace at **Villa Cimbrone** or wandering romantic hillside gardens at **Villa Rufolo**. Above the gardens towers Ravello's 11th-16th century **Cathedral**.

Inspiration abounds during the June–September **Ravello Festival**, with art, movies and dance citywide. From April to October don't miss Ravello Concert Society performances at Villa Rufolo.

Rub elbows with not-exactly-starving artists and celebrities such as Rosie O'Donnell at **Cumpà Cosimo**, where chef Netta Bottone dishes Ravello's trademark *crespolini* (cheese-and-prosciutto–stuffed crepes).

THINGS YOU NEED TO KNOW

Tourist office (www.ravellotime.it; Via Roma 18bis; ⏱9.30am-7pm Apr-Oct, to 5pm Nov-Mar). SITA operates hourly buses from Amalfi (€1.20, 25 minutes). **Villa Cimbrone** (☎089 85 74 59; adult/under 12yr & over 65yr €6/4; ⏱9am-sunset); **Villa Rufolo** (☎089 85 76 21; admission €5; ⏱9am-sunset); **Cumpà Cosimo** (☎089 85 71 56; Via Roma 44-46; pizzas €6-12, meals €45)

Car & Motorcycle
Exit the A3 autostrada at Vietri sul Mare and follow the SS163 along the coast.

Train
From Naples, take the Circumvesuviana to Sorrento, then continue eastwards along the Amalfi Coast by SITA bus.

Amalfi

POP 5340

It is hard to grasp that pretty little Amalfi, with its sun-filled piazzas and small beach, was once a maritime superpower with a population of more than 70,000. Just around the headland, neighbouring Atrani is a picturesque tangle of whitewashed alleys and arches centred on a lively, lived-in piazza and popular beach.

 Sights

CATTEDRALE DI SANT'ANDREA
Duomo, Museum

(089 87 10 59; Piazza del Duomo; 9am-6.45pm Apr-Jun, 9am-7.45pm Jul-Sep, reduced hrs off season) Dominating Piazza del Duomo, Amalfi's iconic cathedral makes an imposing sight at the top of its sweeping flight of stairs. It's a melange of architectural styles: the two-toned masonry is largely Sicilian Arabic-Norman while the interior is pure baroque. To the left of the cathedral's porch, the pint-sized **Chiostro del Paradiso** (089 87 13 24; adult/11-17yrs €3/1; 9am-6.45pm Apr-Jun, 9am-7.45pm Jul-Sep, reduced hrs off season) was built in 1266 to house the tombs of Amalfi's prominent citizens.

GROTTA DELLO SMERALDO
Grotto

(admission €5; 9am-4pm Mar-Oct, 9am-3pm Nov-Feb) Four kilometres west of Amalfi, Conca dei Marini is home to this haunting cave, named after the eerie emerald colour that emanates from the seawater. SITA buses regularly pass the car park above the cave entrance (from where you take a lift or stairs down to the rowing boats). Alternatively, **Coop Sant'Andrea** (089 87 31 90; www.coop santandrea.it; Lungomare dei Cavalieri 1) runs hourly boats from Amalfi (€14 return) between 9am and 3pm daily from May to October. Allow around one hour for the round trip.

MUSEO DELLA CARTA
Museum

(Paper Museum; 089 830 45 61; www.museo dellacarta.it; Via delle Cartiere; admission €4; 10am-6.30pm Apr–mid-Nov, 10am-3pm Tue, Wed & Fri-Sun mid-Nov–Mar) Housed in a 13th-century paper mill (the oldest in Europe), this fascinating museum lovingly

Outdoor market, Positano (p305)

preserves the original paper presses, which are still in full working order, as you'll see during the 15-minute guided tour (in English).

Sleeping

HOTEL LUNA CONVENTO
TOP CHOICE
Hotel €€€

(☎089 87 10 02; www.lunahotel.it; Via Pantaleone Comite 33; s €220-280; d €240-300; P ❄ @ ⚲ ☲) This former convent was founded by St Francis in 1222. Rooms in the original building, in the former nuns' cells, have bright tiles, balconies and sea views; the newer wing features religious frescoes over the beds.

HOTEL CENTRALE
Hotel €€

(☎089 87 26 08; www.amalfihotelcentrale.it; Largo Duchi Piccolomini 1; s €60-120, d €70-140; ❄ @ ⚲) The entrance is on a tiny little piazza in the *centro storico*, but many rooms actually overlook Piazza del Duomo (24 is a good choice). The bright green and blue tile work gives the place a vibrant, fresh look, and the views from the rooftop terrace are magnificent.

Eating

RISTORANTE LA CARAVELLA
Traditional, Modern Italian €€€

(☎089 87 10 29; www.ristorantelacaravella.it; Via Matteo Camera 12; meals €65, tasting menu €75; ☺Wed-Mon, closed Nov & early Jan-early Feb) One of the few places in Amalfi where you pay for the food rather than the location, this celebrated dining den serves a mix of simple, soulful classics and regional grub with a nouvelle twist – think lemon risotto with cooked and raw prawns and grey mullet roe. The 1,750-plus wines are an aficionado's dream.

LE ARCATE
Traditional Italian €€

(Largo Orlando Buonocore Atrani; pizzas from €6, meals €40; ☺closed early Jan–mid-Feb & Mon Sep-Jun) On a sunny day it's hard to beat the dreamy harbourside location. Pizzas are served at night, while daytime fare includes the house speciality, *scialatielli* pasta with shrimp and zucchini.

Tempio di Nettuno (Temple of Neptune; p309), Paestum

Detour:
Paestum

Offerings to Poseidon, the Greek god of the sea, once graced the temples of ancient Paestum. With Poseidon's blessing, Paestum remained an important Greek seaport from 6th century BC until the Romans arrived in 273BC – when it became cursed with malaria.

Paestum was abandoned to mosquitos, snakes and scorpions until 18th century road-builders arrived. But those accursed pests kept looters away, and today Paestum's three well-preserved temples are Unesco-protected. With modern pest-control, Paestum makes a pleasant Amalfi Coast road trip.

The **tourist office** (www.infopaestum.it; Via Magna Grecia 887; ⊙9am-1pm & 2-4pm) offers information on **Paestum Ruins** (☑0828 81 10 23; admission €4, incl museum €6.50; ⊙8.45am-2hrs before sunset).

Highlights include:

◦ **Tempio di Cerere** (Temple of Ceres) The first temple after the entrance dates from the 6th century BC.

◦ **Agorà** (Piazza) In this square are ruins of the *heroon* (Poseidon shrine) and an ancient swimming pool.

◦ **Foro** (Forum) Framing this grassy rectangle are ruins of a housing complex, an Italic temple, the **Bouleuterion** (Senate Hall) and amphitheatre.

◦ **Tempio di Nettuno** (Temple of Neptune) Paestum's largest and best preserved temple dates from 450 BC, and despite the name, recent studies have claimed that it was, in fact, dedicated to Apollo.

◦ **Basilica** From this mid-6th century BC temple to the goddess, majestic columns and ruins of the sacrificial altar remain.

◦ **Museum** (☑0828 81 10 23; admission €4, incl ruins €6.50; ⊙8.30am-7.30pm, last entry 6.45pm, closed 1st & 3rd Mon of month) Stop by to see weathered *metopes* (bas-reliefs) and 5th-century-BC Tomba del Truffatore (Tomb of the Diver), with a carved diver in mid-air representing the passage from life to death.

ℹ Information

Tourist office (www.amalfituristoffice.it; Corso delle Repubbliche Marinare 27; ⊙9am-1pm & 2-6pm Mon-Sat, 9am-1pm Sun, closed Sun Apr, May & Sep, closed Sat & Sun Oct-Mar) Good for bus and ferry timetables.

ℹ Getting There & Away

Boat

Between April and October there are services to Positano (€7, seven daily) and Capri (€17, one daily).

Bus

SITA buses run from Piazza Flavio Gioia to Sorrento (€2.80, 1½ hours, around 30 daily) via Positano (€1.50, 40 minutes), and also to Ravello (€1.20, 25 minutes, every 30 minutes). There are only two daily connections to Naples (€4, two to three hours), so you're better off catching a bus to Sorrento and then the Circumvesuviana train to Naples. Buy tickets and check schedules at Bar Il Giardino delle Palme (Piazza Flavio Gioia), opposite the bus stop.

Sicily &
Southern
Italy

From volcano-view beaches to cave hotels, Italy's south is set to stun.

Why would anyone live under a volcano? Sicilians have their reasons: beaches, history and food, for starters. Of all those who harboured on these dramatic shores over the last 25 centuries – Greeks, Arabs, Spaniards – few seemed inclined to leave, hence the island's multicultural history. Pistachios, almonds and citrus thrive in this volcanic soil, and star in Sicily's signature pastries and gelato.

But save some travel time and appetite for the heel of Italy's boot, where Puglia and Basilicata have somehow managed to keep Unesco World Heritage sites and Italy's most satisfying rustic cuisine more or less to themselves since the 8th century BC. Here you can sleep like a caveman in a subterranean hotel or a gnome in a stone hut, without straying far from sandy beaches.

Vieste (p341)

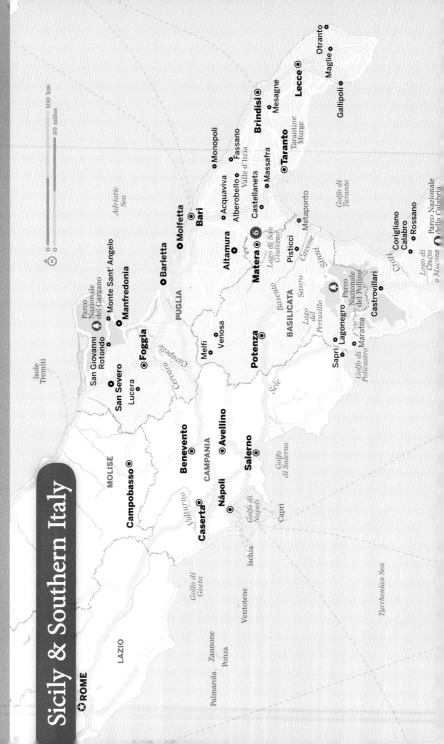

Sicily & Southern Italy

Sicily & Southern Italy Highlights

① Culinary Sicily

Sicilian food is all about bold flavours, a festive spirit and a sense of participation. Exotic ingredients reflect centuries of foreign domination, while the simple, casual recipes reflect Sicilian nonchalance. The cook's tastebuds are the driving force behind a meal to remember.

Need to Know

BEST EDIBLE SOUVENIRS Almond biscotti and pasta reale (marzipan) fruits **FAVOURITE SUMMER TREATS** Almond granita, fruit gelato and Palermo.

Culinary Sicily
Don't Miss List

BY ALESSIO FANGANO,
SICILIAN GOURMAND

1 STREET FOOD

Street food is a great tradition in Sicily, even if we buy most of it in bars and bakeries. King of the savouries is the *arancino*, a deep-fried rice cone traditionally filled with meat, tomato, peas, hardboiled egg and mozzarella. Hold it upside down and eat it from the base. Other snacks include *diavole* (deep-fried dough stuffed with prosciutto, mozzarella and black olives) and *sfincione* (a spongy, oily pizza topped with onions and *caciocavallo* cheese).

2 MARKETS

The atmosphere at Sicilian markets such as Palermo's Mercato di Ballarò (p322) is electric – the bellowing of competing vendors shoots over your head like bullets in a crossfire. Here, rituals have changed little since our Arabic cousins ruled the island, and locals come to exchange gossip on who just died, got married or divorced. Best of all, each season brings new things to try, from wild herbs and asparagus to handpicked snails. Generally, the best periods are spring and autumn.

3 SICILIAN WINES

Sicily is home to many interesting wines, amongst them the Nero d'Avola, a full-bodied, assertive red. For a fresh, sharp white, try Bianco d'Alcamo or Grecanico. Sweet marsala wine is usually served after dessert or with *biscotti*. For something less sweet, try a *passito* (both the *passito di Pantelleria* and the Zibibbo are good bets). Indeed, a cold glass of a good *passito* is the perfect cap to the most Lucullan of meals.

4 FESTIVE SPECIALITIES

During Carnevale, look out for *mpagnuccata* (unsweetened deep-fried dough tossed in soft caramel). The Festa di San Giuseppe on 19 March is famous for cigar-shaped *crispelle di riso* (citrus-scented rice fritters tossed in honey), and November's All Saints Day is time for *mostaccioli* and *moscardini* (spiced biscuits). One traditional type is called *ossa dei morti* (dead-people bones) because they're shaped like long thin logs and covered with dusting sugar.

Go Greek in Syracuse

In its Hellenic heyday, Syracuse (p335) was the Broadway of Magna Graecia (Greater Greece), with top-billing playwrights like Aeschylus. If productions flopped, directors could take it up with the gods at Ara di Gerone II, a sacrificial altar where up to 450 oxen were slaughtered. Today Syracuse boasts the only school of classical Greek drama outside Athens, with spectacular productions staged each May and June at the Teatro Greco.

Hit the Beach at Taormina

You're in for grand old times in the medieval beach town of Taormina (p332). The ancient Greek theatre still hosts summer concerts, shops still sell handmade ceramics and local capers and wooden fishing boats still bob off the cove of Isola Bella. Welcome modern upgrades include cable-car access from the hillside town to Lido Mazzaro beach, and sunset toasts with creative cocktails at Shatulle

Peek into the Volcano atop Mt Etna 4

Sicilians live dangerously in the shadow of this still-active volcano, but you can top that: take the cable car and hike up to the crater zone to see Mt Etna (p334) smouldering. You probably won't see any spewing magma – and that's a good thing – but there was a lava flow as recently as 2002. To keep a safe(r) distance, hop on the Ferrovia Circumetnea train circling the volcano's base.

5 Snooze in a Sassi

Maybe cavemen had the right idea, judging from Matera's incredible *sassi* (cave dwellings; p346). This is the most extensive troglodyte complex in the Mediterranean, one of the oldest human settlements on earth, and a World Heritage Site. Wander through staircases and rooms hewn from rock, and you'll find ancient frescoed churches, snug pigpens and two-storey buildings – plus refurbished caves turned into hotels, complete with solar panels and subterranean swimming pools.

6 Glimpse Heaven inside the Palatine Chapel

The church structure is Byzantine Christian, but the interiors of the Palatine Chapel (p326) are interfaith marvels. Iraqi-style calligraphy weaves through 11th- to 12th-century mosaics, and Islamic stars converge into a cross on the dome. No matter what standpoint you choose, these views are heavenly.

Sicily & Southern Italy's Best...

Beach Spots

◦ **Vieste, Puglia** (p341)
Dazzling whitewashed town with white-sand beaches

◦ **Cefalù, Sicily** (p331)
Mountains at your back, sand at your feet, boutiques handy

◦ **Vulcano, Sicily** (p330)
Dramatic black volcanic beaches on a remote island

◦ **Taormina, Sicily** (p332)
Hop the scenic cable car down to a sparkling cove

Unesco World Heritage Treasures

◦ **Matera, Basilicata** (p346)
Surreal cave dwellings and frescoed underground churches

◦ **Alberobello, Puglia** (p345) A truly fascinating town of *trulli*, whitewashed stone cottages shaped like Santa hats

◦ **Aeolian Islands, Sicily** (p330) Green hills, black lava and turquoise waters

◦ **Syracuse, Sicily** (p335) High Greek drama atop an ancient city

◦ **Castel del Monte, Puglia** (p342) An Islamic-inspired, eight-sided castle

Cheap Thrills

◦ Enjoying 360-degree views of Mt Etna from the **Ferrovia Circumetnea** (p334) train

◦ Bargaining for beach picnic supplies in Palermo's vibrant **Mercato di Ballarò** (p322)

◦ Restorative hot springs and pungent mud-baths on **Vulcano** (p330)

◦ Dodging Bari's Colonna della Giustizia in the **Piazza Mercantile** (p343), where debtors were once whipped

◦ Hanging out with the mummified virgins in Palermo's **Catacombe dei Cappuccini** (p327)

Foodie Experiences

○ Toasting with wine from community vineyards at **Libera Terra** (p329)

○ Hearing the seafood vendors call at Catania's fish market, **La Pescheria** (p332)

○ Resisting filling up on Puglian olive oil and bread before mains at Bari's **La Locandi di Federico** (p343)

○ Trying *cassata, torrone* (nougat) and granita at Noto's **Caffè Sicilia** (p339).

○ Savouring seafood pasta studded with island-grown capers at **Al Cappero** (p330) on the island of Salina

Left: Pastries, Cefalù (p331)
Above: Stromboli, Aeolian Islands (p330)

Need to Know

ADVANCE PLANNING

○ **Three months before** Book accommodation if travelling during peak beach season – late June through August – or planning a stay in a Matera cave-hotel or *trulli* cottage around Alberobello or Locorotondo

○ **One to two months before** Scan the online Taormina Arte festival (p332) and Syracuse Greek theatre festival programmes for promising performances

○ **One week before** Make reservations at Noto's Il Liberty (p340) and Matera's Ristorante Il Cantuccio (p347)

RESOURCES

○ **Sicilian Tourist Board** (www.regione.sicilia.it/turismo/web_turismo)

○ **Best of Sicily** (www.bestofsicily.com)

○ **Travel in Puglia** (www.viaggiareinpuglia.it) Key info and itineraries in Puglia

○ **Ferula Viaggi** (www.materaturismo.it) Dedicated to Basilicata

GETTING AROUND

○ **Air** European routes service Palermo's Falcone-Borsellino airport, Catania's Fontanarossa airport and Bari's Palese airport

○ **Walk** In towns, around ancient ruins, along beaches and up volcanoes

○ **Train** Efficient coastal service; slower to interior towns. Frequent services between Bari and Matera and Puglian towns.

○ **Bus** Handy to cross Sicily's interior and reaching towns not covered by trains

○ **Car** Outside the cities, an ideal way to explore

○ **Ferries & Hydrofoils** Regular summer services between Sicily and the Aeolian Islands; reduced services the rest of the year. Services between Sicily and the mainland, especially to Calabria, and overnight ferries to Naples.

BE FOREWARNED

○ **Museums** Many close Monday or Tuesday

○ **Pickpockets and bag snatchers** Particularly active in Palermo; mind your belongings on crowded beaches July to August.

Sicily & Southern Italy Itineraries

Between the Arabesque elegance of Sicilian seaside towns and the architectural quirks of villages in Puglia, the South may leave you breathless. To return to your senses, try local remedies: sandy beaches and gelato.

MONTENEGRO

MACEDONIA

1 VIESTE

ALBEROBELLO
2 LOCOROTONDO

MATERA 5 3

ALBANIA

4 LECCE

Tyrrhenian Sea

Ionian Sea

GREECE

PALERMO
1

3 CEFALÙ

MONREALE 2

PALERMO TO CEFALÙ
Arabesque Sicily

With its domed roofs and sweet-and-spicy flavours, Sicily seems just a mosaic tile's throw across the Mediterranean to the Middle East. Once the jewel of the Arab-influenced Norman Empire, the Arab heritage of **(1) Palermo** still shines through in its most beloved local landmarks: from the gleaming Palatine Chapel to raucous, souk-like Mercato di Ballarò. If you're not dazzled dizzy yet, check out the Arabesques gracing Palermo's majolica-cupola-topped cathedral, or on intricately hand-painted local ceramics at Le Ceramiche di Caltagirone. Recover afterwards in Palermo's steamy, marble-clad hammam, or watch puppets re-enact ancient

Arab-Norman legends of heroic battles and star-crossed romance at the Museo Nazionale delle Marionette.

Start the next morning with *pane e pannelle* (chickpea fritters) – one of several Sicilian street foods with Middle Eastern flavour – then bus it to Sicily's finest Arab-Norman creation, the shimmering cathedral of **(2) Monreale**. Back in Palermo, catch an afternoon train to **(3) Cefalù**, one of Sicily's favourite resort towns and home to the Arab-Norman beauty of Cefalù Duomo. Another relic of Cefalù's Arabic heritage is Salita Saraceno, a staircase that winds along ancient city walls for stunning views.

VIESTE TO MATERA

Italy's Wild Southwest

The views from the heel of Italy's boot are among the country's wildest and weirdest. In this striking, sunbleached landscape edged with sapphire sea coves, locals have made themselves at home in the most unbelievable places: two-storey cave dwellings, cone-headed stone cottages, and baroque sandstone palaces that look like elaborate sandcastles.

Ease yourself into the scenery by driving across Puglia's white bluffs to the beaches and secret sea caves of **(1) Vieste**. Hit the road the next day to **(2) Alberobello**, which looks like a gnome neighbourhood with tubby little *trulli* cottages capped with

comical, conical roofs. Spend an evening in a snug *trulli* before heading on to **(3) Locorotondo** to stroll around its all-white historic quarter and maybe pick up a few Puglian cooking secrets in a *trulli* kitchen at Truddi. Head onward into the sea castle sandstone beach town of **(4) Lecce**, where you can bunk in baroque splendour at Palazzo Rollo. But nothing you've seen so far can prepare you for Basilicata's **(5) Matera**, where the hillsides are dotted with ancient *sassi* (cave dwellings) and zig-zagged with staircases hewn from the rock.

Duomo, Cefalù (p331)

Discover Sicily & Southern Italy

Basilica di Santa Croce, Lecce (p344)

DAVID BORLAND/LONELY PLANET IMAGES ©

SICILY
Palermo
POP 656,000

A former Arab emirate and seat of a Norman kingdom, Palermo is a treasure trove of palaces, castles and churches. Palermo became Europe's grandest city in the 12th century, but in recent years it has grabbed headlines for political corruption. Yet in Palermo's sunny piazzas, life continues to be lived in the open, with Palermites upholding the social rituals of their multicultural past.

◉ Sights

Around the Quattro Canti

FONTANA PRETORIA   Fountain
The city bought this huge and ornate fountain in 1573; however, the flagrant nudity of the provocative nymphs proved too much for Sicilian church-goers attending Mass next door, and they prudishly dubbed it the Fountain of Shame.

CHIESA CAPITOLARE DI SAN CATALDO   Church
(Piazza Bellini 3; admission €2; ⊙9.30am-1.30pm & 3.30-5.30pm Mon-Sat, 9.30am-1.30pm Sun) This 12th-century church in Arab-Norman style is one of Palermo's most striking buildings, with its dusky-pink bijoux domes, solid square shape, blind arcading and delicate tracery.

Albergheria

MERCATO DI BALLARÒ   Market
Snaking for several city blocks southeast of Palazzo dei Normanni is Palermo's busiest

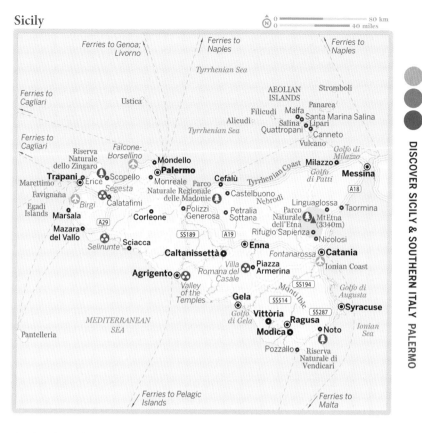

street market with fresh produce, fish, meat, olives and cheese.

Capo

CATHEDRAL   Cathedral

(www.cattedrale.palermo.it; Corso Vittorio Emanuele; ⏱8am-5.30pm Mon-Sat, 7am-1pm & 4-7pm Sun) A feast of geometric patterns, ziggurat crenulations, majolica cupolas and blind arches, Palermo's cathedral is a prime example of the extraordinary Arab-Norman style unique to Sicily. The **crypt** and **treasury** (adult/reduced €3/1.50; ⏱9.30am-5.30pm Mon-Sat) contain various jewels belonging to Queen Costanza of Aragón, a bejewelled Norman crown and a tooth extracted from Santa Rosalia, Palermo's patron saint.

La Kalsa

GALLERIA D'ARTE
MODERNA   Art Gallery

(☎091 843 16 05; www.galleriadartemoderna palermo.it, in Italian; Via Sant'Anna 21; adult/reduced €7/5; ⏱9.30am-6.30pm Tue-Sun, to 11pm Fri & Sat) This lovely museum is housed in a 15th-century *palazzo* (mansion), which metamorphosed into a convent in the 17th century. The collection of 19th- and 20th-century Sicilian art is beautifully displayed, and there's a regular program of modern-art exhibitions here, as well as an excellent bookshop and gift shop.

MUSEO INTERNAZIONALE DELLE
MARIONETTE   Puppet Museum

(☎091 32 80 60; www.museomarionettepalermo .it, in Italian; Piazzetta Antonio Pasqualino 5; adult/reduced €5/3; ⏱9am-1pm & 2.30-6.30pm

Palermo

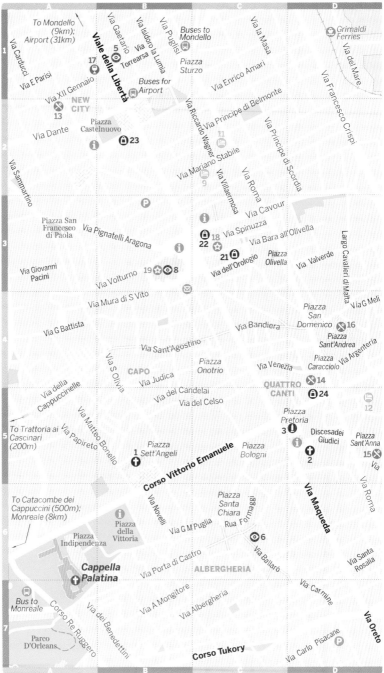

To Mondello (9km); Airport (31km)

Via Carducci

Via E Parisi

Viale della Libertà

Via Gaetario

Via Isidoro la Lumia

Via Puglisi

Buses to Mondello

Via la Masa

Via XII Gennaio

17

5

Via Torrearsa

Piazza Sturzo

Grimaldi Ferries

Via del Mare

Via Enrico Amari

Buses for Airport

Via Francesco Crispi

NEW CITY

13

Piazza Castelnuovo

23

Via Dante

Via Ricardo Wagner

Via Principe di Belmonte

Via Principe di Scordia

Via Sammartino

Via Mariano Stabile

11

Via Roma

Via Villaermosa

9

Piazza San Francesco di Paola

Via Pignatelli Aragona

P

Via Cavour

Via Spinuzza

18

22

Via Bara all'Olivella

Largo Cavalieri di Malta

Via Giovanni Pacini

Via Volturno

19

8

21

Piazza Olivella

Via Valverde

Via dell'Orologio

Via Mura di S Vito

Via G Meli

Via G Battista

Piazza San Domenico

16

Via Bandiera

Piazza Sant'Andrea

Via Sant'Agostino

Piazza Onotrio

Via Argenteria

CAPO

Via S Olivia

Via Judica

Via Venezia

Piazza Caracciolo

Via della Cappuccinelle

Via del Candelai

QUATTRO CANTI

14

Via del Celso

24

Via Matteo Bonello

Via Papireto

12

To Trattoria ai Cascinari (200m)

1

Piazza Sett'Angeli

Corso Vittorio Emanuele

Piazza Bologni

Piazza Pretoria

3

Discesadei Giudici

Piazza Sant'Anna

2

15

Via Roma

To Catacombe dei Cappuccini (500m); Monreale (8km)

Piazza Indipendenza

Piazza della Vittoria

Via Novelli

Via G M Puglia

Piazza Santa Chiara

Rua Formaggi

Via Maqueda

Cappella Palatina

Via Porta di Castro

ALBERGHERIA

Via Ballarò

6

Via Santa Rosalia

Bus to Monreale

Corso Re Ruggero

Via del Benedettini

Via A Mongitore

Via Albergheria

Via Carmine

Via Oreto

Parco D'Orleans

Corso Tukory

Via Carlo Pisacane

P

Palermo

Mon-Sat, 10am-1pm Sun) Housing over 3500
puppets and marionettes from Italy,
Japan, southeast Asia, Africa, China and
India, this whimsical museum also stages
delightful puppet shows most Tuesdays
and Fridays at 5.30pm from October
through June.

The 19th-Century City

TEATRO MASSIMO Opera House
(☎ tour reservations 091 605 32 67; www.teatro
massimo.it; Piazza Giuseppe Verdi; guided tours
adult/reduced €7/5; ☉10am-2.30pm Tue-Sun)

RUSSELL MOUNTFORD/LONELY PLANET IMAGES ©

Don't Miss Palatine Chapel

Bright-eyed saints leap to life from the golden mosaics like comic-book superheroes, but they were completed 900 years before Superman came along: the wonders never cease at the **Palatine Chapel**. The stories these characters enact come from the Old and New Testaments, yet Islamic influences are everywhere in this Christian chapel, from the intricate geometry of its inlaid marble floors to its Arabic *muqarnas* (honeycomb-carved) wooden ceiling. Designed by Roger II in 1130, the chapel was restored in 2008 to its full Arab-Norman glory and remains Sicily's finest monument to its multicultural history.

The chapel is located in the middle level of the three-tiered loggia of **Palazzo dei Normanni**, once a magnificent medieval court and now the seat of the Sicilian parliament. Four days a week government officials vacate the building, allowing visitors access to the **parliamentary chambers and royal apartments** – don't miss stunning mosaics of Persian peacocks and leaping leopards in **Sala di Ruggero II**, which was the king's bedroom.

THINGS YOU NEED TO KNOW

Cappella Palatina; ☎091 626 28 33; www.federicosecondo.org; Piazza Indipendenza 1; Palatine Chapel only adult/reduced €7/5, combined ticket incl palace rooms & Palatine Chapel adult/reduced €8.50/6.50; ☺chapel 8.15am-5pm Mon-Sat, 8.15-9.45am & 11.15am-12.15pm Sun

An iconic Palermo landmark, this grand neoclassical opera house took more than 20 years to complete and has become a symbol of the triumph and tragedy of the city. Appropriately, the operatic closing scene of *The Godfather: Part III* was filmed here.

Suburbs

MONREALE DUOMO — Cathedral

(☎ 091 640 44 03; Piazza del Duomo; ☺8am-6pm) Just 8km southwest of Palermo is the finest example of Norman architecture in Sicily, incorporating Norman, Arab, Byzantine and classical elements. The interior, completed in 1184 and executed in shimmering mosaics, depicts 42 Old Testament stories. Outside the cathedral, the **cloister** (admission €6; ☺9am-7pm) is a tranquil courtyard with elegant Romanesque arches, slender columns and mosaics. To reach Monreale (€1.30, 35 minutes, half-hourly) take bus 389 from Piazza Indipendenza in Palermo.

CATACOMBE DEI CAPPUCCINI — Catacomb

(☎ 091 21 21 17; Piazza Cappuccini; admission €3; ☺9am-1pm & 3-6pm) These catacombs house the mummified bodies and skeletons of some 8000 Palermitans who died between the 17th and 19th centuries. Earthly power, gender, religion and professional status are still rigidly distinguished, with men and women occupying separate corridors, and a first-class section set aside for virgins. From Piazza Independenza, it's a 15-minute walk.

 **Activities**

HAMMAM — Bathhouse

(☎ 091 32 07 83; www.hammam.pa.it; Via Torrearsa 17d; admission €40; ☺women only 2-9pm Mon & Wed, 11am-9pm Fri, men only 2-9pm Tue & Thu, 10am-8pm Sat) For a sybaritic experience, head to this luxurious marble-lined Moorish bathhouse, where you can indulge in a vigorous scrub-down, a steamy sauna and many different types of massages and therapies. There's a one-off charge (€10) for slippers and a hand glove.

 Sleeping

BUTERA 28 — Apartment €

(☎ 333 316 54 32; www.butera28.it; Via Butera 28; 2-/4-/8-person apt per day from €50/100/150; ✸ 🛜) The bilingual owner of Butera 28, Nicoletta, offers cooking classes and 11 well-equipped, comfortable apartments. Four apartments face the sea (apartment number 9 is especially nice), and all have CD and DVD players, plus kitchens stocked that are well-stocked with essentials.

B&B MAXIM — B&B €€

(☎ 091 976 54 71; www.bbmaxim.it; Via Mariano Stabile 136a; s €80-90, d €110-130, ste €160-190; ✸ 🛜) Owner Massimo has spared no expense in creating this little B&B with restrained tones of cream, beige and brown. Perks include ambient sound, chromotherapy lighting in the showers, and state-of-the art designer fixtures throughout.

GRAND HOTEL PIAZZA BORSA — Hotel €€

(☎ 091 32 00 75; www.piazzaborsa.com; Via dei Cartari 18; s €115-181, d €154-208, ste €340-569; P ✸ @ 🛜) This grand new 4-star opened in 2010 in Palermo's former stock exchange. Three separate buildings house the 127 rooms; the nicest ones are the high-ceilinged suites with Jaccuzi tubs and windows facing Piazza San Francesco.

GRAND HOTEL ET DES PALMES — Hotel €€€

(☎ 091 602 81 11; www.hotel-despalmes.it; Via Roma 398; r €230-265; P ✸ @ 🛜) Dating from 1874, this is one of the most historically fascinating hotels located in Palermo. The grand salons are still impressive with their chandeliers and gigantic mirrors, while the rooms are regally luxurious.

Eating

TRATTORIA AI CASCINARI Sicilian €

(091 651 98 04; Via d'Ossuna 43/45; meals €20-23; lunch Tue-Sun, dinner Wed-Sat) Locals pack this Slow Food–recommended labyrinth of back rooms, while waiters load blue-and-white-checked tablecloths with plates of scrumptious seasonal antipasti and divine main dishes.

OSTERIA DEI VESPRI Gastronomic €€€

(091 617 16 31; www.osteriadeivespri.it; Piazza Croce dei Vespri 6; meals €55-70, tasting menu €80; lunch & dinner Mon-Sat) In the summer, sit out under the shadow of the *palazzo* and tuck into dishes such as pasta with fennel and red prawns; spicy tuna with nutmeg-potato croquettes and mint-flavoured rice; or suckling pig with leeks, mushrooms and mandarin compote.

FERRO DI CAVALLO Trattoria €

(091 33 18 35; Via Venezia 20; meals €18-20; lunch Mon-Sat, dinner Thu-Sat) Religious

portraits beam down from red walls at this little trattoria, where nothing is more than €8 on the menu of Sicilian classics.

SANT'ANDREA Modern Sicilian €€

(091 33 49 99; www.ristorantesantandrea.eu; Piazza Sant'Andrea 4; meals €30-35; dinner Mon-Sat) Tucked into the corner of a ruined church in a shabby piazza, Sant'Andrea's location doesn't inspire much confidence, but its superbly creative Sicilian dishes and congenial high-ceilinged dining room keep well-heeled customers picking their way across the broken flagstones nightly.

 Drinking

KURSAAL KALHESA Bar

(091 616 00 50; www.kursaalkalhesa.it, in Italian; Foro Umberto I 21; noon-3pm & 6pm-1am Tue-Sun) Recline on sofas and sip a cocktail beneath the high-vaulted ceilings. A lively unpretentious crowd is attracted by the good program of music and literary events.

PIZZO & PIZZO   Wine Bar
(091 601 45 44; www.pizzoepizzo.
com; Via XII Gennaio 5; closed Sun)
Sure, this sophisticated wine bar is a great
place for *aperitivi,* but the buzzing atmosphere and the tempting array of cheeses,
cured meats, and smoked fish may just
convince you to stick around for dinner.

Entertainment

TEATRO MASSIMO   Opera House
(091 605 35 80; www.teatromassimo.it; Piazza
Verdi 9) Ernesto Basile's art-nouveau masterpiece stages opera, ballet and music
concerts. The theatre's program runs
from October to May.

CUTICCHIO MIMMO   Puppet Theatre
(091 32 34 00; www.figlidartecuticchio.com;
Via Bara all'Olivella 95; 6.30pm Sat & Sun Sep-
Jul) This theatre is a charming low-tech
choice for children (and adults), staging
traditional shows with fabulous handcrafted puppets.

Shopping

Check out the puppet workshop of the
Cuticchio family, **Il Laboratorio Teatrale**
(Via Bara all'Olivella 48-50).

For ceramics and pottery (albeit at
higher prices than you'd find in Sicily's
hinterland) stop by **Le Ceramiche di
Caltagirone** (caltagironeceramiche@alice.it;
Via Cavour 114) or **Mercurio** (www.casamerlo.it;
Corso Vittorio Emanuele 231).

For edible souvenirs with a dollop of
social consciousness, consider buying
some wine, olive oil or pasta – all grown
on land confiscated from the Mafia – at
Libera Terra (; www.liberapalermo.org; Piazza
Castelnuovo 13), an organization actively
working to resist the Mafia's influence in
Sicilian society.

On Sundays, there's a good **antiques
market** on Piazza Marina south of the
port.

Detour:
Aeolian Islands

Not content with glorious cobalt waters lapping tranquil beaches, the seven Aeolian Islands of Lipari, Vulcano, Salina, Panarea, Stromboli, Alicudi and Filicudi are overachievers. With millennia of seafaring adventures to their credit, they landed a featured role in Homer's *Odyssey*. A highlight of the 200km volcanic ridge that runs between Mt Etna and the threatening mass of Vesuvius above Naples, these islands show off the entire range of volcanic geological traits – a feat that's earned them a Unesco World Heritage commendation.

Boat service from Sicily's **Siremar** (www.siremar.it) and **Ustica Lines** (www.usticalines.it) to/from Cefalù (€29.10, 3¼ hours), Milazzo (€16.80, 1 hour) and Palermo (€39.30, 4 hours) is most frequent July to August, when Aeolian beaches have rock-star followings. Highlights include the following:

○ **Lipari** The island's citadel holds a treasury of 6000 years of Aeolian history at **Museo Archeologico Eoliano** (✆090 988 01 74; www.regione.sicilia.it/beniculturali/museolipari; Castello di Lipari; adult/reduced €6/3; ◷9am-1pm & 3-6pm Mon-Sat, 9am-1pm Sun). Lipari's **Tourist Office** (✆090 988 00 95; www.aasteolie.191.it, in Italian; Corso Vittorio Emanuele 202; ◷9am-1pm & 4.30-7pm Mon-Fri year-round, 9am-1pm Sat Jul-Aug) provides tour and accommodation info for all the islands.

○ **Vulcano** Aptly named for its main feature, a 391m volcano (admission €3) responsible for the black-sand beach of **Spiaggia Sabbia Nera** and the warm, sulphurous glop long used to treat arthritis and skin disorders. Test those claims at Laghetto di Fanghi mud baths (admission €2) – mind the eyes (it burns), wear an old swimsuit (it reeks) and no gold jewellery (it tarnishes) – and jump into the hot springs afterwards.

○ **Salina** Scenery that's good enough to eat: freshwater springs feed lush vineyards, edible wildflowers and capers fields – try them in simple pasta dishes at **Al Cappero** (✆090 984 41 33; www.alcappero.it; Pollara; meals €20-25; ◷lunch & dinner June–mid-Sep). The dramatic bluffs of **Pollara** make a perfect backdrop for romance, as seen in the 1994 classic romance *Il Postino*.

ⓘ Information

Medical Services

Ospedale Civico (✆091 666 11 11; www.ospedalecivicopa.org; Via Carmelo Lazzaro) Emergency facilities.

Tourist Information

Tourist office (www.palermotourism.com) airport (✆091 59 16 98; ◷8.30am-7.30pm Mon-Sat); city centre (✆091 605 83 51; Piazza Castelnuovo 34; ◷8.30am-2pm & 2.30-6pm Mon-Fri) Friendly, multilingual staff and abundant brochures.

ⓘ Getting There & Away

Air

Falcone-Borsellino airport (PMO; ✆091 702 01 11; www.gesap.it) is at Punta Raisi, 31km west of Palermo.

Boat

SNAV (✆091 601 42 11; www.snav.it; Calata Marinai d'Italia) Overnight service to Naples (€55, 10½ hours, one daily).

Ustica Lines (✆0923 87 38 13; www.usticalines.it) Summer hydrofoil to Lipari (€39.30, 4½ hours, two daily) and other points on the Aeolian Islands.

Bus

Cuffaro (📞091 616 15 10; www.cuffaro.info; Via Paolo Balsamo 13) Services to Agrigento (€8.10, two hours, three to nine daily).

SAIS (📞091 616 60 28, 091 617 11 41; www.saisautolinee.it, www.saistrasporti.it; Via Paolo Balsamo 16) Services to Catania (€14.20, 2¾ hours, at least nine daily), Messina (€15.10, 2¾ hours, three to seven daily), Naples (€37.50, 10 hours, one nightly) and Rome (€45.50, 10½ hours, one nightly).

Segesta (📞091 616 90 39; www.segesta.it; Via Paolo Balsamo 26) Services to Trapani (€8.60, two hours, at least 10 daily). Also sells Interbus tickets to Syracuse (€11, 3¼ hours, two to three daily).

Car & Motorcycle

Palermo is accessible on the A20-E90 toll road from Messina and the A19-E932 from Catania via Enna. Agrigento and Palermo are linked by the SS121, a state road through the island's interior.

Train

Regular trains leave for Agrigento (€8.10, 2¼ hours, seven to 12 daily) and Cefalù (€5, one hour, 10 to 19 daily). There are also InterCity trains to Reggio di Calabria, Naples and Rome.

Getting Around

To/From the Airport

Prestia e Comandè (📞091 58 63 51; www.prestiaecomande.it) Half-hourly bus service from the airport to the centre of town (€5.80). Buy tickets on the bus.

Taxis from the airport to downtown Palermo costs €45.

Bus

City buses (AMAT; 📞848 80 08 17; www.amat.pa.it, in Italian) are frequent but often crowded and slow. Tickets (per 1½ hours €1.30, per day €3.50) must be purchased before you get on the bus, from *tabacchi* (tobacconists) or AMAT booths at major transfer points.

Car & Motorcycle

Driving is frenetic in the city and best avoided. Vehicle theft is also a problem; use an attended car park in town (€12 to €20 per day).

Cefalù
POP 13,800

This popular holiday resort wedged between a dramatic mountain peak and sweeping stretch of sand has the lot: a great beach; a truly lovely historic centre with a grandiose cathedral; and winding medieval streets lined with restaurants and boutiques.

 Sights & Activities

DUOMO Duomo
(Piazza del Duomo; ⏱8am-5.30pm winter, to 7.30pm summer) Cefalù's imposing cathedral is an Arab-Norman jewel, with a towering figure of Christ Pantocrator as the focal point of the elaborate 12th-century Byzantine mosaics.

LA ROCCA Viewpoint
An enormous staircase, the **Salita Saraceno**, winds up through three tiers of city walls, a 30-minute climb nearly to the summit for stunning views of the town below and the ruined 4th-century **Tempio di Diana**.

Sicilia Divers Diving
(📞347 685 30 51; www.sicilia-divers.com; Hotel Kalura, Via Vincenzo Cavallaro 13; dives from €45, courses from €60) Organises dives and courses for all ages.

Sleeping

HOTEL KALURA Hotel €€
(📞0921 42 13 54; www.hotel-kalura.com; Via Vincenzo Cavallaro 13; d €89-159; P ❄ @ ☞) East of town on a rocky outcrop, this German-run, family-oriented hotel has its own pebbly beach, restaurant and fabulous pool. It's a 20-minute walk into town.

B&B DOLCE VITA B&B €
(📞0921 92 31 51; www.dolcevitabb.it; Via Bordonaro 8; r €60-120; ❄ @ ☞) This popular B&B has a lovely terrace with deck chairs overlooking the sea and a barbecue for warm summer evenings, and rooms that are airy and light.

Eating & Drinking

AL PORTICCIOLO   Seafood, Pizzeria **€€**
(☏ 0921 92 19 81; Via Carlo Ortolani di Bordonaro 66/86/90; pizzas €5-12, meals €20-35; ☺closed Wed Oct-Apr) Dine in a five-star setting without breaking your credit card at this waterfront eatery; in summer everyone piles out onto the ample outdoor terrace.

LA GALLERIA   Bar, Fusion **€€**
(☏ 0921 42 02 11; www.lagalleriacefalu.it; Via Mandralisca 23; cocktails €5, meals €30-40; ☺noon-3pm & 7pm-midnight Fri-Wed) Here you'll find a literary cafe, sophisticated cocktail bar, and tasteful art gallery combined into a supercool dinner venue.

ℹ Information

Tourist office (☏ 0921 42 10 50; strcefalu@ regione.sicilia.it; Corso Ruggero 77; ☺9am-1pm & 3-7.30pm Mon-Sat) English- speaking staff, lots of leaflets and good maps.

ℹ Getting There & Away

BOAT From June to September, **Ustica Lines** (www.usticalines.it) runs daily hydrofoils at 8.15am from Cefalù to the Aeolian Islands. **TRAIN** Hourly trains link Cefalù with Palermo (€5, one hour).

Catania
POP 296,000

Constructed from the lava that engulfed the city in a 1669 eruption, much of Catania is lava-black in colour, as if a fine dusting of soot permanently covers its elegant buildings. Today Catania's central square is a Unesco World Heritage site, with sinuous buildings and a grand cathedral built in the unique local baroque style of contrasting lava and limestone.

◉ Sights

PIAZZA DEL DUOMO   Central Square
In the centre of the Unesco-acclaimed piazza the smiling **Fontana dell'Elefante** (built in 1736), a Roman-era black-lava

elephant topped by an Egyptian obelisk believed to possess magical powers that help to calm Mt Etna's restless activity.

DUOMO   Cathedral
(☏ 095 32 00 44; Piazza del Duomo; ☺8am-noon & 4-7pm) Catania's other defence against Mt Etna is St Agata's cathedral, with its impressive marble facade. Inside the cool, vaulted interior lie the remains of the city's patron saint, the young virgin Agata, who resisted the advances of the nefarious Quintian (AD 250) and was horribly mutilated.

LA PESCHERIA   Fish Market
(Via Pardo; ☺7am-2pm) The best show in Catania is this bustling fish market, where vendors raucously hawk their wares in Sicilian dialect alongside the colourful **food market** (Via Naumachia; ☺7am-3pm) where you can shop for fruit, cheese and sandwich fillings.

🛏 Sleeping

BAD   B&B **€**
(☏ 095 34 69 03; www.badcatania.com; Via C Colombo 24; s €40-55, d €60-80, apt €90-140; ❄ 🛜) An uninhibitedly colourful, modern sense of style prevails at this trendy B&B. All rooms feature local artwork and TVs with DVD players.

IL PRINCIPE   Hotel **€€**
(☏ 095 250 03 45; www.ilprincipehotel.com; Via Alessi 24; d €109-189, ste €129-209; ❄ @ 🛜) This boutique hotel in an 18th-century building features luxurious rooms on one of the liveliest nightlife streets in town (thank goodness for double glazing!). Perks include international cable TV, free wi-fi and fluffy bathrobes to wear on your way to the Turkish steam bath.

Eating & Drinking

TRATTORIA DI DE FIORE   Trattoria **€**
(☏ 095 31 62 83; Via Coppola 24/26; meals €15-25; ☺closed Mon) This neighbourhood

RUSSELL MOUNTFORD/LONELY PLANET IMAGES ©

Don't Miss **Taormina**

Between smouldering Mt Etna and the sea, the gorgeous medieval town of **Taormina** has reduced noteworthy writers, artists and royalty to babbling romantics for centuries – and top talents still flock to **Taormina Arts Festival**, held from June to August. Events are held at **Teatro Greco**, a horseshoe-shaped Greek ampitheatre framing views of Mt Etna.

Directly below Taormina is **Lido Mazzarò** beach, reached by scenic **cable car**. Southwest of the beach is minuscule **Isola Bella**, a stunning cove dotted with wooden fishing boats. Shoppers may prefer the scenery along **Corso Umberto I**, lined with antiques, designers and Sicilian gourmet emporium **La Torinese**.

Long days of sunbathing end with sunset cocktails on the piazza at **Shatulle**, followed by sublime modern Sicilian dishes like aromatic orange-saffron red mullet at **Casa Grugno** or seafood antipasti and spinach-ricotta gnocchi at **Licchio's**.

Call it a night at **Isoco Guest House**, with guestrooms dedicated to artists from Botticelli to Herb Ritts and an outdoor Jacuzzi on the sundeck. Fragrant gardens and sea views might inspire romantic poetry at 1902 **Villa Belvedere**.

THINGS YOU NEED TO KNOW

Teatro Greco (☎0942 2 32 20; Via Teatro Greco; adult/reduced €8/4; ⏰9am-1hr before sunset); **Casa Grugno** (☎0942 2 12 08; www.casagrugno.it; Via Santa Maria dei Greci; meals €70-80; ⏰dinner Mon-Sat); **Licchio's** (☎0942 62 53 27; Via Patricio 10; meals €30-40; ⏰lunch & dinner, closed Thu Nov-Mar); **Isoco Guest House** (☎0942 2 36 79; www.isoco.it; Via Salita Branco 2; s €65-120, d €85-120; ⏰Mar-Nov; P ✳ @); **Villa Belvedere** (☎0942 2 37 91; www.villabelvedere.it; Via Bagnoli Croce 79; d with inland view €124-184, with sea view €144-236; ⏰Mar-Nov; P ✳ @ ⏰ ☒)

trattoria is presided over by septuagenarian chef Mamma Rosanna, who uses organic flour and fresh, local ingredients to recreate her great-grandmother's recipes, including the best *pasta alla Norma* you'll taste anywhere in Sicily.

PHILIP & KAREN SMITH/LONELY PLANET IMAGES ©

Don't Miss Mt Etna

Looming large over eastern Sicily and visible from the moon, Mt Etna (elevation 3329m) erupts frequently from four summit craters and from slopes pock-marked with fissures. The most devastating eruption to date was in 1669, when lava poured down Etna's southern slope for 122 days, engulfing most of Catania. But Etna's not done yet: in 2002, lava flows caused an explosion in nearby Sapienza. The land surrounding the volcano was wisely set aside for the **Parco dell'Etna**, which remains the largest unspoilt wilderness in Sicily.

The AST bus from Catania drops you off at **Rifugio Sapienza**, which offers meals and lodging. Here **Funivia dell'Etna** runs a cable car up the mountain to 2500m. From the upper cable car station, it's a 3½-to-four-hour return trip up the winding track to the authorised crater zone (2920m). Leave enough time to get up *and* down before the last cable car leaves at 4.45pm. Alternatively, you can pay €24 extra for a guided 4WD tour to take you up from the cable car to the crater zone.

You can circle Etna on the private **Ferrovia Circumetnea** train. Catch the metro from Catania's main train station to FCE station at Via Caronda (metro stop Borgo). The train follows a 114km trail around the base of the volcano, providing fabulous views of Etna's snowy, smouldering cone.

THINGS YOU NEED TO KNOW

Rifugio Sapienza (B&B/half-board/full board €55/75/90); **Funivia dell'Etna** (☏095 91 41 41; www.funiviaetna.com; cable car one-way/return €14.50/27; ☉9am-4.30pm); **Ferrovia Circumetnea** (FCE; ☏095 54 12 50; www.circumetnea.it; Via Caronda 352a; one-way/return €4.85/7.80, 2hrs)

OSTERIA ANTICA MARINA   Seafood €€
(☏095 34 81 97; Via Pardo 29; meals €35-45; ☉closed Wed) This rustic but classy

trattoria behind the fish market is *the* place to come for seafood. A variety of tasting menus showcases everything from swordfish to scampi, cuttlefish to calamari.

AGORÁ BAR Bar
(www.agorahostel.com; Piazza Curró 6) This bar occupies a neon-lit cave 18m below ground, with its own subterranean river. The Romans once used it as a spa.

 Entertainment

TEATRO MASSIMO
BELLINI Opera House
(☎ 095 730 61 11; www.teatromassimobellini. it; Via Perrotta 12; guided tours €2; ⊙season Oct-May, tours 9.30am & 10.30am Tue, Thu & Sat) Ernesto Basile's art-nouveau theatre stages opera, ballet and music concerts.

ZÒ Cultural Centre
(☎ 095 53 38 71; www.zoculture.it; Piazzale Asia 6) Catania's former sulphur works, Le Cimin-iere has been renovated into a very cool cultural centre featuring films, live music, dancing, and a bar-cafe-restaurant.

Getting There & Away

Air

Catania's airport, Fontanarossa (☎ 095 723 91 11; www.aeroporto.catania.it), is 7km southwest of the city centre.
Airport shuttles:

Alibus 457 (€1, 30min, every 20 minutes) Departs from outside the train station.

Etna Trasporti/Interbus (☎ 095 53 03 96; www.interbus.it) Runs a regular shuttle to Taormina (€7, 1½ hours, six to 11 daily).

Boat

TTT Lines (☎ 800 91 53 65, 095 34 85 86; www.tttlines.it; seat €38-60, cabin per person €52-165, car €75-115, 11hr) runs nightly ferries from Catania to Naples.

Bus

Interbus (☎ 095 53 03 96; www.interbus.it; Via d'Amico 187) runs buses to Taormina (€4.70, 1¼-2 hours, eight to 17 daily), (€5.70, 1½ hours, hourly Monday to Friday).

SAIS (☎ 095 53 61 68; www.saisautolinee.it, www.saistrasporti.it; Via d'Amico 181) serves Palermo (€14.20, 2¾ hours), Agrigento (€12.40, 3hrs, nine to 15 daily) and Messina (€7.70, 1½ hours, hourly Monday to Saturday, nine on Sunday). It also has an overnight service to Rome (€47, 11 hours).

Car & Motorcycle

Catania is easily reached from Messina on the A18 autostrada and from Palermo on the A19. The centre is pedestrianised, so parking is scarce.

Train

Trains to Messina (€6.80, 1¾ hours, hourly), Syracuse (€6.20, 1¼ hours, nine daily), Agrigento (€10.20, 3¾ hours, two daily) Palermo (€12.30, 3 hours, daily).

Getting Around

AMT city buses (☎ 095 751 96 11; www.amt. ct.it, in Italian) Runs a special June–September service (bus D-Est) to the local beaches.

Radio Taxi Catania (☎ 095 33 09 66) Taxi service.

Syracuse

POP 123,800

Settled by colonists from Corinth in 734 BC, Syracuse was considered to be the most beautiful city of the ancient world, rivalling Athens in power and attracting luminaries such as philosopher Plato, mathematician Archimedes and Greek tragedy pioneer Aeschylus. The ancient island neighbourhood of Ortygia contin-ues to seduce visitors with its atmospher-ic squares, narrow alleyways and lovely waterfront, while the Parco Archaeologico della Neapolis, 2km across town, remains one of Sicily's great classical treasures.

Sights

Ortygia

DUOMO Duomo
(Piazza del Duomo; ⊙8am-7pm)
The baroque facade of the Duomo, de-signed by Andrea Palma, barely hides the Temple of Athena skeleton beneath, and

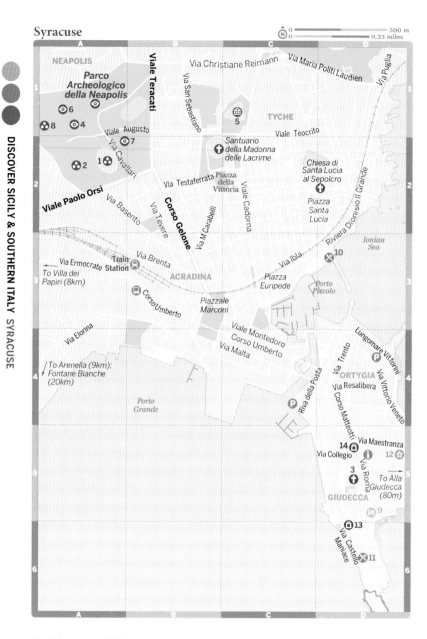

the 5th-century-BC Doric columns are still visible both inside and out.

LA GIUDECCA   Neighbourhood
Simply walking through Ortygia's maze of alleys is an atmospheric experience, especially down the lanes of **Via Maestranza**, the heart of the old guild quarter, and the crumbling Jewish ghetto of **Via della Giudecca**. At the Alla Giudecca hotel you can visit an ancient Jewish **miqwe** (ritual bath; ☎ 0931 2 22 55; Via Alagona 52; hourly tours €5;

Syracuse

◎ 11am, noon, 4pm, 5pm & 6pm Mon-Sat, 11am & noon Sun) 20m below ground level. Blocked up in 1492 when the Jewish community was expelled from Ortygia, the baths were rediscovered during renovations.

Mainland Syracuse

MUSEO ARCHEOLOGICO
PAOLO ORSI   Museum
(☏0931 46 40 22; Viale Teocrito; adult/reduced €8/4; ◎9am-6pm Tue-Sat, 9am-1pm Sun) In the grounds of Villa Landolina, 500m east of the archaeological park, the wheel-chair accessible museum contains one of Sicily's largest and most interesting archaeological collections.

BEACHES   Beaches
In midsummer, when Ortygia steams like a cauldron, people flock to the beaches south of town at **Arenella** (take bus 23 from Piazza della Posta) and **Fontane Bianche** (bus 21 or 22); note that there are charges on certain sections.

🛏 Sleeping & Eating

B&B DEI VIAGGIATORI, VIANDANTI E
SOGNATORI   B&B €
(☏0931 2 47 81; www.bedandbreakfastsicily.it; Via Roma 156; s €35-50, d €55-70; ❄️ 🛜) An old *palazzo* at the end of Via Roma cradles this lovely B&B. Rooms are colourfully and styl-ishly decorated, with supercomfy beds.

ALLA GIUDECCA   Hotel €€
(☏0931 2 22 55; www.allagiudecca.it; Via Alagona 52; s €60-100, d €80-120; ❄️ @ 🛜) Located in the old Jewish quarter, this charming hotel boasts 23 suites with warm terracotta-tiled floors, exposed wood beams and lashings of heavy white linen.

RED MOON   Seafood €
(☏0931 6 03 56; Riva Porto Lachio 36; meals €25; ◎lunch & dinner Thu-Tue) This place serves some of the best seafood in Syracuse under its tented octagonal roof, including *spaghetti ai ricci* (spaghetti with sea-urchin roe), *fritto misto* (fried shrimp and squid) and grilled fish from the case. Finish with a refreshing lemon sorbet.

TABERNA SVEVA   Sicilian €€
(☏0931 2 46 63; Piazza Federico di Svevia; meals €25-35; ◎closed Wed) Food is top-notch, from *primi* like *gnocchi al pistacchio* (with olive oil, parmesan, pepper, garlic and grated pistachios) to a delicious tiramisu to wrap things up.

⭐ Entertainment

Piccolo Teatro dei Pupi   Puppet Theatre
(☏0931 46 55 40; www.pupari.com; Via della Giudecca 17) Syracuse's thriving puppet theatre hosts regular performances; see their website for a calendar.

🔒 Shopping

Ortygia is full of quirky shops such as **Circo Fortuna** (www.circofortuna.it; Via dei Tolomei 20) which produces ceramics and **Massimo Izzo** (www.massimoizzo.com; Piazza

DAMIEN SIMONIS/LONELY PLANET IMAGES ©

Don't Miss Ancient Syracuse

Talk about drama: hewn from white limestone above Syracuse, 5th-century-BC **Teatro Greco** knows how to set a scene. Testing the acoustics is a highlight of visits to **Parco Archaeologico della Neapolis**. The last tragedies of pioneering Greek playwright Aeschylus premiered at this theatre, with the playwright himself in attendance. From May to June you can hear Greek choruses wail here at **Ciclo di Rappresentazioni Classiche**, with Italy's finest performers reviving Greek classics.

Beside the theatre is **Latomia del Paradiso**, its deep limestone quarries riddled with catacombs and filled with citrus and magnolia trees. This mysterious site was an ancient prison camp, holding 7000 survivors of the war between Syracuse and Athens in 413 BC. Caravaggio called one 23m by 3m deep grotto **Orecchio di Dionisio** after the tyrant Dionysius, who is said to have used the almost perfect acoustics of the quarry to eavesdrop on his prisoners.

Outside this site is the entrance to the 2nd-century-AD **Anfiteatro Romano**, originally used for gladiatorial combats and horse races. Spanish colonists largely destroyed the site in the 16th century, using it as a quarry to build Ortygia's city walls. West of the amphitheatre is 3rd-century-BC **Ara di Gerone II**, a monolithic sacrificial altar to Heron II where up to 450 oxen could be killed at one time.

THINGS YOU NEED TO KNOW

To reach the park, take bus 1, 3 or 12 from Ortygia's Piazza Pancali and get off at the corner of Corso Gelone and Viale Teocrito. The walk to the park from Ortygia takes about 30 minutes.
Parco Archaeologico della Neapolis (☎0931 6 50 68; Viale Paradiso; adult/reduced €9/4.50; ⏰9am-1hr before sunset, to 4.30pm during theatre festival)

Archimede 25), specialising in jewellery handcrafted from Sciacca coral and gold. For a more affordable souvenir, check out the hand-painted cards made from local papyrus at **Galleria Bellomo** (www.bellomogalleria.com; Via Capodieci 15).

ℹ Information

Tourist office (☏ 0800 05 55 00; infoturismo@provsr.it; Via Roma 31, Ortygia; ◷ 9am-7pm) English-speaking staff, city maps and lots of good information.

ℹ Getting There & Away

Bus

Interbus (☏ 0931 6 67 10; www.interbus.it) runs buses to Catania (€5.70, 1½ hours, 19 daily Monday to Saturday, eight on Sunday) and its airport, and Palermo (€11, 3¼ hours, two to three daily).

AST (☏ 0931 46 27 11; www.aziendasiciliana trasporti.it) offers services to Noto (€3.20, 55 minutes, two to 10 daily).

Car & Motorcycle

A18 and SS114 highways connect Syracuse with Catania and points north. Traffic on Ortygia is restricted, but the large Talete parking garage on Ortygia's north side is free between 5am and 9pm, and only €1 for overnight parking.

Train

Trains depart daily for Catania (€8.50/6.20, 1¼ hours) and Noto (€3.30, 30 minutes).

ℹ Getting Around

For travel between the bus and train stations and Ortygia, catch the free AST shuttle bus 20 (every 20 to 60 minutes). To reach Parco Archeologico della Neapolis from Ortygia, take AST city bus 1, 3 or 12 (two-hour ticket €1.10), departing from Ortygia's Piazza Pancali.

Noto

POP 23,900 / ELEV 160M

Flattened in 1693 by an earthquake, Noto is now a Unesco World Heritage site and the finest baroque town in Sicily.

♥ If You Like… Dessert

Sicily offers pure bliss to anyone with a sweet tooth, not to mention job security for dentists. Local specialties include extra-creamy gelato; sculptural marzipan; chocolate spiked with red-hot chilli; *granita* (shaved ice) with coffee or locally grown fruit, pistachio or almonds; and, of course, the pastry that inspired the most memorable line in *The Godfather* (1972): 'Leave the gun. Take the cannoli.' Let Sicily disarm your diet with these top three sweet detours:

1 **CAFFÈ SICILIA, NOTO**
(☏ 0931 83 50 13; Corso Vittorio Emanuele 125, Noto) Dating from 1892 and especially renowned for its *granite*, this local landmark adds 10 customers for every degree temperatures inch upward in summer.

2 **DOLCERIA CORRADO COSTANZO, NOTO**
(☏ 0931 83 52 43; Via Silvio Spaventa 9, Noto) Notable beyond Noto for its gelato, *torrone* (nougat), *dolci di mandorla* (almond sweets) and *cassata* (with ricotta, chocolate and candied fruit).

3 **CAPPELLO, PALERMO**
(Via Nicolò Garzilli 10, Palermo; cake slices €2.50) The *setteveli* (seven-layer chocolate cake) was invented at this hole-in-the-wall bakery, which makes a mean *delizia di pistachio*, pistachio cake with creamy icing.

◉ Sights

PIAZZA MUNICIPIO Piazza
San Nicoló Cathedral stands in the centre of Noto's most graceful square, Piazza Municipio, surrounded by elegant town houses such as Palazzo Ducezio (Town Hall) and Palazzo Landolina, once home to Noto's oldest noble family.

PALAZZO NICOLACI DI
VILLADORATA Palazzo
(☏ 320 556 80 38; www.palazzonicolaci.it, in Italian; Via Nicolaci; adult/reduced €4/2; ◷ 10am-1pm & 3-7.30pm) Recently restored to its

former glory, with wrought-iron balconies supported by a swirling pantomime of grotesque figures. Although the palazzo is empty of furnishings, its brocaded walls and frescoed ceilings give an idea of the sumptuous lifestyle of Sicilian nobles.

PIAZZA XVI MAGGIO — Piazza

Noto's elegant 19th-century **Teatro Comunale** is worth a look, as is the Sala degli Specchi (Hall of Mirrors) in the **Palazzo Ducezio** (admission to either €2, combined ticket €3; ☉9.30am-1.30pm & 2.30-6.30pm). For sweeping rooftop views of Noto's baroque splendour, climb the *campanile* (bell tower) at **Chiesa di San Carlo al Corso** (admission €2; ☉9am-12.30pm & 4-7pm) or **Chiesa di Santa Chiara** (admission €1.50; ☉9.30am-1pm & 3-7pm).

🛏 Sleeping & Eating

LA CORTE DEL SOLE — Rural Inn €€

(☎320 82 02 10; www.lacortedelsole.it; Contrada Bucachemi; d €84-206; P ❄ @ 🛜 ☒) A few kilometres downhill from Noto, overlooking the Vendicari bird sanctuary is this rural retreat set around a central courtyard. Other amenities include an in-house restaurant, a breakfast area built around an ancient olive oil press, bike hire, cooking courses and a shuttle bus to the nearby beach.

HOTEL DELLA FERLA — Hotel €€

(☎0931 57 60 07; www.hoteldellaferla.it; Via A Gramsci; s €48-78, d €84-120; P ❄ 🛜) This friendly family-run hotel in a residential area near the train station offers large, bright rooms with pine furnishings and small balconies, plus free parking.

TOP CHOICE IL LIBERTY — Modern Sicilian €€

(☎0931 57 32 26; Via Cavour 40; meals €27-35) An excellent local wine list supplements the inspired menu, which moves from superb appetisers like *millefoglie* – wafer-thin layers of crusty cheese and ground pistachios layered with minty sweet-and-sour vegetables – straight through to desserts like warm cinnamon-ricotta cake with homemade orange compote.

RISTORANTE IL CANTUCCIO — Modern Sicilian €€

(☎0931 83 74 64; Via Cavour 12; meals €30-35; ☉dinner Tue-Sun, lunch Sun) Sample chef Valentina's exquisite *gnocchi al pesto*

Tempio di Castore e Polluce (Temple of Castor and Pollux; p341), Valley of the Temples

JOHN ELK III/LONELY PLANET IMAGES ©

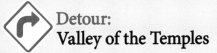

Detour:
Valley of the Temples

Below the modern-medieval town of **Agrigento** is a Unesco-certified, ancient Greek wonder: **Valley of the Temples**, inside the **Parco Archeologico** (0922 49 72 26; adult/reduced €8/4, incl Museo Archeologico €10/5; 9am-11.30pm Jul & Aug, 9am-7pm Tue-Sat, 9am-1pm Sun & Mon Sep-Jun). Five Doric temples stand along a ridge, a salute to 5th century BC Greek sailors returning to their city of Akragas.

East of the entry at Piazzale dei Templi is spectacular **Tempio di Ercole** (Temple of Hercules), built in the 6th century BC with roughly the same dimensions as the Parthenon. Magnificent, c440 BC **Tempio della Concordia** (Temple of Concord) is the only temple to survive relatively intact. High on the ridge stands **Tempio di Giunone** (Temple of Juno), with an impressive sacrificial altar. West across Via dei Templi are the ruins of colossally over-ambitious, 5th-century-BC **Tempio di Giove** (Temple of Jupiter), which was never completed. Nearby **Tempio di Castore e Polluce** (Temple of Castor and Pollux) was partly reconstructed in the 19th century. Artefacts found onsite are displayed inside **Museo Archeologico** (0922 4 01 11; Contrada San Nicola; adult/reduced €6/3; 9am-7pm Tue-Sat, 9am-1pm Sun & Mon).

For maximum romance, visit February to March to see the valley carpeted with almond blossoms, or stick around after sunset to see the temples illuminated. Book rooms with views of Tempio della Concordia at swanky **Villa Athena** (0922 59 62 88; www.hotelvillaathena.it; Via Passeggiata Archeologica 33; d €190-350; P ❄ @ 🛜 🏊).

From Agrigento Centrale station (Piazza Marconi), trains run regularly to **Palermo** (€8.10, 2¼ hours) and **Catania** (€10.20, 3¾ hours).

del Cantuccio (ricotta-potato dumplings with basil, parsley, mint, capers, almonds and cherry tomatoes), then move on to memorable main courses such as lemon-stuffed bass with orange-fennel salad.

ℹ Information

Tourist office (0931 57 37 79; www.comune.noto.sr.it; Piazza XVI Maggio; 9am-1pm & 3-8pm) An excellent and busy information office with multilingual staff and free maps.

ℹ Getting There & Around

BUS From the Giardini Pubblici just east of Noto's historic centre, AST and Interbus serve Catania (€7.70, 1½ to 2½ hours, 11 to 17 Monday to Saturday, six on Sunday) and Syracuse (€3.20, one hour, 16 to 19 Monday to Saturday, four on Sunday).

TRAIN There's frequent service to Syracuse (€3.30, 30 minutes, 10 daily except Sunday).

PUGLIA
Vieste
POP 13,890

Vieste is an attractive whitewashed town above a gleaming beach, backed by sheer white cliffs and overshadowed by a towering rock monolith. Superb sandy beaches surround the town including Spiagga del Castello, Cala San Felice and Cala Sanguinaria.

 Tours

AGENZIA SINERGIE Tours

(338 840 62 15; www.agenziasinergie.it) Arranges tours of the Gargano and visits to **La Salata** (admission adult/child €4/free; 5.30-6.15pm Jun-Aug, 4-4.45pm Sep, Oct-May on request), a 4th- to 6th-century grotto graveyard 9km out of town with tombs cut into the rock wall.

If You Like...
Fantasy Architecture

Minds boggled by the gnome-homes of Alberobello (p345), lava-rock palaces of Catania (p332) and sandstone baroque buildings of Lecce (p344) will be blown away by these Southern wonders:

1 CASTEL DEL MONTE
Perched on a Puglian hilltop is enigmatic, octagonal **Castel del Monte** (☎0883 56 99 97; www.casteldelmonte.beniculturali.it; admission €31.50; ☾9am-6pm Oct-Feb, 10.15am-7.45pm Mar-Sep), a Unesco World Heritage site. No one knows why Frederick II built it, nobody ever lived here, and it serves no military purpose – there are eight octagonal towers, but no kitchens or defenses. Historians speculate it served a spiritual purpose, given its marble columns and Islamic-inspired geometry. By car, it's about 35km from Trani.

2 LOCOROTONDO
Bring your sunglasses: except for scarlet geraniums bursting from window-boxes, Locorotondo's *centro storico* is dazzlingly white. Unwind in sun-bleached traditional homes rented through **Sotto le Cummerse** (☎080 431 32 98; www.sottolecummerse.it; Via Vittorio Veneto 138; apt €82-230 incl breakfast; ❄), or stay in *trulli* cottages clustering like mushrooms in the vineyards outside town at **Truddi** (☎080 443 13 26; www.trulliresidence.it; C da Trito 292; d 65-80, apts 100-150, per week €450-741; ❄ P), where you can also take cooking courses (per day €80). Trains run often to/from Bari (€4.50, 1½ to 2 hours).

AGENZIA SOL — Tours
(☎0884 70 15 58; www.sol vieste.it; Via Trepiccioni 5; ☾9.20am-1.15pm & 5-9pm winter, to midnight in summer) Organises hiking, cycling, boat, jeep and gastronomy tours.

Leonarda Motobarche — Boat Tour
(☎0884 70 13 17; www.motobarcheleonarda. it; per person €15; ☾Apr-Sep) Boat tours of marine caves.

Sleeping & Eating

B&B ROCCA SUL MARE — B&B €
(☎0884 70 27 19; www.roccasul mare.it; Via Mafrolla 32; per person €25-70; @) In a former convent in the old quarter, this popular place has charm, with large, comfortable, high-ceilinged rooms. Meals and bike hire available.

HOTEL SEGGIO — Hotel €€
(☎0884 70 81 23; www.hotelseggio.it; Via Veste 7; d €80-150; ☾Apr-Oct; P ❄ ⛱ @ 🛜) A butter-coloured *palazzo* in the town's historic centre with steps that spiral down to a pool and sunbathing terrace with the backdrop of the sea.

TAVERNA AL CANTINONE — Traditional Italian €€
(☎0884 70 77 53; Via Mafrolla 26; meals €25-30; ☾lunch & dinner Wed-Mon) Run by a charming Italian-Spanish couple who have a passion for cooking; the food is exceptional, seasonal and exquisitely presented.

OSTERIA AL DUOMO — Osteria €
(☎0884 70 82 43; www.osterialduomo.it; Via Alessandro III 23; meals €25; ☾lunch & dinner Mar-Nov) Tucked away in a narrow alley in the heart of the old town, this *osteria* has a cosy cave interior and outdoor seating under a shady arbour. Home-made pastas with seafood sauces feature prominently.

ℹ Getting There & Around

Boat
In summer, Navigazione Libera del Golfo (☎0884 70 74 89; www.navlib.it) heads to the Isole Tremiti (€16.50-20, 1½ hours).

Bus
Pugliairbus (☎080 580 03 58; http://pugliairbus.aeroportidipuglia.it) runs a service to Vieste, from Bari airport (€20, 3½ hours, four daily May to September).

Trulli (whitewashed stone houses), Alberobello (p345)

OLIVER STREWE/LONELY PLANET IMAGES ©

Bari

POP 320,150

Bari is Puglia's capital and one of the south's most prosperous cities. The historic old town of Bari Vecchia is a medieval labyrinth of tight alleyways, piazzas, 40 churches and 120 shrines.

 Sights

BASILICA DI SAN NICOLA　　Basilica

(Piazza San Nicola; www.basilicasannicola.it; ⊙7am-1pm & 4-7pm Mon-Sat, 7am-1pm & 4-9pm Sun) One of the south's first Norman churches, the basilica is a great example of Puglian-Romanesque style, built to house the relics of St Nicholas (better known as Father Christmas), which were stolen from Turkey in 1087 by local fishermen.

PIAZZA MERCANTILE　　Piazza

This beautiful piazza is fronted by the **Sedile**, the headquarters of Bari's Council of Nobles. In the square's northeast corner is the **Colonna della Giustizia** (Column of Justice), where debtors were once tied and whipped.

Sleeping & Eating

B&B CASA PIMPOLINI　　B&B €

(☑080 521 99 38; www.casapimpolini.com; Via Calefati 249; s/d €60/80; ❄ @) This lovely B&B in the new town is within easy walking distance to shops, restaurants and Bari Vecchia. The rooms are warm and welcoming, and the home-made breakfast a treat.

HOTEL ADRIA　　Hotel €€

(☑080 524 66 99; www.adriahotelbari.com; Via Zuppetta 10; s/d €70/110; P ❄ @) A dusky-pink building fronted by wrought-iron balconies, this is a good choice near the train station. Rooms are comfortable, bright and modern.

LA LOCANDA DI FEDERICO　　Trattoria €€

(☑080 522 77 05; www.lalocandadifederico.com; Piazza Mercantile 63-64; meals €30; ⊙lunch & dinner) With domed ceilings, archways and medieval-style artwork on the walls, this restaurant oozes atmosphere. The menu is typical Pugliese, the food delicious and the price reasonable.

Detour: Lecce

About 40km southeast of Brindisi, easily accessible by bus or train, Lecce is a glorious architectural confection of palaces and churches, intricately sculpted from the soft local sandstone. Swooning 18th-century traveller Thomas Ashe thought it 'the most beautiful city in Italy', but the less-impressed Marchese Grimaldi said the facade of Santa Croce made him think a lunatic was having a nightmare. Either way, it's a lively, graceful university town packed with upmarket boutiques, antique shops, restaurants and bars.

Historical attractions abound. The magnum opus of Puglian architect Giuseppe Zimbalo, the **Basilica di Santa Croce** (☏0832 24 19 57; www.basilicasantacroce.eu; Via Umberto I; ☺9am-noon & 5-8pm) raises ornamentation almost to the level of hallucination, with a legion of cherubs, wild animals and mythical beasties writhing across its sandstone facade. More *barocco leccese* (Lecce baroque) masterpieces crowd the **Piazza del Duomo**, where the tower of the 12-century **Duomo di Lecce** (☺8.30am-noon & 4-6.30pm) soars dramatically above the cobbled streets.

VINI E CUCINA Osteria €
(☏338 212 03 91; Strada Vallisa 23; meals €10; ☺lunch & dinner) Run by the same family for more than a century, this boisterous *osteria* chalks up its daily specials of well-prepared and filling Pugliese dishes.

Dangers & Annoyances

Petty crime is a problem, so don't leave anything in your car; don't display money or valuables; and watch out for bag-snatchers on scooters.

ⓘ Information

Hospital (☏080 559 11 11; Piazza Cesare)

Tourist office (☏080 990 93 41; www.viaggiareinpuglia.it; 1st fl, Piazza Moro 33a; ☺8.30am-1pm & 3-6pm Mon-Fri, 10am-1pm Sat); Information kiosk (☺9am-7pm May-Sep) in front of the train station in Piazza Aldo Moro.

ⓘ Getting There & Away

Air
Bari's Palese airport (☏080 580 03 58; www.aeroportidipuglia.it) is served by a host of international and budget airlines, including British Airways, Alitalia and Ryanair.

Pugliairbus (☏080 580 03 58; http://pugliairbus.aeroportidipuglia.it) connects to Bari airport, Vieste (€20, 3½ hours, four daily May to September) and to Matera (€5, 1¼ hours, four daily).

Bus
Ferrovie Appulo-Lucane (☏080 572 52 29; www.fal-srl.it, in Italian) Buses serving Matera.

Ferrovie del Sud-Est (FSE; ☏080 546 21 11; www.fseonline.it, in Italian) From Largo Ciaia for Alberobello (€3.90, 1¼ hours) and to Locorotondo.

Train
From the main train station (☏080 524 43 86) Eurostar trains go to Milan (from €85, about 8 hours) and Rome (from €51, 4 hours). Ferrovie Appulo-Lucane (☏080 572 52 29; www.fal-srl.it) serves Matera (€4.50, 1½ hours, 12 daily).

FSE trains (☏080 546 21 11; www.fseonline.it, in Italian) service Alberobello (€4.50, 1½ hours, hourly) from the station in Via Oberdan.

ⓘ Getting Around

Central Bari is compact – a 15-minute walk will take you from Piazza Aldo Moro to the old town.

To/From the Airport
Tempesta shuttle bus (€4.14, 30 minutes, hourly) leaves from the main train station.

Alberobello

POP 11,000

Unesco World Heritage site Alberobello resembles a mini urban sprawl – for gnomes. The Zona dei Trulli on the western hill of town is a dense mass of 1500 beehive-shaped historic limestone houses, white-tipped as if dusted by snow.

Sights

Alberobello spreads across two hills. Within the old town quarter of **Rione Monti** over 1000 *trulli* (whitewashed stone houses), most of which are now souvenir shops, cascade down the hillside. To its east, on the other side of Via Indipendenza, is **Rione Aia Piccola**. This neighbourhood is much less commercialised, with 400 *trulli*, many still used as family dwellings.

In the modern part of town, the 18th-century **Trullo Sovrano** (☑080 432 60 30; www.trullosovrano.it; Piazza Sacramento; admission €1.50; ◷10am-6pm) is the only two-floor *trullo*, built by a wealthy priest's family. It's a small museum giving something of the atmosphere of *trullo* life, with sweet, rounded rooms which include a re-created bakery, a bedroom and a kitchen. The souvenir shop here has a wealth of literature on the town and surrounding area.

Sleeping & Eating

TRULLIDEA Apartment €€
(☑080 432 38 60; www.trullidea.it; Via Monte San Gabriele 1; 2-person trullo from €63-149) A series of 15 renovated *trulli* in Alberobello's Trulli Zone, these are quaint, cosy and atmospheric. They're available on a self-catering, B&B, or half- or full-board basis.

TRATTORIA AMATULLI Trattoria €
(☑080 432 29 79; Via Garibaldi 13; meals €16; ◷Tue-Sun) Excellent trattoria with a cheerily cluttered interior papered with photos of smiley diners, plus superb down-to-earth dishes like *orecchiette scure con*

cacioricotta pomodoro e rucola ('little ears' pasta with cheese, tomato and rucola).

IL POETA CONTADINO Traditional Italian €€€
(☑080 432 19 17; www.ilpoetacontadino.it; Via Indipendenza 21; meals €65; ◷Tue-Sun Feb-Dec) The dining room here has a medieval banqueting feel with its sumptuous decor and chandeliers. Dine on a poetic menu which includes the signature dish, fava bean purée with *cavatelli* and seafood.

ℹ Information

The tourist office (☑080 432 51 71; Via Garibaldi; ◷8am-1pm Mon-Fri, plus 3-6pm Tue & Thu) is just off the main square. In the Zona dei Trulli is another tourist information office (☑080 432 28 22; www.prolocoalberobello.it; Monte Nero 1; ◷9am-7.30pm).

ℹ Getting There & Away

Alberobello is easily accessible from Bari (€4.10, 1½ hours, hourly) on the FSE Bari-Taranto train line.

BASILICATA

Matera

POP 60,530 / ELEV 405M

Approach Matera from virtually any direction and your first glimpse of its famous *sassi* (stone houses carved out of the caves and cliffs) is sure to be etched in your memory forever.

Sights

MUSEO DELLA SCULTURA CONTEMPORANEA Museum
(MUSMA; ☑366 935 77 68; www.musma.it; via San Giacomo; adult/reduced €5/3.50; ◷10am-2pm Tue-Sun & 4-8pm Sat & Sun) Housed in Palazzo Pomarici, MUSMA is a fabulous contemporary sculpture museum. Some of the exhibits are artfully displayed in atmospherically lit caves. You can also book a tour to visit the **Cripta del Peccato Originale** (the Crypt of Original Sin) which has well-preserved frescoes from the late 8th century.

DAMIEN SIMONIS/LONELY PLANET IMAGES ©

Don't Miss Matera's Sassi

Dotting Matera's serpentine alleyways and staircases are some 3000 habitable *sassi* (cave dwellings), declared a Unesco World Heritage Site in 1993. Far from crude cavemen habitats, these carved-rock structures include elaborate frescoed *chiese rupestri* (cave churches) created between the 8th and 13th centuries.

By the 1950s over half of Matera's population lived in the *sassi,* with a typical cave sheltering six children. But conditions were hardly ideal, and with rampant malaria, infant mortality reached 50%. In his book *Christ Stopped at Eboli,* Carlo Levi recalls children begging for quinine to stave off the deadly disease before local swamps were drained.

Today many *sassi* have been refurbished, including a two-storey **monastic complex** containing the 10th- to 11th-century **Chiesa Madonna delle Virtù** downstairs and frescoed **Chiesa di San Nicola del Greci** upstairs. **Casa-Grotta di Vico Solitario** offers a glimpse of life as it was lived for centuries in the *sassi*: bed in the kitchen, a room for manure, and a section for a pig and a donkey. For overnights stays in a *sasso* – minus the livestock, and plus modern amenities from subterranean swimming pools to solar panels – see p347.

THINGS YOU NEED TO KNOW

Monastic complex (Via Madonna delle Virtù; ⏰10am-7pm Sat & Sun); **Casa-Grotta di Vico Solitario** (off Via Bruno Buozzi; admission €1.50)

PIAZZA VITTORIO VENETO

The focus of the town is this bustling meeting point for an evening *passeggiata* (stroll). It's surrounded by elegant churches and richly adorned *palazzi,* with their backs to the *sassi;* an attempt by the bourgeois to block out the shameful poverty the *sassi* once represented.

Tours

Ferula Viaggi (📞0835 33 65 72; www.matera turismo.it; Via Cappelluti 34; ⏰9am-1.30pm & 3.30-7pm Mon-Sat) Runs *sassi* walking tours, cycling tours and cooking courses.

Cooperativa Amici del Turista (📞0835 33 03 01; www.amicidelturista.it; Via Fiorentini 28-30) Offers *sassi* tours.

Sleeping

TOP CHOICE HOTEL IN
PIETRA Boutique Hotel €€
(📞0835 34 40 40; www.hotelinpietra.it; Via San Giovanni Vecchio 22; Barisano; s €70, d €110-150, ste 220; ✳ @) The lobby here is set in a former 13th-century chapel complete with soaring arches, while the eight rooms combine soft golden stone with the natural cave interior. Furnishings are Zen-style with low beds, while the bathrooms are stylish and include vast sunken tubs.

LOCANDA DI SAN MARTINO Hotel €€
(📞0835 25 66 00; www.locandadisanmartino. it; Via Fiorentini 71; d €89-200; ✳ 🛜 ☰) A sumptuous hotel where you can swim in a cave – in a subterranean underground swimming pool. The cave accommodation, complete with niches and rustic brick floors, is set around a warren of cobbled paths and courtyards.

LA DOLCE VITA B&B B&B €
(📞0835 31 03 24; www.ladolcevitamatera.it; Rione Malve 51; s €40-60, d €60-80; 🛜) This eco-friendly B&B in Sasso Caveoso has self-contained apartments with solar panels and recycled rain water for plumbing.

Eating & Drinking

TOP CHOICE RISTORANTE IL
CANTUCCIO Trattoria €€
(📞0835 33 20 90; Via delle Becchiere 33; meals €25; ⏰Tue-Sun) This quaint, homey trattoria near Piazza Vittorio Veneto is as welcoming as its chef and owner, Michael Lella. The menu is seasonal and the dishes traditional and delicious.

BACCANTI Traditional Italian €€€
(📞0835 33 37 04; www.baccantiristorante. com; Via Sant'Angelo 58-61; meals €50; ⏰lunch & dinner Tue-Sat, lunch Sun) The design here is simple glamour against the low arches of the cavern; the dishes are delicate and complex, using local ingredients.

OI MARÌ Pizzeria €
(📞0835 34 61 21; Via Fiorentini 66; pizzas from €6.50; ⏰dinner nightly, lunch Sat & Sun) In Sasso Barisano, this big convivial cavern is styled as a Neapolitan pizzeria – and has a great cheery atmosphere and excellent substantial pizzas to match.

19A BUCA WINERY? Wine Bar
(📞0835 33 35 92; www.diciannovesimabuca. com; Via Lombardi 3; ⏰11am-midnight Tue-Sun) This ultrachic wine bar-restaurant-cafe-lounge has white space-pod chairs, a 19-hole indoor golf course surrounding an ancient cistern and an impressive wine cellar and degustation menu (meals €30).

ℹ Information

Basilicata Turistica (www.aptbasilicata.it)

Sassiweb (www.sassiweb.it) Informative website on Matera.

ℹ Getting There & Away

Bus

SITA (📞0835 38 50 07; www.sitabus.it) Serves many small towns in the province.

Marozzi (📞06 225 21 47; www.marozzivt.it) Runs three daily buses to Rome (€34, 6½ hours).

Pugliairbus (📞080 580 03 58; pugliairbus. aeroportidipuglia.it) Operates a service to Bari airport (€5, 1¼ hours, four daily).

Train

Ferrovie Appulo-Lucane (FAL; 📞0835 33 28 61; www.fal-srl.it) Runs regular trains (€4.50, 1½ hours, 12 daily) and buses to Bari.

Italy

In Focus

Monte Rosa (p154), Aosta
CHRISTIAN ASLUND/LONELY PLANET IMAGES ©

Italy Today

Nuns visiting the Colosseum (p72), Rome.

if Italy were 100 people

92 would be Italian

4 would be Albanian & Eastern European

3 would be Other

1 would be North African

belief systems
(% of population)

91 Roman Catholic

4 Other Christians

3.5 Other Religions

1.5 Muslims

population per sq km

♟ = 30 people

Rome Italy USA

Trials & Tribulations

It might be the home of *dolce vita*, but Italy has one hell of a *mal di testa* (headache). Unemployment rose from 6.2% in 2007 to 8.4% in 2010, while Italy's public debt remains above 115% of GDP. Unnerving memories of the social unrest that marked the 1970s came to the fore in late 2010, with nationwide rallies protesting education reforms, and anarchist mail bombs at Rome's Swiss and Chilean embassies.

On the political front, former Prime Minister Silvio Berlusconi's string of scandals led a growing number of Italians to question his ability to tackle the country's chronic problems. Among them was Naples' on-again, off-again rubbish crisis: in May 2011, 170 troops were deployed to help clear 2000 tonnes of litter from the city's streets, three years after Berlusconi's promise to resolve the region's waste-disposal woes.

In early 2011, Italy's Constitutional Court overturned a law granting legal immunity to

WILL SALTER/LONELY PLANET IMAGES ©

Mahroug from detention on unrelated theft charges.

On 13 February 2011, close to one million Italians took part in rallies demanding his resignation. In May the same year, Berlusconi's centre-right coalition lost control of both Milan and Naples in local elections. The defeat of Milan mayor Letizia Moratti to centre-left lawyer Giuliano Pisapia had been declared 'unthinkable' by Berlusconi, confident that his powerbase and hometown would prove him to be the seasoned survivor once more.

Italy's failing economy led to the resignation of Berlusconi on 12 November 2011. The country turned to the European Commission veteran Mario Monti as its new prime minister to deal with Italy's economic woes.

the prime minister and senior ministers. As a result, four criminal cases against Berlusconi were reactivated, spanning everything from alleged tax evasion to the alleged bribing of British lawyer, David Mills, in two corruption trials in the 1990s.

The most sensational trial, however, was Rubygate. In it, Berlusconi was accused of paying for sex with Karima El Mahroug, a nightclub dancer nicknamed Ruby Rubacuori (Ruby Heartstealer), while she was still 17. The encounters reputedly took place at so-called *bunga bunga* sessions – sex parties held at several of Berlusconi's villas. The scandal embroiled a number of public figures, including Nicole Minetti. A showgirl-turned-regional councillor for Lombardy, the Anglo-Italian was accused of procuring young women for Berlusconi's parties. Berlusconi was further accused of providing false information to a Milan police chief in order to release El

Refugee Crisis

Already a hot potato in Italy, the immigration debate heated up in 2011 as tens of thousands of boat people swamped Lampedusa, a tiny Italian island and Europe's southernmost point. More than 20,000 reached the island between January and March alone, mostly Tunisians escaping post-revolution uncertainty.

Italy's decision to grant temporary residency permits to 30,000 of the refugees caused consternation among several EU nations. Among the most vocal were France and Germany, who accused Italy of trying to fob off its illegal immigrants to other Schengen Treaty countries. On 17 April 2011, the issue escalated when France temporarily closed its border with Italy to prevent a trainload of immigrants from entering French territory. Far from impressed, the Italian government accused France of lacking solidarity over a problem it sees as European, and not just Italian.

History

MARTIN MOOS/LONELY PLANET IMA*

Italy has seen it all – imperial domination, quarrelling city-states, international exploration, crushing poverty and postwar booms. This operatic story features a colourful cast of characters: perverted emperors, ambitious invaders, Machiavellian masterminds, and above all, ordinary Italians who have repeatedly shown themselves capable of extraordinary, history-changing feats.

Etruscans, Greeks & Ancient Rome

Long before Renaissance palazzi and baroque churches, the Italian peninsula was riddled with caves and hill towns built by the Etruscans, who dominated the land by the 7th century BC. Little is known about them, since they spoke a language that today has barely been deciphered.

c 700,000 BC

Primitive tribes lived in caves and hunted elephants and other hefty beasts on the Italian peninsula.

Though impressive as seafarers, warriors and farmers, they lacked cohesion.

Greek traders set up a series of independent city-states along the coast and in Sicily in the 8th century BC, collectively known as Magna Graecia. These Greek settlements flourished until the 3rd century BC, and the remains of magnificent Doric temples still stand in Italy's south (at Paestum) and on Sicily (at Agrigento, Selinunte and Segesta).

The Etruscans tried and failed to conquer the Greek settlements, but the real threat to both civilisations came from an unexpected source – the grubby but growing Latin town of Rome.

According to legend, Italy's future capital was founded by twins Romulus and Remus on 21 April 753 BC, on the site where they had been suckled by a she-wolf as orphan infants. Romulus later killed Remus and the settlement was named Rome after him. Over the following centuries, this fearless and often ruthless town become Italy's major power, sweeping aside the Etruscans by the 2nd century AD.

The Best...
For Archaeo-
logical Booty

1 Vatican Museums, Vatican City (p89)

2 Capitoline Museums, Rome (p69)

3 Museo Archeologico Nazionale, Naples (p289)

4 Museo Archeologico Paolo Orsi, Syracuse (p337)

5 Museo e Villa Borghese, Rome (p92)

IN FOCUS HISTORY

The Roman Republic

Although Roman monuments were emblazoned with the initials SPQR (Senatus Populusque Romanus, or the Senate and People of Rome), the Roman people initially had precious little say in their republic. Known as plebeians (literally 'the many'), the disenfranchised majority slowly wrested concessions from the patrician class by 280 BC, though only a small political class qualified for positions of power in government.

Slowly at first, Roman armies conquered the Italian peninsula. Defeated city-states were not taken over directly, but were obliged to become allies, providing troops on demand for the Roman army. Wars with rivals like Carthage in the east gave Rome control of Sardinia, Sicily, Corsica, mainland Greece, Spain, most of North Africa and part of Asia Minor by 133 BC. Rome became the most important city in the Mediterranean, with a population of 300,000.

2000 BC

The Bronze Age reaches Italy. Copper and bronze are used to fashion tools and arms.

264–241 BC

War rages between Rome and the Carthage empire, across North Africa and into Spain, Sicily and Sardinia.

AD 79

Mt Vesuvius showers molten rock and ash upon Pompeii and Herculaneum.

Beware the Ides of March

Born in 100 BC, Gaius Julius Caesar would become one of Rome's most masterful generals, lenient conquerors and capable administrators. After quelling revolts in Spain, Caeser received a Roman mandate in 59 BC to govern Gallia Narbonensis, today's southern France. Caesar raised troops to hold off an invasion of Helvetic tribes from Switzerland, and in 52 to 51 BC stamped out Gaul's last great revolt under the leader Vercingetorix. Diplomatic Caesar was generous to defeated enemies, and the Gauls became his staunchest supporters.

Jealous of the growing power of his one-time protégé, Gnaeus Pompeius Magnus (Pompey) severed his political alliance with Caesar, and convinced the Senate to outlaw Caesar in 49 BC. On 7 January, Caesar crossed the Rubicon River into Italy, sparking civil war. Caesar's three-year campaign ended in decisive victory, and upon his return to Rome in 46 BC, he assumed dictatorial powers.

Caesar launched a series of reforms, overhauled the Senate and embarked on a building program, but by 44 BC, it was clear Caesar had no plans to restore the Republic. Dissent grew in the Senate, and on the Ides (15th) of March, 44 BC, a band of

Mosaic, Terme di Nettuno (p84), Ostia Antica
MARTIN MOOS/LONELY PLANET IMAGES ©

312
Constantine becomes the Roman Empire's first Christian leader.

962
Otto I is crowned Holy Roman Emperor in Rome, the first in a long line of Germanic rulers.

1271
Venetian merchant Marco Polo embarks on a 24-year journey to Central Asia and China.

conspirators led by former supporter Marcus Junius Brutus stabbed Caesar to death in a Senate meeting.

In the years following Caesar's death, his lieutenant, Mark Antony (Marcus Antonius), and nominated heir, great-nephew Octavian, plunged into civil war against Caesar's assassins. Octavian took control of the western half of the empire and Antony headed to the east – but when Antony fell head over heels for Cleopatra VII in 31 BC, Octavian and Antony turned on one another. Octavian claimed victory over Antony and Cleopatra in Greece, and when he invaded Egypt, Antony and Cleopatra committed suicide and Egypt became a province of Rome.

Augustus & the Glories of Empire

By 27 BC, Octavian was renamed Augustus (Your Eminence) and conceded virtually unlimited power by the Senate, effectively becoming Rome's emperor. Under Augustus, the arts flourished and buildings were restored and constructed, including the Pantheon.

By AD 100, 1.5 million inhabitants thronged the capital's marble temples, public baths, theatres, circuses and libraries. Poverty was rife, and Augustus created Rome's first police force under a city prefect (praefectus urbi) to curb mob violence and quell dissent among the poor, politically underrepresented masses.

Under Hadrian (76–138), the empire reached its greatest extent, including Britain and most of the modern-day Middle East, from Turkey to northern Morocco. But by the time Diocletian (245–305) became emperor, the Empire was faced with attacks from outside and revolts from within. Diocletian's response to the rise of Christianity was persecution, a policy reversed in 313 under Christian Constantine I (c 272–337).

The Empire was later divided in two, with the second capital in Constantinople (modern-day Istanbul) founded by Constantine in 330. The Byzantine eastern empire survived, while Italy and Rome were overrun.

Papal Power & Family Feuds

In a historic twist, the minority religion Emperor Diocletian tried so hard to stamp out preserved Rome's glory. While most of Italy succumbed to invasion from Germanic tribes, Byzantine reconquest and Lombards in the north, the papacy established itself in Rome as a spiritual and secular force.

**The Best...
For Ancient
Awe**

1 Pantheon, Rome (p73)

2 Colosseum, Rome (p72)

3 Pompeii, Campania (p298)

4 Valley of the Temples, Sicily (p341)

5 Ostia Antica, Lazio (p84)

1309
Pope Clement V shifts the papacy to Avignon in France (for almost 70 years).

1321
Dante Alighieri completes his epic poem *La divina commedia* (The Divine Comedy). He dies the same year.

1452
Leonardo da Vinci is born 15 April in Vinci, near Florence.

Imperial Insanity

Bribes? Booty jokes? Bunga bunga parties? Modern Italy's political shenanigans bring to mind the ancient Romans, who suffered their fair share of eccentric leaders.

14–37 Tiberius A steady governing hand but prone to depression, Tiberius had a difficult relationship with the Senate and withdrew in his later years to Capri, where he apparently devoted himself to drinking, orgies and fits of paranoia.

37–41 Gaius (Caligula) Sex with his sisters and gratuitous violence were Caligula's idea of entertainment. He emptied the state's coffers and suggested naming a horse consul before being assassinated.

41–54 Claudius Apparently timid as a child, he was ruthless with enemies (including 35 senators) and relished watching their executions. According to English historian Edward Gibbon, he was the only one of the first 15 emperors not to take male lovers (standard at the time).

54–68 Nero Fiddle-playing Nero had his pushy stage mum murdered, his first wife's veins slashed, his second wife kicked to death, and his third wife's ex-husband killed. The people accused him of fiddling while Rome burned to the ground in 64 – but Nero blamed the disaster on the Christians. He executed the evangelists Peter and Paul, and had others thrown to wild beasts in grisly public spectacles.

In return for formal recognition of the pope's control of Rome and surrounding Papal States, the Carolingian Franks were granted a powerful position in Italy and their king, Charlemagne, was given the title of Holy Roman Emperor. The bond between the papacy and the Byzantine Empire was broken, and political power shifted north of the Alps, where it remained for more than 1000 years.

Meanwhile, Rome's aristocratic families battled to control the papacy and the right to appoint politically powerful bishops. Across the peninsula, two camps emerged: Guelphs (Guelfi, who backed the pope) and Ghibellines (Ghibellini, in support of the emperor).

The Wonder of the World

Marriage was the ultimate merger between Henry VI, son of Holy Roman Emperor Frederick I (Barbarossa), and Constance de Hauteville, heir to Sicily's Norman throne. The power couple's son, Frederick II (1194–1250), became one of the most colourful figures of medieval Europe. Frederick was a German who grew up in southern Italy and called Sicily home and, as Holy Roman Emperor, allowed freedom of worship to

1506

Work starts on St Peter's Basilica in Rome, to a design by Donato Bramante.

St Peter's Basilica (p90), Rome

1508–12

Pope Julius II commissions Michelangelo to paint the ceiling frescoes in the restored Sistine Chapel.

Muslims and Jews. A warrior and scholar, Frederick was nicknamed *Stupor Mundi* (the Wonder of the World) for his talents as a poet, linguist, mathematician, philosopher and military strategist.

After reluctantly carrying out a (largely diplomatic) Holy Land crusade in 1228–29 under threat of excommunication, Frederick returned to Italy to find papal troops invading Neapolitan territory. Frederick soon had them on the run, and expanded his influence to city-states in central and northern Italy. Battles ensued, which continued after Frederick's death in 1250.

Rise of the City-States

While the south of Italy tended to centralised rule, the north did not. Port cities such as Genoa, Pisa and especially Venice increasingly ignored edicts from Rome, and Florence, Milan, Parma, Bologna, Padua, Verona and Modena resisted Roman meddling in their affairs.

Between the 12th and 14th centuries, these cities developed new forms of government. Venice adopted an oligarchic, 'parliamentary' system in a limited democracy. Tuscan and Umbrian city-states created a *comune* (town council), a form of republican government dominated initially by aristocrats, then by wealthy middle classes. Family dynasties shaped their hometowns, such as the Medici in Florence, and the Visconti and Sforza in Milan.

War between the city-states was constant, and Florence, Milan and Venice absorbed their neighbours to become regional military and trading powers. Venice was most successful with its Mediterranean merchant empire; Florence thrived with its wool trade and financial institutions; and Milan negotiated and fought its way to European political power. Italy's dynamic, independent-minded city-states led a sea change in thinking known as the Renaissance, ushering in the modern era with scientific discoveries, publishing houses and compelling new visions for the world in art.

A Nation Is Born

Centuries of war, plague, and occasional religious purges took their toll on Italy's divided city-states, whose role on the world stage was largely reduced by the 18th century to a vacation playground. Napoleon marched into Venice in 1797 without much of a fight, ending 1000 years of Venetian independence and creating the so-called Kingdom of Italy in 1805. But just 10 years later, the reactionary Congress of Vienna restored all the foreign rulers to their places in Italy.

The Best... For Medieval Mystique

1 Siena, Tuscany (p250)

2 Bologna, Emilia-Romagna (p207)

3 San Gimignano, Tuscany (p256)

4 Assisi, Umbria (p263)

5 Verona, Veneto (p204)

1582
Pope Gregory XIII replaces the Julian calendar (introduced by Julius Caesar) with the modern-day Gregorian calendar.

1600
Naples is Europe's biggest city, boasting a population of over 300,000.

1805
Napoleon is proclaimed king of the newly constituted Kingdom of Italy, comprising most of the north of the country.

Florence's Trials by Fire

In 1481, fat-lipped Dominican friar Girolamo Savonarola began prophesying apocalyptic days ahead for Florence unless the city changed its wayward habits, from the cardinal sin of adultery to the fashion crime of wearing large jewellery. With the horrors of war fresh in their minds and vivid accounts of Florentine plague by Boccacio and Dante, Savonarola's bloodcurdling predictions struck fear in many Florentine hearts. Savonarola developed a following, and called for the establishment of a strict theocratic government for Florence.

When Florence's Medici clan rulers fell into disgrace in 1494, the city's fathers ceded to Savonarola's demands. Books, clothes, jewellery, fancy furnishings and art were torched on 'bonfires of the vanities'. Drinking, whoring, partying, gambling, flashy fashion and other sinful behaviours were banned – and a vibrant Florentine underground scene was born. To purge these rebels, bands of children marched around the city ferreting out Florentines still attached to old habits and possessions. Florence's economy stagnated; no one knew what goods and services Savonarola would ban next.

Florentines soon tired of this fundamentalism, as did the rival Franciscan religious order and Pope Alexander VI (possibly the least religiously inclined pope of all time). To test Savonarola's commitment to his own methods, the Franciscans invited him to submit to trial by fire. Savonarola sent an emissary instead, but the hapless youth was saved when the trial was cancelled on account of rain. Finally the city government had the fiery friar arrested. After weeks at the hands of the city rackmaster, he was hanged and burned at the stake as a heretic alongside two supporters on May 22, 1498.

Inspired by the French Revolution and outraged by their subjugation to Napoleon and Austria, Italians began to agitate for an independent, unified nationhood. Count Camillo Benso di Cavour (1810–61) of Turin, prime minister of the Savoy monarchy, became the diplomatic brains behind the Italian unification movement. He won British support for the creation of an independent Italian state and negotiated with the French in 1858 to create a northern Italian kingdom, in exchange for parts of Savoy and Nice.

The bloody 1859–61 Franco-Austrian War ensued, and is now better known as the war for Italian Independence. Pro-Independence forces took over Lombardy and forced the Austrians to relinquish the Veneto. Revolutionary Giuseppe Garibaldi claimed Sicily and southern Italy in the name of Savoy King Vittorio Emanuele II in 1860, and Cavour and the king claimed parts of central Italy (including Umbria and Le

1861
By the end of the 1859–61 Franco-Austrian War, Vittorio Emanuele II is proclaimed king of a newly united Italy.

1915
Italy enters WWI on the side of the Allies to win Italian territories still in Austrian hands.

1922
A fearful King Vittorio Emanuele III entrusts Mussolini and his Fascists with the formation of a government.

Marche). The unified Italian state was founded in 1861, with Tuscany, the Veneto and Rome incorporated into the fledgling kingdom by 1870 and parliament established in Rome in 1871. However, women were denied the right to vote until after WWII.

Mussolini and World Wars

When war broke out in Europe in July 1914, Italy chose to remain neutral, despite being a member of the Triple Alliance with Austria and Germany. Under the terms of the Alliance, Austria was due to hand over northern Italian territory – but Austria refused.

After Austria's deal-breaker, Italy joined the Allies, and plunged into a nightmarish 3½-year war with Austria. When the Austro-Hungarian forces collapsed in November 1918, the Italians marched into Trieste and Trento – but the post-war Treaty of Versailles failed to award Italy the remaining territories it sought.

This humiliation added insult to injury. Italy had lost 600,000 men in the war, and while a few war profiteers had benefitted, the rest of the populace was reduced to abject poverty. From this despair rose a demagogue: Benito Mussolini (1883–1945).

A former socialist newspaper editor and one-time draft dodger, Mussolini volunteered for the front and returned wounded in 1917. Frustrated at Italy's treatment in Versailles,

San Gimignano (p256)
JEAN-PIERRE LESCOURRET/LONELY PLANET IMAGES ©

1929

Catholicism is declared Italy's sole religion and the Vatican an independent state.

1940

Italy enters WWII on Nazi Germany's side and invades Greece, which quickly proves to be a mistake.

1944

Mt Vesuvius explodes back into action on March 18.

Mussolini formed an extremist Italian right-wing militant political group. By 1921, the Fascist Party was feared and admired for its black-shirted street brawlers, Roman salute and its self-anointed Duce (Leader), Mussolini. After his march on Rome in 1922 and victory in the 1924 elections, Mussolini took full control of the country by 1926, banning other political parties, independent trade unions, and free press.

As the first step to creating a 'new Roman empire', Mussolini invaded Abyssinia (Ethiopia) in 1935–36. Condemned by the League of Nations for his invasion, Mussolini allied with Nazi Germany to back fascist rebel General Franco in Spain. Yet Italy remained aloof from WWII battles until June 1940, when Germany's blitz of Norway, Denmark and much of France made it look like a winning campaign. Instead, allying with Italy caused Germany setbacks in the Balkans and North Africa.

By the time the Allies landed in Sicily in 1943, the Italians had had enough of Mussolini and his war, and the king had the dictator arrested. Italy surrendered in September – but the Germans rescued Mussolini, occupied the northern two-thirds of the country and reinstalled the dictator.

The painfully slow Allied campaign up the peninsula was aided by the Italian Resistance sabotage of German forces, until northern Italy was finally liberated in April 1945. Resistance fighters who were caught fleeing Mussolini, shot him and his lover, Clara Petacci, and strung up their corpses in Milan's Piazzale Lotto.

The Best...
For
Renaissance
Elegance

1 Duomo, Florence (p226)

2 Galleria degli Uffizi, Florence (p227)

3 Urbino, Marche (p263)

4 Isola di San Giorgio Maggiore, Venice (p189)

5 Da Vinci's *The Last Supper*, Milan (p127)

Red Scares & Lead Years

In the aftermath of war, the left-wing Resistance was disarmed and Italy's political forces scrambled to regroup. With the US Marshall Plan funding reconstruction in Italy and strategically limiting communism across Europe, Italy's left was shut out of power positions. Instead, the government formed in December 1945 was headed by the newly formed right-wing Democrazia Cristiana (DC; Christian Democrats), under Alcide de Gasperi. Italy became a republic in 1946, and De Gasperi's DC won the first elections under the new constitution in 1948.

Yet despite being systematically kept out of government until the 1980s, the Partito Comunista Italiano (PCI; Italian Communist Party) played a crucial role in Italy's social and political development. The party's popularity in Italy fuelled red scares across

1946
Italians vote in a national referendum to abolish the monarchy and create a republic.

1957
Italy joins France, West Germany and the Benelux countries to sign the Treaty of Rome.

1960
Rome hosts the Games of the XVII Olympiad.

Going the Distance for the Resistance

In 1943–44, the Assisi Underground hid hundreds of Jewish Italians in Umbrian convents and monasteries, while the Tuscan Resistance forged travel documents for them – but the refugees needed those documents fast, before they were deported to concentration camps by fascist officials. Enter the fastest man in Italy: Gino Bartali, world-famous Tuscan cyclist, Tour de France winner, and three-time champion of the Giro d'Italia. After his death in 2003, documents revealed that during his 'training rides' throughout the war years, Bartali had carried Resistance intelligence and falsified documents to transport Jewish refugees to safe locations. Bartali was interrogated at the dreaded Villa Triste in Florence, where suspected anti-fascists were routinely tortured – but he revealed nothing. Until his death, the long-distance hero downplayed his efforts to rescue Jewish refugees, even with his children, saying, 'One does these things, and then that's that'.

Europe and sabotage efforts that some reports suggest involved the CIA and NATO – possibly at high levels. Today little is known about Operation Gladio, an underground paramilitary organisation apparently formed to undermine the credibility of the Communist Party and lay the groundwork for a right-wing coup in case of Communist victory at the polls.

Neo-fascist terrorists struck with a bomb blast in Milan in 1969, the first of a series of random attacks that would define Italy in the 1970s – an era now known as the *anni di piombo* (years of lead). Retaliation and counter-attacks between extreme right and militant left Brigate Rosse (Red Brigades) killed bystanders and political targets alike, leaving the nation in a constant state of shock, outrage and mourning. After the Brigate Rosse kidnapped and murdered former DC prime minister Aldo Moro in 1978, public outcry helped curb extremist violence.

The 1970s was also a time of changing gender politics. Divorce became legal, abortion legalised, and antisexist legislation allowed women to keep their own names after marriage.

The Rise, Fall & Rise of Berlusconi

Despite its political turbulence, Italy grew into one of the world's leading economies in the 1980s. But high unemployment, inflation and national debt culminated in a crisis in the mid-1990s, and the government introduced draconian measures to cut public spending in order to join the European market and convert to a single currency (the euro) in 2001.

1980
On 25 November, a 6.8-Richter-scale earthquake strikes Campania killing almost 3000 people.

1995
Maurizio Gucci, heir to the Gucci fashion empire, is gunned down outside his Milan offices.

2001
Silvio Berlusconi's right-wing Casa delle Libertà coalition wins an absolute majority in national polls.

The Italian political scene was also rocked by the *Tangentopoli* (Kickback City) scandal, which broke in Milan in 1992. Corruption investigations known as *Mani Pulite* (Clean Hands) implicated thousands of politicians and businesspeople in scandals ranging from bribery and kickbacks to theft. The old centre-right political parties collapsed in the wake of these trials, and the promise of new leadership shifted power to media magnate Silvio Berlusconi and his Forza Italia (Go Italy) in 2001. Ongoing corruption investigations, sex scandals over his 'bunga bunga' parties and unpopular support for war in Iraq contributed to Berlusconi's unseating by centre-left former European Commission head Romano Prodi in 2006. But Berlusconi regained his position in April 2008, heading a majority coalition known as Popolo della Libertà (People of Liberty) that includes Gianfranco Fini's right-wing (and former Fascist) Alleanza Nazionale (National Alliance) and the controversial separatist Lega Nord (Northern League). However, it was money, rather than controversy which finally toppled Il Cavaliere. With Italy's debts soaring to €1.9 trillion, sparking panic across the Eurozone, Berlusconi finally gave into the inevitable and resigned on 12 November 2011. He was replaced by European Commission veteran Mario Monti, who immediately appointed a technocratic cabinet and assumed the dual roles of Prime Minister and Minister of Economy & Finance.

Pantheon (p73), Rome

2005
Pope John Paul II dies aged 84, prompting a wave of sorrow.

2009
Italy's Constitutional Court overturns a law giving Berlusconi immunity from prosecution while in office.

2011
After a string of vice and corruption scandals, Berlusconi resigns to restore confidence in the ailing Italian economy.

Family Travel

Pompeii (p298)

PHILIP & KAREN SMITH/LONELY PLANET IMAGES ©

Kids love Italy because it lets them tell adults 'I told you so'. Aha, you actually can survive on pizza and ice cream: Naples shows how it's done. Look, mermaids do live inside sea caves: Romans called them water sprites, and left offerings inside Capri's Blue Grotto. Gladiators, volcanoes, gondolas...Italy is a storybook come true.

Inspiration

How do you get kids to go along with vacation plans, and let them think it's their idea? Italy makes it easy, with sights and activities that appeal to kids and grown-ups alike. Sprawling ancient Roman sites give kids a chance to run around, and let adults daydream about what life was like thousands of years ago, before kids. Caves and catacombs are worthy dares, and those piles of bones might inspire some creepy Halloween craft projects. Grand villa estates have gardens for picnics and playtime and art for contemplation and downtime. Agriturismi (farmhouse stays) are money-savers that may include rustic meals, a pool and farm animals.

Everyone's a winner with Italian island beach vacations, with plenty of other kids around and sometimes hot springs for parents. Across Italy, there is gelato and *calcio* (soccer, aka English football) on every major piazza. For more information and ideas, see Lonely Planet's *Travel with Children* and the superb Italy-focused website www.italiakids.com.

Planning

Italians love children, but there are few special amenities. In this book, look for the family-friendly icon [👪] highlighting places that are especially welcoming to families. Book accommodation in advance, and ask about extra beds. Reserve train seats whenever possible to avoid finding yourselves standing.

Budgeting

Stretch your family holiday budget further in Italy:

◦ **Sights** Admission to many tourist attractions is free or heavily discounted for children under 18 (listed as 'reduced' in this book).

◦ **Transport** Discounts are often available for children under age 12.

◦ **Hotels & Agriturismi** Many often offer special rates on room and board for kids. Check the handy website www.booking.com, which details the 'kid policy' for every hotel it lists, including what extra charges apply to kids' breakfasts and extra beds.

◦ **Restaurants** Kids' menus are uncommon, but you can ask for a *mezzo piatto* (half-plate), usually at half-price.

The Best...
Destinations
for Kids

1 Sicily (p322)

2 Venice (p170)

3 Capri (p300)

4 Rome (p64)

5 Amalfi Coast (p304)

The Nitty Gritty

◦ **Baby formula and sterilising solution** Available at pharmacies.
◦ **Disposable nappies (diapers)** Available at supermarkets and pharmacies.
◦ **High chairs** Request ahead at restaurants.
◦ **Change facilities** Rare outside airports and fast-food restaurants.
◦ **Cots** Request ahead at hotels.
◦ **Strollers** Bring your own.
◦ **Infant car seats** Reserve from car-rental firms.

Art & Architecture

Head of Constantine, Capitoline Museums (p69), Rome

Head of Constantine, Capitoline Museums (p69), Rome

SEAN CAFFREY/LONELY PLANET IMAGES ©

With more Unesco World Heritage sites than any other country, Italy is one place you can hardly throw a stone without hitting a master-piece. Italian architecture is more than just a wall to hang the art on, with geniuses like Michelangelo creating spaces that alternately give a sense of intimacy and inclusion, steadfastness and momentum.

Classical Era

Ancient Romans initially took their cue from the Greeks – only what the Greeks did first, the Romans made bigger. The Greeks invented Doric, Ionic and Corinthian orders of columns, but Romans installed them in the Colosseum.

Harmonious proportions were key to Roman designs, including the Pantheon's carefully balanced, coffered dome showcasing a Roman innovation: concrete. Unlike the Greeks, Roman sculptors created accurate, brutally honest busts. You'll recognise Emperors Pompey, Titus and Augustus across the rooms at the Palatine Museum from their respective facial features: bulbous nose, square head, sunken eyes.

Roman emperors like Augustus used art as a PR tool, using it to celebrate great military victories – the Colonna di Traiano

(Trajan's Column) and the Ara Pacis Augustae (Altar of Peace) in Rome are especially gorgeous propaganda.

Byzantine Glitz

After Constantine became Christianity's star convert, the empire's architects turned their talents to Byzantine churches: domed brick basilicas, plain on the outside, with mosaic-encrusted interiors. One early example is Cattedrale Santa Maria Assunta (p190) in Torcello. Instead of classical realism, Torcello's *Last Judgment* mosaic conveys a clear message in compelling cartoon shorthand: repent, or snickering devils will drag you off by the hair. Torcello's golden Byzantine mosaics are echoed in Venice's Basilica di San Marco (p185) and as far away as Palermo's Palatine Chapel (p326).

Medieval Graces

Italians didn't appreciate over-the-top French Gothic cathedrals – instead, they took Gothic further over the top. A signature Moorish Gothic style graced Venice's palazzi, including the Ca' d'Oro. Milan took Gothic to extremes in its flamboyant Duomo, and the Sienese came up with a novelty for Siena's cathedral: storytelling scenes inlaid in the church floor.

Florentine painter Giotto di Bondone (1266–1337) added another twist. Instead of Byzantine golden cartoon saints, Giotto featured furry donkeys in the life story of St Francis in the Basilica di San Francesco di Assisi (p263). Pot-bellied pack animals dot Giotto's frescoed Assisi landscape, and when the donkey weeps at the death of the patron saint of animals, it's hard not to well up with him.

Meanwhile, in Siena, Ambrogio Lorenzetti (1290–1348) set a trend for secular painting with his *Allegories of Good and Bad Government* (1337–40), using convincing perspective to make good government seem perfectly achievable, with Peace, Prudence, happy merchants and a wedding party – it's like a medieval Jane Austen novel illustration.

The Renaissance

Plague cut short the talents of many artists and architects in the 14th century, and survivors regrouped. Floating, wide-eyed Byzantine saints seemed far removed from reality, where city-state wars and natural disasters loomed large. Florentine sculptors like Lorenzo Ghiberti (1378–1455) and Donatello (1386–1466) brought Byzantine ideals down to earth, creating anatomically accurate figures with classical principles of perspective and scale.

Architect Filippo Brunelleschi (1377–1446) also looked to the classics as inspiration for Florence's Duomo (p226) – specifically Rome's Pantheon – and created a vast dome of mathematically exacting proportions to distribute its massive weight. Critics were sure it would collapse; it still hasn't. But if Brunelleschi studied the classics, neoclassist Palladio pillaged them, borrowing architectural elements of temples, villas and forums for Venice's San Giorgio Maggiore (p189). The idea of creative repurposing wasn't new – the art of reusing old buildings, *spolia,* had been practiced in Italy for centuries – but Palladio's conceptual *spolia* was accomplished with easy grace.

The Best... Museums

1 Galleria degli Uffizi (p227), Florence

2 Vatican Museums (p89), Vatican City

3 Gallerie dell'Accademia (p181), Venice

4 Museo del Novecento (p122), Milan

5 Villa e Museo Borghese (p92), Rome

Classical laws of harmonious proportions had not been mastered in Roman painting, so Sandro Botticelli (1444–1510) took on the task. Though his early works seem stiff, his *Birth of Venus* (1485) in Florence's Uffizi is a model of poise. Instead of classicism, Leonardo Da Vinci (1452–1519) smudged the contours of his lines – a technique called *sfumato,* still visible in his faded *Last Supper* in Milan. Michelangelo applied the same chiselled perfection to his *David* at Florence's Accademia and to his image of Adam brought to life by God on the ceiling of the Sistine Chapel.

Mannerism

By 1520, artists such as Michelangelo and Raphael had mastered naturalism, and discovered its expressive limitations – to make a point, the Mannerists decided, sometimes you had to exaggerate for effect. One glorious example is *Assunta* (Ascension, 1516–18) by Titian (1490–1576) in Venice's I Frari, where the glowing Madonna rises to heaven in a swirl of red drapery. Milanese-born Michelangelo Merisi da Caravaggio (1573–1610) had no interest in classical conventions of ideal beauty. Instead he concentrated on revealing and concealing truth through skilful contrasts of light and shadow – or *chiaroscuro* – in his *Conversion of St Paul* and the *Crucifixion of St Peter,* both in Rome's Chiesa di Santa Maria del Popolo (p77).

Baroque

The Renaissance's insistence on restraint and pure form led to an exuberant backlash. Baroque religious art served as a kind of spiritual cattle prod, with works by sculptor Gianlorenzo Bernini (1598–1680) simulating religious ecstasy with frantic urgency.

With sculptural flourishes, baroque architecture was well suited to the showplace piazzas of Rome and shimmering reflections in Venice's Grand Canal. But in high-density Naples, the only place to go for baroque was indoors – hence the kaleidoscope of coloured, inlaid marbles inside Naples' Certosa di San Martino.

St Mark's Basilica (p185), Venice

Italian Export Art

By the 18th century, Italy was chafing under foreign domination by Napoleon and Austria. Dependent on foreign admirers, impoverished Italy turned out landscapes for European dandies as 'Grand Tour' souvenirs. The best-known *vedutisti* (landscapists) are Francesco Guardi (1712–93) and Giovanni Antonio Canaletto (1697–1768). Neoclassical sculptor Antonio Canova (1757–1822) took a more daring approach, with a nude sculpture of Napoleon's sister, Pauline Bonaparte Borghese, as a reclining *Venere Vincitrice* (Conquering Venus) in Rome's Museo e Galleria Borghese (p92).

Modern & Contemporary

Stilted by convention and bedraggled by industrialisation, Italy found a creative outlet in European art nouveau, called 'Liberty' in Italian. But some found the style decadent and frivolous. Led by poet Filippo Tommaso Marinetti (1876–1944) and painter Umberto Boccioni (1882–1916), the 1909 *Futurist Manifesto* declared, 'Everything is in movement, everything rushes forward, everything is in constant swift change'. Though the look of futurism was co-opted by fascism, its impulse could not have been more different: fascism was an extreme nostalgia for a heroic Italian empire that wasn't exclusively Italian or heroic. Today, futurism is highlighted at Milan's Museo del Novecento (p122). In the 1960s, radical *Arte Povera* (Poor Art) used simple and found materials to trigger associations, and the impact is still palpable at Turin's Galleria Civica d'arte Moderna e Contemporanea (GAM; p147).

In architecture, on the few midcentury high points is the 1956 Pirelli Tower, designed by architect Giò Ponti and engineer Pier Luigi Nervi. Today, Italian architecture is back on the world stage, ranging from Massimiliano Fuksas' whimsical glass sailboat Fieramilano to Renzo Piano's Turin's Fiat factory creatively repurposed into Slow Food showcase, Eataly.

The Best... Churches

1 St Peter's Basilica (p90), Vatican City

2 Basilica di San Marco (p185), Venice

3 Duomo (p143), Milan

4 Basilica di San Francesco (p263), Assisi

5 Duomo (p226), Florence

The Italian Table

Spaghetti alle Vongole, Naples

JEAN-BERNARD CARILLET/LONELY PLANET IMAGES ©

Let's be honest: you came for the food, right? Wise choice. Just don't go expecting the stock-standards served at your local Italian back home. In reality, Italian cuisine is a handy umbrella term for the country's diverse regional cuisines. Has anything ever tasted this good? Probably not. Will it ever again? Probably tomorrow. Buon appetito.

Regional Cuisine

Italian city-state rivalries once settled with castle sieges and boiling oil poured on enemies are now settled through considerably friendlier culinary competition – though there may still be some boiling oil involved. Visitors in spring may not be allowed to leave Rome without trying *carciofi alla giudía* (Roman artichokes in the Jewish tradition, flattened into a blossom and fried) or Venice without trying *violetti di Sant'Erasmo* (tiny purple artichokes from the lagoon island of Sant' Erasmo, fried or marinated and devoured in a single mouthful). But in this stiff regional competition for gourmet affections, there is a clear winner: travellers, who get to sample regional variations on Italy's seasonal specialty produce, seafood and meats.

Rome

Italy's capitol offers more than just Viagra-strength espresso at Caffè Tazza d'Oro (p102) and glorious gelato (p100). Must-try menu items include thin-crust pizza, *saltimbocca* (veal sautéed with prosciutto and sage) and calorific pasta classics spaghetti carbonara (with bacon, egg and cheese) and *bucatini all'amatriciana* (tube pasta with tomato, *pecorino romano* and *guanciale,* or pigs' cheeks). Rome is the spiritual home of nose-to-tail noshing, where staples like *trippa alla Romana* (tripe with tomato and mint) and *pajata* (a pasta dish of milk-fed calf's intestines in tomato sauce) beckon brave gourmands.

Piedmont to Milan

The Piedmont town of Bra is the home of Slow Food – Italy's artisan food alternative to globalised fast-food – and Turin's Eataly (p150) fills a former Fiat factory with Italy's best artisan specialties. Piedmont's alpine winters are perfect for rich risotto, specialty cheeses, white Alba truffles and warming Barolo red wines. No Piedmont dining extravaganza is complete without coffee roasted to nutty perfection and Turin-made chocolate at Turin's famous cafes. The Ligurian coast south of Turin is famed for pesto and focaccia, best enjoyed with staggering seaside views in the coves of Cinque Terre (p154).

Milan puts meat on supermodels' bones with *risotto alla milanese con ossobucco* (Milanese-style veal shank and marrow with saffron rice) and *bresaola* (air-dried salted beef). Milan's latest culinary trend is *latterie* (milk bars), comfort-food restaurants emphasising cheese, vegetables and simple homemade pasta.

Bologna to Venice

Culinary culture shock may occur between lunch and dinner in the northeast, where you can lunch on Bologna's namesake pasta (*spaghetti bolognese,* with rich beef and pork belly *ragú*) and then dine on Venetian polenta with *sarde in saor* (marinated sardines with onions, pine nuts and sultanas).

Bolognese cuisine stars two world-renowned local products: *parmigiano reggiano* (Parmesan) and aged Modena balsamic vinegar. While bloodlust isn't strictly required in Bologna, carnivores rejoice over meat-stuffed tortellini and cold-cut platters featuring *prosciutto di Parma* (thin-sliced cured ham from Parma), salami, mortadella, *zampone* (trotters) and *coppa,* a surprisingly tasty combo of neck meat and lard cured in brine.

Venice celebrates its lagoon location and spice-trading past in dishes like squid-ink risotto and *granseole* (spider-crab) graced with star anise. Venetian dandies kicked off the European trend for hot chocolate at cafes ringing Piazza San Marco, and you can still enjoy a decadent, gooey cup in baroque splendour at Caffè Florian (p198).

Central Italy

The Tuscans have a special way with meat, herbs and olive oil – think whole boar, pheasant, or rabbit on a spit, or pampered Maremma beef in *spiedino toscano* (mixed grill). Tuscany's celebrity butcher, Dario Cecchini, serves the finest cuts at Chianti's Solociccia (p255). Another must for carnivores is the tender, hulking *bistecca alla fiorentina,* the bone-in steak served in slabs 'three fingers thick' at Florence's Trattoria Mario (p239). Peasant soup (*acquacotta,* literally 'cooked water') becomes a royal feast in the Tuscan town of Lucca, with the addition of farm-fresh eggs, local pecorino, toasted bread and Lucca's prized golden olive oil.

In neighbouring Umbria, locals can be found foraging alongside the local boars for wild asparagus, mushrooms and the legendary black Norcia truffles – grate some atop fresh *tagliatelle* egg pasta to discover one of the most instantly addictive flavours on the planet. Don't miss Perugia's legendary chocolate desserts at Sandri (p260).

Quale Vino? Which Wine?

Not ordering wine with a sit-down lunch or dinner in Italy can cause consternation – are you pregnant or in recovery, or was it something the waiter said? The question isn't whether you're having wine, but which one of Italy's hundreds of specialty wines will best complement the cuisine. When in doubt, keep it local: below are wines to watch for in each region.

○ **Rome & Around** Est! Est!! Est!!! (dry herbal/mineral white)

○ **Venice & Verona** Prosecco (Italy's most popular sparkling white), Amarone (dark, brooding red with velvety tannins), Soave (crisp, minerally white), Tocai (unctuous, fruity/floral white), Valpolicella (versatile, medium-bodied red)

○ **Bologna** Lambrusco (sparkling red)

○ **Milan & Lakes** Franciacorta (Italy's top-quality sparkling white), Bardolino (light, satiny red)

○ **Piedmont & Around** Barolo (Italy's favourite red; elegant and structured), Asti (aka Asti Spumante; sparkling white), Cinque Terre (minerally/grassy white), Gavi (dry, aromatic white), Barbera d'Alba (pleasantly acidic, tomato-friendly red), Dolcetto (light-hearted, aromatic red), Sciacchetrá (Cinque Terre's aromatic dessert wine)

○ **Tuscany** Chianti Classico (big-hearted red, earthy character), Brunello di Montalcino (Italy's biggest, most complex vintage red), Super Tuscan IGT (bombastic, Sangiovese-based reds), Morellino di Scansano (floral, medium-weight red)

○ **Umbria** Orvieto (light, grassy/floral white), Sagrantino di Montefalco secco (dry, oak-barrel-aged Perugian red)

○ **Naples & Amalfi Coast** Falanghina (dry, minerally white)

○ **Sicily** Marsala (sweet fortified wine), Nero d'Avola (volcanic, mineral red)

Naples, Pompeii & the Amalfi Coast

Sun-soaked Mediterranean flavours sparkle in Naples and its coastal turf, where hot capsicums (peppers), citruses and prized San Marzano tomatoes thrive in the volcanic soils that buried Pompeii. Local buffalo-milk mozzarella with basil and tomato sauce piled on pizza dough makes Naples' most famous export: pizza *margherita*. In Naples' Centro Storico (p291), the street food is sublime in the historic *friggitorie* (fast-food kiosks), from *arancini* (mozzarella-filled rice balls) to tempura-style eggplant. Naples was the playground of French conquerors and Spanish royalty, whose influence is savoured in *sfogliatelle* (pastries filled with cinnamon-laced ricotta) and *rum baba,* French rum cake made Neapolitan with Vesuvius-like eruptions of cream.

South of Naples, you'll know you're approaching the Amalfi Coast with a whiff of perfumed Amalfi lemons. The local citrus stars alongside the day's seafood catch and in *limoncello,* Amalfi's sweet lemon digestif.

Sicily & Southern Italy

While past poverty lingers in rustic Pugliese fare like *strascinati con la mollica* (pasta with breadcrumbs and anchovies) and *tiella di verdure* (baked vegetable casserole), ancient Arab influences make Sicily's pasta dishes velvety and complex. Italy's most famous seafood is reason enough to visit Sicily, where wild-caught tuna baked in a salt

crust, local-anchovy-studded *fiori di zucca ripieni* (cheese-stuffed squash blossoms) and *arancini siciliani* (risotto balls) may forever spoil you for lesser versions.

Begin southern food adventures at Catania's La Pescheria (p332), the legendary fish market, and don't skip dessert in Noto (p339), where Sicilian *dolci* (sweets) include local pistachio gelato and sculpted marzipan. Save some room for Puglia, which rivals Lucca for the title of Italy's most satisfying peasant cuisine and takes the prize for Italy's crustiest bread.

Menu Decoder

Tutti a tavola! (Everyone to the table!) Traffic lights are merely suggestions and queues fine ideas in theory, but this is one command every Italian heeds without question. To disobey would be unthinkable – what, you're going to eat your pasta cold? And insult the cook? Even anarchists wouldn't dream of it. You're not obliged to eat three courses – or even two – but here is a rundown of your menu options.

Antipasti (appetiser)

Tantalising offerings on the antipasti menu may include the house *bruschetta* (grilled bread with a variety of toppings, from chopped tomato and garlic to black-truffle spread), seasonal treats like *prosciutto e melone* (cured ham and cantaloupe), and such regional delights as *friarelle con peperoncino* (Neapolitan broccoli with chilli). At this stage, bread (and sometimes *grissini* – Turin-style breadsticks) are deposited on the table as part of your €1 to €4 *pane e coperto* (bread and 'cover', or table service).

Primo (first course)

Starch is the star in Italian first courses, including pasta and gnocchi (especially in south and central Italy) to risotto and polenta (northern Italian specialties). *Primi* menus usually include ostensibly vegetarian or vegan options, such as pasta *con pesto* – the classic northwestern basil pasta with *parmigiano reggiano* (Parmesan) and pine nuts – or *alla norma* (with eggplant and tomato, Sicilian style), or the extravagant *risotto al Barolo* (Piedmont risotto cooked in high-end Barolo wine). But even if a dish sounds vegetarian in theory, ask about the stock used in that risotto or polenta, or the ingredients in that suspiciously rich tomato sauce – there may be beef, ham or ground anchovies involved.

Secondo (second course)

Light lunchers usually call it a day after the *primo,* but *buongustai* (foodies) pace themselves for meat, fish or *contorni* (side dishes) in the second course. Options may range from ambitious meats (especially in Tuscany and Rome) and elegant seafood (notably in Venice and Sicily) to lightly grilled vegetables such as *radicchio di Treviso* (feathery red rocket). A less inspiring option is *insalata mista* (mixed green salad), typically unadorned greens with vinegar and oil on the side – croutons, cheeses, nuts, and other frou-frou ingredients have no business in classic Italian salads.

Frutti e dolci

'*Siamo arrivati alla frutta*' ('We've arrived at the fruit') is an idiom roughly meaning 'we've hit rock bottom' – but hey, not until you've had one last tasty morsel. Imported pineapple has been a trendy choice of late, but your best bets on the fruit menu are local and seasonal. *Formaggi* (cheeses) are an excellent option in Piedmont, but in the south, do the *dolci* (sweets). Think beyond dental-work-endangering *biscotti* (twice-baked biscuits) and consider *zabaglione* (egg and marsala custard), cream-stuffed profiteroles or Sicily's cream-stuffed shell pastries immortalised in *The Godfather:* 'Leave the gun. Take the cannoli.'

Caffè (Coffee)

No amount of willpower or cajoling is going to move your feet into a museum after a proper Italian lunch, so you must administer espresso immediately. Sometimes your barista will allow you a *cappuccino* with a *cioccolatino* (a square of chocolate) or grant you a tiny stain of milk in a *caffè macchiato*. On the hottest days of summer, you may be allowed a *granita di caffè* (coffee with shaved ice and whipped cream). But usually you'll be expected to take espresso as it comes: no milk, no apologies.

The Best... Wine & Cooking Courses

1 **Città del Gusto** (☏ 06 551 11 21; www.gamberorosso.it, in Italian; Via Fermi 161, Rome)

2 **Italian Food Artisans** (www.foodartisans.com/workshops)

3 **International Wine Academy of Roma** (☏ 06 699 08 78; www.wineacademyroma.com; Vicolo del Bottino 8)

4 **Culinary Adventures** (www.peggymarkel.com)

5 **Eataly** (www.eatalytorino.it, in Italian)

Lifestyle

Locals taking coffee standing, Venice

JULIET COOMBE /LONELY PLANET IMAGE

Imagine your own Freaky Friday moment: you wake up and discover you're Italian. Not that it's obvious at first – your pyjamas just have a subtly more elegant cut. But when you open your wardrobe, there's the dead giveaway: the shoes. What might it be like walking in those butter-soft, richly coloured shoes for the day, and what could you discover about Italy?

A Day in the Life of Italy

Sveglia! You're woken not by an alarm but by the burble and clatter of the *caffettiera,* the ubiquitous stovetop espresso maker. If you're between the ages of 18 and 34, there's a 60% chance that's not a roommate making your morning coffee: it's *mamma* or *papá.* This is not because Italy is a nation of pampered *mammoni* (mama's boys) and spoilt *figlie di papá* (daddy's girls) – at least, not entirely. With youth unemployment hitting a record 29% and many university graduates underemployed in short-term contracts, what's the hurry to leave home?

Running late, you bolt down your coffee scalding hot (an acquired Italian talent) and walk blocks out of your way for a morning paper from Bucharest-born Nicolae – your favourite news vendor and (as a Romanian) part of Italy's largest migrant community.

On your way to work you scan the headlines: a postponement of Berlusconi's latest trial, today's match-fixing scandal and new EU regulations on cheese. Outrageous! The cheese regulations, that is; the rest is to be expected. At work, you're buried in paperwork until noon, when it's a relief to join friends for lunch and a glass of wine.

Afterwards you toss back another scorching espresso at your favourite bar, and find out how your barista's latest audition went – turns out you went to school with the sister of the director of the play, so you promise to put in a good word. This isn't just a nice gesture, but an essential career boost. As a Ministry of Labour study recently revealed, most people in Italy still find employment through personal connections. About 30% of Italians have landed a job through family connections, and in highly paid professions, that number rises as high as 40% to 50%. In Europe's most ancient, entrenched bureaucracy, social networks are also essential to get things done: on average, Italians spend the equivalent of two weeks annually on bureaucratic procedures required of working Italian citizens.

Back at work by 2pm, you multitask Italian-style, chatting with co-workers as you dash off work emails, text your schoolmate about the barista on your *telefonino* (mobile phone), and surreptitiously check *l'Internet* for employment listings – your work contract will expire soon. After a busy day like this, *aperitivi* are definitely in order, so at 6.30pm you head directly to the latest happy-hour hot spot. The decor is very stylish, the vibe very cool and the DJ extra hot, until suddenly it's time for your English class – everyone's learning it these days, if only for the slang.

The Best... Books about Italians, by Italians

1 **The Italians**
(Luigi Barzini)

2 **History of the Italian People**
(Giuliano Procacci)

3 **La Bella Figura: A Field Guide to the Italian Mind**
(Beppe Severgnini)

The People

Who are the people you'd encounter every day as an Italian? On average, about half your co-workers will be women – quite a change from 10 years ago, when women represented just a quarter of the workforce. But a growing proportion of the people you'll meet are already retired: one out of five Italians is over 65. You might also notice a striking absence of children. Italy's birth rate is the lowest in Europe, at just under one child per woman.

Like Nicolae the news vendor, 7.1% of Italy's population today are immigrants. Though this is a relatively small number in global terms, it's a reversal of a historical trend: from 1876 to 1976, Italy was a country of net emigration. With some 30 million Italian emigrants dispersed throughout Europe, the Americas and Australia, remittances from Italians abroad helped keep Italy's economy afloat after Independence and WWII.

Political and economic upheavals in the 1980s brought new arrivals to Italy from Central Europe, Latin America and North Africa – including Italy's former colonies in Tunisia, Somalia and Ethiopia – while recent arrivals hail from the Philippines, China and Bangladesh. These new arrivals are vital for the country's economic health. Fewer Italians are entering blue-collar agricultural and industrial fields, so without immigrant workers to fill the gaps, Italy would be sorely lacking in tomato sauce and shoes.

By filling low-paid service positions like restaurant dishwashers and hotel maids, immigrants also keep Italy's vital tourism economy afloat.

But not all Italians are putting out their welcome mats. In 2008, a young Jewish-Romanian immigrant was beaten to death by neo-Nazi groups in Verona, and two Roma camps in Naples were torched by neo-Nazi gangs allegedly tied to Naples' Camorra crime syndicate. In 2010, the shooting of an immigrant worker in Rosarno, Calabria, sparked Italy's worst race riots in years.

Yet not all Italians are willing to let extremists have the last word. In May 2009, a radical law to punish undocumented immigrants – including potential refugees – with summary deportation and fines was denounced by Italian human rights groups, the Vatican and the UN, and caused mass protests in Rome. As writer Claudio Magris observed in *The Times,* recalling Italy's recent past as a nation of emigrants, 'We, above all, should know what it is like to be strangers in a strange land'.

Religion, Loosely Speaking

Although you read about the Church in the news headlines, you didn't actually attend Mass on your day as an Italian. According to a 2007 Church study, only 15% of Italy's population regularly attends Sunday mass – yet when Pope John Paul II died in April 2005, four million mourners poured into Rome in one week. In 2009, an Umbrian teacher's suspension for removing the crucifix from his public classroom sparked arguments over the appropriate division of church and state in Italy.

The Church remains a cultural force, from the relief work of Caritas (Catholic charity) to boisterous celebrations of Christmas and Easter – no generic 'happy holidays' wishes here – plus myriad festivals organised around patron saints. Every year in Naples, thousands cram into the Duomo to witness the ancient blood of San

Inter Milan football fans, Piazza del Duomo, Milan

Italian Women Say *Basta!*

On 13 February 2011, nearly one million Italian women took to the streets of 230 Italian cities, carrying signs with an unequivocal message: *Basta!* (Enough!) Sparked by allegations that Prime Minister Silvio Berlusconi had held sex parties with an underage dancer, they not only demanded his dismissal, but also an end to representation of women on Berlusconi-backed Italian media as hovering mothers or vapid *veline* (showgirls).

Unlike their popular image in Italian media, Italian women are notably accomplished. They represent 65% of college graduates, are more likely than men to pursue higher education (53% to 45%), and twice as likely to land responsible positions in public service. Yet the World Economic Forum's 2010 Global Gender Gap Report ranked Italy 121st in wage parity and 74th overall for its treatment of women.

The situation isn't necessarily better at home: a 2010 survey by the Organisation of Economic Co-Operation and Development (OECD) found that Italian men enjoy almost 80 more minutes of leisure time daily than their female counterparts. Despite the indulgent mamma stereotype, not all Italian women relish the extra housework. According to official statistics, Italian women aged 29 to 34 are increasingly choosing careers and a home life without children. When Italian women take time out of their demanding schedules to say *basta!*, believe it.

Gennaro miraculously liquefy in the crystal vial that contains it. When the blood turns from powdery to watery, the city breathes a sigh of relief – it symbolises another year safe from disaster. When it didn't in 1944, Mt Vesuvius erupted. Coincidence? Perhaps. But even the most cynical Neapolitan would rather see San Gennaro's blood wet than dry... just in case.

Italy's Other Religion: *Calcio*

As an Italian, your true religion is likely to be *calcio* (soccer, aka English football). In the late 19th century, English factory barons of Turin, Genoa and Milan established teams to keep their workers fit – though during World Cups, UK supporters may wish they'd never shown the Italians how it's done. Not that it's always a fair fight: according to French forward Zinedine Zidane, Italian opponent Marco Materazzi insulted the womenfolk of his family during the 2006 World Cup finals. Zidane was red-carded for violently defending his family honour; Italy won the Cup. The same year, match-fixing 'Calciopoli' scandals resulted in revoked championship titles and temporary demotion of Serie A (top-tier national) teams, including the mighty Juventus.

Scandals and all, Italians have an almost literal romance with their national sport. Rita Pavone's song *La partita di pallone* (The football match) topped the charts in the 1960s with a refrain that resonated nationwide: '*Perchè, perchè la domenica mi lasci sempre sola per andare a vedere la partita di pallone?*' (Why, why do you always leave me alone on Sunday so you can go and watch the football match?). Nine months after Italy's 2006 World Cup victory against France, hospitals in northern Italy reported a baby boom.

Outdoor Experiences

Aosta (p154), Piedmont

GARETH MCCORMACK/LONELY PLANET IMAGE

Naturally blessed with rolling hills, mountain peaks, volcanic lakes and 7600km of coastline, Italy offers much more than Roman ruins and Renaissance art. Adrenaline spikes come with stirring views here: there's swimming and windsurfing in the Lakes, mountain biking and skiing in the Dolomites, and volcano summits and scuba-diving in Sicily. Less daunting, Tuscany's rolling landscapes offer scenic cycling between vineyards, and Capri and the Amalfi Coast offer blissful snorkelling.

Hiking & Walking

Thousands of kilometres of *sentieri* (marked trails) criss-cross the peninsula, from mountain treks to lakeside ambles. For coastal hikes with varied challenge levels and sweeping views, don't miss Cinque Terre (p154). Most people may think of Capri (p300) and Ischia (p304) as summer playgrounds, but they both offer fantastic walking trails away from beach crowds. The Amalfi Coast (p304) is laced with age-old paths winding through wooded mountains and ancient olive groves.

The prime volcano hike is Sicily's Mt Etna (p334), but on the Sicilian Aeolian Island of Vulcano (p330), you can descend to an extinct volcano's crater floor. The jagged peaks of Veneto's Dolomites provide superb walking end of June to September, and trails are lined with wildflowers in spring – no wonder Unesco declared this unique mountain ecosystem a Heritage site in 2009.

Tourist offices and visitor centres provide some information resources and basic maps for easier tourist routes. For longer hikes and climbing information on the Dolomites, consult **Club Alpino Italiano** (CAI; www.cai.it).

Cycling

Whether you want a gentle ride between trattorias, a 100km road race or a teeth-rattling mountain descent, you'll find a route to suit in Italy. Tourist offices can provide details on trails and guided rides, and Lonely Planet's *Cycling Italy* is handy.

Tuscany's famously rolling countryside is a favourite with cyclists, particularly the wine-producing Chianti area south of Florence. Further north, Piedmont's terraced vineyards of Barolo are also ideal for pedal-powered wine-tasting. Puglia's rolling countryside and coastal paths make moderate challenges, while the Dolomites are a prime spot for summer mountain-biking.

Diving

Diving is one of Italy's most popular summer pursuits, and there are hundreds of schools that offer a wide range courses, dives for all levels, and equipment for hire. Most diving schools open seasonally from June to October – but try to avoid August, when the Italian coast is swamped with visitors and prices are inflated. Information is available from the local tourist offices and online at **DiveItaly** (www.diveitaly.com, in Italian).

Prime Italian diving destinations include Sicily's Aeolian Islands (p330), with warm waters and sea grottoes around inactive volcanoes. In the Bay of Naples, Capri (p300), Ischia (p304) and Procida (p304) offer exceptional diving and underwater photo ops in glowing sea grottoes. To the north, Cinque Terre Marine Reserve teems with life around ancient pirate's coves.

The Best... Cycling Destinations

1 Chianti (p255)

2 Appian Way (p91)

3 Lucca (p247)

4 Barolo (p152)

5 Bologna (p207)

Winter Hotspots

Most of Italy's top ski resorts are in the northern Alps. Facilities at the bigger centres in the Dolomites and around Aosta are generally world-class, with pistes ranging from nursery slopes to tough black runs. The ski season runs from December to late March, although there is year-round skiing on Mont Blanc (Monte Bianco) and the Matterhorn in the Valle d'Aosta.

Fashion & Design

Prada (p136), Milan

Prada (p136), Milan

RICHARD I'ANSON/LONELY PLANET IMAGE

Better living by design: what could be more Italian? Though the country could get by on its striking good looks, Italy is ever-mindful of design details. They are everywhere you look, and many places you don't: the acid-yellow silk lining inside a sober grey suit sleeve, the glove compartment of a newly reissued Fiat 500 car, the toy duck hidden inside your chocolate uova di pasqua (Easter egg).

Italian Fashion

Italians have strong opinions about aesthetics and aren't afraid to share them. A common refrain is *Che brutta!* (How hideous!), which may strike visitors as tactless. But consider it from an Italian point of view – everyone is rooting for you to look good, and who are you to disappoint? The shop assistant who tells you with brutal honesty that yellow is not your colour is doing a public service, and will consider it a personal triumph to see you outfitted in orange instead. After all, Italy's centuries-old reputation for style is at stake.

Trend-setters and Fashion Victims

Italians have been style trend-setters since the Middle Ages, when Venetian merchants imported dyes and silks from the East and Florence's wool guild rose to political prominence and funded a Renaissance. Clothes became markers of social status, and not only nobles set trends: courtesans and trophy wives were so widely imitated that sumptuary laws were passed restricting low necklines and growing train lengths. Italy's local fashions went global through the dissemination of Florentine art and illustrated pamphlets from Venice's publishing houses – predecessors of billboards and Italian *Vogue*. The Venetian innovation of eyeglasses was initially mocked by monocle-sporting English dandies, who eventually saw the light – and their descendants now pay impressive sums for Italian designer sunglasses.

Italy has also had its share of fashion victims over the centuries. After political crusader Savonarola demanded Florentines surrender their extravagant statement jewellery under pain of flagellation, he was burned at the stake. So many Venetian noblewomen were hobbled emulating courtesans in their staggering platform heels that 1430 sumptuary laws set maximum shoe heights of around 2ft. Siena was more practical, requiring its prostitutes to wear flat shoes. Today, staggering platforms and chic flats still make the rounds of Milan runways.

**The Best...
Italian
Design Icons**

1 Bialetti cafeteria

2 Cinzano vermouth

3 Acqua di Parma cologne

4 Piaggio Vespa

5 Olivetti 'Valentine' typewriter

IN FOCUS FASHION & DESIGN

Italy's Fashion Powerhouses

Cobblers and tailors in Florence who once made only made-to-measure designs began to present seasonal lines in the 1950s to '60s, launching the empires of psychedelic-print maestro Emilio Pucci, logoed leather-goods magnate Guccio Gucci and shoe maven Salvatore Ferragamo. But Milan literally stole the show from Florence in 1958, hosting Italy's first Fashion Week. With its ready factories, cosmopolitan workforce and long-established media, Milan created ready-to-wear fashion for global markets from Armani, Missoni, Versace, Dolce & Gabbana and Prada. Rome remains Italy's political capitol and the home of Valentino and his signature red dress, but Milan was Italy's top (and the world's fourth-biggest) fashion exporter in 2011.

Today, Italian fashionistas are combining mass fashion with artisan-made style signatures. This trend is recession-friendly: artisan-made items are made to last and singular, hence less trend-sensitive. Fashion-forward artisan hotspots include Florence (cobblers, jewellers), Naples (tailors) and Venice (eyewear, fashion, accessories).

Bargain Fashion

Never mind the recession: Italians still rock Missoni knitwear, Fendi bags, Prada shoes and Gucci shades. Their fashion secret: annual *saldi* (sales) in January and July, offering 30% to 50% discounts. Year-round, Italians hit up discount outlets in Milan (see p136) and outdoor markets such as Rome's Porta Portese (p104) and Naples' Mercato Nolano (p291) for factory seconds and vintage finds.

Modern Italian Design

During centuries of domination by Napoleon and other foreign powers, Italy ceded ground as global tastemaker to French and Austrian art nouveau and English arts and crafts – until the industrial era. Italian futurism inspired radical, neoclassical streamlining more suited to Italian manufacturers than French decorators or English craftspeople. The dynamic deco style of futurist paintings was co-opted in fascist propaganda posters, architecture, furniture and design, like cogs in a political machine.

The rise of fascism required modern factories for the war industry, and after WWII, repurposed military industrial complexes in Turin and Milan became centrepieces of a new global, consumer-centric economy. Turin's strength was industrial design, from Lavazza espresso machines to the Fiat 500 car; Milan focused on fashion and home decor. As seen in Italian film and pioneering Italian lifestyle magazines like *Domus*, Italy's mass-produced design objects seemed both aspirational and attainable.

Design Showcases

Though Italian design is distributed globally, seeing it in its home context offers fresh appreciation – and critical perspective. While the Vatican Museums showcase pre-20th-century objects of power – from saints' reliquaries to papal thrones – Milan's Triennale Museum (p132) focuses on 20th-century secular talismans, including mid-century Vespas to 1980s Memphis Group chairs. Like churches, Italian designer showcases are carefully curated to offer beauty and belonging, from the 1950s Scarpa-designed Olivetti showroom in Venice's Piazza San Marco (p171) to Alessi's new flagship store in Milan (p132) – but this fully branded lifestyle can seem impersonal. Milan's Salone del Mobile is the world's largest design fair, with 2500 companies represented – yet differences in corporate design can seem slight, and easily outshone by 700 independent designers in the satellite fair (p113).

Survival
Guide

Gelati, Naples
JEAN-BERNARD CARILLET/LONELY PLANET IMAGES ©

Directory

Accommodation

Accommodation in Italy can range from the sublime to the ridiculous, with prices to match. Hotels and *pensioni* (guesthouses) make up the bulk of the offerings, while other options include charming B&B-style places, villa and apartment rentals, and *agriturismi* (farmhouse accommodation). Some *agriturismi* are working farms, others converted farmhouses (often with a pool).

For reservations, hotels usually require confirmation by fax or, more commonly, a credit-card number. In the latter case, if you don't show you will be docked a night's accommodation.

RATES

Prices can fluctuate enormously depending on the season, with Easter, summer and the Christmas-New Year period typical peak tourist times. There are many variables. Expect to pay top prices in the mountains during the ski season (December to March). Summer is high season on the coast, but in the parched cities can be low season. In August especially, many city hotels charge as little as half price.

In this book a range of prices is quoted from low to high season; these are intended as a guide only. Half-board equals breakfast and either lunch or dinner; full board includes breakfast, lunch and dinner.

Accommodation in this book is listed according to three price categories, as follows:

CATEGORY	SYMBOL	PRICE RANGE
budget	€	under €100
midrange	€€	€100-200
top end	€€€	over €200

AGRITURISMI

Holidays on working farms, or *agriturismi*, are popular with travellers and property owners looking for extra revenue. Accommodation can range from simple, rustic affairs to luxury locations where little actual farming is done and the swimming pool sparkles. *Agriturismo* business has boomed in Tus-

cany and Umbria, but is gaining ground in other regions too.

Local tourist offices can usually supply lists of operators. For detailed information on *agriturismo* facilities throughout Italy check out **Agriturist** (www.agriturist.com) and **Agriturismo.com** (www.agriturismo.com). Other sites include **Network Agriturismo Italia 2005** (www.agriturismo-italia2005.com), which in spite of its name is updated annually, **Agriturismo-Italia.Net** (www.agriturismo-italia.net), **Agriturismoitalia.com** (www.agriturismoitalia.com) and **Agriturismo Vero** (www.agriturismovero.com).

B&BS

B&B options include everything from restored farmhouses, city *palazzi* and seaside bungalows to rooms in family houses. Tariffs per person cover a wide range from around €25 to €75. For more information, contact **Bed & Breakfast Italia** (☎ 06 687 86 18; www.bbitalia.it; Corso Vittorio Emanuele II 282, 00186).

CONVENTS & MONASTERIES

Some convents and monasteries let out cells or rooms as a modest revenue-making exercise and happily take in tourists, while others are single-sex and only take in pilgrims or people who are on a spiritual retreat. Convents and monasteries generally impose a fairly early curfew. Charges hover around €40/75/100 for a single/double/triple, although some charge more like €05/100 for singles/doubles

As a starting point, take a look at the website of the **Chiesa di Santa Susana** (www.santasusanna.org/coming torome/convents.html) and www.monasterystays.com.

HOTELS & PENSIONI

There is often little difference between a *pensione* and an *albergo* (hotel). However, a *pensione* will generally be of one- to three-star quality and traditionally it has been a family-run operation, while an *albergo* can be awarded up to five stars. *Locande* (inns) long fell into much the same category as *pensioni,* but the term has become a trendy one in some parts and reveals little about the quality of a place. *Affittacamere* are rooms for rent in private houses. They are generally simple affairs.

One-star hotels/*pensioni* tend to be basic and usually do not offer private bathrooms. Two-star places are similar but rooms will generally have a private bathroom. At three-star joints you can usually assume reasonable standards. Four- and five-star hotels offer facilities such as room service, laundry and dry-cleaning.

Prices are highest in major tourist destinations. They also tend to be higher in northern Italy. A *camera singola* (single room) costs from €25. A *camera doppia* (twin beds) or *camera matrimoniale* (double room with a double bed) will cost from around €40.

Tourist offices usually have booklets with local accommodation listings. Many hotels are also signing up with (steadily proliferating) online accommodation-booking services. You could start your search here:

Practicalities

o Use the metric system for weights and measures.

o Since 2005, smoking in closed public spaces (from bars to elevators, offices to trains) has been banned.

o If your Italian is up to it, try *Corriere della Sera,* the country's leading daily; *Il Messaggero,* a popular Rome-based broadsheet; or *La Repubblica,* a centre-left daily with a flow of Mafia conspiracies and Vatican scoops. For the Church's view, try the *Osservatore Romano*.

o Tune into Vatican Radio (www.radiovaticana.org; 93.3 FM and 105 FM in the Rome area) for a run-down on what the pope is up to (in Italian, English and other languages); or state-owned Italian RAI-1, RAI-2 and RAI-3 (www.rai. it), which broadcast all over the country and abroad. Commercial stations such as Rome's Radio Centro Suono (www.centrosuono.com) and Radio Città Futura (www.radiocittafutura.it), Naples' Radio Kiss Kiss (www. kisskissnapoli.it) and Milan-based left-wing Radio Popolare (www.radiopopolare.it) are all good for contemporary music.

o Switch on the box to watch the state-run RAI-1, RAI-2 and RAI-3 (www.rai.it) and the main commercial stations (mostly run by Silvio Berlusconi's Mediaset company): Canale 5 (www.canale5.mediaset.it), Italia 1 (www.italia1.mediaset.it) and Rete 4 (www.rete4.mediaset.it) and La 7 (www.la7.it).

Alberghi in Italia (www.alberghi-in-italia.it)

All Hotels in Italy (www.hotelsitalyonline.com)

Hotels web.it (www.hotelsweb.it)

In Italia (www.initalia.it)

Travel to Italy (www.travel-to-italy.com)

VILLA RENTALS

Cuendet (www5.cuendet.com) An old hand in this business; operates from the heart of Siena province in Tuscany.

Ilios Travel (www.iliostravel. com) UK-based company with villas, apartments and castles in Venice, Tuscany, Umbria, Lazio, Le Marche, Abruzzo and Sardinia.

Invitation to Tuscany (www. invitationtotuscany.com) A wide range of properties across Tuscany, Umbria and Liguria.

Long Travel (www.long-travel. co.uk) From Lazio and Abruzzo south, including Sardinia.

Simpson (www.simpson-travel. com) Concentrates on Tuscany, Umbria, the Amalfi coast and Sicily. Also has properties in Rome, Florence and Venice.

Think Sicily (www.thinksicily. com) Strictly Sicilian properties.

385

Climate

In the Alps, temperatures are lower and winters can be long and severe. The Alps shield northern Lombardy and the Lakes area, including Milan, from the extremes of the northern European winter.

Venice can be hot and humid in summer and, although not too cold in winter, it can be unpleasant if wet or when the sea level rises and *acque alte* (literally 'high waters') inundate the city. This is most likely in November and December.

In Florence, encircled by hills, the weather can be quite extreme, but as you travel towards the tip of the boot, temperatures and weather conditions become milder. Rome has an average July and August temperature in the mid-20s (Celsius), although the impact of the sirocco (a hot, humid wind blowing from Africa) can produce stiflingly hot weather in August, with temperatures in the high 30s for days on end. Winters are moderate and snow is rare in Rome, although winter clothing (or at least a heavy overcoat) is still a requirement.

The south of Italy and the islands of Sicily have a Mediterranean climate. Summers are long, hot and dry, and winter temperatures tend to be relatively moderate, with daytime averages not too far below 10°C.

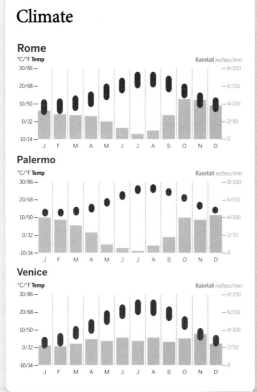

Climate

Rome

°C/°F **Temp**   Rainfall inches/mm

Palermo

°C/°F **Temp**   Rainfall inches/mm

Venice

°C/°F **Temp**   Rainfall inches/mm

Customs Regulations

Duty-free sales within the EU no longer exist (but goods are sold tax-free in European airports). Visitors coming into Italy from non-EU countries can import, duty free: 1L of spirits (or 2L wine), 50g perfume, 250mL eau de toilette, 200 cigarettes and other goods up to a total of €175; anything over this limit must be declared on arrival and the appropriate duty paid. On leaving the EU, non-EU citizens can reclaim any Value Added Tax (VAT) on expensive purchases.

Discount Cards

At museums and galleries, never hesitate to enquire after discounts for students, young people, children, families or the elderly. When sightseeing and wherever possible buy a *biglietto cumulativo*, a ticket that allows admission to a number of associated sights for less than the combined cost of separate admission fees.

SENIOR CARDS

Admission to most museums in Rome is free for over-60s but in other cities (such as Florence) often no concessions are made for nonresidents. In numerous places, EU seniors have free entry to sights, sometimes only on certain days. Always ask.

STUDENT & YOUTH CARDS

Free admission to some galleries and sites is available to under-18s.

Electricity

Italy uses plugs with two or three round pins. The current is 220V to 230V, 50Hz; older buildings may still use 125V.

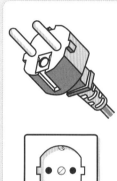

230V/50Hz

230V/50Hz

Food

A meal as defined in this book includes a *primo* (first course), a *secondo* (second course), house wine and a dessert. Budget categories are as follows:

CATEGORY	SYMBOL	PRICE RANGE
budget	€	under €25
midrange	€€	€25-45
top end	€€€	over €45

Most eating establishments have a cover charge (called *pane e coperto;* usually around €1 to €4) and *servizio* (service charge) of 10% to 15%.

Gay & Lesbian Travellers

Homosexuality is legal in Italy and well tolerated in the major cities. However, overt displays of affection by homosexual couples could attract a negative response in the more conservative south, and smaller towns. .

The useful website **Gay. it** (www.gay.it, in Italian) lists gay bars and hotels across the country. **Arcigay & Arcilesbica** (☑ 051 649 30 55; www.arcigay.it; Via Don Minzoni 18, Bologna) is a worthy national organisation for gay men and lesbians.

Check out the English-language **GayFriendlyItalia. com** (www.gayfriendlyitaly. com), which is produced by Gay.it. It has information on everything from hotels to homophobia issues and the law.

Health
BEFORE YOU GO

While Italy has reasonable health care (although public hospitals tend to be less impressive the further south you travel), prevention is the key to staying healthy while abroad. Bring medications in their original, clearly labelled containers. A signed and dated letter from your physician describing your medical conditions and medication, including generic names, is also a good idea. If carrying syringes or needles, be sure to have a physician's letter documenting their medical necessity.

Insurance

If you're an EU citizen (or from Switzerland, Norway or Iceland), a European Health Insurance Card (EHIC) covers you for most medical care in public hospitals free of charge, but not for emergency repatriation home or non-emergencies. Citizens from other countries should find out if there is a reciprocal arrangement for free medical care between their country and Italy (Australia, for instance, has such an agreement; carry your Medicare card).

If you do need health insurance, make sure you get a policy that covers you for the worst possible scenario, such as an accident requiring an emergency flight home. Find out in advance if your insurance plan will make payments directly to providers or reimburse you later for overseas health expenditures.

Recommended Vaccinations

No jabs are required to travel to Italy. The World Health Organization (WHO), however, recommends that all travellers should be covered for diphtheria, tetanus, the measles, mumps, rubella and polio, as well as hepatitis B. Lonely Planet's *Travel with Children* includes travel health advice for younger children.

IN ITALY

Availability of Health Care

If you need an ambulance anywhere in Italy, call 118. For emergency treatment, head straight to the *pronto soccorso* (casualty) section of a public hospital, where you can also get emergency dental treatment. Pharmacists can give you valuable advice and sell over-the-counter medication for minor illnesses. Condoms are readily available but emergency contraception is not, so take the necessary precautions.

Bites, Stings & Insect-Borne Diseases

Italian beaches are occasionally inundated with jellyfish. Their stings are painful but not dangerous. Dousing in vinegar will deactivate any stingers that have not fired. In coastal areas with sandflies, avoid sandfly bites by covering up and using repellent.

Italy's only dangerous snake, the viper, is found throughout the country except on Sardinia. To minimise the possibilities of being bitten, always wear boots, socks and long trousers when walking through undergrowth where snakes may be present. Don't put your hands into holes or crevices, and be careful when collecting firewood. If bitten, seek medical help, if possible with the dead snake for identification.

Always check all over your body if you have been walking through a potentially tick-infested area, as ticks can cause skin infections and other more serious diseases such as Lyme disease and tick-borne encephalitis. If a tick is found attached, press down around the tick's head with tweezers, grab the head and gently pull upwards.

Insurance

A travel-insurance policy to cover theft, loss and medical problems is a good idea. It may also cover you for cancellation or delays to your travel arrangements. Paying for your ticket with a credit card can often provide limited travel accident insurance and you may be able to reclaim the payment if the operator doesn't deliver. Ask your credit-card company what it will cover.

For information on health insurance, see p387.

Internet Access

Throughout this guide we use the @ icon to indicate venues that offer an internet terminal (physical computer) for guests' use, and the ⓦ icon to designate places with a wi-fi network.

Internet access in Italy has improved markedly in the past couple of years, with Rome, Bologna, Venice and other municipalities instituting city-wide hotspots, and an increasing number of hotels, B&Bs, hostels and even *agriturismi* now offering free wi-fi. On the downside, internet cafes remain thinner on the ground than elsewhere in Europe, signal strength is variable, and access is not yet as widespread in rural and southern Italy as in urban and northern areas. You'll still have to pay for access at many top-end hotels (upwards of €10 per day) and at internet cafes (€2 to €6 per hour).

If you plan to carry your computer with you, carry a universal AC adaptor for your appliance (most are sold with these).

Certain provisions of Italy's antiterrorism law, which required all internet users to present a photo ID and allowed the government to monitor internet usage, were rescinded in January 2011, but internet cafes will still sometimes request identification before allowing you to use their facilities.

Legal Matters

The average tourist will only have a brush with the law if robbed by a bag-snatcher or pickpocket.

ALCOHOL & DRUGS

Those caught in possession of 5g of cannabis can be considered traffickers and prosecuted as such. The legal limit for blood-alcohol level is 0.05% and random breath tests do occur. The same applies to tiny amounts of other drugs. Those caught with amounts below this threshold can be subject to minor penalties.

POLICE

If you run into trouble in Italy, you are likely to end up dealing with the *polizia statale* (state police) or the *carabinieri* (military police).

The *polizia* deal with thefts, visa extensions and permits (among other things). They wear powder blue trousers with a fuchsia stripe and a navy blue jacket.

The *carabinieri* deal with general crime, public order and drug enforcement (often overlapping with the *polizia*). They wear a black uniform with a red stripe and drive light blue cars with a red stripe.

Other police include the *vigili urbani,* basically local traffic police. You will have to deal with them if you get a parking ticket or your car is towed away.

YOUR RIGHTS

Italy still has antiterrorism laws on its books that could make life difficult if you are detained. You should be given verbal and written notice of the charges laid against you within 24 hours by arresting officers. You have no right to a phone call upon arrest. The prosecutor must apply to a magistrate for you to be held in preventive custody awaiting trial (depending on the seriousness of the offence) within 48 hours of arrest. You have the right not to respond to questions without the presence of a lawyer. If the magistrate orders preventive custody, you have the right to then contest this within the following 10 days.

●●●

Money

The euro is Italy's currency. The seven euro notes come in denominations of €500, €200, €100, €50, €20, €10 and €5. The eight euro coins are in denominations of €2 and €1, and 50, 20, 10, five, two and one cents.

Exchange rates are given on the inside front cover of this book. For the latest rates, check out www.xe.com.

CASH

There is little advantage in bringing foreign cash into Italy. True, exchange commissions are often lower than for travellers cheques, but the danger of losing the lot far outweighs such gains.

CREDIT & DEBIT CARDS

Bancomats (ATM machines) are widely available throughout Italy and are the best way to obtain local currency. International credit and debit cards can be used in any Bancomat displaying the appropriate sign. Visa and MasterCard are among the most widely recognised, but others like Cirrus and Maestro are also well covered. Only some banks give cash advances over the counter, so you're better off using ATMs. Cards are also good for payment in most hotels, restaurants, shops, supermarkets and tollbooths.

Check any charges with your bank. Most banks now build a fee of around 2.75% into every foreign transaction. In addition, ATM withdrawals can attract a further fee, usually around 1.5%.

If your card is lost, stolen or swallowed by an ATM, you can telephone toll free to have an immediate stop put on its use:

Amex (☎ 06 7290 0347 or your national call number)

Diners Club (☎ 800 864064)

MasterCard (☎ 800 870866)

Visa (☎ 800 819014)

MONEYCHANGERS

You can change money in banks, at the post office or in a *cambio* (exchange office). Post offices and banks tend to offer the best rates; exchange offices keep longer hours, but watch for high commissions and inferior rates.

TAXES & REFUNDS

A value-added tax of around 20%, known as IVA (Imposta di Valore Aggiunto), is slapped onto just about everything in Italy. If you are a non-EU resident and spend more than €155 (€154.94 to be more precise!) on a purchase, you can claim a refund when you leave. The refund only applies to purchases from affiliated retail outlets that display a 'tax free for tourists' (or similar) sign. You have to complete a form at the point of sale, then have it stamped by Italian customs as you leave. At major airports you can then get an immediate cash refund; otherwise it will be refunded to your credit card. For information, visit **Tax Refund for Tourists** (www.taxrefund.it) or pick up a pamphlet on the scheme from participating stores.

TIPPING

You are not expected to tip on top of restaurant service charges but you can leave a little extra if you feel service warrants it. If there is no service charge, the customer should consider leaving a 10% tip, but this is not obligatory. In bars, Italians often leave small change as a tip (as little as €0.10). Tipping taxi drivers is not common practice, but you are expected to tip the porter at top-end hotels.

TRAVELLERS CHEQUES

Visa, Travelex and Amex are widely accepted brands. Get most of your cheques in fairly large denominations to save on per-cheque commission charges. Amex exchange offices do not charge commission to exchange travellers cheques. Take along your passport as identification when you go to cash travellers cheques.

Phone numbers to report lost or stolen cheques:

Amex (☎ 800 914912)

MasterCard (☎ 800 872050)

Visa (☎ 800 874155)

Public Holidays

Most Italians take their annual holiday in August, with the busiest period occurring around August 15, known locally as Ferragosto. This means that many businesses and shops close for at least a part of that month. Settimana Santa (Easter week) is another busy holiday period for Italians.

Individual towns have public holidays to celebrate the feasts of their patron saints. National public holidays include the following:

New Year's Day (Capodanno or Anno Nuovo) 1 January

Epiphany (Epifania or Befana) 6 January

Easter Monday (Pasquetta or Lunedì dell'Angelo) March/April

Liberation Day (Giorno della Liberazione) On 25 April – marks the Allied Victory in Italy, and the end of the German presence and Mussolini, in 1945.

Labour Day (Festa del Lavoro) 1 May

Republic Day (Festa della Repubblica) 2 June

Feast of the Assumption (Assunzione or Ferragosto) 15 August

All Saints' Day (Ognissanti) 1 November

Feast of the Immaculate Conception (Immaculata Concezione) 8 December

Christmas Day (Natale) 25 December

Boxing Day (Festa di Santo Stefano) 26 December

Telephone

DOMESTIC CALLS

Italian telephone area codes all begin with ☎ 0 and consist of up to four digits. The area code is followed by a number of anything from four to eight digits. The area code is an integral part of the telephone number and must always be dialled, even when calling from next door. Mobile-phone numbers begin with a three-digit prefix such as 330. Toll-free (free-phone) numbers are known as *numeri verdi* and usually start with 800. Nongeographical numbers start with 840, 841, 848, 892, 899, 163, 166 or 199. Some six-digit national-rate numbers are also in use (such as those for Alitalia, rail and postal information).

As elsewhere in Europe, Italians choose from a host of providers of phone plans and rates, making it difficult to make generalisations about costs.

INTERNATIONAL CALLS

The cheapest options for calling internationally are free or low-cost computer programs such as Skype, cut-rate call centres or international calling cards, which are sold at newsstands and tobacconists. Cut-price call centres can be found in all of the main cities, and rates can be considerably lower than from Telecom payphones for international calls. You simply place your call from a private booth inside the centre and pay for it when you've finished. Direct international calls can also easily be made from public telephones with a phonecard. Dial ☎00 to get out of Italy, then the relevant country and area codes, followed by the telephone number.

To call Italy from abroad, call the international access number (☎011 in the United States, ☎00 from most other countries), Italy's country code (☎39) and then the area code of the location you want, including the leading ☎0.

DIRECTORY ENQUIRIES

National and international phone numbers can be requested at ☎1254 (or online at 1254.virgilio.it).

MOBILE/CELL PHONES

Italy uses GSM 900/1800, which is compatible with the rest of Europe and Australia but not with North American GSM 1900 or the totally different Japanese system (though some GSM 1900/900 phones do work here). If you have a GSM phone, check with your service provider about using it in Italy and beware of calls being routed internationally (very expensive for a 'local' call).

Italy has one of the highest levels of mobile-phone penetration in Europe, and you can get a temporary or prepaid account from several companies if you already own a GSM, dual- or tri-band cellular phone. You will usually need your passport to open an account. Always check with your mobile-

service provider in your home country to ascertain whether your handset allows use of another SIM card. If it does, it can cost as little as €10 to activate a local prepaid SIM card (sometimes with €10 worth of calls on the card). Alternatively, you can buy or lease an inexpensive Italian phone for the duration of your trip.

Of the main mobile phone companies, TIM (Telecom Italia Mobile), Wind and Vodafone have the densest networks of outlets across the country.

PAYPHONES & PHONECARDS

Partly privatised Telecom Italia is the largest telecommunications organisation in Italy. Where Telecom offices are staffed, it is possible to make international calls and pay at the desk afterwards. Alternatively, you'll find Telecom payphones throughout the country, on the streets, in train stations and in Telecom offices. Most payphones accept only *carte/schede telefoniche* (phonecards), although some also accept credit cards. Telecom offers a wide range of prepaid cards for both domestic and international use; for a full list, see www.telecomitalia.it/telefono/carte-telefoniche. You can buy phonecards (most commonly €3, €5 or €10) at post offices, tobacconists and newsstands. You must break off the top left-hand corner of the card before you can use it. All phonecards have an expiry date, printed on the face of the card.

● ● ●
Time

Italy is one hour ahead of GMT. Daylight-saving time, when clocks are moved forward one hour, starts on the last Sunday in March. Clocks are put back an hour on the last Sunday in October. Italy operates on a 24-hour clock.

● ● ●
Tourist Information

The quality of tourist offices in Italy varies dramatically. Four tiers of tourist office exist: local, provincial, regional and national.

LOCAL & PROVINCIAL TOURIST OFFICES

Throughout this book, offices are referred to as tourist offices rather than by their more elaborate titles. All deal directly with the public, and most will respond to written and telephone requests for information. Staff can usually provide a city map, lists of hotels and information on the major sights. English, and sometimes French or German, is spoken at tourist offices in larger towns and major tourist areas.

The Azienda Autonoma di Soggiorno e Turismo (AAST) is the local tourist office in many towns and cities of the south. AASTs have town-specific information and should also know about bus routes and museum opening times. The Azienda di Promozione Turistica (APT) is the provincial (ie main) tourist office, which should have information on the town you are in and the surrounding province. Informazione e Assistenza ai Turisti (IAT) has local tourist office branches in towns and cities, mostly in the northern half of Italy. Pro Loco is the local office in small towns and villages and is similar to the AAST office. Most tourist offices will respond to written and telephone requests for information.

Information booths at most major train stations tend to keep similar hours but in some cases operate only in summer. Staff can usually provide a city map, list of hotels and information on the major sights.

Tourist offices are generally open from 8.30am to 12.30pm or 1pm and 3pm to 7pm Monday to Friday. Hours are usually extended in summer, when some offices also open on Saturday or Sunday.

REGIONAL TOURIST AUTHORITIES

Regional offices are generally more concerned with planning, budgeting, marketing and promotion than with offering a public information service. However, they still maintain some useful websites, as listed below. In some cases you'll need to look for the Tourism or Turismo link within the regional site.

Abruzzo
(www.abruzzoturismo.it)

Basilicata
(www.aptbasilicata.it)

Calabria
(www.turiscalabria.it, in Italian)

Campania
(www.in-campania.com)

Emilia-Romagna
(www.emiliaromagnaturismo.it)

Friuli Venezia Giulia
(www.turismo.fvg.it)

Lazio
(www.ilmiolazio.it, in Italian)

Le Marche
(www.le-marche.com)

Liguria
(www.turismoinliguria.it)

Lombardy (www.turismo.regione.lombardia.it)

Molise (www.regione.molise.it/turismo, in Italian)

Piedmont (www.regione.piemonte.it/turismo, in Italian)

Puglia
(www.pugliaturismo.com)

Sardinia
(www.sardegnaturismo.it)

Sicily
(www.regione.sicilia.it/turismo)

Trentino-Alto Adige
(www.visittrentino.it,
www.suedtirol.info)

Tuscany
(www.turismo.intoscana.it)

Umbria
(www.regioneumbria.eu)

Valle d'Aosta
(www.regione.vda.it/turismo)

Veneto (www.veneto.to)

TOURIST OFFICES ABROAD

The **Italian National Tourist Office** (ENIT; www.enit.it) maintains offices in over two dozen cities on five continents. Contact information for all offices can be found on their website.

Travellers with Disabilities

Italy is not an easy country for disabled travellers and getting around can be a problem for wheelchair users. Even a short journey in a city or town can become a major expedition if cobblestone streets have to be negotiated. Although many buildings have lifts, they are not always wide enough for wheelchairs. Not an awful lot has been done to make life for the deaf and/or blind any easier either.

The Italian National Tourist Office in your country may be able to provide advice on Italian associations for people with a disability and information on what help is available.

Italy's national rail company, **Trenitalia** (www.trenitalia.com) offers a national helpline for disabled passengers at ☎199 303060 (7am to 9pm daily).

A handful of cities also publish general guides on accessibility, among them Bologna, Milan, Padua, Reggio Emilia, Turin, Venice and Verona. In Milan, **Milano per Tutti** (www.milanopertutti.it) is a helpful resource.

Organisations that may help include the following:

Accessible Italy (www.accessibleitaly.com) A San Marino–based company that specialises in holiday services for people with a disability, ranging from tours to the hiring of adapted transport to romantic Italian weddings. This is the best first port of call.

Consorzio Cooperative Integrate (www.coinsociale.it) This Rome-based organisation provides information on the capital (including transport and access) and is happy to share its contacts throughout Italy. Its 'Turismo per Tutti' program seeks to improve infrastructure and access for tourists with a disability.

Tourism for All (www.tourismforall.org.uk) This UK-based group has information on hotels with access for guests with a disability, where to hire equipment and tour operators dealing with travellers with a disability.

● ● ●
Visas

Italy is one of 25 member countries of the Schengen Convention, under which 22 EU countries (all but Bulgaria, Cyprus, Ireland, Romania and the UK) plus Iceland, Norway and Switzerland have abolished permanent checks at common borders.

Legal residents of one Schengen country do not require a visa for another. Residents of 28 non-EU countries, including Australia, Brazil, Canada, Israel, Japan, New Zealand and the USA, do not require visas for tourist visits of up to 90 days (this list varies for those wanting to travel to the UK and Ireland).

The standard tourist visa is valid for up to 90 days. You must apply for a Schengen visa in your country of residence. A Schengen visa issued by one Schengen country is generally valid for travel in other Schengen countries. It is worth checking visa regulations with the consulate of each country you plan to visit.

All non-EU and non-Schengen nationals entering Italy for more than 90 days, or for any reason other than tourism (such as study or work) may need a specific visa. For details, visit www.esteri.it/visti/home_eng.asp or contact an Italian consulate.

PERMESSO DI SOGGIORNO

Non-EU citizens planning to stay at the same address for more than one week are supposed to report to the police station to receive a *permesso di soggiorno* (a permit to remain in the country). Tourists staying in hotels are not required to do this.

A *permesso di soggiorno* only really becomes a necessity if you plan to study, work or live in Italy.

● ● ●
Women Travellers

Italy is not a dangerous country for women to travel in. Clearly, as with anywhere in the world, women travelling alone need to take certain precautions and, in some parts of the country, be prepared for more than their fair share of unwanted attention. Eye-to-eye contact is the norm in Italy's daily flirtatious interplay. Eye contact can become outright staring the further south you travel.

Lone women may find it difficult to remain alone. In many places, local Lotharios will try it on with exasperating insistence, which can be flattering or a pain. Foreign women are particular objects of male attention in tourist towns like Florence and more generally in the south. Usually the best response to undesired advances is to ignore them. If that doesn't work, politely tell your interlocutors you're waiting for your *marito* (husband) or *fidanzato* (boyfriend) and, if necessary, walk away. Avoid becoming aggressive as this may result in an unpleasant confrontation. If all else fails, approach the nearest member of the police.

Watch out for men with wandering hands on crowded buses. Either keep your back to the wall or make a loud fuss if someone starts fondling your behind. A loud '*Che schifo!*' (How disgusting!) will usually do the trick. If a more serious incident occurs, report it to the police, who are then required to press charges.

Avoid walking alone in dark streets, and look for hotels that are centrally located.

Transccript... Transport

●●●
Getting There & Away

Competition between airlines means you should be able to pick up a reasonably priced fare to Italy, even from as far away as Australia. There are plenty of rail and bus connections, especially with northern Italy. Flights, tours and rail tickets can be booked online at www.lonelyplanet.com/travel_services.

ENTERING THE COUNTRY

EU and Swiss citizens can travel to Italy with their national identity card alone. All other nationalities must have a valid passport and may be required to fill out a landing card (at airports).

By law you are supposed to have your passport or ID card with you at all times. You'll need one of these documents for police registration every time you check into a hotel.

In theory, there are no passport checks at land crossings from neighbouring countries, but random customs controls do occasionally still take place between Italy and Switzerland

✈ AIR

High seasons are generally June to September, Christmas and Easter, although it depends in part on your destination. Shoulder season is often from mid-September to the end of October and again in April. Low season is generally November to March.

Airports

Italy's main intercontinental gateways are Rome's **Leonardo da Vinci Airport** (Fiumicino; www.adr.it) and Milan's **Malpensa Airport** (www.sea-aeroportimilano. it). Cut-rate airlines, led by Ryanair and Easyjet, fly from a growing number of European cities to over two dozen Italian destinations, typically landing in smaller airports such as Rome's **Ciampino** (www.adr.it). Plenty of flights from other European cities fly to regional capitals; the leading mainstream carriers include Alitalia, Air France, British Airways, Lufthansa and KLM.

Tickets

The internet is increasingly becoming the easiest way of locating and booking reasonably priced seats. Full-time students and those under 26 sometimes have access to discounted fares, especially on longer-haul flights from beyond Europe.

LAND

There are plenty of options for entering Italy by train, bus or private vehicle. Bus is the cheapest option, but services are less frequent, less comfortable and significantly longer than the train.

Border Crossings

The main points of entry to Italy from France are the coast road from Nice, which becomes the A10 motorway along the Ligurian coast, and the Mont Blanc Tunnel near Chamonix, which connects with the A5 for Turin and Milan.

Regular trains on two lines connect Italy with France in the west (one along the coast and the other via the French Alps to Turin). Trains from Milan head for Switzerland and on into France and the Netherlands. Two main lines head for the main cities in Austria and on into Germany, France or Eastern Europe.

🚌 BUS

Eurolines (www.eurolines. com) is a consortium of European coach companies that operates across Europe with offices in all major European cities.

🚗 CAR & MOTORCYCLE
Continental Europe

When driving in Europe, always carry proof of vehicle ownership and evidence of third-party insurance. If driving an EU-registered vehicle, your home-country insurance is sufficient. Ask your insurer for a European Accident Statement (EAS) form, which can simplify matters in the event of an accident.

A European breakdown assistance policy is a good investment and can be obtained through the Automobile Club d'Italia.

Every vehicle travelling across an international border should display a nationality plate of its country of registration.

Italy's scenic roads are tailor-made for motorcycle touring, and motorcyclists swarm into the country every summer. With a bike you rarely have to book ahead for ferries and can enter restricted-traffic areas in cities. Crash helmets and a motorcycle licence are compulsory. The US-based **Beach's Motorcycle Adventures** (www.beachs -mca.com) offers two-week tours through north-central Italy in May and October.

For longer-term auto leasing (14 days or more) or camper-van and motorhome hire, check **IdeaMerge** (www.ideamerge.com).

UK
You can take your car across to France by ferry or via the Channel Tunnel on **Eurotunnel** (☎ 0870 535 3535; www.eurotunnel.com).

🚆 TRAIN
Depending on distances travelled, rail can be highly competitive with air travel. Those travelling from neighbouring countries to northern Italy will find it is frequently more comfortable, less expensive and only marginally more time-consuming than flying. You avoid all the airport hassle and generally can rely on trains being on time.

It is also a much greener way to go – the same trip by rail can contribute up to 10 times less carbon dioxide emissions per person than by air.

Continental Europe
The *European Rail Timetable* (UK£13.99), updated monthly, is available from **Thomas Cook Publishing** (www.thomascook publishing.com).

Reservations on international trains to/from Italy are always advisable, and sometimes compulsory. Some international services include transport for private cars. Consider taking long journeys overnight, as the supplemental fare for a sleeper costs substantially less than Italian hotels.

UK
The **Eurostar** (☎ 08432 186186; www.eurostar.com) train travels between London and Paris, or London and Brussels. Alternatively you can get a train ticket that includes crossing the Channel by ferry.

For the latest fare information on journeys to Italy, including the Eurostar, contact the **Rail Europe Travel Centre** (☎ in UK 08448 484064; www.raileurope.co.uk) or **Rail Choice** (☎ 0871 231 0790; www.railchoice.com).

⚓ BOAT
Multiple ferry companies connect Italy with countries throughout the Mediterranean. Many routes only operate in summer, when ticket prices also rise. Prices for vehicles vary according to their size. The helpful website www.traghettionline.com (in Italian) covers all the ferry companies in the Mediterranean.

Climate Change & Travel
Every form of transport that relies on carbon-based fuel generates CO_2, the main cause of human-induced climate change. Modern travel is dependent on aeroplanes, which might use less fuel per kilometre per person than most cars but travel much greater distances. The altitude at which aircraft emit gases (including CO_2) and particles also contributes to their climate-change impact. Many websites offer 'carbon calculators' that allow people to estimate the carbon emissions generated by their journey and, for those who wish to do so, to offset the impact of the greenhouse gases emitted with contributions to portfolios of climate-friendly initiatives throughout the world. Lonely Planet offsets the carbon footprint of all staff and author travel.

Getting Around
Italy's network of train, bus, ferry and domestic air transport allows you to reach most destinations efficiently and relatively affordably.

With your own vehicle, you'll enjoy greater freedom, but *benzina* (petrol) and *autostrada* (motorway) tolls are expensive. For many, the stress of driving and parking in urban areas may outweigh the delights of puttering about the countryside. One solution is to take public transport between large cities and rent a car only to reach remoter rural destinations.

✈ AIR

The privatised national airline, Alitalia, is the main domestic carrier. Its many cut-rate competitors within Italy include **Meridiana** (www.meridiana. it), **Air One** (www.flyairone.it), **Ryanair** (www.ryanair.com), **EasyJet** (www.easyjet.com), **Windjet** (www.volawindjet. it) and **AirAlps** (www.airalps. at). A useful search engine for comparing multiple carriers' fares and purchasing low-cost domestic flights is **AZfly** (www.azfly.it).

Airport taxes are factored into the price of your ticket.

👓 BICYCLE

Cycling is very popular in Italy. Bikes are prohibited on the autostrada, but there are few other special road rules.

If bringing your own bike, you'll need to disassemble and pack it for the journey, and may need to pay an airline surcharge. Make sure to include tools, spare parts and for safety's sake, a helmet, lights and a secure bike lock.

Bikes can be wheeled onto any domestic train displaying the bicycle logo. Simply purchase a separate bicycle ticket, valid for 24 hours (€3.50). Certain international trains, listed on Trenitalia's 'In treno con la bici' page, also allow transport of assembled bicycles for €12. Bikes dismantled and stored in a bag can be taken for free, even on night trains. Most ferries also allow free bicycle passage.

In the UK, **Cyclists' Touring Club** (☏ 0844 736 8450; www.ctc.org.uk) can help you plan your tour or organise a guided tour. Membership

costs £37 for adults, £23 for seniors and £12 for under-18s.

Hire

Both city and mountain bikes are available for hire in most Italian towns. In Florence, for instance, there are several private outlets and a municipal scheme. City bikes start at €10/50 per day/week; mountain bikes a bit more.

BOAT

Navi (large ferries) service Sicily and Sardinia; *traghetti* (smaller ferries) and *aliscafi* (hydrofoils) service smaller islands. The main embarkation points for Sicily are Naples and Villa San Giovanni in Calabria (near Reggio Calabria), and the main points of arrival are Palermo and Messina.

The comprehensive website **Traghettionline** (www. traghettionline.com, in Italian) includes links to multiple Italian ferry companies, allowing you to compare prices and buy tickets.

For other relevant destinations, see the Getting There & Away sections of individual chapters. Most ferries carry vehicles.

BUS

Numerous companies provide bus services in Italy, from meandering local routes to fast and reliable intercity connections. Buses are usually priced competitively with the train and are often the only way to get to smaller towns.

It's usually possible to get bus timetables from local tourist offices. In larger cities most of the intercity bus companies have ticket offices or sell tickets through

agencies. In villages and even some good-size towns, tickets are sold in bars or on the bus.

Advance booking, while not generally required, is advisable in the high season for overnight or long-haul trips.

🚗 CAR & MOTORCYCLE

Italy boasts an extensive privatised network of autostradas, represented on road signs by a white A followed by a number on a green background. The main north–south link is the Autostrada del Sole (the 'Motorway of the Sun'), which extends from Milan to Reggio di Calabria (called the A1 from Milan to Rome, the A2 from Rome to Naples, and the A3 from Naples to Reggio di Calabria).

There are tolls on most motorways, payable by cash or credit card as you exit. For information on traffic conditions, tolls and driving distances, see www. autostrade.it (in Italian).

There are several additional road categories, listed below in descending order of importance.

Strade statali (state highways) Represented on maps by 'S' or 'SS'. Vary from toll-free, four-lane highways to two-lane main roads. The latter can be slow, especially in mountainous regions.

Strade regionali (regional highways connecting small villages) Coded SR or R.

Strade provinciali (provincial highways) Coded SP or P.

Strade locali Often not even paved or mapped.

ROAD DISTANCES (KM)

Note
Distances between Palermo and mainland towns do not take into account the ferry from Reggio di Calabria to Messina. Add an extra hour to your journey time to allow for this crossing

	Bari	Bologna	Florence	Genoa	Milan	Naples	Palermo	Perugia	Reggio di Calabria	Rome	Siena	Trento	Trieste	Turin	Venice
Bologna	681														
Florence	784	106													
Genoa	996	285	268												
Milan	899	218	324	156											
Naples	322	640	534	758	858										
Palermo	734	1415	1345	1569	1633	811									
Perugia	612	270	164	432	488	408	1219								
Reggio di Calabria	490	1171	1101	1325	1389	567	272	816							
Rome	482	408	302	526	626	232	1043	170	664						
Siena	714	176	70	296	394	464	1275	103	867	232					
Trento	892	233	339	341	218	874	1626	459	1222	641	375				
Trieste	995	308	414	336	420	948	1689	543	1445	715	484	279			
Turin	1019	338	442	174	139	932	1743	545	1307	702	460	349	551		
Venice	806	269	265	387	284	899	799	394	1296	567	335	167	165	415	
Verona	808	141	247	282	164	781	1534	377	1139	549	293	97	250	295	120

Automobile Associations

The **Automobile Club d'Italia** (ACI; www.aci.it) is a driver's best resource in Italy. For 24-hour roadside emergency service, dial ☏803116 from a landline or ☏800 116800 from a mobile phone. Foreigners do not have to join but instead pay a per-incident fee.

Bring Your Own Vehicle

Cars entering Italy from abroad need a valid national licence plate and an accompanying registration card. All vehicles must be equipped with any necessary adjustments for the Italian market; for example, left-side-drive cars will need to have their headlamps adjusted.

Driving Licence

All EU member states' driving licences are fully recognised throughout Europe. In practice, many non-EU licences (such as Australian, Canadian, New Zealand and US licences) are accepted by car-hire outfits in Italy. Travellers from other countries should obtain an International Driving Permit (IDP) through their national automobile association. If you want to hire a car or motorcycle you'll need to produce your driving licence.

Fuel

Italy's petrol prices are among the highest in Europe and vary from one service station (*benzinaio, stazione di servizio*) to another. As this book went to press, lead-free gasoline (*senza piombo;* 95 octane) was averaging €1.57 per litre, with diesel (*gasolio*) costing €1.44 per litre.

Hire
CARS

Pre-booking via the internet often costs less than hiring a car in Italy. Renters must generally be aged 25 or over, with a credit card and home country driving licence or International Driving Permit. Consider hiring a small car, which will reduce your fuel expense and help you negotiate narrow city lanes and tight parking spaces.

Check with your credit-card company to see if it offers a Collision Damage Waiver, which covers you for additional damage if you use that card to pay for the car.

Multinational car rental agencies:

Auto Europe
(www.autoeurope.com)

Autos Abroad
(www.autosabroad.com)

Avis (www.avisautonoleggio.it)

Budget
(www.budgetautonoleggio.it)

Europcar (www.europcar.com)

Hertz (www.hertz.it)

Holiday Cars
(www.holidaycars.com)

Italy by Car
(www.italybycar.it)

Maggiore (www.maggiore.it)

MOTORCYCLE

You'll have no trouble hiring a small Vespa or scooter. There are numerous rental agencies in cities where you'll also be able to hire larger motorcycles for touring. Prices start around €20/140 per day/week for a 50cc scooter, or upwards of €80/400 per day/week for a 650cc motorcycle. Note that many places require a sizable deposit, and you could be responsible for reimbursing part of the cost of the bike if it is stolen.

Most agencies will not hire motorcycles to people under 18.

Insurance

You need insurance when bringing your own car to Italy. Car-hire companies offer various insurance options. Be careful to understand what your liabilities and excess are and what waivers you are entitled to in case of accident or damage to the hire vehicle.

Road Rules

Cars drive on the right side of the road and overtake on the left. Unless otherwise indicated, you must always give way to cars entering an intersection from a road on your right. Seat belt use (front and rear) is required by law; violators are subject to an on-the-spot fine.

In the event of a breakdown, a warning triangle is compulsory, as is use of an approved yellow or orange safety vest if you leave your vehicle. Recommended accessories include a first-aid kit, spare-bulb kit and fire extinguisher.

Italy's blood-alcohol limit is 0.05%, and random breath tests take place. If you're involved in an accident while under the influence, the penalties can be severe.

Speeding fines follow EU standards and are proportionate with the number of kilometres that you are caught driving over the speed limit, reaching up to €2000 with possible suspension of your driving licence. Speed limits are as follows:

Autostradas: 130km/h to 150km/h

Other main highways: 110km/h

Minor, non-urban roads: 90km/h

Built-up areas: 50km/h

On all two-wheeled transport, helmets are required. The speed limit for mopeds is 40km/h. You don't need a licence to ride a scooter under 50cc but you should be aged 14 or over and you can't carry passengers or ride on an autostrada. To ride a motorcycle or scooter up to 125cc, you must be aged 16 or over and have a licence (a car licence will do). For motorcycles over 125cc you need a motorcycle licence. Do not venture onto the autostrada with a bike of less than 150cc.

Motorbikes can enter most restricted traffic areas in Italian cities, and traffic police generally turn a blind eye to motorcycles or scooters parked on footpaths.

Headlights are compulsory day and night for all vehicles on the autostradas, and advisable for motorcycles even on smaller roads.

LOCAL TRANSPORT

Major cities all have good transport systems, including bus and underground-train networks. In Venice, the main public transport is on *vaporetti* (small passenger ferries).

Bus & Underground Trains

Purchase bus and metro tickets before boarding and validate them once on board. Passengers with unvalidated tickets are subject to a fine (up to €50 in most cities).

There are extensive *metropolitane* (underground systems) in Rome, Milan, Naples and Turin, plus smaller metros in Genoa and Catania and a space-age *minimetro* in Perugia connecting the train station with the city centre. As this book went to press, Turin, Naples and Rome were all significantly expanding their metro systems.

Express Trains: Times & Prices Compared

FROM	TO	FRECCIAROSSA/AV TRAIN		INTERCITY	
		Duration (Hr)	Price (€)	Duration (Hr)	Price (€)
Turin	Naples	5½	111	9¾	63
Milan	Rome	3–3½	91	6½	49.50
Venice	Florence	2	43	3¼	24
Rome	Naples	1¼	45	2¼	22
Florence	Bologna	37min	25	1	10.50

Every city or town of any size has an efficient *urbano* (urban) and *extraurbano* (suburban) system of buses. Services are generally limited on Sundays and holidays.

Tickets can be bought from a *tabaccaio* (tobacconist), newsstands, ticket booths or dispensing machines at bus stations and in underground stations, and usually cost around €1 to €1.30. Most cities offer good-value 24-hour or daily tourist tickets.

Taxi

You can catch a taxi at the ranks outside most train and bus stations, or simply telephone for a radio taxi. Note that radio taxi meters start running from when you've called rather than when you're picked up.

Charges vary somewhat from one region to another. Most short city journeys cost between €10 and €15. Generally, no more than four people are allowed in one taxi.

TRAIN

Trains in Italy are relatively cheap compared with other European countries, and the better train categories are fast and comfortable.

Trenitalia (☎ 892021 in Italian; www.trenitalia.com) is the partially privatised, state train system that runs most services. Other private lines are noted throughout this book.

There are several types of trains. *Regionale* or *interregionale* trains stop at all or most stations. Intercity (IC) trains, and their international counterparts known as Eurocity (EC), are faster services that operate between major cities. Even faster *pendolini* (tilting trains) capable of reaching speeds of 250 to 300km per hour are collectively known as Eurostar Italia (ES).

In late 2009, Italy's newest, fastest trains – the Alta Velocità (High Speed) services variously known as Frecciarossa, Frecciargento, AV and ESAV – began operating on the Turin-Milan-Bologna-Florence-Rome-Naples-Salerno line, revolutionising train travel on that route. As shown in the table above, AV trains cost almost twice as much as traditional Intercity express trains, but get you to your destination nearly twice as fast.

Classes & Costs

Prices vary according to the class of service, time of travel and how far in advance you book. Most Italian trains have 1st- and 2nd-class seating; a 1st-class ticket typically costs from a third to half more than the 2nd-class ticket.

Travel on Intercity, Eurostar and Alta Velocità

Stamp it!

Countless foreign travellers in Italy learn the hard way that their train tickets must be stamped in the yellow machines (usually found at the head of rail platforms) just before boarding. Failure to do so usually results in fines, although the cry of 'I didn't know' sometimes elicits an indulgent response from ticket controllers. So stamp that ticket!

Eurail & Interrail Passes

You'll need to cover a lot of ground to make a rail pass worthwhile. Before buying, consider where you intend to travel and compare the price of a rail pass to the cost of individual tickets on the **Trenitalia** (www.trenitalia.com) website.

InterRail (www.interrailnet.com) passes, available online and at most major stations and student travel outlets, are for people who have been resident in Europe for more than six months. A Global pass encompassing 30 countries comes in five versions, ranging from five days' travel within a 10-day period to a full month's unlimited travel. There are four age brackets: child (4 to 11), youth (12 to 25), adult (26 to 59) and senior (60+), with different prices for 1st and 2nd class. The InterRail one-country pass for Italy can be used for three, four, six or eight days in one month, and does not offer senior discounts. See the website for full price details. Cardholders get discounts on travel in the country where they purchase the ticket.

Eurail (www.eurail.com) passes, available to non-European residents, are good for travel in 22 European countries (not including the UK). They can be purchased online or from travel agencies outside of Europe.

The original Eurail pass, now known as the **Global Pass**, is valid for a continuous period of 15 days, 21 days, one, two or three months. Youth under 26 are eligible for a 2nd-class pass; all others must buy the more expensive 1st-class pass (offered at half-price for children aged between four and 11).

Eurail offers several alternatives to the traditional Global Pass:

⊙ Two or more people travelling together can save 15% by purchasing the **1st-Class Saver Pass**.

⊙ The **Global Flexi Pass** allows you to choose 10 or 15 days of travel within a 2-month period in all 22 Eurail countries.

⊙ The **Select Pass** allows five to 15 days of travel within a 2-month period in three to five bordering countries of your choice.

⊙ The two-country **Regional Pass** (France–Italy, Spain–Italy or Greece–Italy) allows four to 10 days of travel within a 2-month period in the country pair selected.

⊙ The **One Country Pass** allows three to 10 days travel in Italy in a 2-month period.

trains means paying a supplement, determined by the distance you are travelling and included in the ticket price. If you have a standard ticket for a slower train and end up hopping on an IC train, you'll have to pay the difference on board. (You can only board a Eurostar or Alta Velocità train if you have a booking, so the problem does not arise in those cases.)

Reservations

Reservations are obligatory on Eurostar and AV trains. Otherwise they're not and, outside of peak holiday periods, you should be fine without them. You can make reservations at railway station counters, travel agents and, when they haven't broken down, at the automated machines sprinkled around most stations. Reservations carry a small extra fee.

Train Passes

Trenitalia offers various discount passes, including the Carta Verde for youth and Carta d'Argento for seniors, but these are mainly useful for residents or long-term visitors, as they pay for themselves with regular use over an extended period.

More interesting for short-term visitors are Eurail and Interrail passes (see above).

Language

Italian pronunciation isn't difficult as most sounds are also found in English. The pronunciation of some consonants depends on which vowel follows, but if you read our pronunciation guides below as if they were English, you'll be understood just fine. Just remember to pronounce double consonants as a longer, more forceful sound than single ones. The stressed syllables in words are in italics in our pronunciation guides.

To enhance your trip with a phrasebook, visit **lonelyplanet.com**. Lonely Planet iPhone phrasebooks are available through the Apple App store.

BASICS

Hello.
Buongiorno./Ciao. (pol/inf)   bwon·*jor*·no/chow
How are you?
Come sta?   *ko*·me sta
I'm fine, thanks.
Bene, grazie.   *be*·ne *gra*·tsye
Excuse me.
Mi scusi.   mee *skoo*·zee
Yes./No.
Sì./No.   see/no
Please. (when asking)
Per favore.   per fa·*vo*·re
Thank you.
Grazie.   *gra*·tsye
Goodbye.
Arrivederci./Ciao. (pol/inf)   a·ree·ve·*der*·chee/chow
Do you speak English?
Parla inglese?   *par*·la een·*gle*·ze
I don't understand.
Non capisco.   non ka·*pee*·sko
How much is this?
Quanto costa?   *kwan*·to *ko*·sta

ACCOMMODATION

I'd like to book a room.
Vorrei prenotare   vo·*ray* pre·no·*ta*·re
una camera.   *oo*·na *ka*·me·ra
How much is it per night?
Quanto costa per   *kwan*·to *kos*·ta per
una notte?   *oo*·na *no*·te

EATING & DRINKING

I'd like ..., please.
Vorrei . . ., per favore.   vo·*ray* . . . per fa·*vo*·re
What would you recommend?
Cosa mi consiglia?   *ko*·za mee kon·*see*·lya
That was delicious!
Era squisito!   *e*·ra skwee·*zee*·to
Bring the bill/check, please.
Mi porta il conto,   mee *por*·ta eel *kon*·to
per favore.   per fa·*vo*·re

I'm allergic (to peanuts).
Sono allergico/a   *so*·no a·*ler*·jee·ko/a
(alle arachidi). (m/f)   (*a*·le a·*ra*·kee·dee)
I don't eat ...
Non mangio . . .   non *man*·jo . . .

fish	*pesce*	*pe*·she
meat	*carne*	*kar*·ne
poultry	*pollame*	po·*la*·me

EMERGENCIES

I'm ill.
Mi sento male.   mee *sen*·to *ma*·le
Help!
Aiuto!   a·*yoo*·to
Call a doctor!
Chiami un medico!   *kya*·mee oon *me*·dee·ko
Call the police!
Chiami la polizia!   *kya*·mee la po·lee·*tsee*·a

DIRECTIONS

I'm looking for (a/the) ...
Cerco . . .   *cher*·ko . . .

bank		
la banca		la *ban*·ka
... embassy		
la ambasciata de . . .		la am·ba·*sha*·ta de . . .
market		
il mercato		eel mer·*ka*·to
museum		
il museo		eel moo·*ze*·o
restaurant		
un ristorante		oon rees·to·*ran*·te
toilet		
un gabinetto		oon ga·bee·*ne*·to
tourist office		
l'ufficio del turismo		loo·*fee*·cho del too·*reez*·mo

Behind the Scenes

Our Readers

Many thanks to the travellers who used the last edition and wrote to us with helpful hints, useful advice and interesting anecdotes: Barbara, Aleksander Braathen, Sauwoon Li, Mariana Mesquita, Yamini Misra, Francesco Poggio, Julie Robles, Deborah Sadler, Carla Wesby, Regina Zamel

Author Thanks

ALISON BING

Mille grazie e tanti baci a le mie famiglie a Roma and Stateside, the Bings, Ferrys and Marinuccis; editorial mastermind Joe Bindloss; local experts Alberto Toso Fei, Claudio Bonoldi, Alessandra Spisni, Fra Mirko, Patrizio Osticresi, Valentina Vellusi, Alessio Zito, Vincenzo Maccarrone, Rita Annunziata and Alessio Fangano; managing editor Brigitte Ellemor; ace editor Alison Ridgway; intrepid Italy coauthors, especially Christian Bonetto and Paula Hardy; *ma sopra tutto a* Marco Flavio Marinucci.

Acknowledgments

Climate map data adapted from Peel MC, Finlayson BL & McMahon TA (2007) 'Updated World Map of the Köppen-Geiger Climate Classification', *Hydrology and Earth System Sciences*, 11, 163344.

Illustrations pp70-1, pp176-7, pp232-3, pp296-7 by Javier Zarracina.

Cover photographs: Front: Gondolas and Chiesa di San Giorgio Maggiore, Venice, Leue Holger/Lonely Planet Images; Back: Poppy field near Montalcino, Tuscany, David Tomlinson/Lonely Planet Images. Many of the images in this guide are available for licensing from Lonely Planet Images: www.lonelyplanetimages.com.

This Book

This 2nd edition of Lonely Planet's *Discover Italy* guidebook was written and researched by Alison Bing, Abigail Blasi, Cristian Bonetto, Gregor Clark, Joe Fullman, Duncan Garwood, Paula Hardy, Robert Landon, Virginia Maxwell, Olivia Pozzan, Brendan Sainsbury, Donna Wheeler and Nicola Williams. The previous edition was researched by Damien Simonis, Alex Leviton and Josephine Quintero. This guidebook was commissioned in Lonely Planet's London office, and produced by the following:

Commissioning Editor Joe Bindloss
Coordinating Editor Alison Ridgway
Coordinating Cartographer Valentina Kremenchutskaya
Coordinating Layout Designer Jessica Rose
Managing Editors Brigitte Ellemor, Kirsten Rawlings
Managing Cartographer Mandy Sierp
Managing Layout Designers Chris Girdler, Jane Hart
Assisting Editors Elizabeth Anglin, Emma Gilmour, Carly Hall, Gabrielle Innes, Asha Ioculari, Shawn Low, Angela Tinson, Saralinda Turner, Fionn Twomey, Jeanette Wall
Assisting Cartographer James Leversha
Cover Research Naomi Parker
Internal Image Research Aude Vauconsant
Language Content Annelies Mertens
Thanks to Nicholas Colicchia, Erin Corrigan, Ryan Evans, Yvonne Kirk, Annelies Mertens, Trent Paton, Peter Shields, Gerard Walker

NOTES

Index

000 Map pages

How to Use This Book

These symbols will help you find the listings you want:

- ⊙ Sights
- 🐠 Beaches
- ➊ Activities
- ⊜ Courses
- ⊘ Tours
- ✷ Festivals & Events
- ▤ Sleeping
- ✕ Eating
- 🍺 Drinking
- ✪ Entertainment
- 🔒 Shopping
- ℹ Information/Transport

Look out for these icons:

FREE No payment required

🍃 A green or sustainable option

Our authors have nominated these places as demonstrating a strong commitment to sustainability – for example by supporting local communities and producers, operating in an environmentally friendly way, or supporting conservation projects.

These symbols give you the vital information for each listing:

- ☏ Telephone Numbers
- ⊙ Opening Hours
- P Parking
- ⊖ Nonsmoking
- ❄ Air-Conditioning
- @ Internet Access
- ☎ Wi-Fi Access
- ☒ Swimming Pool
- ✔ Vegetarian Selection
- 📖 English-Language Menu
- 👪 Family-Friendly
- 🐾 Pet-Friendly
- ▣ Bus
- ⛴ Ferry
- M Metro
- S Subway
- ⊖ London Tube
- ▣ Tram
- ▣ Train

Reviews are organised by author preference.

Map Legend

Sights
- 🐠 Beach
- ⚑ Buddhist
- ⊛ Castle
- ✚ Christian
- ☫ Hindu
- ☪ Islamic
- ✡ Jewish
- ❶ Monument
- 🏛 Museum/Gallery
- ⊙ Ruin
- ⊛ Winery/Vineyard
- 🐾 Zoo
- ⊙ Other Sight

Activities, Courses & Tours
- ⊖ Diving/Snorkelling
- ⊜ Canoeing/Kayaking
- 🎿 Skiing
- 🏄 Surfing
- 🏊 Swimming/Pool
- 🚶 Walking
- 🏄 Windsurfing
- ➕ Other Activity/Course/Tour

Sleeping
- ▤ Sleeping
- ⛺ Camping

Eating
- ✕ Eating

Drinking
- 🍺 Drinking
- ☕ Cafe

Entertainment
- ✪ Entertainment

Shopping
- 🔒 Shopping

Information
- ✉ Post Office
- ℹ Tourist Information

Transport
- ✈ Airport
- ⊗ Border Crossing
- 🚌 Bus
- 🚠 Cable Car/Funicular
- 🚲 Cycling
- ⛴ Ferry
- Ⓜ Metro
- 🚝 Monorail
- P Parking
- S S-Bahn
- 🚕 Taxi
- 🚉 Train/Railway
- 🚊 Tram
- ⊜ Tube Station
- Ⓤ U-Bahn
- • Other Transport

Routes
- Tollway
- Freeway
- Primary
- Secondary
- Tertiary
- Lane
- Unsealed Road
- Plaza/Mall
- Steps
-)=(Tunnel
- Pedestrian Overpass
- Walking Tour
- Walking Tour Detour
- Path

Boundaries
- International
- State/Province
- Disputed
- Regional/Suburb
- Marine Park
- Cliff
- Wall

Population
- ✪ Capital (National)
- ◉ Capital (State/Province)
- ● City/Large Town
- ● Town/Village

Geographic
- 🏠 Hut/Shelter
- 🔦 Lighthouse
- ⊙ Lookout
- ▲ Mountain/Volcano
- ⊛ Oasis
- ➊ Park
-)(Pass
- ⊛ Picnic Area
- ⊛ Waterfall

Hydrography
- River/Creek
- Intermittent River
- Swamp/Mangrove
- Reef
- Canal
- Water
- Dry/Salt/Intermittent Lake
- Glacier

Areas

- Beach/Desert
- Cemetery (Christian)
- Cemetery (Other)
- Park/Forest
- Sportsground
- Sight (Building)
- Top Sight (Building)